Architecting Google Cloud Solutions

Learn to design robust and future-proof solutions with Google Cloud technologies

Victor Dantas

BIRMINGHAM—MUMBAI

Architecting Google Cloud Solutions

Copyright © 2021 Packt Publishing

Group Product Manager: Wilson D'souza

Publishing Product Manager: Rahul Nair

Senior Editor: Shazeen Iqbal

Content Development Editor: Romy Dias

Technical Editor: Yoginee Marathe

Copy Editor: Safis Editing

Project Coordinator: Shagun Saini

Proofreader: Safis Editing

Indexer: Rekha Nair

Production Designer: Joshua Misquitta

First published: March 2021
Production reference: 1110321

Published by Packt Publishing Ltd.
Livery Place
35 Livery Street
Birmingham
B3 2PB, UK.

ISBN 978-1-80056-330-8
www.packt.com

Contributors

About the author

Victor Dantas has a PhD in software-defined networking and cloud systems and is a solutions architect currently working at AWS. He has professional cloud certifications from Google Cloud, Azure, and AWS. With a background ranging from software development and systems engineering to technology consulting, he has accumulated experience in software engineering, cloud migrations, hybrid cloud infrastructure, cloud solutions architecture, and Agile/DevOps practices working with organizations of all sizes. Victor also writes practical guides and labs on cloud computing for Pluralsight. Beyond the cloud, his interests include big data, AI / Machine Learning, and the **Internet-of-Things (IoT)**.

I want to express my gratitude for the lockdown policies implemented in response to COVID-19. Not only have they kept many of us safe, the lack of social life that ensued made writing this book a little easier.

About the reviewers

Shantanu De is a principal architect and consultant at Royal Mail Group, specializing in application development and integration projects. With over 20 years of experience in his field, he has gained mastery in various products, including those by SAP, IBM, Oracle, GCP, JDA, Microsoft, and AWS, along with vast industry experience in logistics, retail, utilities, banking, insurance, manufacturing, telecommunications, and transportation.

He did his master's in technology in material science before starting his professional career. He holds various professional certificates, such as SAFe Agile, TOGAF, and GCP Professional Cloud Architect. While he is accredited with many other certifications, these are the most relevant to today's climate.

I am extremely grateful to my uncle, who was my tutor in my early childhood – he taught me discipline, manners, respect, and so much more that has helped me succeed in life. I would also like to thank my daughter and wife, who have always stood by me. Reviewing this book has been an absolute pleasure, and to work with Victor – it has been challenging and engaging to have a hand in such a fantastic book.

David das Neves lives with his wife and a small Norwich Terrier close to Dachau, Germany. He was born and grew up in Germany, but his name is Portuguese and means "from the snow."

He is a typical IT guy and started his career as a software engineer. Afterward, he moved into consultancy and customer-facing roles at companies such as Microsoft and Google, with the latest stop being Media Markt Saturn. There, he works as a principal engineer focusing on cloud topics, directly reporting to the VP level.

Besides his work, he is strongly connected to the community, writes articles, frequently posts on LinkedIn, organizes several User Groups and events in EMEA, and speaks at international conferences.

I want to thank my wife, who tolerates my huge time investments towards my work and this book. You allow me to do so.

Table of Contents

Section 2: Designing Great Solutions in Google Cloud

3
Designing the Network

4
Architecting Compute Infrastructure

5
Architecting Storage and Data Infrastructure

6
Configuring Services for Observability

7

Designing for Security and Compliance

Section 3: Designing for the Modern Enterprise

8

Approaching Big Data and Data Pipelines

9

Jumping on the DevOps Bandwagon with Site Reliability Engineering (SRE)

10

Re-Architecting with Microservices

11

Applying Machine Learning and Artificial Intelligence

12

Achieving Operational Excellence

Preface

Google Cloud is a powerful and highly scalable cloud platform that has seen rising demand and interest from enterprises seeking digital transformation and looking to modernize their workloads. With best-of-breed technologies in the areas of AI and big data, among others, **Google Cloud Platform** (**GCP**) is capable of delivering unique value to businesses. This book is a comprehensive introduction to solutions architecture with Google Cloud that focuses on much more than just an overview of Google Cloud services. Beyond the fundamentals, it covers the timeless principles of great solutions architecture, architectural best practices, and how to get the best out of Google Cloud.

Who this book is for

This book is for cloud architects who are responsible for designing and managing cloud solutions with GCP. You'll also find the book useful if you're a systems engineer or enterprise architect looking to learn how to design modern solutions using Google Cloud. Moreover, cloud architects who already have experience with other cloud providers and are now beginning to work with Google Cloud will benefit from this book. Although a basic-level understanding of cloud computing and distributed applications is required, working experience in the public and hybrid cloud domain is not mandatory.

What this book covers

Chapter 1, An Introduction to Google Cloud for Architects, looks at cloud economics, motivations, delivery models, Google Cloud's key differentiators, and getting started with GCP.

Chapter 2, Mastering the Basics of Google Cloud, covers **Identity and Access Management** (**IAM**), cost discipline on GCP, and a simple case study.

Chapter 3, Designing the Network, looks at networks and subnetworks, routes, firewalls, load balancing, hybrid connectivity options on GCP, and common network designs.

Chapter 4, Architecting Compute Infrastructure, introduces **Google Compute Engine** (**GCE**), Compute platforms on GCP, Kubernetes, and designing a Compute solution.

Chapter 5, *Architecting Storage and Data Infrastructure*, looks at choosing the right storage solution, identifying data types, relational and structured datastores on GCP, and non-relational and unstructured datastores on GCP.

Chapter 6, *Configuring Services for Observability*, addresses monitoring basics and best practices, configuring and analyzing logs and metrics, investigating application performance issues, and designing for observability.

Chapter 7, *Designing for Security and Compliance*, goes into identity security, network security, data security, compliance, security monitoring, and security best practices.

Chapter 8, *Approaching Big Data and Data Pipelines*, looks at big data services on GCP, building data pipelines, streaming and analyzing data, and a big data case study.

Chapter 9, *Jumping on the DevOps Bandwagon with Site Reliability Engineering (SRE)*, goes into automation and **Infrastructure-as-Code** (**IaC**) in Google Cloud, SRE practices, error budgets, development agility, and designing for reliability.

Chapter 10, *Re-Architecting with Microservices*, looks at microservices architecture, designing APIs, Kubernetes, and a microservices case study.

Chapter 11, *Applying Machine Learning and Artificial Intelligence*, goes into AI and ML basics, business motivations, ML APIs on GCP, building ML models on GCP, and productionizing ML with MLOps.

Chapter 12, *Achieving Operational Excellence*, looks at cloud strategy, the cloud operating model, organizational culture, operations best practices, disaster recovery, chaos engineering, and SRE.

To get the most out of this book

Software/Hardware covered in the book	OS Requirements
Any of the latest versions of Google Chrome, Mozilla Firefox, Microsoft Edge, Microsoft Internet Explorer 11+, and Apple Safari 8+. Safari in private browser mode is not supported.	Windows, macOS, and Linux (Any)

You will need a personal GitHub account for the hands-on activity in Chapter 9, Jumping on the DevOps Bandwagon with Site Reliability Engineering (SRE).

If you are using the digital version of this book, we advise you to type the code yourself or access the code via the GitHub repository (link available in the next section). Doing so will help you avoid any potential errors related to the copying and pasting of code.

Download the example code files

You can download the example code files for this book from GitHub at `https://github.com/PacktPublishing/Architecting-Google-Cloud-Solutions`. In case there's an update to the code, it will be updated on the existing GitHub repository.

We also have other code bundles from our rich catalog of books and videos available at `https://github.com/PacktPublishing/`. Check them out!

Code in Action

Code in Action videos for this book can be viewed at `http://bit.ly/3sMc1cX`.

Download the color images

We also provide a PDF file that has color images of the screenshots/diagrams used in this book. You can download it here: `http://www.packtpub.com/sites/default/files/downloads/9781800563308_ColorImages.pdf`.

Conventions used

There are a number of text conventions used throughout this book.

`Code in text`: Indicates code words in text, database table names, folder names, filenames, file extensions, pathnames, dummy URLs, user input, and Twitter handles. Here is an example: "Mount the downloaded `WebStorm-10*.dmg` disk image file as another disk in your system."

A block of code is set as follows:

```
apiVersion: v1
kind: Service
metadata:
  name: dinner-recommendation-service
```

When we wish to draw your attention to a particular part of a code block, the relevant lines or items are set in bold:

```
spec:
  selector:
    app: dinnerapp
    department: it
  type: ClusterIP
```

Any command-line input or output is written as follows:

```
$ gcloud projects create --name chapter-4 --set-as-default
```

Bold: Indicates a new term, an important word, or words that you see onscreen. For example, words in menus or dialog boxes appear in the text like this. Here is an example: "Note the **SSH** button in the **Connect** column on the right."

> **Tips or important notes**
> Appear like this.

Get in touch

Feedback from our readers is always welcome.

General feedback: If you have questions about any aspect of this book, mention the book title in the subject of your message and email us at customercare@packtpub.com.

Errata: Although we have taken every care to ensure the accuracy of our content, mistakes do happen. If you have found a mistake in this book, we would be grateful if you would report this to us. Please visit www.packtpub.com/support/errata, selecting your book, clicking on the Errata Submission Form link, and entering the details.

Piracy: If you come across any illegal copies of our works in any form on the Internet, we would be grateful if you would provide us with the location address or website name. Please contact us at copyright@packt.com with a link to the material.

If you are interested in becoming an author: If there is a topic that you have expertise in and you are interested in either writing or contributing to a book, please visit authors.packtpub.com.

Reviews

Please leave a review. Once you have read and used this book, why not leave a review on the site that you purchased it from? Potential readers can then see and use your unbiased opinion to make purchase decisions, we at Packt can understand what you think about our products, and our authors can see your feedback on their book. Thank you!

For more information about Packt, please visit `packt.com`.

Section 1: Introduction to Google Cloud

In this section, you will get an overview of cloud computing technologies and the economics of cloud computing, as well as an introduction to Google Cloud. You will learn how to make a case for Google Cloud and the essential concepts to master for a strong start.

The following chapters will be covered in this section:

- *Chapter 1, An Introduction to Google Cloud for Architects*
- *Chapter 2, Mastering the Basics of Google Cloud*

1

An Introduction to Google Cloud for Architects

Is the "cloud" just someone else's data center? Some may see it that way, but there is much more to **cloud computing** than that. Cloud computing builds on infrastructure virtualization technologies to deliver services on demand, enabling not only a technological but a cultural shift in the way we work with IT systems. Furthermore, cloud computing has facilitated a new economic model for infrastructure services and has lowered the entry barrier for highly demanding applications, particularly in the areas of **big data** and **artificial intelligence** (**AI**), making it easier for smaller players to join the data-driven market. Foundational knowledge of cloud business and **Google Cloud** is a fundamental first step in a **cloud architect's** journey toward designing solutions with confidence using Google Cloud, so this is where we will start. In this chapter, you will learn about the enabling technologies of cloud computing and the motivations for its adoption, as well as develop a basic understanding of cloud economics and different cloud delivery models. You will then be provided with an overview of Google Cloud services and learn about some of its competitive advantages and best-of-breed technologies. Finally, you will get hands-on with Google Cloud by setting up an account, installing the **SDK**, and running a minor deployment.

In this chapter, we're going to cover the following main topics:

- Understanding the motivations and economics of cloud computing
- Making the business case for cloud adoption (and Google Cloud)
- Learning about Google Cloud's key differentiators – big data and AI
- Getting an overview of Google Cloud for cloud architects
- Getting started with **Google Cloud Platform** (**GCP**)

Technical requirements

Check out the following link to see the Code in Action video: `https://bit.ly/3bYNoEv`

Understanding the motivations and economics of cloud computing

At what point do we stop calling it just a data center, and start calling it the "cloud"? **The National Institute of Standards and Technology** (**NIST**) defines the following five essential traits that characterize cloud computing:

- On-demand, self-service
- Broad network access
- Resource pooling
- Rapid elasticity or expansion
- Measured service

The ability to deliver elastic services that can scale to adapt to varying demand, while paying only for the resources that you use, is what makes cloud computing so appealing and powerful.

The main enabling technology is that of infrastructure virtualization (or *cloudification*, as it is sometimes referred to), which has been made possible in the past few decades by the commoditization of hardware and new paradigms such as **software-defined networking** (**SDN**), in which the system's "intelligence" (control plane) is decoupled from the system's underlying hardware processing functions (the data plane).

These new technologies have allowed for increased levels of *programmability* of the infrastructure, where provisioned infrastructure resources can be abstracted and services can be exposed through **application programming interfaces** (**APIs**), in the same way that software applications' resources are. For example, with a few REST API calls, you can deploy a virtual network environment with virtual machines and public IP addresses. This has made cloud computing much more accessible to professionals working in roles beyond those of traditional enterprise IT or solution architects. It has also facilitated the emergence of the **Infrastructure-as-Code** (**IaC**) paradigm and the **DevOps** culture.

It has done this by enabling infrastructure resources to be defined in text-based declarative language and source-controlled in a code repository, and deployments to be streamlined via pipelines. At the time of writing, there is nothing standing between a team of developers and a complete infrastructure ready to run application workloads at any scale, except perhaps the required budget for doing so.

The NIST definition also lists four *cloud deployment models*:

- Private
- Community
- Public
- Hybrid

These models relate to the ownership of the hosting infrastructure. This book is about Google Cloud, which is owned and operated by Google as the cloud service provider and delivered over the internet through the **public cloud** model. In a public cloud, the infrastructure resources are shared between organizations (or cloud "tenants"), which means that within the same physical hosting infrastructure, several different virtualized systems from different customers may be running alongside each other. This, along with the lack of control and visibility over the underlying physical infrastructure, is one of the most criticized aspects of the public cloud model since it raises security and privacy concerns. It is the reason some organizations are reluctant to seriously consider migrating their infrastructure to the public cloud, and also the reason several others settle "somewhere in the middle" with a hybrid cloud deployment, in which only part of their infrastructure is hosted in a public cloud environment (the remaining part being privately hosted).

What makes cloud computing so disruptive and appealing, however, is not solely the new technological model that's enabled by virtualization technologies and commodity hardware, but the economic model that ensues (at least for the players in the market with deep enough pockets), which is that of *economies of scale* and *global reach*. While IT systems are generally expensive to purchase and maintain, being able to buy resources in massive quantities and build several data centers across the globe enables you to reduce and amortize those costs greatly, and then pass those savings on to your customers, who themselves can benefit from the consumption-based model and avoid large upfront investments and commitments. It's a win-win situation.

This is the shift from **Capital Expenditures** (**CAPEX**) to **Operational Expenditures** (**OPEX**) that we hear about so often, and is one of the tenets of cloud computing.

CAPEX versus OPEX

Instead of purchasing your own expensive infrastructure with a large upfront investment (the CAPEX model), you can benefit from the pay-as-you-go pricing model offered in the public cloud as a monthly consumption fee with no termination penalty (the OPEX model). Pay-as-you-go simply means you pay only for the resources you consume, while you consume them, and it's a bundled price that includes everything from any potential software licenses down to maintenance costs of the physical infrastructure running the service. This is in contrast to acquiring your own private infrastructure (or private cloud), in which case you would size it for the expected maximum demand and commit with a large upfront investment to this full available capacity, even if you only utilize a fraction of that capacity most of the time.

For organizations whose line-of-business applications have varying demands based on, for example, day of the week or time of the year (indeed, this is the case for most web-based applications today), the ability to only pay for extra resource allocation only during the few hours or days that those extra resources are needed is very beneficial financially. Resource utilization efficiency is maximized. What is even better is that such scaling events can be done automatically, and they require no on-call operations personnel to handle them.

The shift from CAPEX to OPEX also has implications on cash flow. Rather than having to pay a large, upfront infrastructure cost (the price commitment for which may go beyond the budget of smaller organizations, which would force them to borrow money and deal with interest costs), organizations can smooth out cash flows over time and drive improved average margin per user. In addition, it offers a much lower financial "penalty" for start - ups that pivot their business in a way that would drive major changes in the infrastructure architecture (in other words, it costs less to "pull the plug" on infrastructure "purchase" decisions).

Technology enablement

Cloud technologies are also powering a new range of applications that require immense distributed computing power and AI capabilities. The possibility to scale compute needs on-demand and pay only for what you use means that many more companies can benefit from this powerful and virtually limitless capacity, as they don't need to rely on prohibitively expensive infrastructure of their own to support such high-demand workloads.

Google has invested heavily over the years in their infrastructure and machine learning models since services such as *Google Search*, *Google Maps*, and *YouTube* – some of the most powerful data-driven services at the highest scale you can think of today – run on the same infrastructure and use the same technologies that Google now makes available for Google Cloud customers for consumption.

The NIST definition for cloud computing also lists three "service models" that, together with the deployment models, characterize the ways services are delivered in the cloud:

- **Software-as-a-Service**, also known as **SaaS**

- **Platform-as-a-Service**, also known as **PaaS**

- **Infrastructure-as-a-Service**, also known as **IaaS**

These relate to which layers of the infrastructure are managed and operated by the cloud provider (or the infrastructure owner) and which are your responsibility as a consumer.

In a public cloud, such as Google Cloud, the delivery models are easy to reason about when you're visualizing the stack of infrastructure layers against your – and the cloud provider's – responsibility for managing and operating each layer:

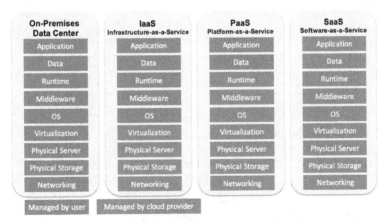

Figure 1.1 – Difference in management responsibilities (on-premises versus IaaS versus PaaS versus SaaS)

Organizations with a medium to large digital estate and several different types of workloads will typically acquire not one but a mix of services across different models, based on the specific requirements and technical constraints of each workload. For example, you may have a stateless application that you developed with a standard programming language and framework hosted on a PaaS service, while you may have another application in the same cloud environment that relies heavily on custom libraries and features, and is therefore hosted on a virtual machine (IaaS). As we will see throughout this book, there are several considerations and design trade-offs to take into account when choosing which delivery model is best, but typically, it comes down to a tug of war between control over the underlying platform (things such as patch and update schedules, the configurability of the application runtime and framework, access to the operating system's filesystem, custom VM images, and so on) and low management overhead (low to no platform operation, smaller and more independent application teams).

Cloud-native or cloud-first organizations will typically consume more of the PaaS and SaaS services, and rely less on IaaS VMs. This reduces dependencies on infrastructure teams and allows development-focused teams to quickly and easily deploy code to a platform whose infrastructure management is delegated to the cloud provider. This is one reason why the public cloud has a very strong appeal to smaller organizations and start - up software companies.

For other organizations, you may need to make a convincing case for the public cloud to get executive buy-in. Next, we'll explore how to make the business case for cloud adoption.

Making the business case for cloud adoption (and Google Cloud)

An important decision-making tool for companies considering cloud adoption is the **Return on Investment** (**ROI**) calculation, which can be obtained as follows:

$$ROI = \frac{\text{Gain from investment} - \text{Initial investment}}{\text{Initial investment}}$$

Let's take a look at this calculation in more detail:

- The *gain from investment* is the net positive cost savings obtained by migrating on-premises infrastructure to the cloud. This can be estimated by obtaining a quote (for instance, from the Google Cloud Pricing Calculator) and subtracting it from the **Total Cost of Ownership** (**TCO**) of the on-premises data center. This includes capital costs of equipment, labor costs, and other maintenance and operational costs, such as software license fees.

- The *initial investment* is the sum of costs involved in the migration project itself. This involves primarily labor and training costs.

A positive ROI will help you make a stronger case for the business value of cloud adoption to the executives in the organization you're working with. A cloud solution architect will often be involved in this financial exercise.

It is also useful (and even more important) to identify, as a cloud architect, the main motivations and business drivers behind a cloud adoption project beyond cost savings, as this knowledge will help shape the solution's design. Each organization is unique and has different needs, but some of the most common motivations for enterprises are as follows:

- You can avoid large capital expenditures and infrastructure maintenance in order to focus on application development.
- You can reduce technical complexity and integrate complex IT portfolios.
- You can optimize and increase the productivity of internal operations.
- You can improve the reliability and stability of online applications.
- You can increase business agility and innovation with self-service environments.
- You can scale to meet market demands.

Once you have identified these motivations, the next thing you must do is align those motivations with your expected business outcomes. These are observable and measurable results, such as increased profitability, improved customer satisfaction, improved team productivity, and so on. For each business outcome, success metrics should be defined that describe how such benefits are going to be measured. The ROI we discussed earlier is one example of such a metric, but there could be several others that measure, in some way or another, the degree of success of the cloud adoption (which, of course, depends on the organization's own definition of success). The following diagram shows an example of a *motivation + outcome + metric* triad:

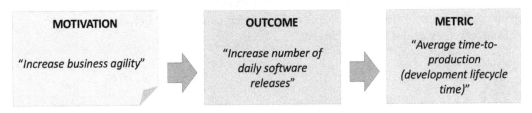

Figure 1.2 – Sample motivation, outcome, and metric triad as a cloud adoption strategy

This exercise is not just something to wind up on a slide presentation at a meeting room full of executives during a boring Tuesday afternoon. It should be taken seriously and become an integral part of the organization's overall strategy. In fact, in a recent Unisys' Cloud Success Barometer report (`https://www.unisys.com/cloudbarometer`), it has been shown that, globally, *one in three cloud migrations fail because the cloud is not part of the business' core strategy.* On the other hand, organizations that make the cloud a part of a broader business transformation strategy are substantially more likely to succeed. Let that sink in.

Establishing a cloud adoption business strategy is outside the scope of this book, but Google's Cloud Adoption Framework (`https://cloud.google.com/adoption-framework`) was developed to provide a streamlined framework to guide organizations throughout their cloud adoption efforts. It is freely available online and is based on four themes (**Learn, Lead, Scale, and Secure**) and three phases that reflect the organization's maturity level (**Tactical, Strategic, and Transformational**).

Deciding whether or not to migrate to the public cloud may not be a very difficult decision to make. We are well past the phase of early adoption and uncertainty, and the public cloud model is now very mature and well into its adulthood. A perhaps more difficult question, however, is: *why Google Cloud?*

You've learned about the economics of cloud computing and how to make the business case for cloud adoption. Now, let's see where Google fits into the picture and the reasons you can present to organizations as to why they should choose Google Cloud.

Learning about Google Cloud's key differentiators – big data and AI

The cloud business is a real fight of titans, with the "titans" being Microsoft, Amazon, Google, Alibaba, and a few others. They are among the biggest organizations in the world in terms of network and infrastructure footprint. Competition is good for any business, of course, but for us customers, it can make it difficult for us to decide between the options we have when they are all seemingly great.

Why Google?

Google Cloud was late to the cloud business. And it didn't speak to the early adopters when it decided to focus on PaaS services primarily (as opposed to the more familiar IaaS option), something the world wasn't yet ready for in the early days of cloud computing. But things are now changing. Google Cloud offers some of the best-of-breed services for the development of modern, containerized applications, using sophisticated analytics and AI capabilities that are cost-competitive. Google is the inventor of *Kubernetes* and some of the cutting-edge big data technology innovations such as *TensorFlow*, *MapReduce*, and *BigTable*. Google knows how to handle large-scale distributed applications and very large amounts of data probably better than anyone, because this is exactly what it has been doing (and doing really well) for about two decades now. It also knows how complex these systems are, which is why it is presenting them to its customers as a friendly, serverless, and easy-to-consume service in the cloud.

The reluctance of many enterprises to consider Google Cloud is understandable. Amazon's *AWS* is very mature and reliable, and their client portfolio certainly speaks for the success and maturity of their platform. Microsoft's *Azure* is a natural best choice too if all your existing IT systems are based on Microsoft products and services, such as Active Directory, Windows Servers, and **Microsoft** (**MS**) Office applications. Microsoft has dominated the enterprise IT business for years (and probably still does, with its strong appeal to enterprise customers due to existing relationships and its level of maturity), and they are certainly making sure that a transition to the Azure cloud would be as seamless as possible. Plus, they understand the needs of enterprises deeply, their security and compliance concerns, their need for protecting users' identities, and their need for reliability and strong Service-Level Agreements. This is all very true, but an unfair assumption that's often made in that line of reasoning is that Google does not have any of that expertise or credibility themselves. People will often say Google Cloud is "cool," but it is not as safe a bet as AWS or Azure. That might have been true once, but now, that is an assumption that you, as a cloud architect, can learn to challenge.

Firstly, Google Cloud has a growing list of high-profile customers, some of which are:

- PayPal
- HSBC
- Target
- eBay
- Twitter
- Verizon
- Spotify
- Deutsche Bank

These are just a few. They have all reported that they have realized benefits with Google Cloud, especially around big data and AI capabilities, but not exclusively so. PayPal's CTO Sri Shivananda has stated that PayPal turned to Google as their cloud provider *"because it has the fastest network in terms of throughput, bandwidth, and latency."* It's not very difficult to understand why Google's global network is hard to beat: it powers latency- and bandwidth-sensitive services such as *Google Search* and *YouTube*. Twitter runs on a distributed Hadoop system that hosts more than 300 PB of data across tens of thousands of servers on Google Cloud. Parag Agrawal, CTO of Twitter, said "*Google Cloud Platform provides the infrastructure that can support this and the advanced security that well serves not just our company but also our users. This peace of mind is invaluable.*"

Multi-cloud friendly

More and more companies are also evaluating so-called multi-cloud strategies to benefit from the best of two or more cloud platforms. Google seems very much on board with this, facilitating multi-cloud strategies and even developing products that work on multiple cloud platforms. Organizations that would like to leverage, for example, Microsoft Azure to migrate their existing Windows-based systems and Active Directory identities can still do so, while more modern applications can be migrated to Google Cloud to reap the benefits of modern capabilities. You can have yet another piece of your application in AWS too, should you consider that platform to be best suited for it. The one drawback of multi-cloud deployments is the higher management overhead and the more diverse skillset required within the organization to manage multiple platforms, which may increase the needs for internal training and/or hiring (and therefore drive costs).

Once again, however, the strategic discussions around business motivations and business outcomes become very relevant in identifying ways to actually obtain a higher ROI through a multi-cloud deployment model, by aiming to explore the best of what each cloud provider has to offer. With the right strategy and the right execution, multi-cloud certainly pays off.

Big data and AI

One important consideration when it comes to making the case for Google Cloud is to adopt an innovation-led development mindset and understand industry trends. We may be in a moment now where big data and AI are somewhat what cloud computing itself used to be in its early days: a shiny new object, a cool-but-maybe-not-for-me-yet technology. Now, nearly everyone is in a rush to get to the cloud, and some probably regret not being among the early adopters. The same could happen with AI and big data: this may likely be the right window to get in, and should you decide to do so, it is hard to dispute the fact that Google Cloud is leading the way and offering the very best you can get in that arena. Google firmly believes in the saying that "*every company is a data company*," or at least that this will eventually be true, because it seems to be seeding the ground for a future where the best big data capabilities will be the deciding factor on who's going to win the war for cloud market share.

In a 2019 PwC study, it was estimated that AI will provide a potential contribution of $15.7 trillion to the global economy by 2030, with high potential use cases across several different industries. What is already a reality in 2020, however, is that companies are investing heavily in cognitive software capabilities to analyze data and inform decision-making or to build more personalized and profitable products and campaigns. Other areas of focus of AI currently include supply chain optimizations, mobile features (such as real-time speech translation), enhancing customer experience (by providing, for example, always-on chat bots or contact center AI), and improved security (with features such as fraud and threat detection).

The common theme underlying these use cases is not old technologies being replaced (or people, at least not for the time being), but rather the improvement, enhancement, or augmentation of existing ones to provide more value and profitability. The field of AI has many aspirations and ambitions for the future, and those are the ones we tend to hear about the most in the press, which gives us the impression that AI still only belongs to the realm of imagination and research. But it is very real already, and companies have been reaping its benefits for years. Jumping on the AI and big data bandwagon is likely one of the safest bets tech organizations can place today, especially considering the entry barrier has never been this low, with easy-to-consume, pay-as-you-go AI services that are on the bleeding edge of the field.

And it gets better. You don't need to lock yourself in with Google Cloud products if you want to leverage these capabilities – you can simply build your applications on open source tools you might already be familiar with.

Open source

If you work with an organization involved in the open source world (be it as a contributor, or purely as a consumer), Google's heavy involvement and strategic partnerships with leading open source companies may appeal to them. These partnerships have allowed Google to integrate open source tooling and services into Google Cloud, making it easy for enterprise customers to build and use apps by using those services in ways that feel very similar to the experience of using cloud-native resources. If vendor lock-in is a concern in your organization, you can see how Google Cloud embraces not only the open software culture, but also the multi-cloud model, by allowing several of these services to seamless integrate with systems that are hosted in other public clouds or on-premises data centers (in a hybrid cloud model). And because open source software does not rely on proprietary libraries and technologies, they are easier to port to another cloud provider, should you decide to do so. One of the best examples is Kubernetes, an open source container orchestration platform where you can run service-oriented applications completely agnostic to the underlying infrastructure. In fact, one of Google's latest developments is *Anthos*, a new and also open platform service that lets you run applications anywhere inside Kubernetes clusters, unmodified, across different clouds and/or private on-premises environments. It is a fully fledged hybrid- and multi-cloud solution for modern application development.

You have now gotten a better understanding of the many strengths of Google Cloud and some reasons why organizations should consider it, as well as how you can make a convincing case for it. Next, let's dive into Google Cloud and its technologies.

Getting an overview of Google Cloud

As we discussed in the previous section, some of Google Cloud's key market differentiators are its democratized big data and AI innovations and its open source friendly ecosystem. Data-driven businesses that already work with open source tools and frameworks such as **Kubernetes, TensorFlow, Apache Spark, and Apache Beam** will find Google to be a well-suited cloud provider as these services are first-class citizens on **Google Cloud Platform (GCP)**. Although you can technically deploy open source software on any cloud platform using VMs, Google has gone to some greater lengths than its competitors have by offering several of these services through a cloud-native experience with its PaaS offerings.

GCP also has one of the world's largest high-speed software-defined networks. At the time of writing, Google Cloud is available in over 200 countries and territories, with 24 cloud regions and 144 network edge locations. It would come as no surprise, however, if by the time you're reading this that these numbers have increased.

In this section, we're going to explore how GCP is structured into regions and zones, what its core services are, and how it approaches the security of the platform and its resource hierarchy.

Regions and zones

GCP is organized into regions and zones. Regions are independent and broad geographic areas, such as *europe-west1* or *us-east4*, while zones are more specific locations that may or may not correspond to a single physical data center, but which can be thought of as single failure domains. Networked locations within a region typically have round-trip network latencies *under 5ms, often under 1ms.*

Most regions have three or more zones, which are specified with a letter suffix added to the region name. For example, region *us-east4* has three zones: *us-east4-a*, *us-east4-b*, and *us-east4-c*. Mapping a zone to a physical location is not the same for every organization. In other words, there's not a location Google calls "zone A" within the *us-east4* region. There are typically at least three different physical locations, and what a zone letter corresponds to will be different for each organization since these mappings are done independently and dynamically. The main reason for this is to ensure there's a resource balance within a region.

Certain services in Google Cloud can be deployed as multi-regional resources (spanning several regions). Throughout this book, we will look at the options and design considerations for regional or multi-regional deployments for various services.

Core Google Cloud services

In this section, we'll present a bird's-eye overview of the core GCP services across four different major categories: compute, storage, big data, and machine learning. The purpose is not to present an in-depth description of these services (which will happen in the chapters in section two as we learn how to design solutions), but to provide a quick rundown of the various services in Google Cloud and what they do. Let's take a look at them:

- **Compute**

    Compute Engine: A service for deploying IaaS virtual machines.

    Kubernetes Engine: A platform for deploying **Kubernetes** container clusters.

App Engine: A compute platform for applications written in **Java, Python, PHP, Go, or Node.js.**

Cloud Functions: A serverless compute platform for executing code written in **Java, Python, Go, or Node.js.**

- **Storage**

Bigtable: A fully managed **NoSQL** database service for large analytical and operational workloads with high volumes and low latency.

Cloud Storage: A highly durable and global object storage.

Cloud SQL: A fully managed relational database service for **MySQL, PostgreSQL, and SQL Server.**

Cloud Spanner: A fully managed and highly scalable relational database with strong consistency.

Cloud Datastore: A highly scalable **NoSQL** database for web and mobile applications.

- **Big Data**

BigQuery: A highly scalable data warehouse service with serverless analytics.

Pub/Sub: A real-time messaging service.

Data Fusion: A fully managed, cloud-native data integration service.

Data Catalog: A fully managed, highly scalable data discovery service.

Dataflow: A serverless stream and batch data processing program based on Apache Beam.

Dataproc: A data analytics service for building **Apache Spark, Apache Hadoop, Presto, and other OSS clusters.**

- **Machine Learning**

Natural Language API: A service that provides natural language understanding.

Vision API: A service with pre-trained machine learning models for classifying images and detecting objects and faces, as well as printed and handwritten text.

Speech API: A service that converts audio into text by applying neural network models.

Translation API: A service that translates text between thousands of language pairs.

AutoML: A suite of machine learning products for developing machine learning models with little to no coding.

AI Platform: A code-based development platform with an integrated tool chain that can help you run your own machine learning applications.

Naturally, similar services to the ones presented here could be deployed to virtual machines with the full power of customization that comes with them. However, a self-hosted IaaS-based service is evidently not managed nor offered any service-level guarantees (beyond that of the virtual machines themselves) by the cloud provider, although they are viable options when migrating applications – sometimes the only option – as will be discussed in later chapters.

Multi-layered security

Security is a legitimate concern for many organizations when considering cloud adoption. For many, it may feel like they're taking a strong business risk in handing over their data and line-of-business applications to some other company to host within their data centers. Cloud providers know about such concerns very well, which is why they have gone to great lengths to ensure that they're designing security into their technical infrastructure. After all, the major cloud providers in the market (Google, Amazon, and Microsoft) are themselves consumer technology companies that have to deal with security attacks and penetration attempts on a daily basis. In fact, these organizations have years of experience safeguarding their infrastructure against **Denial-of-Service (DoS)** attacks and even things such as social engineering. In fact, an argument could be made that security concerns over hosting private data and intellectual property by a third party is somewhat offset by the fact that the third party's infrastructure is likely to be more secure and impenetrable than a typical private data center facility. The infrastructure security personnel of a cloud service provider certainly outnumbers that of a typical organization, offering more manpower and more concentrated effort toward preventing and mitigating security incidents at the infrastructure layer.

The following are some of the measures taken by Google with its multi-layered security approach to cloud infrastructure:

LAYER	MEASURES
Hardware Infrastructure	Securing boot stack and machine identity, custom hardware design, and the security of physical premises, for example, based on Titan chip + Reference.
Service Deployment	Access management, encryption of inter-service communication, service isolation.
User Identity	Authentication and login abuse protection.
Storage Services	Encryption at rest and DoS protection.
Internet Communication	Google Front End (GFE), TLS certificates, and DoS protection.
Operational Security	Intrusion detection, insider risk reduction, safe employee devices and credentials, and safe software development.

Because of the sheer scale of Google, it can deliver a higher level of security at the lower layers of the infrastructure than most of its customers could even afford to. Several measures are taken to protect users against unauthorized access, and Google's systems are monitored 24 hours a day, 365 days a year by a global operations team.

With that being said, it is important to recognize that security in the cloud is a shared responsibility. *Customers are still responsible for securing their data properly, even for PaaS and SaaS services.*

Security is a fundamental skill for cloud architects, and incorporating security into any design will be a central theme throughout this book.

Resource hierarchy

Resources in GCP are structured similar to how you would structure artifacts when working in any other types of projects.

The project level is where you enable and manage GCP capabilities such as specific APIs to be used, billing, and other Google services, and is also where you can add or remove collaborators. Any resources that are created are connected to a project and belong to exactly one project. A project can have multiple owners and users, and multiple projects can be organized into folders. Folders can nest other folders (sub-folders) up to 10 levels deep, and contain a combination of projects and folders.

One common way to define a folder hierarchy is to have each folder represent a department within the company, with sub-folders representing different teams within the department, each with their own sub-folders representing different applications managed by the team. These will then contain one or more projects that will host the actual cloud resources. At the top level of the hierarchy is the organization node.

If this sounds a little confusing, then take a look at the following diagram, which helps illustrate an example hierarchy. Hopefully, this will make things a little clearer to you:

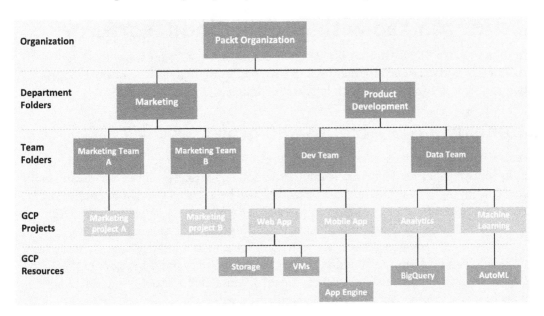

Figure 1.3 – Resource hierarchy in GCP

At every level in this hierarchy (and down to the cloud resources for certain types of resources), **Identity and Access Management (IAM)** policies can be defined, which are inherited by the nodes down the hierarchy. For example, a policy applied at the organization node level will be automatically inherited by all folders, projects, and resources under it.

Folders can also be used to isolate requirements for different environments, such as production and development. You are not required to organize projects into folders, but it is a recommended best practice that will greatly facilitate management (and access management in particular) for your projects. An organization node is also not a requirement, and not necessarily something you have to obtain if, for example, you have a GCP project for your own personal use and experimentation.

One important thing to note is that an access policy, when applied at a level in the hierarchy, cannot take away access that's been granted at a lower level. For example, a policy applied at project A granting user John editing access will take effect even if, at the organization node (the project's parent level), view-only access is granted. The less restrictive (that is, more permissive) access is applied in this case, and user John will be able to edit resources under project A (but still not under other projects belonging to the same organization).

Getting started with Google Cloud Platform

In this section, we will get started with GCP by setting up an account and a project, installing the **Software Development Kit** (**SDK**), and using BigQuery to query *Wikipedia* articles and get you warmed up with big data in Google Cloud.

Setting up a GCP account and project

From a web browser, navigate to `https://console.cloud.google.com/` and sign in with your personal Gmail account (if you don't have one, go ahead and create one before continuing). If you're a first-time user, you will be asked to select your country and agree with the Terms of Service, and you will also see a prompt for activating a free trial so that you can get $300 to explore Google Cloud. This may be a banner on the top, or a button on the **Home** page. Activate your trial, keeping in mind that you will be asked for a valid credit card number. But don't worry – you won't be charged even after the trial ends, unless you manually upgrade to a paid account. There should be a clarifying statement on the trial activation page that confirms this.

Once you've gone through that so that your account has been set up and your trial has been activated, you should be directed to the Google Cloud console. A project named **My First Project** (or something similar) will be automatically created for you. On the top bar within the console, you can see which project you're currently working under from the top-left corner:

Figure 1.4 – GCP console project view

If you click on the small down arrow next to the name of the project, it will open the project selection menu, as shown in the following screenshot. This is where you can choose which project to work on (for now, there will only be one listed). You can also create a new project from here if you wish to do so:

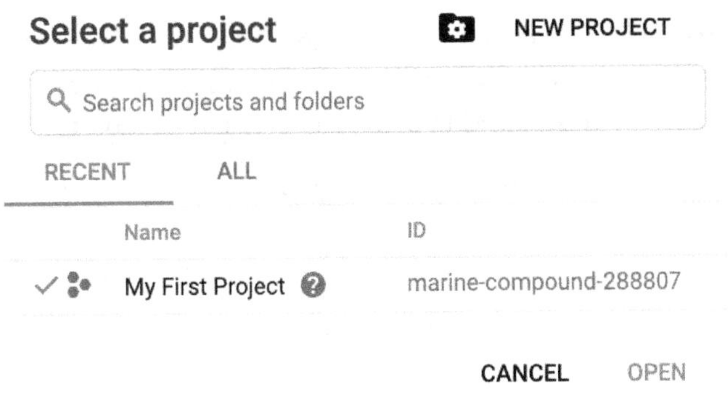

Select a project   ⚙   NEW PROJECT

Q Search projects and folders

RECENT   ALL

Name   ID

✓ ⦂• My First Project ❓   marine-compound-288807

CANCEL   OPEN

Figure 1.5 – GCP project selection menu

For every project in GCP, the following must be defined:

- **Project Name**: Set by you and doesn't need to be globally unique. Can be changed after project creation.

- **Project ID**: Can be set by you but needs to be globally unique and cannot be changed.

- **Project Number**: Assigned by GCP. It is globally unique and cannot be changed.

For now, however, we don't need to create a new project (we will do that in *Chapter 2, Mastering the Basics of Google Cloud*, as well as handling things such as billing and IAM policies. If you're already somewhat familiar with the platform, feel free to skip ahead to the next chapter!).

Installing the Google Cloud SDK and using gcloud

The Google Cloud **Software Development Kit** (**SDK**) is a set of tools for interacting with the platform. This includes the gcloud, gsutil, and bq command-line tools, as well as client libraries and local emulators for developing with Google Cloud.

Go to `https://cloud.google.com/sdk/install` and follow the installation instructions specific to your operating system. Make sure that you complete the last step, which is to run the following on a terminal:

```
$ gcloud init
```

If you're a Windows user, after running this command, there will be an option to select at the end of the installation process. This command will initialize `gcloud` and set some default configurations. You will be asked to sign in to Google Cloud and choose a project.

If you want to see what the active configuration is, you can run the following command:

```
$ gcloud config list
```

This command should list your active configurations, such as the account and project currently being used.

The `gcloud` CLI commands are organized into a nested hierarchy of command groups, each one representing a specific service or feature of the platform or their functional subgroups. So, for example, if you want to run commands against virtual machines, you would start with `gcloud compute instances`. That's how you "drill down" the hierarchy of command groups: you simply append the respective command group name. This is, of course, a very long list to memorize, but you don't have to. As you type in commands, if you're unsure what options are available for the next level, you can simply add the `--help` command suffix flag and you will see the sub-groups and commands you can use from that point on.

For example, if you want to see what you can do with compute instances, you can type in the following:

```
$ gcloud compute instances --help
```

In the output, you should see something similar to the following:

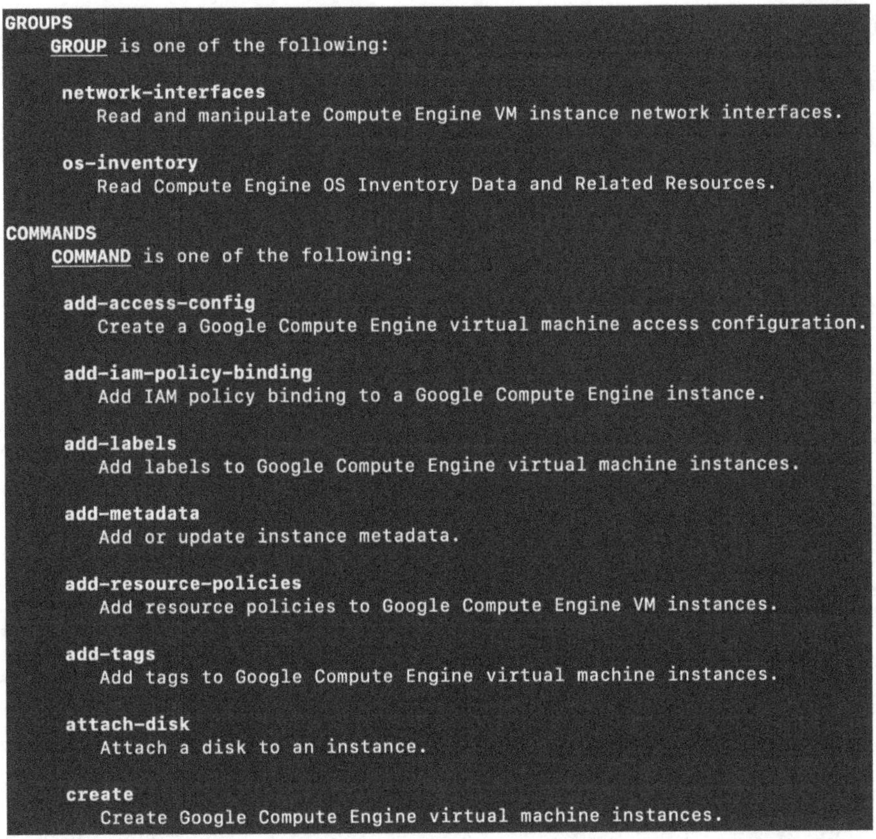

```
GROUPS
    GROUP is one of the following:

     network-interfaces
         Read and manipulate Compute Engine VM instance network interfaces.

     os-inventory
         Read Compute Engine OS Inventory Data and Related Resources.

COMMANDS
    COMMAND is one of the following:

     add-access-config
         Create a Google Compute Engine virtual machine access configuration.

     add-iam-policy-binding
         Add IAM policy binding to a Google Compute Engine instance.

     add-labels
         Add labels to Google Compute Engine virtual machine instances.

     add-metadata
         Add or update instance metadata.

     add-resource-policies
         Add resource policies to Google Compute Engine VM instances.

     add-tags
         Add tags to Google Compute Engine virtual machine instances.

     attach-disk
         Attach a disk to an instance.

     create
         Create Google Compute Engine virtual machine instances.
```

Figure 1.6 – gcloud help command output for compute instances

The GROUPS section lists the command sub-groups available "under" gcloud compute instances. We can see here that we can drill further down into the VM network interfaces or the VM OS inventory data and run commands against those resources.

The COMMANDS section lists the commands that can be applied at the level that you are in (in this case, compute instances). In this example, this include things such as creating a VM, attaching a disk, adding tags, and several others not shown in the preceding screenshot.

It is also a good idea to bookmark the *cheat sheet* from Google so that you can quickly look up commonly used commands:

https://cloud.google.com/sdk/docs/cheatsheet.

Using the bq command-line tool and a primer on BigQuery

The bq command-line tool is a Python-based CLI for BigQuery.

BigQuery is a petabyte-scale analytics data warehouse. It is actually two services in one:

- SQL Query Engine
- Managed Storage

It therefore provides both a serverless analytics engine and storage space for data, and you don't have to manage any of the underlying infrastructure for that. Google also provides a number of publicly available datasets that are ready to consume, so it's very easy to get started. So, let's run a query right away to count the number of Wikipedia articles whose titles contain the word cloud or variations of it. Open a terminal and run the following:

```
$ bq query --use_legacy_sql=false \
'SELECT DISTINCT
    title
 FROM
    `bigquery-public-data`.samples.wikipedia
 WHERE
    title LIKE "%cloud%"'
```

The first time you run the bq command, you may be asked to select a GCP project to be the default one to work with. Simply select the same project you've been working on so far.

This command is simply running a SQL query that selects the title column from the Wikipedia table (under the public dataset called samples), where the title text includes the substring cloud. In other words, we're asking to see all the Wikipedia article titles that include the word cloud in some way.

Your output should look like this:

```
+------------------------------------------------------------------------+
|                                title                                   |
+------------------------------------------------------------------------+
| Stratocumulus cloud                                                    |
| 1970 Propane vapor cloud explosion in Port Hudson                      |
| The Raincloud Man                                                      |
| User talk:Wanderingclouds818                                           |
| File:Chase the clouds.jpg                                              |
| Chaos cloud                                                            |
| Wikipedia:Featured picture candidates/File:Noctilucent clouds bargerveen.jpg |
| Ceiling (cloud)                                                        |
| User talk:Finalcloud33                                                 |
| User talk:The-cloud-atlas                                              |
| Talk:Altocumulus cloud                                                 |
| File:Wildfire in Yellowstone Natinal Park produces Pyrocumulus cloud.jpg |
| User talk:Deathcloud33                                                 |
| Formosan clouded leopard                                               |
| Rock filled cloud                                                      |
| File:LA cloudbasin.jpg                                                 |
| Get off of my cloud                                                    |
| File:Actinoform cloud.jpg                                              |
| Rope cloud                                                             |
| User:Biocloudy                                                         |
| User talk:Qcloudpromo                                                  |
| User:Arianne bustillo/Summary of killing time in st cloud             |
| Wikipedia:Articles for deletion/Crystalclouds                         |
| Rainclouds over Wushan                                                 |
| File talk:Oort cloud Sedna orbit.svg                                   |
| User talk:Nandcloud                                                    |
```

Figure 1.7 – bq query output

The preceding screenshot only shows a part of the full output. As you can see, there are quite a few cloud-related articles on Wikipedia.

In this section, you signed up for GCP, installed the SDK, got up and running with the platform, and with just a short CLI command, you queried the entire Wikipedia dataset in a matter of just a few seconds, without spinning up a single VM or database – and without even paying for it. This was just a taste of the power of Google Cloud. With that, you have gotten up to speed with how to interact with the platform and what some of its capabilities are.

Summary

In this first chapter, you learned about the appeal of cloud computing and how to make the case for cloud adoption and for Google Cloud in particular. You also learned about some of Google Cloud's key differentiators, such as its fast network and its cutting-edge big data and AI services. We had a look at the core services of the platform and things such as regions and zones, the resource hierarchy, and other GCP concepts. Finally, we got started with the platform by setting up an account and installing the Cloud SDK, before teasing out BigQuery's powerful capabilities by running a fast serverless query on a sample public dataset.

In the next chapter, we will get into IAM in Google Cloud and look at ways to improve the cost discipline. To help you truly master the basics, we will end the next chapter with a case study and a small hands-on project.

2

Mastering the Basics of Google Cloud

You might have heard the expression "*Identity is the new perimeter.*" **Identity and Access Management (IAM)** is a key component of any cloud solution design and is a foundational skill. A well-designed identity solution goes a long way in protecting users and businesses in the cloud world. In addition, honing your **cost discipline** by leveraging the ways you can save costs in **Google Cloud**, as well as the different ways you can monitor and keep track of your expenses, will provide you with yet another strong pillar of cloud governance. In this chapter, to establish a strong foundation and allow you to master the basics, you will learn about Google Cloud's approach to IAM and concepts such as the **least privilege principle**. You will then learn how to be cost-effective within Google Cloud. To put all that into practice, you will complete a hands-on assignment based on a case study of a fictional start - up.

In this chapter, we're going to cover the following main topics:

- Understanding IAM
- Practicing the cost discipline on Google Cloud
- Getting hands-on – a case study

Let's get started!

Technical requirements

Check out the following link to see the Code in Action video: `https://bit.ly/388Ay5q`

Understanding IAM

IAM is the discipline that ensures the right access is given to the right individuals and systems. Since the explosion of internet-connected devices and the ease with which company employees can now reach internal IT systems and work apps over the internet (as opposed to from within a firewalled corporate network), it is now generally accepted that identity, not the network, is the *security perimeter*. You might have heard the phrase *"Identity is the new perimeter."* This is because this new perimeter extends well beyond the corporate network environment to include personal computers and devices in remote locations. This means that no matter how well-protected networks are, it is still crucial to have strong security policies in place to secure users' identities and to have measures in place that mitigate risks if – and when – identities are breached. A compromised identity, especially a privileged one, can cause so much damage to the business that you might as well not have any network firewall if your IAM is lax.

In GCP, an IAM policy can be summarized as *"[who] [can do what] [on what resources]."* It has, therefore, three components:

- **who**: This can be a Google account, a Google group, a service account, or an entire G-suite or **Cloud Identity** domain.

- **can do what**: The permissions defined by an IAM role. There are three kinds of roles: *primitive*, *predefined*, and *custom*, as follows:

    a) **Primitive**: These are the broad roles of *owner*, *editor*, and *viewer*. A viewer can examine but not change the state or configuration of a resource (that is, a viewer has read-only access); an editor can do everything a viewer can do, plus change the state and configuration of a resource; and an owner can do everything the editor can do, plus manage roles and permissions on the resource. If they're the owner at the project level, they can also set up billing for that project. The additional primitive role of the *Billing administrator* exists at the project level for access to setting up and managing billing, but not to editing project resources.

b) **Predefined**: These are predefined roles specific to a GCP service that are aligned with the typical job roles of individuals using those services. For example, Compute Engine offers a set of predefined roles that define permissions to Compute Engine resources exclusively, such as `instanceAdmin`, along with a set of permissions necessary to create, modify, and delete **virtual machines (VMs)**; or `imageUser`, which has a more specific set of permissions for listing and reading images. Each service will have its own set of predefined roles.

c) **Custom**: Roles where you can manually specify the list of permissions associated with the role. You must create and manage these types of roles yourself, but they're a fundamental component of the least privilege principle, which we will discuss in more detail later.

- **on what resources**: The specific resources access is assigned for; that is, the scope of the permissions, which can also be a project, folder, or organization node. Since permissions are inherited from parent nodes, an access policy that's applied at any of the parent levels will affect all the resources down the hierarchy. Custom roles can only be applied at project and organization levels (not folders).

Service accounts are used when the "who" is a machine. They control server-to-server interactions, such as when a VM needs to access the Cloud Storage service. It is a crucial component of IAM as it prevents the usage (and storage) of a real user's credentials for this type of authentication. In GCP, service accounts use managed cryptographic keys as opposed to passwords to access resources. You can assign IAM roles to service accounts, just like you would with any user account. They are identified with email addresses, as follows:

- `PROJECT_NUMBER-compute@developer.gserviceaccount.com`
- `PROJECT_ID@appspot.gserviceaccount.com`

Next, we will look at the principle of least privilege and the IAM Recommender.

Principle of least privilege and the IAM Recommender

The principle of least privilege states that an identity (be it a user, a system, or a group) should only be able to access the resources and perform actions that are strictly necessary for the user or system to perform its function. For example, an account created solely to manage databases should not be able to make any configuration changes to the network or anything else other than databases. It doesn't matter if this is a service account being used by a system or script that was designed to configure databases specifically, and which would therefore never "touch" anything else by design. The identity can still be stolen and used by a third party, in which case what really matters is the permissions that have been granted to this identity and not how it is used.

The least privilege principle is one of the components of the **zero trust** security model, which we will discuss in a little more depth in the next chapter.

A well-designed cloud-based solution should have the least privilege principle enforced at all times. Apart from the increased level of security, a nice side effect is that it also prevents accidental and unwanted changes to the system due to human errors and misconfigurations. For example, if a deployment pipeline uses a service account to configure databases, if someone accidentally makes changes to the deployment template so that it includes changes to the network where the database has been deployed to, the lack of permissions on the service account will prevent the deployment from actually happening.

To help you enforce the least privilege principle, Google Cloud offers a recommendation service called **IAM Recommender**. It works by comparing project-level role grants with the permissions that each member actually used in the past 90 days. If there were unused permissions, then the IAM Recommender is likely going to recommend that you either revoke the role or assign a less permissive role instead (often a custom role, with a more specific set of permissions than predefined roles). The IAM Recommender never suggests a change that increases the level of access, and it will never apply recommendations automatically without your review and acceptance. However, there are ways you can automate the process of applying these recommendations.

The IAM Recommender service also uses machine learning to identify situations where a member is likely to need specific permissions, even if they haven't used them in the past 90 days. This prevents "noise" in the recommendation set in cases where users don't necessarily use a specific set of permissions during a long period, but are likely to need it eventually. This also reduces the risk of breaking changes if you automate the process of applying recommendations.

Later in this chapter, you will get the opportunity to put your knowledge of IAM into practice. Now, let's explore another fundamental security principle, which is that of segregation of duties.

Segregation of duties

Another very important best practice in the context of identity management is segregation of duties. Simply put, it means that no one should have all rights, and highly privileged rights are spread among multiple people. Its intention can be divided into two key objectives:

- **Conflict of interest**: This relates to abusing administrative power, and the possibility of wrongful acts being performed by individuals who would be responsible for reporting them themselves and whose acts are unrestricted.

- **Detection of security control failures**: This includes security breaches or theft of information and intellectual property. An individual with influence over the design and implementation of security controls can potentially circumvent them and prevent, for example, reports of fraudulent activities from surfacing.

To reduce business risks and improve the organization's security posture, organizations must strive to apply segregation of duties to highly privileged operations and highly sensitive areas. Responsibilities and rights must be assigned to individuals so that no one single individual could compromise the system, and especially not be able to do so without any trace.

Cloud Identity

Cloud Identity is Google's **Identity-as-a-Service (IdaaS)** solution for centrally managing users and groups. Most IT professionals are likely familiar with **Active Directory (AD)** as an identity provider and **Azure Active Directory (AAD)** as Microsoft's IdaaS solution in the cloud. Cloud Identity works very similar to how AAD does, by providing user authentication and features such as **Single Sign-On (SSO)** and **Multi-Factor Authentication (MFA)**.

Cloud Identity has two editions: a free edition and a premium edition. The free edition comes at no cost, but it lacks several features that are available in the premium edition, such as mobile device management, advanced passcode enforcement, security policies, mobile audit, remote device wipe, secure LDAP, automated user provisioning, and more. A full feature comparison between the two editions is available at `https://cloud.google.com/identity/docs/editions`.

You don't have to necessarily use Cloud Identity to manage user accounts in Google Cloud and apply IAM policies; you can have an external identity provider instead. Also, Cloud Identity can be configured to federate identities between Google and other providers, such as AD and AAD. So, if you have, for instance, AD set up in your on-premises environment or if the partners that you work with are using AD-based solutions, you can still use Cloud Identity and have no integration issues.

Really, the absolute most important thing about any IdaaS solution, be it Cloud Identity or any other, is to *enable MFA for your users*. Recent statistics gathered by Microsoft (which, by their accounts, analyze over 300 million fraudulent sign-in attempts to their cloud services) pointed out that *MFA can block over 99.9 percent of account compromise attacks*. This is typically highly recommended for highly privileged accounts, but it works best when you extend it to your whole user landscape. If you do nothing else but this, you will have already done most of the work toward securing your perimeter. Now, let's explore another fundamental Cloud Architect skill, which is knowing how to save costs.

Practicing the cost discipline on Google Cloud

Before we move on to learning how to design great solutions in Google Cloud, it is essential to be cost-effective by knowing how to save money on GCP. This will help not only you directly if you have a personal "lab" environment that you pay out of your pocket, but also help the organizations you work with by saving their money, regardless of whether you're building test environments or production systems. Cost optimization is a fundamental and well-appreciated skill for any Cloud Architect.

The following has been stated in Google's Cloud Adoption Framework:

> *"With no up-front procurement of IT resources to set a physical limit on the amount of resources that an application can consume and no CAPEX-based, multiyear capacity planning, controlling costs begins with the individual software engineer. [...] Without appropriate dashboards, alerts, and processes in place, managing the cloud expenditure for organizations with multiple projects, teams, or business units can be a cumbersome and time-consuming process."*

With the increased agility and ease of deploying new services in the cloud comes the risk of overspending and overshooting the budget. This may not necessarily be intentional: often times, developers or engineers will spin up a virtual machine for testing purposes, and simply forget to shut it down when it is no longer being used. Or, someone with the right access may deploy a premium tier of a service where a more standard tier would do just fine for what the application requires. Professionals in technology-related roles usually don't factor costs into their decision making; it's just not something most are used to dealing with. They care more about performance. The solution is not to take access away from them entirely or introduce business approval barriers (in most cases, that would go against agility outcomes), but to educate them on cost-saving strategies and how to design cloud budgeting and monitoring solutions in a way that prevents overspending from happening. Therefore, it is essential to master cost discipline within GCP.

It all starts with a budget, which will provide a starting point in terms of cost control by setting expectations on consumption expenses, and to enable the possibility of setting up alert notifications for the cloud governance team to react to over-consumption and uncontrolled usage of resources. A good budgeting strategy is one that is *realistic* in that the budget gives some room for short-term growth and unplanned costs (and is not overly optimistic about what the total expenses will be), as well as being *actionable*; that is, there is a periodic cost review process in place for analyzing costs (actual and/or forecasted) against budgets, and/or an alert strategy that notifies relevant stakeholders at set points of budget consumption. Next, we'll learn how to set up a budget and look at some concrete examples of how budget alerts can be setup in Google Cloud.

Budgets and alerts

With **Cloud Billing** budgets, you can define a budget amount and then set alert threshold rules that will trigger email notifications when the actual spend matches any threshold values. For example, you can set up alerts when you reach 80% and 90% of your set budget (or other percentage values). Let's say, for the sake of this example, that your budget is $1,000. This means that when your actual cost (which, in Google Cloud, is computed continuously, albeit with some delay as you deploy and utilize resources) reaches $800, you will get an email. When it reaches $900, you will get a second email. The number of threshold rules and their values can be defined by you. The goal is to make such alerts useful and actionable. For instance, you could have an alert set at 50% of the budget so that when you receive that email, you can look at the calendar and see if you are at or more than halfway through the billing month. If so, you're on track. If not, then you might want to take action to review how resources are being utilized and find out ways to cut down on costs. When you receive the 90% alert email and you still have quite a few days left in the current billing month, you might want to start thinking about shutting down resources or securing approval to expand the budget.

Budgets can be scoped to an entire *Cloud Billing account*, specifically to one or more projects and/or one or more products. You can apply budget filters to define the scope of your budget more granularly.

By default, alert emails are sent to users that have been assigned the role of *Billing Account Administrator* or *Billing Account User* in the target Cloud Billing account. However, this can be customized using **Cloud Monitoring** so that alert emails are also sent to any other users you specify. You can even use **Cloud Pub/Sub** so that additional services consume the budget alert messages and create programmatic integrations.

> **Important Note**
>
> Setting a budget does not mean that your usage will be capped automatically when you reach the budget amount. The budget is simply a tool that allows you to track what you spend on the cloud continuously. However, there are ways to cap spending programmatically based on budget alert rules, such as disabling Cloud Billing on the project via a Cloud Function that reacts to alerts. Disabling Cloud Billing causes Google Cloud services to terminate all non-free tier services, effectively preventing further costs. However, you need to keep in mind that resources might not shut down gracefully and might not be recoverable, even if you re-enable Cloud Billing.

Google Cloud Free Tier

The Google Cloud Free Tier is a collection of free resources on GCP. The purpose of this offering is for Google Cloud customers to learn about and get hands-on knowledge of Google Cloud services. It also includes a 3-month free trial with $300 credit for you to use on any of the services, something you can only benefit from once if you have not previously signed up for the free trial and have never been a paying customer. Most impressive, however, is the so-called *Always Free* feature, which provides limited access to many common Google Cloud resources at no cost. Always Free coverage and limits vary by service, and you can find an up-to-date list in Google Cloud's documentation on Always Free usage limits (`https://cloud.google.com/free/docs/gcp-free-tier#free-tier-usage-limits`). Some notorious examples are as follows:

- **App Engine**: 28 hours per day of "F" instances, or 9 hours per day of "B" instances (*App Engine Standard Environment* only).

- **BigQuery**: 1 TB of querying and 10 GB of storage per month.

- **Cloud Functions**: 2 million invocations and 5 GB network egress per month.

- **Cloud Storage**: 5 GB per month of regional storage (only in *us-east1*, *us-west1*, and *us-central1* regions).

- **Compute Engine**: 1 f1-micro VM instance per month (only in *us-east1*, *us-west1*, and *us-central1* regions), 30 GB per month of HDD disk storage, and 1 GB network egress from North America to all regions (except China and Australia) per month.

- **Pub/Sub**: 10 GB of messages per month.

There are several other services included, such as **AutoML**, **Cloud Run**, **Cloud Build**, **Kubernetes Engine**, and a few others not listed here, each with a "little something" you can do for free. As you might have already noticed from the values listed here, however, there is plenty you can do in a "lab" environment or when you're just trying things out at no cost whatsoever. Some of these offerings are generous, and you should take advantage of them. There's no program you need to sign up for; it's a part of your billing account and applies automatically.

Keep in mind, however, that this does not apply on top of a free trial account. This means that if you've already signed up for the free trial and your billing account has free trial credits, you won't be entitled to any of the Always Free benefits until that trial expires and you upgrade the billing account. Besides, Always Free is not a credit-based system, and it doesn't accumulate or roll over to the next month if you haven't used free resources.

Sustained use discounts

Sustained use discounts are automatic discounts you get for running specific Compute Engine resources for more than just a few days within a billing month. This applies to vCPUs and the memory usage of most machine types, as well as GPU devices. The discount is automatic, starting at continuous usage for 25% of a month, with the discount applied for every incremental minute you use it. The actual discounts and a detailed breakdown per machine type are available on the *Sustained use discounts* (`https://cloud.google.com/compute/docs/sustained-use-discounts`) documentation page.

It is worth noting that the discount applies across different instances *on their combined vCPU and memory usage* when the machines are of the same type. So, if you, for example, scale up an instance from *n1-standard-4* size (four vCPUs) to *n1-standard-16* size (16 vCPUs) halfway through the billing month, Compute Engine will treat the larger instance as having the same four vCPUs that you allocated at the beginning of the month, plus an additional 12 vCPUs. Therefore, you will be entitled to a full-month usage discount on the four vCPUs, and a half-month usage discount on the additional 12 vCPUs. The same goes for the memory amounts of these instances. The resources are combined and that works to your benefit as it maximizes the discounts you get.

One way to approach this benefit is to also think about its flip side: there's a "penalty" for using VMs for short periods of time. It is not a real penalty, of course; you simply pay the full price (which is still very competitive and comparable to other cloud providers). But this is like a loyalty program. If you "keep coming back" – that is, you keep deploying and utilizing VM resources–you will get discounts and pay less per hour than a user who sporadically spins up a VM and then deletes it.

Committed use discounts

Google Cloud allows you to purchase committed use contracts in return for discounted prices for VM usage. This is like the sustained use discount deal but at the next level, when you contractually commit to using resources for some time. The discounts you get are also greater.

If you're deploying production VMs for an organization or simply VMs that you expect to be running for a significant amount of time (at least 1 year), this is something to look into. The commitment period can be 1 year or 3 years, and the discount can be up to 57% on compute resources and up to 70% for memory-optimized machine types. The low-end machine types of `f1-micro` and `g1-small` are excluded from this.

With a committed use contract, you are billed monthly for the resources you have purchased and for the duration of the term you chose, regardless of whether you have deployed and used those resources. These discounts apply to the aggregate number of vCPUs, memory, GPUs, and local SSDs within a region, so they are not affected by changes in the number of instances, nor in the size of running instances. Resources that are not covered by committed use discounts are eligible for the sustained use discounts that we discussed previously, but you cannot combine these benefits over the same resources.

Some services also offer discounts when you reserve capacity for some minimum duration of time, such as BigQuery, which offers a monthly or annual compute capacity commitment.

For more information and details on the pricing tiers for different machine types, check out the documentation on *Committed Use Discounts* (`https://cloud.google.com/compute/docs/instances/signing-up-committed-use-discounts`).

Preemptible VM instances

A preemptible VM instance is a VM you can create at a much lower price than regular instances, but with one catch: the platform might terminate (preempt) these instances at any time, at short notice (30 seconds!), and certainly after they have been running for 24 hours. This is because preemptible VMs use available *excess Compute Engine capacity*, so their availability varies with usage (from Google Cloud customers in general).

You may be asking yourself, what good is a VM that doesn't last more than 24 hours and can terminate at any time? Well, there's plenty of good use for them. For example, batch processing jobs that are not time-sensitive (that is, those you can afford to wait before they complete) can run on preemptible instances. This could be resizing an image once it has been uploaded, for example. Another case for preemptible VM instances could simply be when you need an accessory VM to be created for troubleshooting or testing.

You have the possibility of defining a script that will run the moment the instance receives notice of termination (through a platform signal) so that you can gracefully terminate whatever process was running in the instance, and maybe record any important state information on an external datastore.

Preemptible VMs can be created in a managed instance group (we will get to that in *Chapter 4, Architecting Compute Infrastructure*, but a managed instance group is essentially a group of VMs that can scale out or in automatically based on usage metrics and certain rules). By specifying a minimum number of instances or a target size for the group, should a VM be terminated, another will be spun up. That way, if a processing job is interrupted by an instance being terminated, another one can pick it up. It slows things down, but it keeps them going (which is why the use case here must not be time-sensitive). One caveat, however, is that the addition of new preemptible instances is still subject to platform availability, and it may not be possible at given times. So, don't have your critical workloads running on preemptible instances! However, you can certainly benefit from it in a dev or test scenario. Knowing that instances can be terminated at any time will actually strengthen your and your team's mindset on always designing for failure, which is an essential system design skill!

Nearline, Coldline, and Archive

If you have data in the cloud that you don't expect to access often or access only very rarely, if at all, you can save costs with the **Nearline**, **Coldline**, or **Archive** Storage classes. Nearline Storage is an ideal choice in scenarios where data is not meant to be retrieved (read or modified) more often than once a month. Coldline Storage is ideal if you plan to read (or modify) your data, *at most*, once a quarter (that is, *no more than once every 3 months*). These storage classes are slightly less available than the Standard Storage class, but they are still highly durable. In other words, you won't lose your data (or it is extremely unlikely that you will), but you may not have it immediately available, should you decide to access it. The difference, however, is not very significant (SLA availability goes from 99.9% within a region with Standard Storage to 99.0% with both Nearline and Coldline, and from 99.95% to 99.9% with multi-regional deployments). What you get in return for that slightly lower availability and high retrieval cost is the *low cost for keeping it* (and only accessing it, at most, once a month or once a quarter). How much are we talking about? Prices can fluctuate in the cloud (or anywhere for that matter), but at the time of writing, the storage cost for Standard Storage is at $0.020 per GB per month, whereas the cost for Coldline Storage, for example, is $0.004 per GB per month. That is five times lower. However, while Standard Storage has no associated cost for data retrieval, with Coldline Storage, you pay $0.02 per GB of data. That is because it is meant for infrequently accessed data, which is why you shouldn't expect to save costs with Coldline Storage if you're accessing the data you put there every month or so.

Archive Storage works in exactly the same way, except it is even cheaper, but with even higher costs for data access and operations. It is meant for data that's accessed *less than once a year*. It has no availability SLA, although its typical availability is comparable to the Nearline and Coldline classes. It is worth noting that one competitive advantage that Google Cloud has is that its Archive Storage makes your data available within milliseconds (should you want to retrieve it), as opposed to hours or days, which is what other cloud providers typically require.

Custom Machine Types

Custom Machine Types is a feature of Compute Engine, in Google Cloud, that allows you to customize a machine's virtual hardware settings by defining the exact amount of CPU and memory you need. This offers more flexibility than a regular predefined machine type, which is a packaged deal. This can be a cost saving strategy when you have a workload that "sits between" two predefined machine types, where the lower type is not quite good enough and the next one in line has more capacity than necessary, either in terms of CPU or memory (or both). With custom machine types, you can be more granular when defining the amount of processing power and memory so that it fits your workload just right and you're not paying for extra capacity that is not needed.

Rightsizing recommendations

Even as you do your best to estimate the capacity needs of your VM, it is not uncommon to wind up in a situation where your VM resources are either being underutilized or overutilized to a large degree. This is when the sizing recommendation feature within GCP comes in handy. Compute Engine will analyze system metrics gathered by the Cloud Monitoring service over the previous 8 days to offer you sizing recommendations for your VMs. This happens automatically under the hood and is a built-in feature of the platform that you don't need to pay or opt-in for. This feature is also known as *rightsizing recommendations*, as it is about finding that sweet spot of resource allocation that meets your usage needs precisely.

The way it works is that if Compute Engine observes that, during the last 8 days, a particular instance has had low/high CPU utilization most of the time, it recommends a different machine type with more/fewer virtual CPUs, respectively. The same goes for memory. The recommended target machine types can either be a standard or even a custom machine type. You will also be given a cost difference estimation that is based on the previous week's usage, extrapolated to 30 days.

You may be asking yourself, why would Google offer such a thing? Wouldn't it be in their best interest to have us all pay for capacity we don't need? Why ever recommend that we downsize a VM? Well, the truth is, Google (or any other cloud provider, for that matter) cares about customer retention more than it does about short-term gains that they could get from not giving you these recommendations. After all, what if paying for capacity you don't need for an extended period ends up being the reason your organization can't become more profitable, and therefore can't scale and generate more revenue (for themselves and, by extension, Google as their cloud provider?). What if it leads smaller organizations to bankruptcy, or for them deciding on using another cloud provider because the costs on GCP are too high? Or even on going back to on-premises data centers? Ultimately, Google wants to provide a platform that is rich in value-added features to its customers so that they may prosper and grow as a business, which will then allow them to scale. And that, of course, is very much in Google's best interests.

Pricing Calculator

Finally, let's look at something that may not necessarily help you save costs directly, but will definitely help you plan and estimate your infrastructure costs and keep you grounded on what is realistic to do in Google Cloud given your budget: the **Google Cloud Pricing Calculator**. It's a web-based tool for estimating the costs of resources based on their specs and deployment region, as well as how long you use them for. You can add several different resources to your estimate to create a consumption quote for an entire infrastructure. You can even factor in things such as *committed use discounts* and *Always Free* usage. *Sustained use discounts* will also be automatically calculated as you define the usage timeframe. Keep in mind, however, that despite being a somewhat high-fidelity estimation of the real costs, the output of this tool is *not binding on either you or Google*. Your actual fees may be higher, or they may be lower. It should be used to obtain estimations, not price guarantees from Google.

This tool can be seen in the following screenshot:

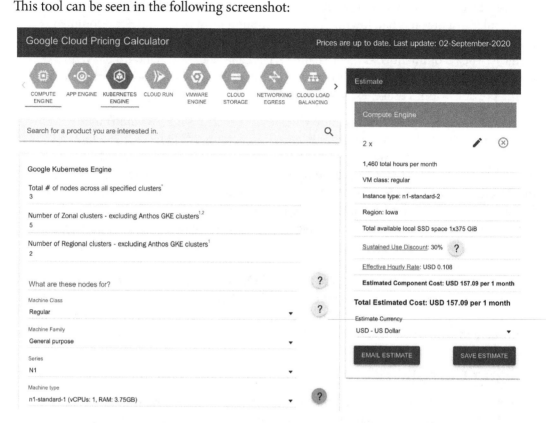

Figure 2.1 – The Google Cloud Pricing Calculator

We've covered some good foundational ground so far by covering the basics of IAM in Google Cloud and the most essential cost-saving features within GCP. Now, it's time to get hands-on.

Getting hands-on – a case study

Let's learn how to set up some necessary IAM policies and a project budget with alert rules in practice. We will introduce a case study that will test the knowledge you've acquired in this chapter by having you think about what a real-world scenario could look like. This will also get you to think like a Google Cloud Architect from the get-go.

Case study

A young unnamed technology start-up has decided to run a proof-of-concept of their web app on Google Cloud Platform and turned to you for guidance. They have a small team of developers and they have allocated only one developer to participate in this pilot. As a small startup in its early stages, they do not currently own a domain, and every user has their own Gmail account that is used for communication. The CEO specified the following requirements:

- *Costs must be kept at a minimum.* For this pilot, we have a budget of $500, and alerts should be sent via email to the CFO when costs have reached 50% and 80% of that value. The CFO should also be able to view all deployed resources.

- The developer who will be working on this *should be able to deploy the application and access the resources he or she needs, but nothing else outside of that.* You, as the Cloud Architect, will be the owner of the project for the duration of the pilot.

- The application is based on *Python 3.8* and, ideally, it should be hosted on a *service that requires no infrastructure operations* as there would be little availability in the team for such tasks.

The team is as follows:

- **CFO**: Mary Jane (`MaryJaneTheCFO@gmail.com`)
- **Developer**: John Doe (`JohnDoeThePythonWizard2020@gmail.com`)

Even though this case study refers to a very simple start - up scenario, it is not uncommon for a somewhat similar scenario and its requirements to come from a large organization that is running a pilot deployment involving a small team of individuals (perhaps more than two individuals where they all probably have their own corporate emails, but the setup is largely the same).

Let's break down the requirements and relate them to what we've discussed in this introductory chapter. Firstly, this is a very cost-conscious company that listed cost control at the top of its requirements, while also mentioning a budget and their wish to be notified of costs reaching their budget limit. What this tells us is that, for this project, a *budget and an alert rule should be defined* and that, whenever possible, any of the cost-saving strategies discussed in the previous section should be applied.

Secondly, they need the developer working on this project to be able to do their job, but they shouldn't have more access than what they strictly need to do it. This is the *least privilege principle* (a concept we will continuously come back to throughout this book), which means that we should create an IAM policy that prevents John Doe from creating or editing resources that are not required to do their job. This way, if their account is ever compromised, the attacker won't be able to "move laterally" and cause a lot more damage than tinkering with the application John Doe is involved with. In addition, the developer's responsibility is separated from, in this case, the Cloud Architect's responsibility around the infrastructure's setup, which is in line with the principle of segregation of duties.

And what resources should John Doe be able to work with? With this, we have come to the third and last requirement: this is a Python 3 application that should be hosted on a PaaS service. *App Engine Standard Environment* is a great candidate for this as it provides the added bonus of downscaling to zero instances when there is no traffic; that is, it won't cost anything when it's not being used. In part two of this book, we will explore how to decide on a compute platform and design a solution based on different application requirements in more depth. This chapter is just a primer on the capabilities of App Engine.

So, knowing that we will be deploying an App Engine Standard Environment and that the developer, John, should only be able to deploy and release code with it, let's look into the App Engine predefined roles to see if we can find one tied to his responsibilities. By taking a quick look at the documentation (`https://cloud.google.com/appengine/docs/standard/python/roles#predefined_roles`), we can find two relevant roles:

Role Title	Capabilities	Target User
App Engine Admin	Read/Write/Modify access to all application configuration and settings.	Application owner/ administrator On-call engineer Sys Admin
App Engine Deployer	Read-only access to all application configuration and settings. Write access only to deploy and create a new version. Delete old versions that are not serving traffic. Cannot modify an existing version, nor change traffic configuration.	Deployment account Release engineer

Now, which one should we pick for John Doe? *App Engine Admin* would allow him to modify application configuration and settings, but does he need to? We know for sure that he needs to deploy code, and we know that he's not a Google Cloud expert, but maybe it would be wise to give him an Admin role (even if it's restricted to App Engine) *just in case* he needs to do something other than deploy code?

Well, that kind of reasoning is often what leads to overly permissive access and security incidents down the road. The least privilege principle requires you to be strict and, when in doubt, start with the most restrictive access. On an as-needed basis, you can expand it to include additional permissions. With that in mind, let's go with the *App Engine Deployer* role.

Now that we have all the necessary information at hand and know exactly what we need to do, let's get to it.

Creating a project

You might already have a project and therefore wish to skip this step, but if you don't, we need to create a project. On the top bar within the console, you can see which project you're currently working under from the top-left corner:

Figure 2.2 – Project indicator in the Google Cloud console

If you click on the small down arrow next to the name of the project, it will open the project selection menu, where you can choose which project to work on (for now, there will be only one listed). You can also create a new project from here.

Click on **New Project** in the top-right corner:

Select a project   ⚙ NEW PROJECT

🔍 Search projects and folders

RECENT   ALL

	Name	ID
✓	My First Project ❓	marine-compound-288807

CANCEL   OPEN

Figure 2.3 – Project selection menu in the Google Cloud console

When you create a project in GCP, the following must be defined:

- **Project Name**: Set by you and doesn't need to be globally unique. Can be changed after project creation.

- **Project ID**: Can be set by you but needs to be globally unique and cannot be changed.

- **Project Number**: Assigned by GCP. It is globally unique and cannot be changed.

Under **Project Name**, type in a name for this project, such as `Pilot Project`. A project ID will be automatically generated based on the name, with some numbers added to it to make it unique. It is a good idea to click on **Edit** and choose something yourself so that it will be easier for you to remember what the project ID is. This ID is often needed in the GCP CLI and across various APIs when you're writing code or scripts to interact with the platform. Even though you can easily check it anytime, it just makes things a little bit easier if you set it to something you can more easily remember. For example, the `pilot-project-2020` ID string is still unique and a lot easier to remember, since I'm writing this in 2020:

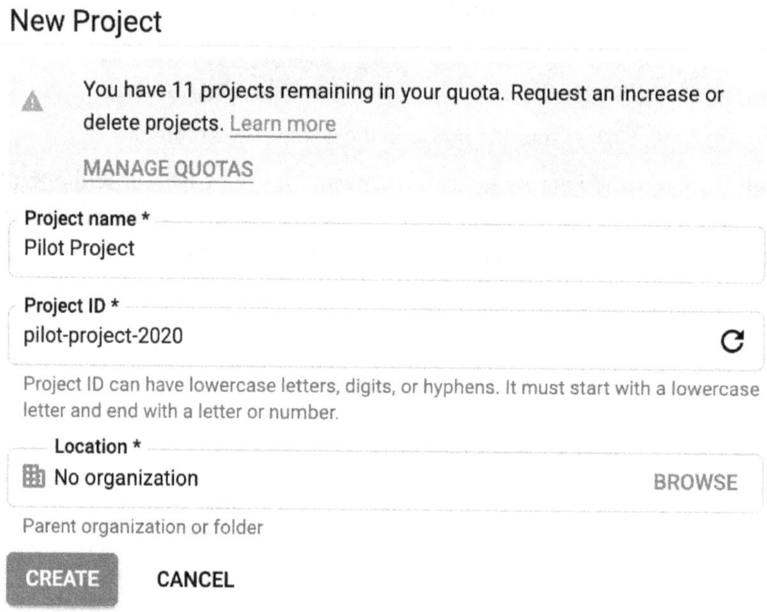

New Project

⚠ You have 11 projects remaining in your quota. Request an increase or delete projects. Learn more

MANAGE QUOTAS

Project name *
Pilot Project

Project ID *
pilot-project-2020   ↻

Project ID can have lowercase letters, digits, or hyphens. It must start with a lowercase letter and end with a letter or number.

Location *
⊞ No organization   BROWSE

Parent organization or folder

CREATE   CANCEL

Figure 2.4 – Project creation menu in the Google Cloud console

In the **Location** field, you can select an organization under which this project is to be created. We have no organization set for this assignment, so you can just leave the default of **No organization** and click on **Create**.

Configuring budget and alerts

Now, we can go ahead and create a budget.

In the console, click on the navigation menu icon in the top-left corner to expand the left-side menu if it's not already expanded. Through this menu, you can get to any GCP service and capability. Click on **Billing**, then click on **Budgets & Alerts** in the new context menu. After that, click on **Create Budget**.

On the budget creation page, first, you will be asked to give it a name and select the scope. Fill in the **Name** field with a descriptive name for the budget, such as Pilot Budget. Then, under the **Projects** drop - down field, select the project you created and leave **All products** selected for **Products**:

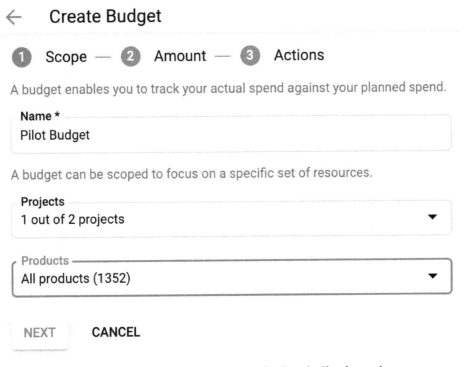

Figure 2.5 – Budget creation menu in the Google Cloud console

Click on **Next**. Under **Budget type,** leave **Specified amount** selected and for the target, amount enter the specified budget for this project ($500). Leave the **Include credits in cost** checkbox selected so that the budget will apply to the total cost minus, the free credits you received for the trial:

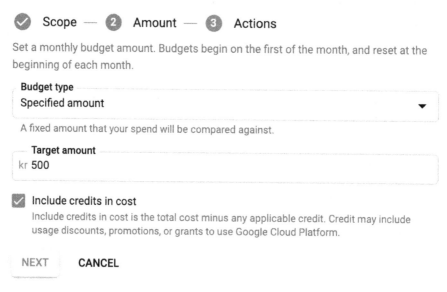

Figure 2.6 – Budget creation menu – budget type and the target amount

Click on **Next**. Note that a different currency is shown here (*Swedish krona* as opposed to *US dollars*), but you get the idea.

Now, we can define the threshold values for alerts. The requirements specify that these should be 50% and 80%, so make sure you specify those values under **Set alert threshold rules** and leave the **Actual** option selected for the **Trigger on** field. This is to ensure the alerts trigger on actual costs and not forecasted costs. Then, in the **Manage notifications** section, leave the **Email alerts to billing admins and users** checkbox selected and the others unselected:

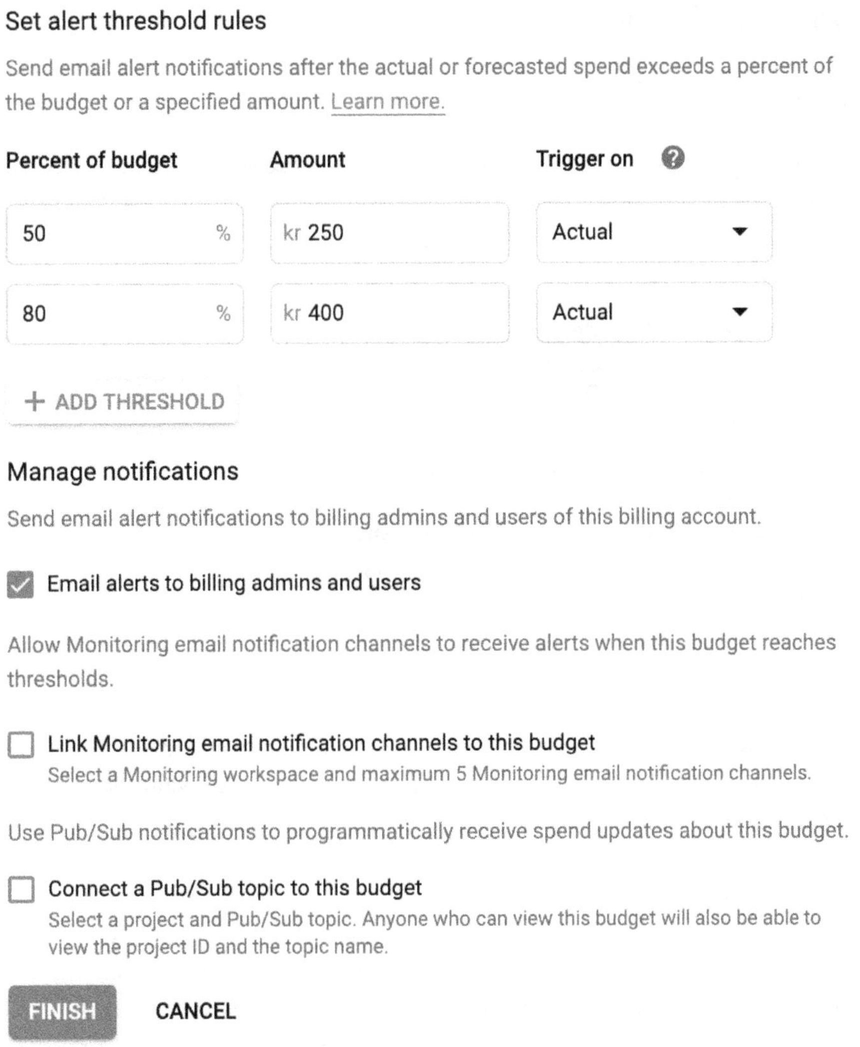

Set alert threshold rules

Send email alert notifications after the actual or forecasted spend exceeds a percent of the budget or a specified amount. Learn more.

Percent of budget	Amount	Trigger on ⑦
50 %	kr 250	Actual ▼
80 %	kr 400	Actual ▼

Manage notifications

Send email alert notifications to billing admins and users of this billing account.

☑ **Email alerts to billing admins and users**

Allow Monitoring email notification channels to receive alerts when this budget reaches thresholds.

☐ **Link Monitoring email notification channels to this budget**
   Select a Monitoring workspace and maximum 5 Monitoring email notification channels.

Use Pub/Sub notifications to programmatically receive spend updates about this budget.

☐ **Connect a Pub/Sub topic to this budget**
   Select a project and Pub/Sub topic. Anyone who can view this budget will also be able to view the project ID and the topic name.

FINISH   **CANCEL**

Figure 2.7 – Budget creation menu – alert threshold rules

Click on **Finish**. Now, we have a budget and alert rule, but no one will receive notifications yet since we haven't assigned the role of *Billing Administrators* to anybody. We'll go ahead and take care of role assignments next.

Configuring an IAM policy

In the GCP console, expand the navigation menu on the left and click on **IAM & Admin**. Then, perform the following steps:

1. On the IAM page, first, verify that you have the project you've created selected on the top bar (if not, click on the down arrow next to the project name and select the right project), then click on **Add** to add a new member to the project, as shown in the following screenshot:

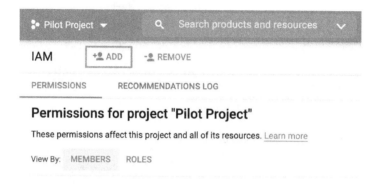

Figure 2.8 – IAM page in the Google Cloud console

2. A form will open up where you will be asked for the email address of the new member. You can enter a Gmail address here, but it must be a valid one (that is, an actual existing email address).

> **Important Note**
>
> The case study in this chapter is fictional, obviously, so the email addresses mentioned in this case study were created for demonstration purposes. If you're following along and don't have a spare Gmail account or someone that can provide theirs, feel free to skip this step and simply read on. But do NOT invite a stranger to your project by typing in a random email address!

3. To add a member, type in an email address into the **New members** field and under the **Select a role** drop-down menu, select **Viewer**, as shown in the following screenshot. *Mary Jane*, the CFO, will need this role in addition to her more specific role of Billing Account Administrator (which cannot be assigned at this point; we will do that next), since one of the requirements was that she should be able to view all the resources in the pilot project:

Add members to "Pilot Project"

Add members, roles to "Pilot Project" project

Enter one or more members below. Then select a role for these members to grant them
access to your resources. Multiple roles allowed. Learn more

New members

maryjanethecfo@gmail.com

Role	Condition
Viewer ▼	Add condition

Read access to all resources.

+ ADD ANOTHER ROLE

☑ Send notification email
This email will inform members that you've granted them access to this role for "Pilot Project"

SAVE   CANCEL

Figure 2.9 – Adding a member to a project and assigning a role

The user `maryjanethecfo@gmail.com` will receive a notification, but the access
is granted immediately (the user doesn't need to "accept" it or take any further action).

4. Next, we need to assign her the role of **Billing Account Administrator**. Because
    this is a role that is tied to a billing account, which is somewhat separate from
    GCP projects (since you can have, for example, one billing account associated with
    different projects), we need to navigate to the **Billing** page in the console (via the
    left-side navigation menu), and then click on **Account management**. You will see
    a page similar to the following:

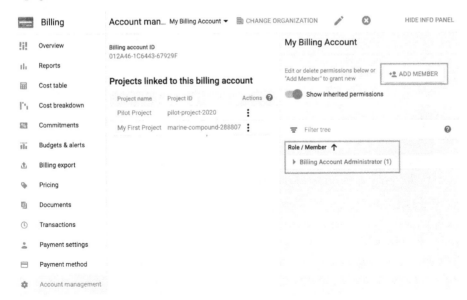

Figure 2.10 – Billing account management in the Google Cloud console

Note the box where it says **Billing Account Administrator (1)** under **Role / Member**. The number indicates how many members there are with this role. This one member is myself (or yourself, in your console), because I am the one who created the billing account (by signing up for the trial).

5. Click on **Add members** on the right-hand side pane under the name of your billing account (if you have more than one billing account, you need to select it from the top bar). A form will open up, as shown in the following screenshot, where we fill in the user's email address and select the role of **Billing Account Administrator**. Optionally, we can select the option to send an email notification, just like we did previously. Finally, click on **Save**:

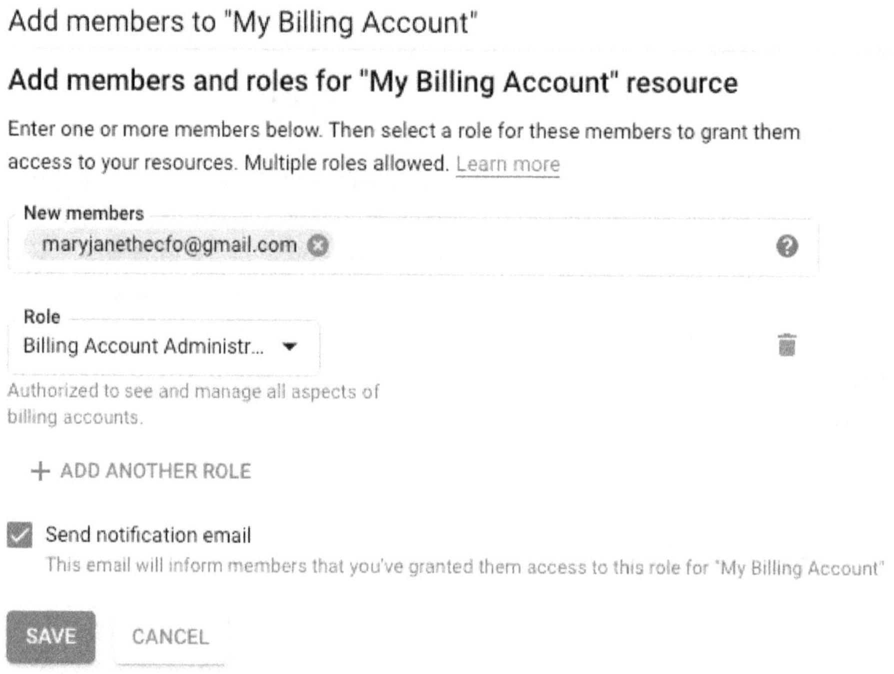

Add members to "My Billing Account"

Add members and roles for "My Billing Account" resource

Enter one or more members below. Then select a role for these members to grant them access to your resources. Multiple roles allowed. Learn more

New members

maryjanethecfo@gmail.com ⊗   ❓

Role

Billing Account Administr... ▼   🗑

Authorized to see and manage all aspects of
billing accounts.

➕ ADD ANOTHER ROLE

☑ Send notification email
This email will inform members that you've granted them access to this role for "My Billing Account"

[SAVE]   CANCEL

Figure 2.11 – Adding a Billing Account Administrator to a billing account

Again, make sure you're not adding strangers to your project.

Now, the user Mary Jane can browse the project and manage the billing account, which is exactly what we wanted. She will be able to change the threshold rules if she wishes to, and also do things such as configure billing exports, view cost information, and manage other user roles on the billing account. If she tries to, for example, navigate to Compute Engine and try to create a VM instance, this is what she will encounter:

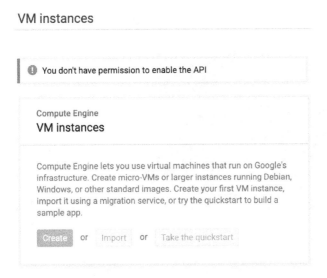

Figure 2.12 – Trying to create VM instances as a Billing Account Administrator

As you can see, she doesn't have the required access to create Compute Engine resources or, for that matter, enable the API for VM instances.

6. Now, we need to onboard the user John Doe. For that, we must navigate back to the **IAM & Admin** page and click on **Add**. Let's fill in *John Doe's* email address and his role of **App Engine Deployer**, as follows:

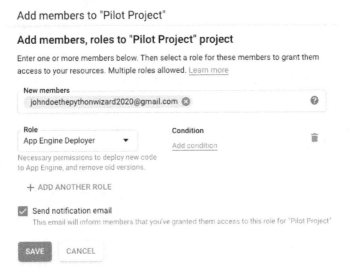

Figure 2.13 – Adding an App Engine Deployer to the project

7. Hit **Save**.

Now, if the user John Doe navigates to App Engine, he will see the following:

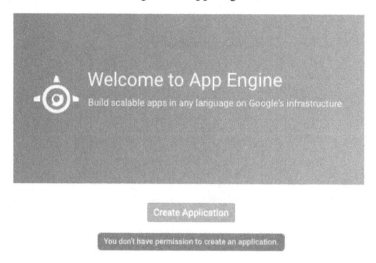

Figure 2.14 – App Engine creation page as an App Engine Deployer user

The **Create Application** button is grayed out. Indeed, he shouldn't be able to create applications (which, here, in GCP, means creating an App Engine environment), only deploy them to an existing App Engine service. We will do that next, as the architect, before handing things over to our fictional developer.

Deploying a Python 3 application on App Engine

We will do these next few steps using gcloud. For this, either open a local terminal (if you have installed the Google Cloud SDK) or go to the console and click on the terminal icon on the top-right corner of the page to open **Cloud Shell**. Cloud Shell is a web-based Linux shell that comes with Google Cloud SDK and several other tools pre-installed. Let's get started:

1. First, we must make sure that we are working on the right project by running the following command (replace pilot-project-2020 with your actual project ID):

```
$ gcloud config set project pilot-project-2020
```

2. Now, simply run the following command:

```
$ gcloud app create
```

Since we selected the project to work with by utilizing the previous command, we don't need to provide one here. The one thing we need to provide is the region where we will deploy App Engine in our project, but you will be prompted to select one, as shown in the following screenshot:

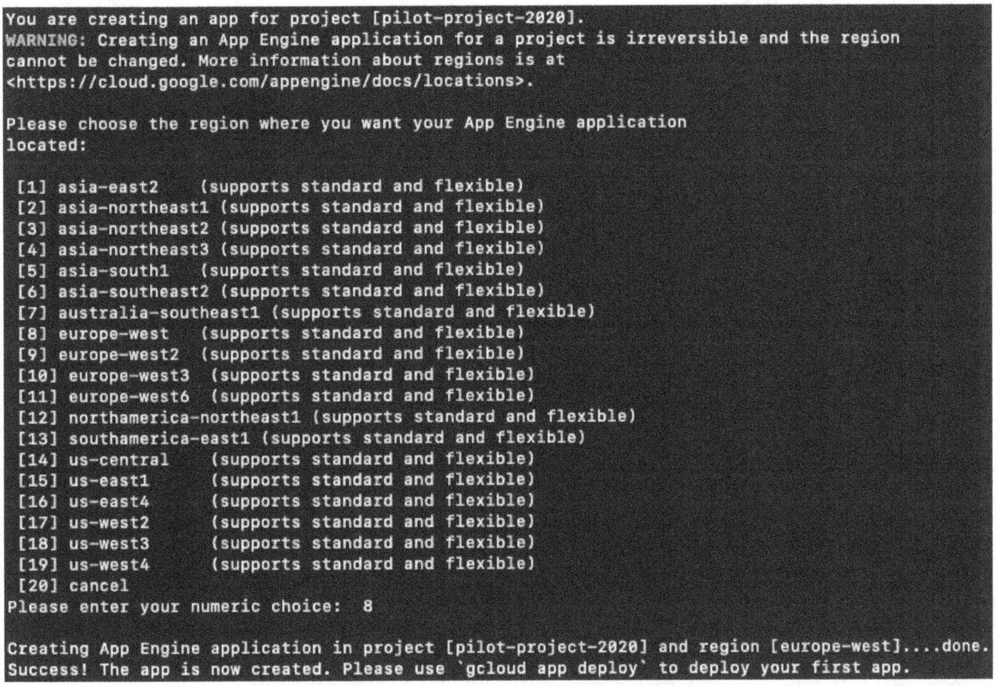

```
You are creating an app for project [pilot-project-2020].
WARNING: Creating an App Engine application for a project is irreversible and the region
cannot be changed. More information about regions is at
<https://cloud.google.com/appengine/docs/locations>.

Please choose the region where you want your App Engine application
located:

 [1] asia-east2    (supports standard and flexible)
 [2] asia-northeast1 (supports standard and flexible)
 [3] asia-northeast2 (supports standard and flexible)
 [4] asia-northeast3 (supports standard and flexible)
 [5] asia-south1   (supports standard and flexible)
 [6] asia-southeast2 (supports standard and flexible)
 [7] australia-southeast1 (supports standard and flexible)
 [8] europe-west    (supports standard and flexible)
 [9] europe-west2  (supports standard and flexible)
 [10] europe-west3 (supports standard and flexible)
 [11] europe-west6 (supports standard and flexible)
 [12] northamerica-northeast1 (supports standard and flexible)
 [13] southamerica-east1 (supports standard and flexible)
 [14] us-central    (supports standard and flexible)
 [15] us-east1     (supports standard and flexible)
 [16] us-east4     (supports standard and flexible)
 [17] us-west2     (supports standard and flexible)
 [18] us-west3     (supports standard and flexible)
 [19] us-west4     (supports standard and flexible)
 [20] cancel
Please enter your numeric choice:  8

Creating App Engine application in project [pilot-project-2020] and region [europe-west]....done.
Success! The app is now created. Please use `gcloud app deploy` to deploy your first app.
```

Figure 2.15 – Region selection prompt when creating an app

As you can see, I selected europe-west. Creating an App Engine service should only take a few seconds since we're not deploying an actual app yet. Note the warning at the top, which states that *creating an App Engine application for a project is irreversible and the region cannot be changed.* This means that from this point on, my Pilot Project will always have App Engine in West Europe. If I want to change the region, I would basically need a new project and a new App Engine deployment.

3. Now, let's take a look at what John Doe can see if he navigates to App Engine:

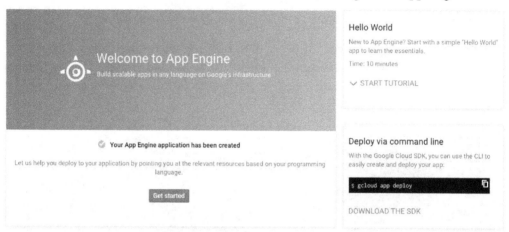

Figure 2.16 – App Engine get started page for app deployments

Because we have created the App Engine environment, John Doe (an App Engine Deployer) can go ahead and deploy apps. If he clicks on **Get started** and then selects the necessary language (Python) on the next screen, what he will see next are instructions for downloading the Cloud SDK and deploying a Python app, along with a link to any necessary documentation and a GitHub page for samples. This will look as follows:

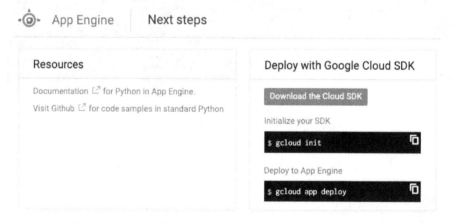

Figure 2.17 – App Engine next steps page for app deployments

That should give him everything he needs to get started. Deploying an app is as simple as running `gcloud app deploy` on a local directory containing the application files, plus a YAML file named `app.yaml` containing App Engine app's settings, such as the Python runtime. For this simple scenario, the file can simply contain one line that reads `runtime: python38` as long as the main application is in a file named `main.py` and an additional `requirements.txt` file is present containing any required non-standard libraries. John Doe can refer to the linked documentation to see what other properties of the environment he can define in the YAML file, as well as how the directory and files should be structured. If you wish to run a test deployment yourself of a "Hello World" Python flask web app, here are the steps you must follow:

```
$ git clone https://github.com/GoogleCloudPlatform/
python-docs-samples

$ cd python-docs-samples/appengine/standard_python3/
hello_world

$ gcloud config set project pilot-project-2020

$ gcloud app deploy
```

The standard output log should look similar to the following:

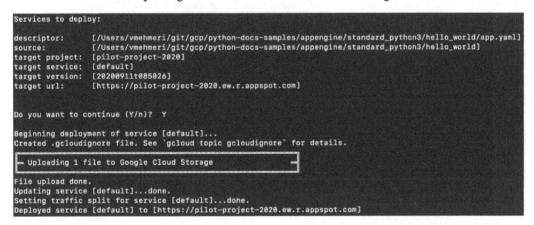

```
Services to deploy:

descriptor:      [/Users/vmehmeri/git/gcp/python-docs-samples/appengine/standard_python3/hello_world/app.yaml]
source:          [/Users/vmehmeri/git/gcp/python-docs-samples/appengine/standard_python3/hello_world]
target project:  [pilot-project-2020]
target service:  [default]
target version:  [20200911t085026]
target url:      [https://pilot-project-2020.ew.r.appspot.com]


Do you want to continue (Y/n)?  Y

Beginning deployment of service [default]...
Created .gcloudignore file. See `gcloud topic gcloudignore` for details.

- Uploading 1 file to Google Cloud Storage

File upload done.
Updating service [default]...done.
Setting traffic split for service [default]...done.
Deployed service [default] to [https://pilot-project-2020.ew.r.appspot.com]
```

Figure 2.18 – App deployment output log for our Python "Hello World" app

At the bottom, you can see an URL for the deployed app, which you can use to access the app through a browser and check if the application was deployed correctly.

Your job is now done! You can hand things over to the developer, who shall now be able to deploy apps without further assistance. Because this is a PaaS service that offers built-in availability and scalability capabilities, there's virtually nothing to be done in terms of maintaining and operating the platform. We're still lacking a vital design component here, which is that of *observability* (monitoring), so that we can get insight into application performance and several metrics that can be useful in not only troubleshooting issues, but finding ways to optimize the user experience for the application. But we will cover that in *Chapter 6, Configuring Services for Observability*.

You have now gotten some hands-on experience with the platform so that it feels more like what a real-world use case would be. You can now feel more confident with creating IAM policies (remember the least privilege principle, always) and being cost-effective in Google Cloud.

Cleaning up

If you've created an App Engine application and want to disable it, go to `https://console.cloud.google.com/appengine/settings`.

Once you've done this, click on the **Disable application** button and follow the prompts.

If you wish to delete the project and everything in it, you can simply run the following command (while replacing `PROJECT_ID` with your project ID):

```
$ gcloud project delete PROJECT_ID
```

To recap, we have created a Google Cloud project for a small proof-of-concept for a cost-conscious start - up organization. We started by setting up a budget and an alert, and then assigning correct roles and permissions to the members involved. We have made decisions in line with the principles of least privilege and segregation of duties. This simple case study illustrates the kind of mental frame a Cloud Architect must be in with such cloud projects: start from the principles, identify the priorities, and apply best practices whenever possible.

Summary

In this chapter, you learned some of the basic skills that are fundamental for any architect working with Google Cloud. You learned about IAM and the least privilege principle. You then learned about how to save costs in Google Cloud and improve your cost discipline overall. Finally, you worked on a case study where you put some of these skills into practice by creating a budget and alert rule, setting IAM policies, and deploying a basic PaaS service for an application pilot deployment.

Now that we have covered the fundamentals and have set the foundation, we'll go even deeper in the next few chapters by learning how to design great solutions with Google Cloud. We shall start with the network.

Section 2: Designing Great Solutions in Google Cloud

In this section, you will learn how to architect and design infrastructure solutions in Google Cloud and choose the right services for your needs. Covering networking, computing, storage, monitoring, security, and compliance, you will learn architectural principles and best practices as well as how to apply them on GCP.

The following chapters will be covered in this section:

3
Designing the Network

The **network** is the foundation of a compute infrastructure, and any design decision you make at this level is very hard to revert later on. Therefore, it is essential to get things right from the start of the network architecture.

In this chapter, you will learn **Google Cloud**'s approach to networking and its available services, as well as the design considerations for building networks and setting up **hybrid connectivity** between an on-premises environment (or another cloud) and Google Cloud. You will also learn how to create a shared **virtual private cloud** (**VPC**) to share networks across projects, as well as how to configure **routes** and **firewall access** on networks. Finally, you will learn about some of the common network designs in Google Cloud.

In this chapter, we're going to cover the following main topics:

- Designing networks and subnetworks
- Understanding routes and firewalls in Google Cloud
- Understanding load balancing in Google Cloud
- Designing for hybrid connectivity
- Mastering common network designs

Let's get started!

Technical requirements

Check out the following link to see the Code in Action video: `https://bit.ly/3c3CVYn`

Designing networks and subnetworks

A network in GCP is called a VPC, and it differs from the way other cloud platforms define virtual networks in that it is a more purely logical construct, with no IP address range defined in it. It is also global by default, spanning all available GCP regions, and it is segmented by **subnetworks** (the equivalent to what is referred to as *subnets* in other cloud platforms), which themselves have IP address ranges and a set region. A GCP project can have up to five VPC networks (although this quota can be increased upon request), and networks can be shared across projects and also peered with each other.

There are three network types (or "modes") in GCP, as follows:

- **Default**: Provided by default to every new project. It contains one subnetwork per region and includes some default firewall rules. These default rules allow all traffic within the network, as well as inbound RDP, SSH, and ICMP from any other network.

- **Auto**: Auto mode creates one subnetwork per region automatically with an expandable address range. The default network is, in fact, an auto mode network. When creating an auto mode network, the default firewall rules (which would be automatically deployed in the default network) are suggested in the creation form. Still, you can select which specific ones you want to deploy and there's the option to not select any of them and, therefore, not deploy any firewall rules on creation. This means every piece of network traffic will be blocked until a rule is created at a later point.

- **Custom**: In this mode, no default subnetworks are created, so you can specify in which regions you want subnetworks in. You also have full control over their IP ranges, as long as they're within the private *RFC 1918* address space. You can convert an already existing auto mode network into a custom mode network to customize it to your needs. However, you cannot convert a custom mode network back into auto mode.

Because subnetworks are regional in scope, they cross all the different zones within each region. This means that two VMs can be in the same subnetwork but deployed to different zones (which often means different data centers).

All networks have managed routing capability, which means you don't need to set up routes yourself for network communication across different subnetworks and regions of a VPC network. In addition, with the default and auto mode networks, firewall rules are also automatically set up (optionally, in the case of auto mode networks) to allow any communication that may occur within the network, even if it's going across different subnetworks and regions. With custom networks, these firewall rules won't be created automatically, but you can create them yourself and customize them to the security level you want.

> **Important Note**
>
> Although default and auto networks have been designed so that you can get started easily, you shouldn't use these options in an enterprise-grade solution. The firewall rules that allow all communications within the network and management protocols (such as RDP, SSH, and ICMP) to the outside world, though convenient, are too permissive and go against network security best practices and the zero trust principle, which we will discuss later in this chapter. The auto mode network could be used for truly global solutions, but generally, the suggested firewall rules should not be selected when creating the network.

Because Google's VPC networks are global, you can connect an on-premises network to all your GCP subnetworks (in different regions) with a single **VPN gateway** service. That way, it becomes significantly easier to extend your on-premises network to global reach with GCP.

Multi-project networking

When working with multiple projects and networks under the same organization in Google Cloud, there are two essential features to consider: **shared VPC** and **VPC peering**.

Let's look at what they are.

Shared VPC

The idea behind a shared VPC is to host a single network within a designated GCP project (referred to as the *host project*), which allows it to be shared with one or more projects (referred to as *service projects*) to centralize and simplify network management and security controls. In this model, the resources in the service projects can be deployed to one of the subnetworks of the shared VPC (belonging to the host project). Network and security policies can be applied to this one single, centralized network.

Security best practices and the least privilege principle are facilitated with the shared VPC model, since network administration tasks can be delegated to and centralized by network and security admins in the shared VPC network. Administrators in the service projects cannot make any changes that impact the network in any way. This also helps keep access control policies consistent across different projects in the organization.

When a project is set as a host project, all existing and new VPC networks will automatically become a shared VPC network. Therefore, *this is a project-level definition, and you can't determine specific networks within a host project that should become shared VPCs.*

When it comes to subnetworks, you can define which subnetworks can be accessed by a specific service project within the host project. This allows you to assign different subnetworks to different projects and keep them segregated (via firewall rules) if needed.

VPC peering

In GCP, two networks can be peered as long as they don't have overlapping IP address ranges. What peering means is that their route tables will be shared, and the underlying platform (Google's software-defined network) will be set up so that these two networks can be reached by each another. This effectively means you will have all your subnetworks (*layer 2* network domains) across both VPC networks connected via a managed *layer 3* router (which you do not need to concern yourself with). One way to think about this is that you're merely extending one of the networks with another network as if to obtain a single VPC network with a larger address space. We are, of course, talking about reachability at the network layer – things still need to be allowed in the firewall for communication to happen, and any IAM permissions granted at the VPC network level won't translate over to peered VPC networks.

VPC peering is non-transitive, which means that if **VPC A** is peered with **VPC B**, and **VPC C** is peered with **VPC B**, the resources in **VPC C** won't be able to reach the resources in **VPC A** (and vice versa) through the peerings. This is because route exchange only supports propagating routes to an immediate peer, not to peers of peers. This has implications on the scalability of, for example, a *hub-and-spoke* network model. Popularized by Microsoft as an ideal topology for sharing managed **Active Directory** (**AD**) installations and other shared services, the *hub-and-spoke* model involves one centralized hub network, and several "spoke" networks that are peered with the hub (and therefore can reach its shared services, such as AD domain controllers). The hub is also where a VPN gateway is deployed to for connectivity to on-premises networks. The general idea is that the resources in any of the "spoke" networks can reach on-premises resources (and vice versa) *through the hub*. However, due to the route exchange limitation of GCP, this design won't work as intended, unless you're deploying a smaller version of a hub-and-spoke model and you have no requirement for reachability between your spokes and on-premises. You can work around this limitation by setting up VPNs between VPCs, as opposed to peerings, though this is non-ideal, given the extra cost of VPN tunnels and extra management overhead on the network. For that reason, if you want to achieve something similar to that of a hub-and-spoke model, you should use a shared VPC.

IP addresses

In GCP, VMs can have two types of IP addresses:

- **Internal IP**: This is an IP in the private space, allocated from the subnetwork range by DHCP. An internal (network-scoped) DNS name is associated with this IP, based on its VM hostname and following the structure:

  `[hostname].c.[project-id].internal`

  Internal IPs can be static (DHCP-reserved) or *ephemeral*, in which case it might change upon, for example, the instance being restarted.

- **External IP**: This is a public IP that is dynamically assigned by GCP from an address pool when configured as *ephemeral*, or with a reserved address when configured as *static*. An external IP is never directly attached to a VM (and therefore not visible from within the VM's operating system). Rather, it's an IP address that is mapped to the VM's internal IP so that, effectively, the external IP "belongs" to the VM. DNS records can be published using existing DNS servers (outside of GCP, or within GCP when hosting the DNS zone for the domain using the **cloud DNS** service – more on that later).

You can also assign a range of IP addresses as *aliases* to a VM instance's primary IP address. This feature allows you to assign separate IPs to separate services running on the same VM instance, making it particularly useful for use cases involving *containerization*. You can also set up a secondary CIDR range in your subnetwork that can be explicitly used to assign alias IPs for that subnet.

In Google Cloud, a VM can have multiple **network interface cards** (**NICs**) belonging to different VPC networks. This means that a VM can belong to more than one network, as long as those networks' IP ranges don't overlap. The internal DNS name is only associated with the first interface (`nic0`), and the *NICs can only be configured during the creation of the instance, not afterward*. One limitation of this is that you can't delete an interface without deleting its actual VM. In other words, you should think of a NIC as not a separate resource from the VM but as a part of it. This approach to network interfaces is slightly different from what you might have seen with other cloud providers. It should guide your design decisions since you don't have the flexibility to add or remove the network interfaces on an existing VM instance. You should also keep in mind that instances support one NIC per vCPU, up to a maximum of eight NICs.

One typical use case for having a VM with multiple NICs would be when the application requires a separation between management access and data access through different networks. It could also be used for VMs performing network functions such as load balancing, or only when you want a VM to privately access two different networks when these networks can't be peered for security reasons (for example, a DMZ and an internal network).

NAT

In Google Cloud, a VM instance without an external IP address cannot communicate with public networks (such as the internet) by default. **Cloud NAT**, Google Cloud's **Network Address Translation** (**NAT**) service, allows such instances to send outbound packets to the internet (and receive corresponding inbound responses on the same established connection). Cloud NAT is a fully managed service and is a distributed, software-defined solution. Therefore, it's not based on virtual appliances or proxy VMs, and all address translation and packet handling functions are carried out in Google Cloud's underlying network infrastructure.

Using a service such as Cloud NAT has security benefits compared to having several external IP addresses assigned to VM instances. You can also manually assign specific NAT IP addresses to be used by the NAT virtual gateway, which allows you to confidently share that set of IP addresses to third parties that require IP whitelisting to provide access. As a fully managed and software-based service, cloud NAT is highly available and scalable by default, with virtually no impact on the bandwidth and network performance of outgoing connections.

For VM instances that only access Google APIs and services, an alternative is **Private Google Access**. This service allows VMs *with only internal IP addresses* to access Google's Cloud and Developer APIs and most Google Cloud services through Google's network.

DNS

Cloud DNS is a very reliable, low-latency DNS service powered by Google's global network. It's the only service in Google Cloud that is offered with 100% availability SLA. That level of availability is typically so difficult to achieve and often so unfeasible that services are almost never provided with 100% availability. However, DNS is such an essential service – since it's something that virtually every other service depends on – that if it goes down, the damage would far exceed the cost of keeping this service up at all times (without name resolution, no system anywhere would be reachable – that would have the same kind of impact as all your services being down, at least from the perspective of end users). Therefore, Google delivers DNS with 100% availability SLA. You can leverage that level of availability for your organization's DNS needs on GCP with cloud DNS. Besides, you also get autoscaling and low latency capabilities with fast anycast name servers distributed globally.

Cloud DNS offers both public zones, for names visible to the internet and that can be resolved by anyone; and private managed DNS zones, for names visible only internally. The service also includes managed **DNS security extensions (DNSSEC)**, which add security capabilities that protect your domains from DNS spoofing and cache poisoning attacks.

To be able to manage and automate DNS records for systems on GCP, it is a good idea to have the relevant DNS zones within Google's cloud DNS by making it the authoritative DNS server for those zones (in case you have your DNS services elsewhere).

Cloud CDN

The cloud **Content Delivery Network (CDN)** is a service that allows you to use Google's global edge network to serve content closer to users. You can reduce latency and speed up access to website content (especially "static" content such as images and JavaScript files) for your users. In addition, by having commonly accessed content distributed globally through Google's edge network, you also reduce the load on your web servers.

This service works with an external load balancer (which we will explore later in this chapter) to deliver content. The load balancing service will provide the frontend IP addresses and ports that receive requests, as well as the backends (referred to as *origin servers*) that provide the content in response to requests. To understand how cloud CDN works, particularly with regard to how it handles caching and cache misses, please refer to `https://cloud.google.com/cdn/docs/overview#how-cdn-works`.

Network pricing and service tiers

Pricing is always an essential factor in any design, so in this section, we'll highlight the basic pricing considerations for networking services in Google Cloud.

General network pricing

Although these prices can change, the following table provides some general pricing information for Google Cloud networking services, at the time of writing, to give you a good idea of what is charged and what the cost structure looks like:

Usage Type	Price
Ingress traffic.	Free
Egress traffic to the same zone (via an internal IP address).	Free
Egress traffic to Google products (YouTube, Maps, Drive, and so on).	Free
Egress traffic to a different GCP service within the same region, except Memorystore for Redis, Filestore, and Cloud SQL.	Free
Egress traffic between zones in the same region .	$0.01 per GB
Egress traffic to the same zone (via an external IP address).	$0.01 per GB
Egress traffic between regions within the US.	$0.01 per GB
Egress traffic between regions not within the US.	Varies by region
Egress traffic to the internet.	Varies by combination of service tier, geolocation, and data volume

Usage Type	Price
Static IP address (dissociated).	$0.010
Static and ephemeral IP addresses associated with standard VM instances.	$0.004
Static and ephemeral IP addresses associated with preemptible VM instances.	$0.002

Further and more up to date information about pricing can be found at `https://cloud.google.com/network-tiers/pricing`.

The following diagram provides a visual illustration of what types of network traffic are charged, as well as what types are not:

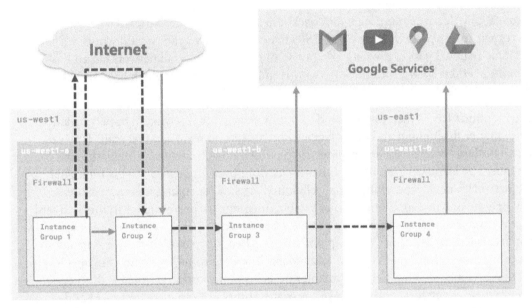

Figure 3.1 – Types of network traffic in GCP – free (solid lines) and charged (dashed lines)

In the preceding diagram, the arrows indicate the direction of the traffic. A solid line shows traffic that is free of charge, while a dashed line shows network traffic that incurs a cost.

As a cloud architect, you may want to explore ways to reduce unnecessary network costs, such as when there are "chatty" applications communicating across different regions when they could have been deployed in the same region. Such design decisions are obviously multi-dimensional and involve trade-offs between cost, performance (bandwidth, latency), availability, and more. Very often, however, the cost aspect is left out of these discussions.

Service tiers

Google Cloud is the first major public cloud provider to offer a tiered cloud network. There are two network service tiers you can choose from: **Premium Tier** and **Standard Tier**.

The main difference is that with the Premium Tier, most or all network traffic is routed through Google's "premium" network backbone. In contrast, the Standard Tier relies on regular **internet service provider (ISP)** networks. This, of course, really only affects the inter-regional part of the network, not so much so the internal networking and the communications between cloud services within the same region, which have similar characteristics in both tiers.

The Premium Tier is therefore tailored to online services that rely on high performance (with higher throughput and lower latency communications) at a global scale. It is well-suited for large enterprises and businesses for which downtime means impactful loss of revenue. The Standard Tier, on the other hand, optimizes for cost by relying on regular ISP networks for internet traffic. It is well-suited for smaller enterprises and businesses that operate only within a single cloud region. The network performance in the Standard Tier is similar to that of other cloud providers, according to Google. Therefore, it is not necessarily to be seen as a "cheap and dirty" networking solution for non-serious businesses, but a solution that is, well, standard. The Premium Tier is then the next level for those seeking the best Google can offer in terms of networking, which is the largest cloud provider network globally (in terms of the number of points of presence) and arguably the best performing one.

Due to the global nature of the premium service tier, the network services and resources that are global in nature, such as global HTTP(S) Load Balancing and Cloud NAT Gateways, are thus always Premium Tier themselves (although they'll likely also have a Standard Tier version that operates only within a single region). In a way, Google is simply packaging its global network services into a Premium Tier offering by keeping everything inside its own high-performing network. It is doing so to draw a line between the performance and pricing characteristics of global and regional networking products, in addition to giving users the option to derive cost savings at the expense of network performance. Keep in mind that the Premium Tier is the default tier when deploying and using GCP networks. In contrast, the Standard Tier is something you have to opt in for when you want to tell Google to use ISP networks (instead of their own) for traffic over the internet.

Getting hands-on – deploying a custom VPC network

If you don't already have a Google Cloud account and project set up, please refer to *Chapter 1, An Introduction to Google Cloud for Architects*, for instructions on how to do so.

In the GCP console, make sure you have the Compute Engine API (required for deploying networks) enabled on your project by going to the following URL:

```
https://console.cloud.google.com/marketplace/product/google/
compute.googleapis.com.
```

Then, click on **Enable**. If you don't have a project selected (via the top bar of the console), you'll be asked to choose the project where you wish to enable the API. If you have a project selected and you don't see this button, this means the API is already enabled on your project.

In the GCP console, expand the navigation menu on the left by clicking on the menu icon (the icon with three stacked horizontal lines) in the top-left corner. Then, search for and click on **VPC network**. Your project likely has a default VPC network, unless you deleted it after creating the project. Explore the default network, observing the subnetworks that were created (one on each of the available regions), and also explore the **Firewall** section to see the default firewall rules. Finally, check the **Routes** section to view the local default routes for each subnetwork, plus a default route to the internet. We'll dive deeper into firewalls and routes in the next section.

Click on **VPC networks** and then on **Create VPC Network**, as shown in the following screenshot:

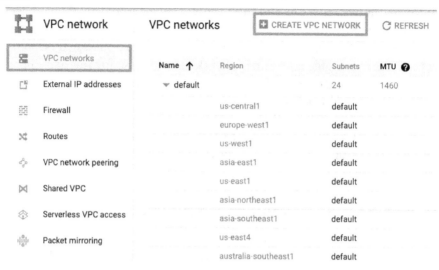

	VPC network	VPC networks	⊕ CREATE VPC NETWORK	C REFRESH

		Name ↑	Region	Subnets	MTU ❷
🖵	External IP addresses	▼ default		24	1460
🖾	Firewall		us-central1	default	
			europe-west1	default	
✕	Routes		us-west1	default	
⟡	VPC network peering		asia-east1	default	
⋈	Shared VPC		us-east1	default	
			asia-northeast1	default	
⟁	Serverless VPC access		asia-southeast1	default	
⣿	Packet mirroring		us-east4	default	
			australia-southeast1	default	

Figure 3.2 – Creating a VPC network

Give it a name (for example, `my-custom-vpc`), a description if you'd like, and then, under the **Subnets** section, select **Custom** under **Subnet creation mode**. Note that you won't have any subnetworks listed as you would if you'd selected automatic mode because, now, how your subnetworks are defined is up to you.

Click on **Add Subnet**. Name it `subnet1-eastus`, and then for **Region**, select `us-east1`, and for **IP address range**, type in `10.10.0.0/20`. In the **Private Google Access** field, select **On**. Under **Flow logs**, select **On**, and then click on **Configure Logs** to expand the flow logs configuration form. After that, select **30 SEC** for **Aggregation Interval**. Leave the remaining options with their default values. Click on **Done**.

Click on **Add Subnet** to add a new subnet. Name it **subnet2-westeu**. For **region**, choose `europe-west1`. In the **IP address range** field, type in `10.20.0.0/20`. This time, select **Off** for both the **Private Google access** and **Flow logs** fields. Click on **Done**.

Under **Dynamic routing mode**, select **Global**. Click on **Create**. On the **VPC networks** page, create your newly created VPC (**my-custom-vpc**). Explore the configuration of your new VPC, which should match the one shown in the following screenshot. Navigate to the **Firewall rules** tab, as well as the **Routes** tab, and see how those lists are empty (except for the default route to the internet and to your subnetworks, which were created for you). With custom VPC networks, you don't get certain things automatically set up for you, but you do have full control over the configurations. When designing networks for enterprise organizations, this is the way you should approach it:

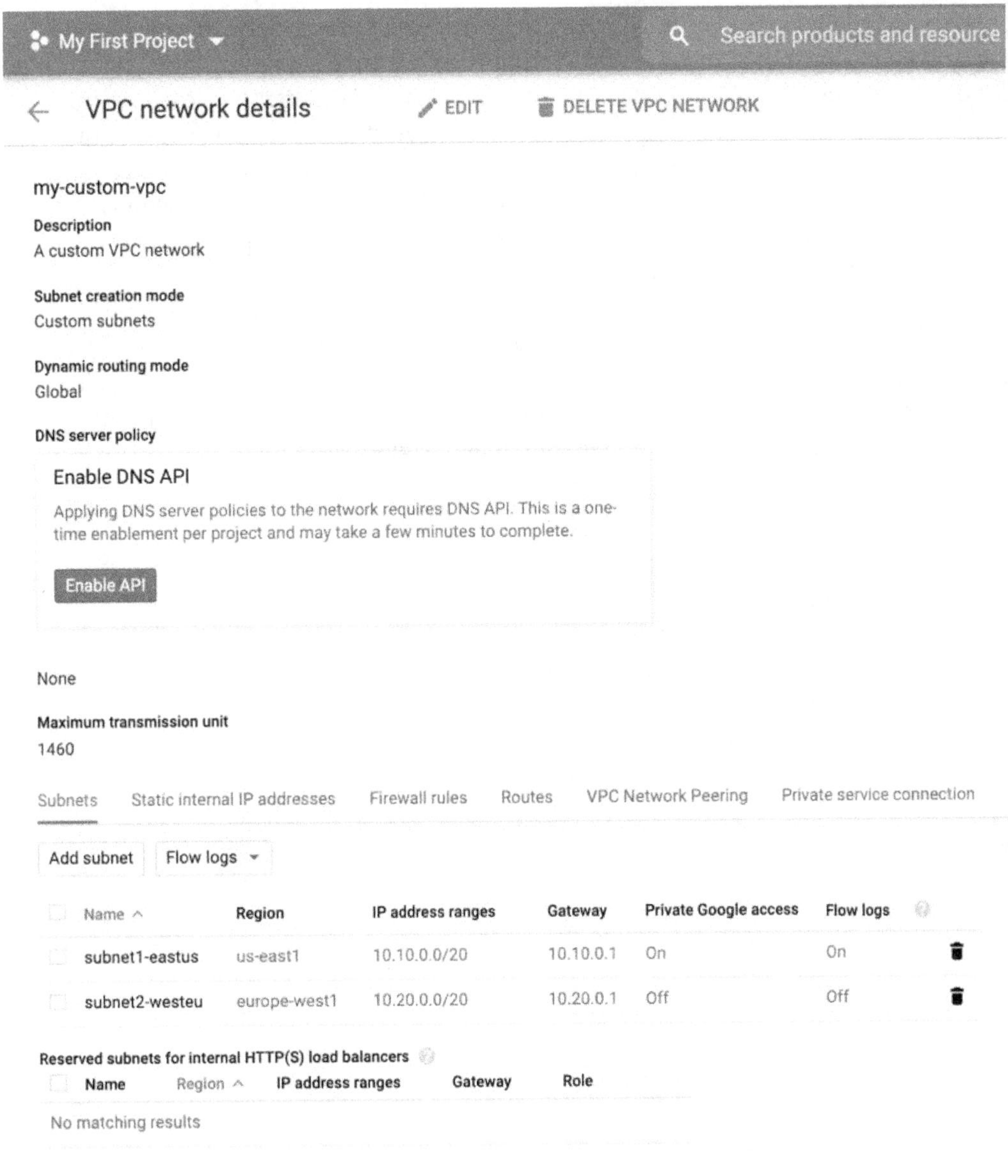

VPC network details

✏ EDIT   🗑 DELETE VPC NETWORK

my-custom-vpc

Description
A custom VPC network

Subnet creation mode
Custom subnets

Dynamic routing mode
Global

DNS server policy

Enable DNS API

Applying DNS server policies to the network requires DNS API. This is a one-time enablement per project and may take a few minutes to complete.

Enable API

None

Maximum transmission unit
1460

Subnets   Static internal IP addresses   Firewall rules   Routes   VPC Network Peering   Private service connection

Add subnet   Flow logs ▾

Name ^	Region	IP address ranges	Gateway	Private Google access	Flow logs	
subnet1-eastus	us-east1	10.10.0.0/20	10.10.0.1	On	On	🗑
subnet2-westeu	europe-west1	10.20.0.0/20	10.20.0.1	Off	Off	🗑

Reserved subnets for internal HTTP(S) load balancers

Name	Region ^	IP address ranges	Gateway	Role

No matching results

Figure 3.3 – A custom VPC network

Now, what did you just create? This is a VPC network with two subnetworks, one located in the East US region and another in the West Europe region. It's a custom VPC network with no default firewall rules. Therefore, no communication is currently allowed in this network. You're starting with tight security. You also have **global dynamic routing** mode enabled, which means that GCP's Cloud Router has visibility to the resources in all regions and will be able to dynamically route traffic to VMs across different regions. For example, if there's a VPN tunnel set up in one of the regions to an on-premises network, VMs in other regions can only reach the tunnel (and the on-premises network) *if global dynamic routing is enabled*. In addition, both subnetworks here (and any additional subnetworks that are created) will be advertised by Cloud Router, and all the VMs in all regions will dynamically learn about on-premises hosts, thanks to dynamic routing. To better understand this, take a look at the following diagram, which depicts a VPC network connected to an on-premises network *without* dynamic global routing:

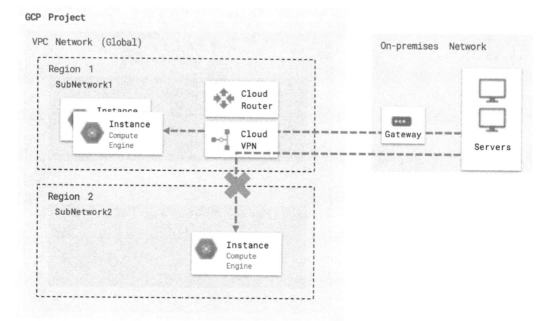

Figure 3.4 – VPC without global dynamic routing

With this regional routing set up, VMs in other regions (different from the one where the VPN tunnel endpoint is) can't be reached by on-premises VMs and aren't able to reach on-premises VMs through the tunnel. They're also not able to learn routes dynamically from the connected on-premises network(s). In other words, without global dynamic routing, your network only "exists" in a single region from the perspective of external networks.

Finally, you enabled Private Google Access and Flow Logs in the East US subnetwork. This means that in this subnetwork, VMs will be able to access Google services and APIs privately (that is, with no need for a public IP address or external access), and a sample of the network flows sent from and received by the VMs in this subnetwork (Flow Logs) will be recorded (every 30 seconds, in our configuration) and be available for use in network monitoring or real-time security analysis. We will explore Flow Logs further in this chapter, but for now, know that this is a crucial network monitoring feature that you can enable at the subnetwork level.

With the basics of networking on GCP out of the way, let's dig into two fundamental elements of any network: routes and firewalls.

Understanding routes and firewalls in Google Cloud

By default, every network in GCP will have routes automatically created to handle reachability between instances in the network (regardless of whether they are on the same subnetwork), and also a default route for traffic leaving the network. The actual network routers along the way are not something you manage or even see. They're entirely abstracted away and treated as a single centralized virtual router, which every instance connects to. Through Google's **Cloud Routes** service, you can create your own custom routes by defining a next hop IP address for traffic destined to any network you specify (via its IP address range). You can also apply tags to routes so that they only apply to specific instances with the corresponding tag, but otherwise, routes apply to all the instances in the network by default.

The Firewall service in GCP functions as a *distributed stateful firewall* across the VPC network. This means that firewall rules are applied to the network as a whole, and there's no determining specific interfaces, contexts, or such things as you would do on a traditional physical firewall. Firewall rules are, however, still applied at the instance level and will be evaluated even on traffic between two instances in the same subnetwork. You can think of there being a firewall appliance between any pair of instances in the network, and between any instance and the outside networks.

A firewall rule can explicitly allow or deny traffic, but the VPC firewall *implicitly denies all ingress* and *allows all egress communications*. In other words, unless explicitly allowed, any ingress traffic will be denied, and unless explicitly denied, any egress traffic will be allowed.

A firewall rule contains a direction, a type (*ingress* or *egress*), one or more sources, one or more destinations (target), a protocol, a port, and an action (*allow* or *deny*). The following screenshot shows an example of an ingress rule (on the left) and an egress rule (on the right):

Figure 3.5 – Firewall rule creation example – ingress (left) and egress (right) rules

Zero trust

As the perimeter becomes more "porous" with the expansion of the mobile workforce, a crucial network design consideration is *zero trust security*. The general idea is never to trust and always verify. It involves a collection of principles and behaviors, one of which is the least privilege principle we discussed previously for access management. Others are to always explicitly verify authentication and authorization requests with all available relevant information, and, most importantly, always *assume breach*. Assuming breach means you make design and governance decisions while not only thinking about ways you can prevent a breach from happening but also how you can *protect the environment when (not if) a breach occurs*. From a networking perspective, the best way to achieve this is to implicitly block any network traffic between any pair of servers in the infrastructure and only explicitly allow communications when and where they're needed, as specifically defined as possible. The goal is to minimize lateral movement, or the "blast radius", of a successful attack by preventing the attackers from reaching any other business-critical systems within the network from a source they managed to access. An example of this would be if someone manages to, through whatever means, open a **secure shell** (**SSH**) to a seemingly unimportant VM instance, such as a developer machine. There might not be any relevant or critical business data inside that VM – not even an application running inside it. However, imagine if the firewall in the underlying network permits any communication between VMs in the environment, because someone once thought "it's inside our environment, it's a trusted zone." Now, the attacker can essentially "jump" into any other machine (through SSH or other means) and eventually land on a machine containing business-critical intellectual property or sensitive data. Even if SSH or **Remote Desktop Protocol** (**RDP**) traffic is blocked and full access to other VMs is prevented, there are other means through which the attacker can obtain information (data exfiltration) or simply cause damage, such as overloading other servers with heavy "dummy" network traffic.

By assuming breach, each request in the network is analyzed as if it could be coming from a compromised server or application or the open internet. Strict security controls are then enforced, regardless of how seemingly harmless an access request may be. A system designed with zero trust security may be more challenging to manage, and it may even hurt business agility at times. But it is likely the best insurance policy a company can have against a security breach event, which, often, businesses cannot recover from.

The implicit deny feature of Google Cloud's Firewall facilitates the zero trust model. For a robust network security foundation, ensure overly permissive firewall rules are never created and that they are periodically reviewed.

Understanding load balancing in Google Cloud

Load balancing is a crucial network function and an important design component as it directly affects the availability and resiliency of a solution. In GCP, load balancing is a fully distributed and software-defined service (this shouldn't come as a surprise to you at this point in this book!). It is not hardware-based, which means no actual physical appliances are being provided, and no infrastructure you have to manage or operate. All load balancing services are *fully managed and scale automatically*. There are a few different types of load balancing in Google Cloud, all of which we will explore in this section.

Layer 7 HTTP/HTTPS load balancing

Load balancers can be categorized broadly by the layer at which they operate. This "layer" refers to the **Open System Interconnection (OSI)** model of networking (`https://en.wikipedia.org/wiki/OSI_model`), which defines seven stacked layers of communication, from the physical layer (layer 1) to the networking layer (layer 4) and all the way "up" to the application layer (layer 7). Because the HTTP protocol is an application layer protocol (hence layer 7), a load balancer that is HTTP-aware is considered to be a layer-7 load balancer (or just simply an HTTP load balancer, since in most cases there are really no other application protocols supported). Most HTTP load balancers also support the more secure HTTPS protocol and therefore can also be referred to as an HTTPS load balancer, or, how Google will typically write it as a catch-all term, an **HTTP(S) Load Balancer**.

What does it mean for a load balancer to be HTTP(S)-aware? This means that it "understands" the HTTP protocol, and it can therefore deliver features such as **URL-based routing** decisions, **cookie-based session affinity**, and **SSL offloading**. We will elaborate more on these features shortly. In Google Cloud, an HTTP(S) Load Balancer can be of two types: external or internal. Let's see what the differences are.

External HTTP(S) load balancing

In the Premium Network Service Tier, external load balancers are distributed globally and have an external **anycast** IP address. An anycast IP address means that even though a single IP address has been defined, multiple geographically distributed devices can share this same IP. Based on the location of a user's request, the closest device to the user will be the one that handles the request. So, even though everyone "sees" the same IP address (which simplifies DNS setup), what that address actually maps to in terms of physical infrastructure will correspond to the closest network entry point to that specific user. In the Standard Network Service Tier, external HTTP(S) Load Balancer is a regional service, and its backend instances are required to all be in the same region.

In Google Cloud, an HTTP(S) Load Balancer is a proxy-based load balancer for HTTP and HTTPS protocols that can also authenticate communications by using **SSL certificates** (in the case of HTTPS). This means unencrypting SSL can be carried out at the load balancer, thus offloading the backend servers from the burden of doing so (this capability is often referred to as *SSL offloading*). You can also control the features of SSL that your HTTP (S) Load Balancer uses to negotiate and establish HTTPS connections with clients by defining **SSL policies**. For example, you can enforce a minimum TLS version of 1.2, thus preventing clients from attempting to use the less secure 1.1 or 1.0 versions.

The fact that it is a *proxy-based* load balancer means that it terminates HTTP(S) connections from clients before reinitiating a connection toward the backend. It can use a **global URL map** that you define to make a forwarding decision based on HTTP attributes (such as URL, cookies, or protocol headers). For cross-regional load balancing (in the Premium Tier), the HTTP(S) Load Balancer can also intelligently route requests from users to the backend instances in the region that is closest to the users. If the closest region instances don't have available capacity, it will forward to the next nearest region instead. Backend capacity is measured by either CPU utilization or **requests per second (RPS)**. A **global health check** periodically monitors the backend instances' health to ensure requests are not routed to unavailable servers.

Content-based routing can be configured by using the URL path attribute. For example, the request path may define different types of served contents, such as video (with the / video path) and images (with the /images path), and therefore can be used to route traffic to the right dedicated backend system according to the type of content being requested. For more complex and global use cases, you can have a combination of cross-regional load balancing (making forwarding decisions based on proximity) and content-based routing. An example of such a case is illustrated in the following diagram:

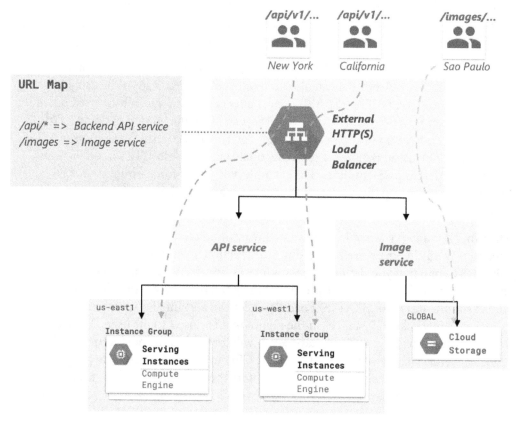

Figure 3.6 – External HTTP(S) Load Balancer with content-based and intelligent global routing

Cloud Armor can be used together with HTTP(S) Load Balancer to add **Distributed Denial of Service (DDoS)** protection to the frontend and the capability to either blacklist or whitelist a set of IP addresses for access. It also provides filtering based on layer 7 attributes, in addition to layers 3 and 4, thus enabling protection against web-based attacks. Preconfigured **Web Application Firewall (WAF)** rules can be added to security policies to protect web servers against common attacks such as **SQL injection (SQLi)** and **cross-site scripting (XSS)**.

An external HTTP(S) Load Balancer can also be configured with a **content delivery network (CDN)**. A CDN leverages globally distributed edge **points of presence (PoP)** to cache content at locations that are close to end users, thus providing faster access and reduced serving costs. In Google Cloud, this capability is offered through the Cloud CDN service, which uses Google's PoP and CDN nodes to provide global scale caching. You can enable Cloud CDN with a checkbox when setting up an HTTP(S) Load Balancer's backend service.

Consider incorporating both Cloud Armor and Cloud CDN services into your network design for web applications. Cloud Amor is an effective WAF service that will protect your web applications against common attacks, such as those identified in the **Open Web Application Security Project (OWASP)** Top Ten list (`https://owasp.org/www-project-top-ten/`). You can also create your own custom rules by applying any combination of filters on the layer 3 through layer 7 parameters of network packets. The cloud CDN service can be "stacked" with Cloud Armor to deliver static content that is less prone to exploitations, while your origin servers (application backend) remains protected for all *cache miss* events that redirect users to your web servers directly.

Internal HTTP(S) load balancing

The HTTP(S) Load Balancer can also be configured as an internal load balancer; that is, a regional layer 7 load balancer with an internal frontend IP address. The load balancing capabilities are the same as the external load balancers'; the only difference is that, since it's a regional load balancer, it doesn't provide any of the intelligent global routing capabilities that an external load balancer does with an anycast IP address. An internal HTTP(S) Load Balancer can be used internally to distribute load among backend services where HTTP-based load balancing features are needed.

For example, in a three-tiered web service, the Web Tier (frontend web servers) can be scaled using a global, external HTTP(S) Load Balancer, the characteristics of which we explored previously. Then, that HTTP(S) traffic can flow from the Web Tier to an Application Tier, consisting of one or more application backend servers behind one or more regional load balancers. Each regional HTTP(S) Load Balancer provides an internal frontend IP address that's used to distribute traffic to the Application Tier servers based on, for example, HTTP header values. This use case is illustrated in the following diagram:

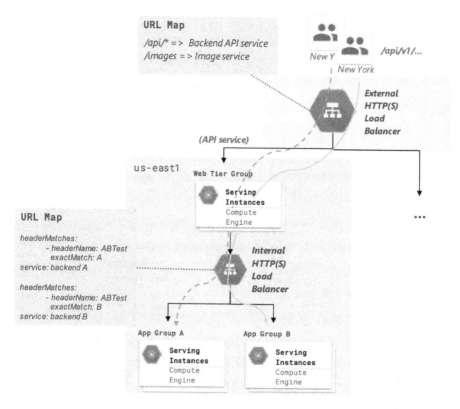

Figure 3.7 – Example use case of an external and internal HTTP(S) Load Balancer

The syntax shown for the **URL Map** in the preceding diagram is expressed at a high level and does not correspond to the actual syntax you would use, but it illustrates the idea. In this example, the web server located in the region that is closest to the end users will serve the traffic and forward requests to one of two backends: **App Group A** or **App Group B**. This routing decision is based on the value of the custom HTTP header, called **ABTest**. Hence, there are two layers of layer 7 routing in this example: URL-based routing (at the web tier with an external HTTP(S) Load Balancer) and header-based routing (at the application tier with an internal HTTP(S) Load Balancer).

Another use case would be when an application is served only internally, typically for security reasons, to clients on another network that has been peered with (or connected to via a VPN) the VPC network where the application is hosted.

Layer 4 TCP/UDP load balancing

The layer 4 load balancers are not aware of the higher-level protocols such as HTTP, so they only make routing decisions based on IP addresses and ports. Things such as URL maps, content-based routing, and other HTTP-related capabilities are not supported. These load balancers are typically used for more straightforward use cases, usually in internal networks, to distribute loads to a cluster of backend instances. However, they can also be used on public networks with an external frontend IP address, in which case they are referred to in Google Cloud as (external) TCP/UDP Network Load Balancers (or just **Network Load Balancers**).

External TCP/UDP load balancing

The Network Load Balancer distributes TCP and UDP traffic (any port) across instances in a region and provides an external IP address to the frontend. Unlike the HTTP(S) Load Balancer, these load balancers do not work as proxies but instead as **pass-through load balancers**. This means that connections are not terminated at the load balancer and reinitiated with the load balancer itself as the source (which would be a normal proxy behavior). Instead, the connections are rerouted to their destination, with the original source IP address preserved. Responses from the backend servers then go directly back to the clients, not through the load balancer. This is referred to as *direct server return*. In other words, the load balancer transparently forwards the traffic to a healthy backend instance and then "gets out of the way." As a layer 4 load balancer, it doesn't inspect packets beyond the network layer and thus does not "read" HTTP headers or application-level protocol details. The Network Load Balancer cannot decrypt SSL traffic, but it has no problem forwarding it (for the backend servers to decrypt themselves).

Internal TCP/UDP load balancing

An internal TCP/UDP Load Balancer has basically the same features and characteristics as the Network Load Balancer, with the main difference being that it only supports an internal IP address as the frontend. It is also a regional, pass-through load balancer that operates at layer 4, with direct server return. It is most commonly used to provide load distribution and internal high availability for backend servers. Both external and internal TCP/UDP Load Balancers work with any TCP/UDP ports.

External SSL proxy and TCP proxy

An alternative to the HTTP(S) Load Balancer for non-HTTP applications that still require a more advanced, proxy-based load balancer (potentially capable of SSL offloading) are SSL Proxy and TCP Proxy Load Balancers.

With **SSL Proxy Load Balancing**, you can terminate user SSL connections at the load balancing layer if your application uses TLS encryption along with an application protocol other than HTTP. For HTTP applications, the HTTP(S) Load Balancer would be the best fit. With the Premium Network Tier, an SSL Proxy Load Balancer can be deployed globally to deliver traffic across multiple regions, with the capability of directing user traffic to their closest region. The SSL Proxy Load Balancing service doesn't work with all TCP ports but with a set list of ports, all of which you can check out by referring to the documentation page: `https://cloud.google.com/load-balancing/docs/ssl`. You can also define your own set of SSL policies, and you can either use your own SSL certificates or Google-managed certificates (in which case, you're required to use port `443` for the frontend).

Don't need SSL encryption with your non-HTTP application, but still need an external proxy-type load balancer? The **TCP Proxy Load Balancing** service is the right choice here. It's very similar to the SSL Proxy offering, apart from the lack of support for SSL. It includes the same intelligent global routing (in the Premium Network Tier), proxy-based load balancing behavior, and it has a similarly restricted list of supported TCP ports, all of which you can find here: `https://cloud.google.com/load-balancing/docs/tcp`.

Design considerations for load balancing

With so many different types of load balancing services in Google Cloud, things can get confusing when you're designing a load balancing solution. However, by understanding how the different load balancing types meet your particular needs, choosing the right one(s) for your design becomes an easier task. The following flowchart consolidates what you've learned so far and should help you do so:

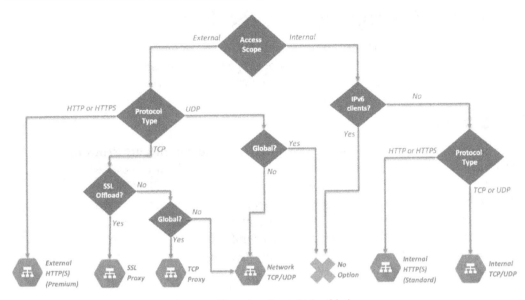

Figure 3.8 – Choosing the right load balancer

Note that **IPv6** clients are only supported by the proxy load balancers, which are external load balancers by design. This is why a decision point was included in the flowchart, to account for that limitation. You may have noticed that *Internal load balancers with IPv6 client support* and *global UDP load balancers* are two service requirements that *don't lead to any available option* on GCP.

When designing a load balancing solution for your application, the first question is whether the service should be global or regional, which will also raise the question of which network service tier you should opt for. Then, you can start thinking about what type of network protocol the application(s) will use, whether SSL offloading is a required or advantageous feature, and potentially whether IPv6 clients should be considered. Remember, no matter what option you choose, high availability and scalability will be built into the solution, and it's not something you have to design for yourself (when it comes to the load balancer itself).

So far, you've learned about the basics of networking in Google Cloud and networking services such as routing, firewalls, and load balancing. You probably have a good enough foundation for designing cloud-native solutions using GCP. However, it is often the case that your VPC networks need to be connected to one or more on-premises networks. This could be due to an ongoing cloud migration, where certain services are still only available on-premises, or due to security and compliance requirements that dictate certain services and/or data must remain on an on-premises infrastructure. For these scenarios, you will need to design a **hybrid connectivity** strategy, the options for which we shall explore next.

Designing for hybrid connectivity

There are mainly three factors that influence which hybrid connectivity service we choose: bandwidth, reliability, and security. The options range from a **Virtual Private Network (VPN)** connection to direct fiber connectivity to Google's network.

Cloud VPN

Google Cloud's VPN service is **Cloud VPN**, which provides an **Internet Protocol Security (IPSec)** tunnel endpoint in your VPC networks, to which you can establish VPN connections from an on-premises (or another cloud's) network via its VPN gateway. A VPN connection is established over public networks (that is, over the internet), though this is often unreliable and has no service-level guarantees. Public networks are also generally unsecure, but the VPN service encrypts traffic between the two gateways with the IPSec protocol, thus overcoming, to some extent, the lack of security in public networks.

Google Cloud offers two types of cloud VPN gateways:

- **HA VPN**: This is a **high availability (HA)** VPN solution that provides an SLA of 99.99% service availability (only on the Google Cloud side of the connection). This works because the VPN gateway in this offering will have two interfaces (with two external IP addresses) to set up two redundant VPN tunnels, which helps overcome the unreliable nature of public networks by establishing a backup tunnel in case one fails. For achieving end-to-end reliability, the peer VPN gateway device must support dynamic BGP routing and be configured with adequate redundancy.

- **Classic VPN**: Classic VPN gateways have a single interface and external IP address and are able to deploy a single tunnel to the same peer gateway. Tunnels can use either dynamic BGP routing or static routing (which can be policy-based or route-based, with the latter being the most common option). This service provides a lower SLA availability of 99.9%.

Each cloud VPN tunnel supports *up to 3 G bps* (gigabits per second) total bandwidth for ingress and egress traffic. Since 1 *byte* equals 8 *bits*, this is equivalent to 375 MBps (megabytes per second). Due to the reliance on public network infrastructure, the actual bandwidth of a VPN connection can oscillate, and performance can be unstable at times.

Cloud Interconnect

For organizations willing to pay for a slightly more reliable connection and higher bandwidth with more stable performance, the options to consider are the **Cloud Interconnect** services: **Partner Interconnect** and **Dedicated Interconnect**.

Partner Interconnect

This service provides connectivity between an on-premises network and a Google Cloud VPC network *through a partner service provider*. Suppose your on-premises data center is at a physical location that can reach a colocation facility where a partner is present through a peering edge. In that case, you can work with that service provider to establish connectivity between their network and your on-premises network. Supported service providers will have existing (physical) network connections to Google's network, so only your "side" of the connection needs to be set up.

Depending on the partner service provider's available offerings, you can configure either **layer 2** or **layer 3** network connectivity. With a layer 2 connection, you establish a BGP session between Google Cloud (via the **Cloud Router** service on GCP) and on-premises routers for each *VLAN attachment* you create. For layer 3 connections, the service provider will establish a BGP session between your Cloud Router and their edge routers for each VLAN attachment, and you don't need to configure BGP yourself on your on-premises router.

Google has two prescriptive configurations for Partner Interconnect: one for 99.99% availability (recommended for production environments) and another for 99.9% availability (for less mission-critical applications). These SLAs do not apply to connectivity between your network and the service provider's, but between the service providers and Google Cloud. Information on how to configure your Partner Interconnect topology for 99.99% availability is available at `https://cloud.google.com/network-connectivity/docs/interconnect/concepts/partner-overview#9999_availability_recommended`.

Network bandwidth for this type of connection ranges *from 50 Mbps to 10 Gbps*. Availability and prices vary by service provider.

Dedicated Interconnect

As the name implies, this dedicated connectivity service does not require a partner service provider and instead provides direct physical connections between an on-premises network and Google's network. For this to be possible, however, *the on-premises network must physically reach Google's network* at a colocation facility. The on-premises network devices must also support specific technical requirements for enabling 10G or 100G fiber-based circuits. A detailed list of requirements can be found at `https://cloud.google.com/network-connectivity/docs/interconnect/concepts/dedicated-overview#before_you_use`.

Similar to the Partner Interconnect service, there are two different configurations for achieving either 99.99% or 99.9% availability. For instructions on how to set up a redundant topology for 99.99% availability, please refer to `https://cloud.google.com/network-connectivity/docs/interconnect/tutorials/dedicated-creating-9999-availability`.

The available bandwidth for a Dedicated Interconnect connection can be *10 Gbps or 100 Gbps per link*.

Cloud peering

Cloud peering offerings (not to be confused with VPC peering) allow you to have a direct (with **direct peering**) or partner-based (with **carrier peering**) link between your business network and Google's edge network. This capability exists outside of Google Cloud and is tailored for businesses that wish to access Google Workspace (formerly G Suite) applications at high throughput.

You should consider including one of these services in your design when working with organizations that rely heavily on Google Workspace applications.

Choosing a hybrid connectivity option

To highlight the differences between the different hybrid connectivity offerings and help you decide which option is best for your solution, take a look at the following comparison table:

Service	Requirements	Bandwidth and SLA	Best for
Cloud VPN	Network appliance with IPSec VPN Tunnel support. Dynamic BGP routing support for HA VPN.	Up to 3 Gbps (375 MBps). 99.9% with Classic VPN and 99.99% with HA VPN.	Low bandwidth requirements, low budget. HA VPN for mission-critical applications.
Partner Interconnect	Physical network reachability to a partner's peering edge, BGP-enabled routers.	50 Mbps to 10 Gbps, depending on the provider. 99.9% or 99.99% availability, depending on the topology setup.	High bandwidth requirements.

Service	Requirements	Bandwidth and SLA	Best for
Dedicated Interconnect	Physical network reachability to Google's network. 10G- or 100G-enabled network device with LACP, 802.1Q VLAN, and EBGP-4 multi-hop routing support.	10 Gbps or 100 Gbps per link. 99.9% or 99.99% availability, depending on the topology setup.	Highest possible bandwidth and reliability.
Cloud Peering	Physical network reachability to a partner's peering edge (with carrier peering) or Google's Edge Point of Presence (with direct peering).	Bandwidth varies by partner and setup, with no prescriptive amounts. Google does not provide a SLA for this service. Partners may offer their own SLAs.	Higher availability and throughput, plus lower latency connections to Google Workspace products. Eliminates the need to maintain a DMZ subnetwork for this traffic.

You should now be familiar with Google Cloud's networking services and things such as routing, firewalls, and load balancing on GCP. You should also have the foundational knowledge to design a network in Google Cloud and design a hybrid connectivity solution. Still, you may be feeling that designing a network sounds like a daunting task, and that's because it is. In the next section, we will look into a few standard network designs and some best practices that will give you some references to lean on when architecting networks in Google Cloud.

Mastering common network designs

In this section, we're going to cover some design considerations and best practices, followed by common designs, for VPC deployments on GCP.

Design considerations and best practices

The network is one of the most fundamental components of an IT infrastructure. For that reason, the design of the VPC network should be given sufficient time and effort in the early stages of the overall solution design. Design decisions at this level can't be easily reversed later, so make sure you're taking in as much input as possible into consideration.

In this final section of this chapter, you're going to learn about the common design patterns you can use to build your own design. But before that, we will highlight a few best practices to keep in mind and guide you through your decisions.

Use a naming convention

This goes for all your resources and not only the network-related ones. But if you're starting your design with the network (a natural starting point), that may be the time to set your naming convention straight. This involves defining how resource names are constructed and setting abbreviations, acronyms, and relevant labels that help users identify a resource's purpose and its associated business unit and location. Some examples of labels you may need to define are as follows:

- Company short name: acm (ACME)

- Department or Business Unit: it, hr, and so on

- Application code: crm (Customer Relationship Management application), pay (Payroll application)

- Region abbreviation: eu-we1 (*europe-west1*), us-ea2 (*us-east2*)

- Environment: dev, test, prod, and so on

Once you have defined some labels and possible values based on your IT environment, you can start defining naming structures for various GCP resources; for example:

- **Department-specific and global network resources**: {company name}-{dept-label}-{environment-label}-{resource type}-{seq#}. For example, if you have one VPC per company department, you apply this to your VPCs; for example, acm-it-test-vpc-1.

- **Department- or application-specific regional/zonal resources**: {company name}-{[APP or DEPT] label}-{region/zone label}-{environment-label}-{resource type}-{seq#}; for example, applied to subnetworks: acm-hr-eu-we1-prod-subnet-01. A naming convention will help ensure consistency in how resources are named and will facilitate several aspects of infrastructure management.

Subnetwork design

Firstly, as we mentioned previously, *avoid using default or auto mode networks* and opt for custom mode networks instead so that you have full control over the subnetwork design and firewall rules. Then, you can deploy subnetworks in the regions that your business operates in and adopt an IP address scheme so that there are no overlaps with any other network (such as on-premises networks) that you intend to peer or integrate with your VPC network.

Also, aim to *group your applications into a few, large subnetworks*. Traditional enterprise networks separate applications into many small address ranges (by using, for example, VLANs). However, in modern cloud networks, fewer subnets with large address spaces are recommended as it facilitates management and reduces complexity at no cost in terms of security. Firewalls, service accounts, and network tags are all features that can be used to segment traffic and isolate network communications as needed.

Shared VPC for multiple projects

If you're designing a multi-project solution in GCP, you may want to consider deploying a shared VPC. As we discussed previously, a shared VPC offers an effective way for you to simplify management and centralize security and network policies in a single host project. In contrast, service projects (which may represent, for example, different company departments or applications) can simply deploy their resources to the same network. This avoids the situation where there are multiple VPC networks to manage, which increases the risks of inconsistent configuration and policies, excessive use of network administration roles, and disruptive changes to the network design.

In terms of the service projects, grant the network user role at the subnetwork level so that each project can only use its assigned subnetwork(s), which will reinforce the principle of least privilege.

Isolate workloads

For isolation between project-specific workloads and for independent IAM controls, you can create VPC networks in different projects. Network-related IAM roles assigned at the project level will apply to all VPC networks within the project, so if you require independent IAM policies per VPC network, create different projects to host those networks. This setup works as an alternative to or in conjunction with a shared VPC model.

If you're working with an organization that deals with compliance regulations (such as *HIPAA* or *PCI-DSS*) and sensitive data that needs to be secured appropriately, then isolate these types of data into dedicated VPC networks. Two different VPC networks in GCP will never be able to reach each other (from a routing perspective) unless they're peered (or are integrated by other means, such as with a VPN gateway or a network appliance). This significantly reduces the risk of unauthorized access to the data or breach of compliance.

Limit external access

Limit the use of external IP addresses and access to public networks as much as possible. Resources with only an internal IP address can still access many Google services and APIs through Private Google Access. You can use a Cloud NAT to provide VMs with external access. By limiting unnecessary external access, you reduce the attack surface on your environment by eliminating the possibility of VMs being reached from external sources (especially when management protocols such as SSH and RDP are not restricted at the firewall level).

Common network designs

In this section, we will look at some of the common network designs that are adopted by enterprises using Google Cloud.

Single VPC network, high availability

A single VPC network, which can be of global scale in Google Cloud, can, in many cases, suffice if you wish to build a robust network design that is easy to manage and maintain. There are two ways of obtaining high availability with a single VPC network:

- **Leveraging different zones within a subnetwork**: By deploying instances to different zones within a subnetwork (and its associated region), you spread your application across different infrastructure failure domains, therefore obtaining improved availability and resiliency against hardware failures (and, in some cases, even the failure of an entire data center).

- **Leveraging different regions (with different subnetworks)**: Deploying instances to different regions allows you to obtain a higher degree of failure independence, which even protects you against regional failures and natural disasters. It's the best design choice for realizing robust global systems. With a global HTTP(S) Load Balancer, you can deliver lower latency for end users with intelligent global routing, as you learned previously.

Whether you opt for multi-zonal or multi-regional deployments on the network, you can obtain high availability without additional security complexity (it's still one single GCP firewall for the network). The following diagram illustrates this design:

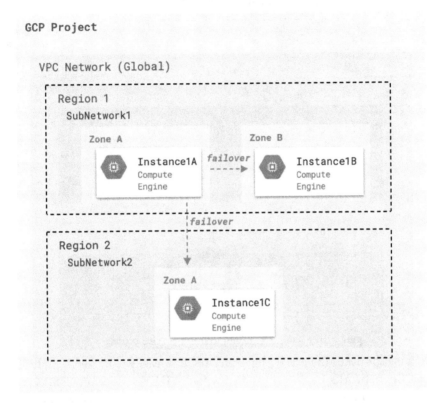

Figure 3.9 – Single VPC network with zonal and regional deployments

In the preceding diagram, VM instance **Instance1B** is a failover instance for **Instance1A** on a different zone that can serve traffic in case **Instance1A** fails to. VM **Instance1C** is a failover instance located in a different region.

Shared VPC and multiple service projects

For a more complex and scalable infrastructure, you can opt for having a shared VPC where network controls can be centralized (that is, the configuration of things such as subnetworks, routes, and firewall rules), with service projects able to share the same network infrastructure. The users in these service projects still have the autonomy to deploy and manage instances and applications, without the risk of impacting the network configuration. This is a great way to prevent breaking changes and inconsistencies in the network configurations.

This design is exemplified in the following diagram:

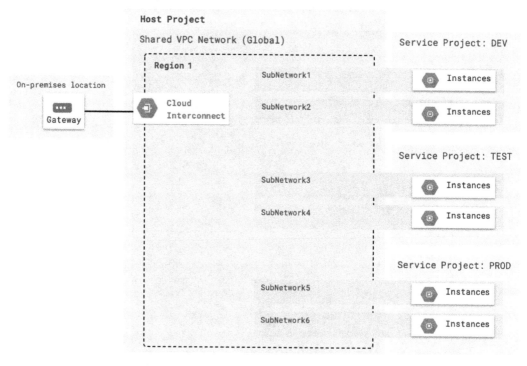

Figure 3.10 – Shared VPC and multiple service projects

Only one region is shown in the preceding diagram, but it easily works with multiple regions as well. Subnetworks 1 and 2 are shared with the **DEV** service project (as you learned previously, you can define which specific subnetworks are shared with which specific service projects). Subnetworks 3 and 4 are used by the **TEST** project, while 5 and 6 are used by the **PROD** project. Network policies are centralized in the host project. Workloads and VM instances are managed within each of the service projects individually, and they can be deployed to the subnetworks that are created in the host project.

Multiple VPC networks bridged by a next-generation firewall (NGFW) appliance

Sometimes, security requirements will dictate that "untrusted" network environments (the portion of the network that's exposed to the internet or outside networks) be more strictly isolated from "trusted" networks (such as the internal networks hosting applications) via a **next-generation firewall (NGFW)**. Google Cloud's native firewall is not an NGFW firewall, the definition of which is a firewall with additional network filtering functions such as deep packet inspection. An NGFW provides you with deeper insights into the packets traversing the network, thus allowing you to detect and prevent network attacks. However, while you lack such capabilities from GCP's built-in firewall service, nothing prevents you from deploying a VM appliance containing a software-based version of an NGFW (several vendors make VM images available for consumption in the cloud).

In this design, an untrusted network (DMZ) is introduced to terminate outside connections (such as hybrid interconnects and connections originating from the internet). The traffic is then filtered in the NGFW, which is deployed to a multi-NIC VM, before reaching trusted networks. The NGFW VM has an NIC on each of the VPC networks, which, in this design, must all reside within the same GCP project. Therefore, you should observe the limits on the number of VPC networks and, most importantly, on the number of NICs supported on a single VM (since the former can be extended upon demand, but the latter has a hard limit of eight as the time of writing).

There are many variations of this design, but the following diagram shows an example of such a topology:

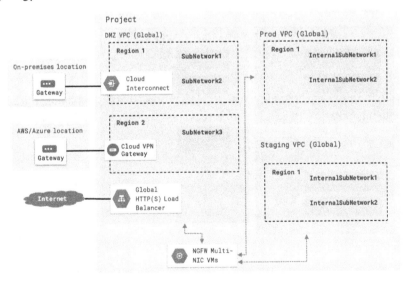

Figure 3.11 – Multiple VPC networks bridged by an NGFW appliance

In a topology diagram, a **DMZ VPC** is where external traffic is terminated. In this example, this is traffic from an on-premises location, from another public cloud network, and the internet. This is the "untrusted" network. Two other trusted networks, **Prod** and **Staging**, represent a production VPC network and a staging VPC network where application instances are deployed to, respectively. Traffic from and to the untrusted zone is filtered through the NGFW firewall.

You could combine this design with that of a shared VPC and service projects so that if you have multiple projects, you won't need to replicate this design over to different projects (which would require numerous NGFW appliances and licenses). For example, the project shown in *Figure 3.8* would become a host project, with the two trusted VPCs being shared with other service projects (used, for example, by different development teams).

Summary

In this chapter, you have learned about the network services in Google Cloud, how to handle routes and firewall rules, and how to make design decisions around load balancing and hybrid connectivity using GCP. You have also learned some best practices and common network designs, and, very importantly, about the zero trust principle. There is one big takeaway from this chapter: *never trust, always verify*. The skills you've learned in this chapter will allow you to bake security into your network design, incorporate the right type of load balancing based on your application needs, and make sure multi-project cloud solutions have a centralized, shared VPC, where network policies are set and controlled from one place.

You should now have a robust foundation to start designing networks in Google Cloud that are global, scalable, and able to offer a resilient and secure infrastructure environment for VMs to be deployed on.

Speaking of which, in the next chapter, you will learn how to architect a compute infrastructure using Google Cloud's compute services (such as VMs, App Engine, Cloud Functions, Cloud Run, and Kubernetes Engine).

4
Architecting Compute Infrastructure

In this chapter, you will learn about the various GCP Compute options and design considerations for choosing and implementing various Compute services. You will learn about **Google Compute Engine (GCE)**, as well as Compute platform services such as **App Engine**, **Cloud Functions**, **Cloud Run**, and **Kubernetes Engine**. Throughout this chapter, you will be learning how to design a Compute solution based on common requirements and scenarios.

In this chapter, we're going to cover the following main topics:

- Architecting with Compute Engine
- Exploring Compute platforms
- Understanding when to use Kubernetes

Let's get started!

Technical requirements

For the hands-on activities in this chapter, you will need a billing-enabled Google Cloud account and, optionally, the Google Cloud SDK installed (if you've followed along with the setup steps in *Chapter 1, An Introduction to Google Cloud for Architects*, you should already have everything in place). The helper scripts and code for this chapter can be found at `https://github.com/PacktPublishing/Architecting-Google-Cloud-Solutions/tree/master/ch4`.

Check out the following link to see the Code in Action video: `https://bit.ly/3bY3IFj`

Architecting with Compute Engine

If you're an IT professional, you're probably already familiar with **virtual machines** (**VMs**) and comfortable working with them. **Google Compute Engine** (**GCE**) is the service in Google Cloud that enables you to create and manage VMs. How is that different from deploying VMs on a traditional data center environment? First and foremost, Google is one of the *hyperscale* cloud providers, which means their hardware capacity is virtually limitless. This allows you to create VMs with powerful enough specifications for the most demanding applications that scale to meet increasing needs. Powered by Google's data centers, GCE also delivers the robustness and resiliency of a platform that is constantly monitored and well-secured. Then, you get things such as managed VM images, marketplace images with preconfigured software, and, in general, easy integration with other cloud services and powerful automation capabilities. In addition, as we mentioned in *Chapter 2, Mastering the Basics of Google Cloud*, GCE will provide you with rightsizing recommendations to help you be cost-effective with your VMs.

The true power of the cloud really lies in its **Platform as a Service** (**PaaS**) offerings, where even things such as scalability and high availability are taken care of and you don't need to worry about them. Google Cloud also offers a few different Compute platform options for when you just need the computing power without the hassle of managing a VM. However, there are many cases where VMs should belong in your architecture. In this section, we'll explore when to use VMs and how to design them for scalability and high availability.

IaaS VMs

In *Chapter 1, An Introduction to Google Cloud for Architects*, we discussed the differences between the IaaS, PaaS, and SaaS delivery models. In the IaaS model, the cloud provider is responsible for managing the infrastructure hardware, up until the virtualization layer of the stack. The customer (you) is then responsible for all the layers above that, starting with the **operating system (OS)**. This means you're responsible for the following:

- Creating and maintaining a VM image with any custom OS or custom OS version currently not available on GCP image marketplace (if a suitable one is available, you don't need to create or maintain images).

- Patching and upgrading the OS as required to remediate known vulnerabilities and keep your systems secure.

- Configuring various OS settings and installing and maintaining application software and libraries.

- Manually setting up the ability to export or stream application logs for observability.

On the flip side, you have the ability to customize at this layer, which means you can, for instance, use custom OS settings and have full access to the VM's underlying filesystem.

Since hardware failures and maintenance activities are expected in the underlying infrastructure, you're also responsible for designing your solution around that to deliver a final product with high availability. In the previous chapter, we highlighted a common network design that involves having subnetworks on multiple regions, or, alternatively, leveraging the default multi-zonal nature of a subnetwork within a region (that is, the fact that a subnetwork *sits* across all zones within a region) to deliver failure independence at no cost of network management overhead. When deploying applications on VMs, you will want to build them as clusters of VMs that are spread across zones at a minimum so that your applications are resilient against hardware faults (a zone maps to one physical fault domain).

Managed instance groups

Another system design component that would have been typically taken care of in PaaS services, but which you have to deal with yourself in IaaS, is that of scalability. Generally, there are two ways to approach system scalability. One way is to scale *up*, which means increasing an individual instance's size by updating its performance specifications, such as the amount of vCPU and memory allocated. Conversely, you can scale back *down* by decreasing the instance's resource allocations. This approach is referred to as *vertical* scaling. The other way is to scale *out*, in which case you add new instances to increase the overall serving capacity of the system. Conversely, you can scale back *in* by removing instances. This approach is referred to as *horizontal* scaling. The difference between these two approaches is illustrated in the following diagram:

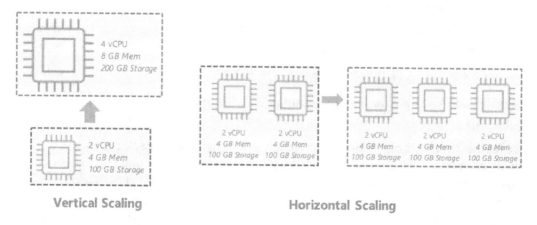

Figure 4.1 – Scaling up (vertical scaling) versus scaling out (horizontal scaling)

With GCE, you can scale VM instances *up* or *down* (which means updating the machine type to a larger or smaller size), but this won't happen automatically based on demand (unless you develop an automation solution around that). Scaling up will also hit a limit very quickly and you won't be able to go very far with it. However, if your application is designed to be either stateless or so that its state is external to the VM's filesystem or memory (for example, recorded on a database service on GCP), then you have the option to scale your VMs *out* (or back *in*) using a **managed instance group**.

A managed instance group is a feature of GCE that allows you to group VM instances together as a cluster, and associate autoscaling policies to that group so that new instances can be added (scaled out) or removed (scaled in) as needed. This capability is also referred to as **horizontal scalability**. You can configure scaling events so that they happen automatically based on load, and they can be one of *CPU utilization, load balancing service capacity*, or *monitoring metrics* (which can be any custom monitoring metrics you create). Instance groups can be load balanced with a GCP load balancing service just like VMs can, and, with the load balancing service capacity option as an autoscaling policy, you can define the capacity of an instance in the load balancer's backend service, which can be based on *backend utilization* or *requests per second*.

Here are a few examples of what autoscaling policies could look like:

- When the average utilization of the VM instances in an instance group is at 80%, scale out by creating and adding a new instance to the group.

- When the requests per second per instance are over 80% of your configured maximum (100 requests per second), scale out by creating and adding a new instance to the load balanced group.

- When your custom monitoring metric, `processing_queue_size`, is over the target level of 100 for instances, scale out by creating and adding a new instance to the group.

Now that you have some understanding about IaaS VMs (and managed instance groups), let's figure out when we should choose them.

When to choose IaaS VMs

In a modern, greenfield, cloud-native project, there would be very few reasons – if any at all – for opting for IaaS VMs as opposed to one of the managed Compute platform services. But not that many projects are like that and often, the best architectural decision is to go with IaaS VMs.

This is the most common in migration projects. Migrating VMs from an on-premises data center to the public cloud by moving them *as-is* is referred to as *rehosting*, or sometimes *lift and shift*. Other migration approaches include *refactoring* or *replacing*, when the workloads are rearchitected to better suit the cloud environment or replaced altogether (by a SaaS service).

In-between these two approaches, there's *replatforming*, which is when you move the application (with little to no code changes) to a PaaS service that supports the specific runtime currently in use. Each of these comes with its own pros and cons, which usually boils down to how much work is involved in it and the long-term efficiency of the solution. For example, refactoring or rearchitecting an application to a more cloud-native, scalable design will likely yield a better end result in the long term, but can be very resource-intensive and add a lot of friction and changes to the way people currently work. This comes with an associated cost and business risk. That is why, oftentimes, the rehosting ("lift and shift") approach is opted for, as it involves no code or architectural changes, it speeds up migration, and it is non-disruptive to existing security and compliance processes. In addition, especially when migrating legacy applications from on-premises environments, you may not find a suitable PaaS offering that provides the runtime and library versions that are needed for that application in the first place, and rearchitecting it may prove extremely difficult or too high of a risk of budget overrun. For such cases, IaaS VMs may the best option you have.

Some enterprise organizations will often set out to create a migration project in different waves, wherein the first wave involves a rehosting approach, while the second and subsequent waves may involve progressively refactoring and rearchitecting applications so that they fit into modern cloud-native services.

Whatever the reason may be for adopting IaaS VMs in Google Cloud, you will need to know how to design them for high availability at a minimum. That's exactly what you will learn about next.

Deploying an application with high availability on VMs

In this section, we're going to get hands-on by deploying two VMs on two different zones within a VPC network, simulating an application cluster spread across two fault domains.

We're going to be using the `gcloud` command-line utility, so if you haven't installed the Google Cloud SDK yet, please refer to *Chapter 1, An Introduction to Google Cloud for Architects*, for instructions on how to do so. Alternatively, simply go to the Google Cloud console and click on the small terminal icon at the top-right corner of the screen to open a **Cloud Shell** session. Cloud Shell is a browser-based Linux shell that comes with `gcloud` and several other Google Cloud utilities pre-installed. And, you can use it for free. If you're a Windows user and you don't have a Linux-based shell (such as Windows Subsystem for Linux), then it's best if you use Cloud Shell since the syntax for a lot of the commands used in this chapter and throughout this book is sometimes based on Bash, which differs from that of PowerShell in some aspects (for example, when applying multi-line commands).

Let's start by creating a project for this chapter:

1. Within a Cloud Shell session or a local terminal with Google SDK installed, make sure you're logged in by running the following command:

```
$ gcloud auth login
```

2. Then, run the following command:

```
$ gcloud projects create --name chapter-4 --set-as-
default
```

A project ID will be automatically generated, and you will be prompted to accept it. Type in *Y* and hit *Enter* to accept the project ID. Remember that it needs to be globally unique, which is why letting GCP determine that for you is the surest and quickest way to get one, but you can optionally try to define one yourself by passing a project ID right after the `create` command word (`project_id` is a positional argument, so you don't have to pass in an argument for it). The `--set-as-default` flag will ensure that the project is automatically set as the default one it will work with when using `gcloud`.

3. Next, we need to associate the existing billing account with this project; otherwise, we won't be able to enable the Compute Engine API and deploy VMs with it. Run the following command to list your billing accounts:

```
$ gcloud beta billing accounts list
```

Note the `beta` command word. This means that, at the time of writing, this command is available in beta and not generally available yet. This may have changed by the time you're reading this, so you can try running the command without the `beta` word in it. If it doesn't work, you will need to run it as `beta`. If you're running this on your local terminal and it's the first time you have run a `beta` command, you will be prompted to install the `beta` extension of the SDK. Do this before continuing by following the instructions on-screen.

4. Once you've successfully run the previous command, you should see an ACCOUNT_
    ID for your billing account listed. Copy this value. If you have more than one
    billing account, decide which one you're going to use for this project and copy the
    corresponding account ID. Remember that if you've signed up for a free trial, you
    will have a billing account associated with that trial, which will include credits that
    you can use for this deployment. If you haven't customized its name, it's likely to be
    called My Billing Account. To associate the billing account with your project,
    run the following command:

    ```
    $ gcloud beta billing projects link [PROJECT_ID]
    --billing-account [ACCOUNT_ID]
    ```

5. Replace PROJECT_ID and ACCOUNT_ID with your project ID (not the project
    name) and billing account ID, respectively. If you don't remember your project ID,
    you can run gcloud projects list to check what it is.

6. Next, enable the Compute Engine API by running the following command:

    ```
    $ gcloud services enable compute.googleapis.com
    ```

    As a newly created project, there will be a default VPC network in it. For our
    purposes, the default VPC will serve us just fine.

7. Run the following command to list all the subnetworks that have been precreated
    for you:

    ```
    $ gcloud compute networks subnets list
    ```

    You might remember from previous chapters that the default network comes with
    one subnetwork per Google Cloud region. In this assignment, we're going to create
    two VMs in the same region (and same subnetwork) but on different zones. Let's
    create the first VM by running the following code:

    ```
    $ gcloud compute instances create ch4vm01 \
            --machine-type n1-standard-1 \
            --network default \
            --zone us-east1-c \
            --image-project debian-cloud \
            --image-family debian-10
    ```

    Note that the region is inferred from the zone that we specify. And, in the case of the
    default network, the subnetwork is inferred from the region. Here, we're deploying
    this VM to the us-east1-c zone, in the us-east1 region and its corresponding
    subnetwork.

8. Let's SSH to this newly created VM. The easiest way is to go to `https://console.cloud.google.com/compute/instances` and select the newly created **chapter-4** project from the top bar of the console (once you've expanded the project list by clicking on the down arrow next to the current project's name, the new project may not be listed under the **Recent** tab, in which case simply switch to the **All** tab and select the project from there). You should see your new VM listed on the page. Note the **SSH** button under the **Connect** column to the right. Click on it to open a new window with an SSH session to the VM. The platform will take care of the SSH key pair handling for us so that we can log into the VM's terminal directly. Once you're in the VM's terminal, run the following commands:

```
$ sudo apt-get install -y git
$ git clone https://github.com/PacktPublishing/
Architecting-Google-Cloud-Solutions.git
$ cd Architecting-Google-Cloud-Solutions/ch4/ha-vms/
$ ./setup.sh
$ python3 webserver.py
```

9. Keep this terminal window open and the web server running. Now, go back to Cloud Shell (or your local shell with `gcloud`) and create the second VM by running the following code:

```
$ gcloud compute instances create ch4vm02 \
          --machine-type n1-standard-1 \
          --network default \
          --zone us-east1-d \
          --image-project debian-cloud \
          --image-family debian-10
```

10. Repeat the previous steps that we completed for the first VM (SSH to the VM and run the necessary commands to install Git, clone the repository, and set up and run the web server).

Now, we need to deploy a load balancer with a health check for our VMs so that, if there's ever a zonal failure (or simply a failure in one of the VMs), traffic can be seamlessly routed to the remaining healthy ones.

We will create a load balancer via the console. Let's get started:

1. Open a browser and go to `https://console.cloud.google.com/net-services/loadbalancing/loadBalancers/list`.

   As always, make sure the right project is selected from the top bar. (Also, make sure you're signed into the right account in the first place. Remember, if you don't find the project under the **Recents** tab in the project selection menu, try the **All** tab.)

2. Click on **Create load balancer**. We're only concerned with providing high availability to our web servers and we don't have any special HTTP-based routing requirements, so let's deploy a TCP load balancer by clicking on **Start configuration** under the **TCP Load Balancing** box, as shown on the left-hand side of the following screenshot:

Figure 4.2 – TCP Load Balancing configuration

3. Next, you will be asked whether this is an external or internal load balancer (**Internet facing or internal only**), and whether it is global or regional (**Multiple regions or single region**). We're doing a multi-zonal deployment within a single region, and we want this to be accessible from the internet. Therefore, let's set this up as a regional external load balancer by selecting the **From Internet to my VMs** and **Single region only** options.

4. Next, you're going to see the load balancing creation wizard. First, give it a name by typing `tcp-lb` under **Name**. Then, click on **Backend configuration**. In **Region**, select **us-east1**. Under **Backends**, click on **Select existing instances**, then **Add an instance**, and select **ch4vm01**. Click on **Add an instance** once more and select **ch4vm02**.

5. Click on **No health check**, then **Create a health check**. This will open up a new form so that you can create a health check configuration object. Name it `tcp-8080-healthcheck`, and for **Port number**, type in `8080`. Leave all the remaining fields with their default values set and click on **Save and continue**.

6. Back on the **Backend configuration** page, verify that your configuration matches the one shown on the left-hand side of the following screenshot:

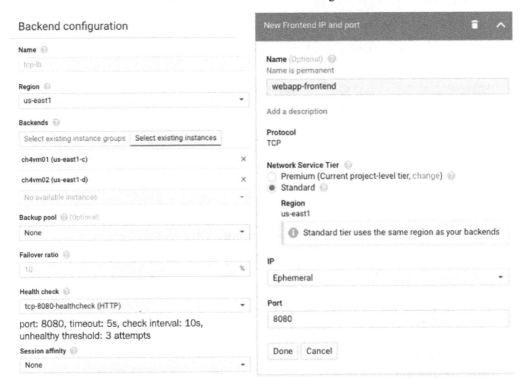

Figure 4.3 – Backend and Frontend configurations for the TCP Load Balancer

7. Click on **Frontend configuration**. Name it `webapp-frontend`. Then, for **Network Service Tier**, select **Standard**. Note that the region will be automatically selected so that it matches that of backend's. Leave **IP** as **Ephemeral** and for the **Port** field, type in `8080`. The frontend configuration is shown on the right-hand side of the preceding screenshot. Click on **Done**.

8. Finally, click on **Create** to create the load balancer. Wait a minute or two until the load balancer is created, and then click on the name of the load balancer (**tcp-lb**) when it appears. Copy the external IP address shown under the **Frontend** section. This is the IP address of the load balancer, which is the frontend to our two web server VMs.

    Now, there's only one thing we need to do before we can test the application in the browser: we need to allow port 8080 traffic in our firewall.

9. Go back to Cloud Shell (you may need to open it again) or your local shell and run the following `gcloud` command to create an ingress firewall rule:

    ```
    $ gcloud compute firewall-rules create allow-http-8080
    --allow tcp:8080 --direction INGRESS --source-
    ranges='0.0.0.0/0'
    ```

10. Now, open a browser tab or window and paste in the external IP address of the frontend you copied previously. Append `:8080` to the IP address to make sure we're on the right TCP port. You should see a simple web page, similar to the one shown in the following screenshot:

I am a webpage

And I am being served by ch4vm01

Figure 4.4 – Web page served by the web servers

Press refresh in your browser a few times until you see the name of the server change from ch4vm01 to ch4vm02 and vice versa.

11. Now, go to one of the open SSH terminals (for example, the one for ch4vm02) and press *Ctrl* + *C* to kill the web server. Let's pretend this was a hardware failure in the data center associated with our zone, *us-east1-d*. If you refresh the page, you should now see that the other server (located on a different hardware failure domain) continues to serve the web page, and the application continues working without any issues. For this to work well in the real world, these web servers (or whichever application component you're doing this for) must not be designed to store state locally in the VM or on some datastore that is confined to the same zone. Ideally, you'd have any state written to a regional (multi-zonal) datastore, so that in the event of a zonal failure, the other web servers in other zones can pick up the slack without losing state information.

a) As a challenge for you, think about how a multi-regional deployment of these web servers would be done. What would be different?

b) What kind of load balancer would you deploy instead?

c) If you still have free trial credits or a budget that allows you to, and you want to continue experimenting, why not go ahead and deploy these VMs in a multi-regional setting?

To prevent unwanted costs or credit consumption, we must clean up the resources.

> **Important Note**
>
> For the next section, we're going to use the same type of VM again, so if you're jumping into this straight away, you can optionally leave one VM running.

12. Run the following commands:

```
$ gcloud compute instances delete ch4vm01 -zone
us-east1-c
$ gcloud compute instances delete ch4vm02 -zone
us-east1-d
```

13. Press *Y* after each command to confirm them.

14. Then, navigate to the load balancing page in the console (on the left-side menu, go to **Network Services** > **Load balancing**). Click on the three dots next to the load balancer you've created and click on **Delete**. When prompted, select the associated health check resource to delete that as well. Finally, go to the **Firewall** page (on the left-side menu, go to **VPC Network** > **Firewall**), select the **allow-http-8080** firewall rule, and click on **Delete** at the top of the page.

With that, you have deployed IaaS VMs in a highly available setup, which is an important hands-on skill to have. However, we still haven't tackled the scalability component of the application, so we'll dive into this with our next assignment.

Deploying an application with autoscaling on VMs

This time, we will recreate our application in two VMs belonging to a regional managed instance group. This will allow the group to scale horizontally (in or out) according to demand. In addition, instances will be spread across different zones within the region to provide high availability. The autoscaling service will attempt to evenly distribute the instances across available zones so that we don't wind up relying too much on one single zone.

As a principle, a system that scales horizontally (by adding or removing instances) relies on all instances being, essentially, clones of each other and undifferentiated in terms of the application running in them. For this reason, to create a **managed instance group** (**MIG**) in Google Cloud, first, we're going to create a virtual machine image and then an instance template that instances will be created from. An instance template defines the disk image, plus additional VM properties such as the machine type (size) and disk size.

To create an image, we're going to need to set up a VM instance with our application so that the application starts automatically at boot, before creating an image from that VM. If you still have a VM instance running from the previous activity, then great – we're going to use that. If not, we will need to create one using `gcloud`:

1. Run the following command:

    ```
    $ gcloud compute instances create ch4vm01 \
            --machine-type n1-standard-1 \
            --network default \
            --zone us-east1-c \
            --image-project debian-cloud \
            --image-family debian-10
    ```

2. Next, SSH to the VM via the console (as you learned to do in the previous section) and run the following commands to install Git and download the repository (you may also skip this step if you're reusing the VM from the previous section):

    ```
    $ sudo apt-get install -y git
    $ git clone https://github.com/PacktPublishing/
    Architecting-Google-Cloud-Solutions.git
    ```

3. Still in the VM's SSH terminal, go to the `autoscaling-mig` directory under the `ch4` parent directory and run the setup script:

    ```
    $ cd Architecting-Google-Cloud-Solutions/ch4/autoscaling-
    mig/
    $ chmod +x setup.sh
    $ sudo ./setup.sh
    ```

4. This script creates a cronjob for starting the web server upon a reboot event. If you see an output message saying *no crontab for root*, don't worry – it's not an error, just a message stating that there was no crontab file set for root previously. Now, we can go ahead and create an image from that instance. First, stop the running VM:

```
$ gcloud compute instances stop ch4vm01 --zone us-east1-c
```

5. Then, create the image:

```
$ gcloud compute images create webserver-image \
    --source-disk ch4vm01 \
    --source-disk-zone us-east1-c
```

6. Now, create an instance template:

```
$ gcloud compute instance-templates create webserver-custom-templ \
--machine-type n1-standard-1 \
--image webserver-image \
--boot-disk-size 25GB
```

7. Finally, create the MIG:

```
$ gcloud compute instance-groups managed create webserver-mig-eastus \
    --template webserver-custom-templ  \
    --size 2 \
    --region us-east1
```

8. Now, let's set an autoscaling policy based on a target CPU utilization threshold of 50%. For that, run the following code:

```
$ gcloud compute instance-groups managed set-autoscaling webserver-mig-eastus \
    --region us-east1 \
    --max-num-replicas 4 \
    --target-cpu-utilization 0.50 \
    --cool-down-period 30
```

> **Important Note**
>
> A CPU utilization threshold of 50% is a lower value than what you'd typically configure in the real world, but it will just make it easier for us to test autoscaling later.

The cooldown period tells the autoscaler how many seconds to wait after a new instance has started before it starts watching the CPU utilization of that instance. You should configure this based on how long it takes, on average, for your instance to boot up and run the application. We have a lightweight application, so 30 seconds will do fine.

9. Finally, let's create a firewall rule before going back to the console to create our load balancer:

```
$ gcloud compute firewall-rules create allow-web
--allow tcp:80,tcp:8080 --direction INGRESS --source-
ranges='0.0.0.0/0'
```

10. In the console, navigate via the left-hand side menu to **Network services** > **Load balancing**. Then, click on **Create load balancer**. This time, we're going to create an HTTP(S) Load Balancer. Under **HTTP(S) Load Balancing**, click on **Start configuration**. Select the **From Internet to my VMs** option and click on **Continue**.

11. For the **Name** field, type in mig-lb. Click on **Backend Configuration**, then click on **Create or select backend services & backend buckets**, and then **Backend services** and **Create a backend service**.

12. Configure the backend service as follows:

    a) **Name**: mig-backend

    b) **Backend type: instance group**

    c) **Protocol: HTTP**

    d) **Named port**: http-8080

    e) **Timeout**: 30

13. Under **New Backend**, add the following configuration:

    a) **Instance group**: webserver-mig-eastus

    b) **Port numbers**: 8080

    c) **Balancing mode: Utilization**

d) **Maximum backend utilization**: 80

e) **Capacity**: 100

14. Then, click on **Done**.

15. Click on **Health check**, then **Create a health check**. This will open up a new form so that you can create a health check configuration object. Name it tcp-8080-healthcheck, and for **Port number**, type in 8080. Leave all the remaining fields with their default values and click on **Save and continue**.

16. In **Host and path rules**, leave all the configurations with their default values. Next, click on **Frontend configuration**. Configure the frontend as follows:

    a) **Name**: mig-frontend

    b) **Protocol**: HTTP

    c) **Network Service Tier**: Standard

    d) **IP version**: IPv4

    e) **IP address**: Ephemeral

    f) **Port**: 80

17. Finally, click on **Create**. Wait a few minutes for the deployment to complete and then, click on **mig-lb** when it appears. Copy the IP address shown under **Frontend** and paste it into your browser (you may need to wait a few minutes for it to work). You should see a web page, as follows:

I am a webpage

And I am being served by webserver-mig-eastus-xs53

Figure 4.5 – Web page served by an instance of a managed instance group

You might see the word debian instead of the instance name (such as webserver-mig-eastus-xs53, as shown in the preceding screenshot). This is because the web server may start before the hostname has been changed by the platform, which happens when an instance is created. If you restart the instances, you will probably see their names. For the purpose of this assignment, however, you don't need to do this.

18. Now, navigate to the managed instance group in the console by expanding the left-hand side menu and going to **Compute Engine | Instance Groups**. Click on **webserver-mig-eastus**. You should see two instances listed with a prefix of `webserver-mig-eastus`. Note the zones that they have been deployed on. They're different because GCE will automatically balance deployments across zones for a regional MIG. Let's simulate some heavy load on the instances by clicking on the **SSH** button next to an instance name to open an SSH terminal. Once the terminal has loaded, run the following command:

```
$ sudo apt-get install stress
$ stress --cpu 8
```

19. This command will install a small utility program that can create stress on the VM's CPU to simulate high load. Open an SSH terminal to the other instance in the group and repeat these steps to create a stress load on the other instance. After a few seconds, you can refresh the console and you should see two more instances being created (we set the maximum number of instances in the group to four to avoid incurring high costs). Now, your MIG should look as follows:

Name	Creation time	Template	Per instance config	Zone
webserver-mig-eastus-22tv	Nov 1, 2020, 5:04:15 PM	webserver-custom-templ		us-east1-c
webserver-mig-eastus-gcd0	Nov 1, 2020, 5:03:52 PM	webserver-custom-templ		us-east1-d
webserver-mig-eastus-xvlk	Nov 1, 2020, 4:54:17 PM	webserver-custom-templ		us-east1-b
webserver-mig-eastus-zlvs	Nov 1, 2020, 4:54:16 PM	webserver-custom-templ		us-east1-c

Figure 4.6 – Managed instance group after a scaling out event

Notice the zone distribution. The US East 1 region has, at the time of writing, three different zones: b, c, and d. Each of the first three instances are in their own separate zones, while the fourth instance has been placed in zone b again (since there were no more zones). This pattern would continue if we kept adding instances to the group, thus obtaining the best possible spread.

Congratulations! Our task is complete and you've deployed an autoscaling application that is also resilient against zonal outages by using regional MIGs. By doing this, you've learned how to create an image from a VM instance and set up a template that you can use to deploy MIG instances.

To clean up the resources, do the following:

1. Go to the console and navigate to **Network services** > **Load Balancing**. Select the **mig-lb** load balancer, then click on **Delete**. When prompted, select the **mig-backend** backend service and the health check **tcp-8080-healthcheck** resources to be deleted along with the load balancer.

2. Next, run the following commands to delete all the remaining resources we created for this assignment, confirming this each time by typing *Y* and hitting *Enter*:

```
$ gcloud compute instance-groups managed delete
webserver-mig-eastus --region us-east1
$ gcloud compute images delete webserver-image
$ gcloud compute instance-templates delete webserver-
custom-templ
$ gcloud compute firewall-rules delete allow-web
```

With that, we've wrapped up our hands-on work with IaaS VMs and MIGs. However, there's one more thing worth mentioning in this section, which is the possibility to have stateful MIGs. Let's see how that works.

Stateful MIGs

Before we move on and look at the various Compute platforms that are available, you should know about **stateful managed instance groups**. If the application you're working with relies on having the unique state of each instance that hosts it preserved (including things such as instance name, data on attached persistent disks, and metadata) upon a restart, recreation, or update event, then stateful MIGs will have you covered. Instances that run stateful workloads can't simply be discarded and recreated in the same way that stateless MIGs can. Therefore, Google Cloud delivers the stateful MIG as a service that allows you to preserve instance state.

Stateful workloads can't be easily scaled horizontally since scaling, in this case, could require data replication, creation or deletion of data shards, or changes to the overall application configuration. However, with stateful MIGs, you can still achieve *autohealing* features and manual horizontal scaling while preserving state. In addition, you also have the capability of applying controlled updates (rolling updates) to the instances. Examples of stateful applications that could benefit from this include **ElasticSearch**, **Kafka**, and **Jenkins** or database applications such as **Cassandra**, **mongoDB**, and **MySQL**.

Stateful MIGs are not separate services in GCP, but rather, a MIG is considered stateful if you have created a stateful configuration. This means that you can convert a "regular" stateless MIG into a stateful MIG after its creation by adding stateful configuration to it. You do that by setting a non-empty stateful policy and/or one or more non-empty per-instance configs. A stateful policy defines items that you want to preserve for *all instances*, whereas a per-instance config defines *instance-specific* items to preserve. GCE will apply your stateful policy configuration to new and existing instances in the MIG automatically, without disrupting running VMs. Converting an existing MIG into a stateful MIG is as simple as running a `gcloud` command, as follows:

```
$ gcloud compute instance-groups managed update MIG_NAME \
  --stateful-disk device-name=DEVICE_NAME
```

You should now be well familiar with the IaaS offerings in Google Cloud, when to use them, and how to design for high availability and/or horizontal scalability with GCE. You're now ready for the next level: Compute platforms.

Exploring Compute platforms

In the previous section, you learned about why you should choose IaaS VMs to host your workloads. If none of them apply to a project you're working on, then you should most certainly consider the Compute platform options on GCP. Some example good candidate scenarios are as follows:

- Organizations with a code-first mentality and a business model centered around shipping software fast.

- Organizations with small or non-existent IT operations teams.

- Innovation-led businesses that wish to modernize existing applications or deploy new applications with modern cloud-native practices.

- Organizations that wish to reduce their operational overhead by re-architecting some of their workloads to fit cloud-based PaaS services.

If you recall from *Chapter 1, An Introduction to Google Cloud for Architects*, the PaaS delivery model implies that the cloud provider is responsible for all the layers of the stack, up until, and including, the runtime environment. You, as a customer, are then responsible for the application and its data. This means that you don't have to concern yourself with OS patching and upgrading or even maintaining a particular application's underlying runtime platform. You can just deploy application code along with its declared dependencies onto the platform, and it will run it. And all that high availability and scalability jazz? Taken care of, at least to some extent.

In most cases, when working with Compute PaaS services, you can't even open an SSH terminal toward the underlying instances running the application (though you typically have access to its standard output or logs sent externally). For system engineers and professionals that have worked with VMs and SSH terminals their entire professional lives, this may cause them to "itch" and yearn for some control or visibility over the underlying system. If that's you, don't worry. The reason you can't do these things is because you really don't need to, and you really shouldn't.

Let's start by exploring what GCP has to offer in terms of Compute platforms and why you would include each of them in your design.

App Engine

Google Cloud's App Engine is a fully managed platform for deploying applications that can grow from zero to global scale. The supported development languages are **Node.js**, **Java**, **Ruby**, **C#**, **Go**, **Python**, and **PHP**. However, you can also supply a **Docker** container to bring any custom library and/or framework to App Engine, effectively customizing your runtime.

Some other useful features of App Engine are as follows:

- **Traffic splitting**: Allows you to route incoming requests to your app to different deployed versions. Useful for **A/B testing** or **incremental feature rollouts**.

- **Application versioning**: Allows you to host different versions of your app and create, for example, different application environments such as development, test, staging, and production.

- **Application Diagnostics**: Allows you to easily integrate with **Cloud Monitoring** and **Cloud Logging** to monitor the health and performance of your running apps, as well as with **Cloud Debugger** and **Error Reporting** for diagnosing and fixing software bugs.

- **Built-in Application Security**: Allows you to set firewall rules right from within App Engine, as well as manage and deploy **SSL/TLS certificates** for custom domains.

The main appeal of App Engine is that, as a fully managed Compute platform that scales as needed, you, as a customer, can simply focus on the coding of the application. Using **Cloud Source Repositories**, you can version your code privately in Google Cloud as a Git repository, along with your App Engine application configuration files (written in YAML), and you would be just a `gcloud` command away from deploying that application to production. Better yet, you can use Cloud Build to automate deployments when code is pushed to your repository, effectively setting **continuous delivery** (**CD**) for your application. Firstly, however, you will need to understand the two types of App Engine environments: **Flexible Environment** and **Standard Environment**.

In the Standard Environment, application instances will run in a sandbox, using the runtime for the supported language and one of the supported versions. This means you can't just run any version of your programming language, but you should be covered if you're running one that is fairly recent. An up to date list of supported language versions can be found at `https://cloud.google.com/appengine/docs/the-appengine-environments#when-to-choose-the-standard-environment`.

What you get in return for those "restrictions" is that your application will be able to achieve very rapid and elastic scaling, and, due to lack of demand, it will actually *scale in to zero*. This means that no instances will be running at all if there is no traffic to your application, and App Engine will charge you nothing. If there's very little traffic, you will also pay very little. You pay for how much your application is used. It's that simple.

In the Flexible Environment, as the name implies, you get a little more flexibility in terms of runtime. You no longer need to write code in one of the supported programming languages necessarily, nor be restricted to any specific set of versions. Your application will run in a Docker container that will include your custom runtime (which you set through a **Dockerfile**), which may comprise any programming language and version. You also get to SSH to instances to do any debugging that needs to be done. The trade-off for that flexibility is that your application won't be able to scale as immediately as with the Standard Environment. The pricing for the Flexible Environment is based on the usage of vCPU, memory, and persistent disks as opposed to instance hours, as is the case with the Standard Environment. You won't get the Flexible Environment for free, even if there's no traffic to your application, since it can't scale in to zero.

You might be thinking that there aren't many differences between App Engine's Flexible Environment and Compute Engine VMs. But keep in mind you still get high availability and scalability without the need to set up load balancing yourself, plus the other App Engine features mentioned previously. And in addition, Flexible Environment instances are restarted weekly to apply any required OS patching and security updates without disruption to your running application. The Standard Environment should be preferred whenever it meets the application requirements. However, for those application components with specific programming language and/or library requirements that fall outside of what the Standard Environment offers, you could and should deploy them to the Flexible Environment. One good design approach is to break your application down into its basic components based on their runtimes, similarly to a microservices design, but not necessarily as a service-oriented architecture (if you're not ready for that). This will allow you to place different components on either the Standard or the Flexible environment as required.

Deploying versioned code to App Engine

Let's learn how to deploy code to App Engine and how it all works in practice:

1. Open a browser and go to the Google Cloud console. Ensure the project for this chapter is selected at the top (if not, then select the **chapter-4** project), then open Cloud Shell by clicking on the shell icon at the top-right corner of the page. Alternatively, you can use a local shell if you have the Google Cloud SDK installed:

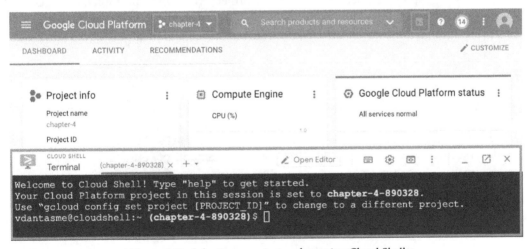

Figure 4.7 – Selecting a project and opening Cloud Shell

2. In the shell, type in the following commands:

```
$ git clone https://github.com/PacktPublishing/
Architecting-Google-Cloud-Solutions.git
$ cd Architecting-Google-Cloud-Solutions/ch4/appengine/
$ gcloud auth login
```

3. After typing in `gcloud auth login`, follow the instructions on-screen to authenticate through your browser. Once you're logged in, you will be informed what your current project is. If it's not the one you set up for this chapter in the previous section, make sure you select it by running the following command:

```
$ gcloud config set project PROJECT_ID
```

Remember, the project ID is different than the project name. If you've been following along, your project name should be `chapter-4`, whereas your project ID is unique to you. You can check what your project ID is by running the following command:

```
$ gcloud projects list
```

4. Finally, without changing directories, run the following command:

```
$ gcloud app deploy
```

As the first App Engine deployment on this project, you will be prompted to select a region for App Engine. Pick a region that is close to you by typing in the number corresponding to the region from the list that appears on your screen. Confirm your choice and wait a few minutes for the deployment to complete.

5. Once the deployment is done, you can run the following command:

```
$ gcloud app browse
```

This should automatically open your app on a new browser tab or window. If it doesn't detect your browser, it will spit out the DNS name of your app so that you can paste in into your browser yourself. You should see a web page similar to the one shown in the following screenshot.

This simple web app prints out some environment variables set by App Engine and the contents of the app.yaml file, which is where you set the configuration of the App Engine environment and its runtime. It is also possible to set custom environment variables in that file that you can access from your application. Of course, I had to add a URL for a cat image:

Hello There!

My instance id is **00c61b117c3412eade0cdeef6ecdacd935664fd192344f78126de22fe4b0745311e773a26d**.

I am running on **standard** environment. My Runtime is **python38**.

Here is the content of my app.yaml:

runtime: python38

instance_class: F2

env_variables:
MY_CUSTOM_ENV_VAR: "https://upload.wikimedia.org/wikipedia/commons/8/86/Cat_yawning_in_park.jpg"

Figure 4.8 – Web page from the web app we deployed to the App Engine Standard Environment

Looking at the contents of the `app.yaml` file printed on the page, you can see the following:

- The definition of the runtime (**Python 3.8**)
- The instance class (**F2**)
- The custom environment variable (**MY_CUSTOM_ENV_VAR**)

The instance class refers to the class within the Standard Environment that determines the amount of memory and CPU available to *each* instance. For the latest generation runtimes, the following instance classes can be set:

Instance Class	Memory Limit	CPU Limit	Scaling Types
F1 (default)	256 MB	600 MHz	automatic
F2	512 MB	1.2 GHz	automatic
F4	1,024 MB	2.4 GHz	automatic
F4_1G	2,048 MB	2.4 GHz	automatic

There are also B-class instances (basic), which have different capacities and do not support automatic scaling. You can check out the full table at https://cloud.google.com/appengine/docs/standard#instance_classes.

Many other things can be defined in the app.yaml file, such as URL handlers that match requests to certain paths (for example, /images) to a destination (for example, the static/images directory). The syntax and full reference documentation for the app.yaml file can be found at https://cloud.google.com/appengine/docs/standard/python3/config/appref.

Now, experiment with making an update to the main code (main.py) or the app configuration file (app.yaml), for example, by changing the custom environment variable to the address of a picture of another cat (or a dog, if you're a dog person). Then, to redeploy the app, simply rerun the following command:

```
$ gcloud app deploy
```

Then, refresh the page. It's that simple.

Cleaning up

To delete the App Engine application, go to the console, expand the left-hand side menu, and navigate to **App Engine** > **Settings**. Make sure your project is selected. On the **Settings** page, click on the **Disable application** button. You will be prompted to confirm this by typing in the application ID. This will effectively delete your entire deployment.

In *Part 3, Designing for the Modern Enterprise,* we're going to learn how to automate App Engine deployments with continuous delivery using Cloud Build. For now, all you need to know is that this is possible to do, so let's continue exploring Compute platforms.

Cloud Functions

Cloud Functions is a **serverless** execution environment for application code. Serverless doesn't mean the thing runs in a vacuum, without any underlying server (we don't have that technology yet). It refers to services that do not require you (as a customer) to provision and manage any servers. Serverless services are also, by design, highly available and have automatic elastic scaling. In addition, you typically only pay for a more precise unit of consumption, such as number of requests, CPU time, and so on. Technically, App Engine offers precisely that. So, what is the difference?

Cloud Functions is meant for lightweight applications with very specific scopes (or *functions*). It's not necessarily meant to host a fully-fledged application (although you could do that), but applications that contain compute-focused *components*. This is something that runs on a trigger to do one specific processing job. It's probably the quickest way to get a piece of code with event-based execution in the cloud. Some examples of source triggers that can trigger your code are as follows:

- **HTTP triggers**: When someone or some application calls an HTTP endpoint
- **Cloud Pub/Sub triggers**: When a message is published to a topic
- **Cloud Storage triggers**: When a new object is created in a bucket (and/or deleted from it)
- **Direct triggers**: When you just want to trigger it directly (via a `gcloud functions call` command)

Other available triggers include **Cloud Firestore** (currently in beta, it's a trigger that's used in response to events using Firestore APIs) and **Firebase**-related triggers (Analytics for Firebase, Firebase Realtime Database, and Firebase Authentication).

To illustrate its functionality, let's create a simple function with an HTTP trigger:

1. Go to the console, make sure the **chapter-4** project is selected at the top, expand the left-hand side menu, and click on **Cloud Functions** in the **Compute** sub-group.

2. Click on **Create Function**. Name it `dinner-suggestion`, and for **Region,** select one that is close to you. Under the **Trigger** section, for **Trigger type**, choose **HTTP**. Select **Allow unauthenticated invocations**. Click on **Save**, and then click on **Next**.

3. Next, in the **Runtime** field, select **Python 3.8**. For **Source code**, select **Inline Editor**. In the code editor section, replace the contents provided with the contents of the file available in this book's GitHub repository at `https://github.com/PacktPublishing/Architecting-Google-Cloud-Solutions/blob/master/ch4/function/function.py`. This is shown in the following screenshot:

Figure 4.9 – Cloud Function inline editor for Python 3

4. For **Entry point**, replace `hello_world` with `what_to_cook_for_dinner`. Click on **Deploy**.

5. Wait a few minutes until the function has been deployed. Then, click on the three dots icon on the right (under **Actions**) and click on **Test function**, as shown in the following screenshot:

Figure 4.10 – Triggering the function from the console to test it

6. Then, click on **Text the function**. After a few seconds, you should see the output, which should be a suggestion for dinner, as shown in the following screenshot:

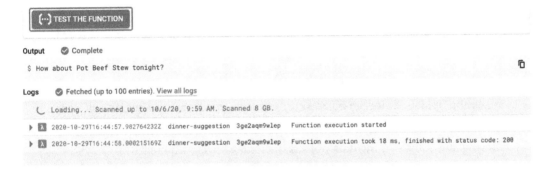

Figure 4.11 – Checking the function's output

As you can see, some logs are also shown, including information about how long the function's execution time was and the response HTTP status code.

7. Now, from the same page, click on the **Trigger** tab. You should see the URL for the HTTP endpoint of your function. You can copy and paste it into a browser, for example, to get a dinner suggestion directly from your browser. You can also use this URL in any HTTP client application, which is what you would typically do when designing solutions with functions. The example we used here is silly (unless you were really out of ideas for dinner). Hopefully, however, this illustrates the point of functions: a scope-bounded, lightweight piece of code that gets executed based on an event that depends on the chosen trigger.

8. Back in the console, click on **Delete** to delete the function and clean up.

Cloud Functions code can be written in Python, Java, Go, or Node.js. It is priced according to a combination of invocation, compute time, and network traffic. At the time of writing, the first 2 million invocations per month are free of charge, and beyond 2 million, they're priced at $0.40 per million. Fees for compute time are variable based on the amount of resources (CPU and memory) that are provisioned for the function (something the platform will figure out based on what the function requires). This goes from about $0.0000100 to $0.0000140 per GHz-second of compute utilization. Finally, network egress is priced at $0.12 per GB, with 5 GB free per month. Remember, prices fluctuate, and these values are just to give you an idea of how, and by how much, Cloud Functions are priced.

It is a reasonably cost-effective service and something to keep in mind when you need to include executable application components in your overall solution. Here are a few real-world examples of when you would use Cloud Functions:

- Automated backups and other batch jobs
- Processing uploaded storage objects (for example, resizing an image once it's been uploaded)
- Filtering and transforming data objects once they have been created
- Event processing for event-driven applications
- Infrastructure automation (for example, start or stop the application, scale up or down, and so on)

Next in line in our exploration of Compute platforms on GCP is Cloud Run. Let's get to it.

Cloud Run

The Cloud Run service is somewhat similar to Cloud Functions in that it is a fully managed "serverless" platform. The main difference is that your code is deployed to containers that listen for requests or events. Since it's a container-based deployment, you can "package" your application along with its dependencies, configurations, and tools. This also means you can develop code in any language of your choice, using any custom library or binary you provide.

A **service** is the main component of Cloud Run. When you deploy an application to Cloud Run, you deploy it as a service resource (that listens for requests). Container instances will be created according to the number of requests your service is receiving, effectively scaling the application according to demand. A service is placed on a specific GCP region and, for high availability, is automatically replicated across multiple zones within the region they are in. In a project, you can have multiple services running in different regions.

Each service deployment creates a **revision**. A revision consists of a particular container image and environment settings such as variables, memory limits, or concurrency value. The latter determines the maximum number of requests that can be sent in parallel to each container instance. A revision is immutable because, once it has been created, it cannot be modified or updated. If a change needs to be made, a new revision will be created to incorporate it. Requests are automatically routed to the latest healthy service revision.

To illustrate how everything comes together in Cloud Run, the following diagram shows two Cloud Run services: **Service A** and **Service B**:

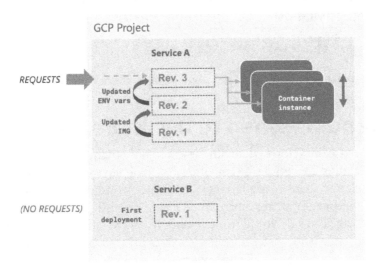

Figure 4.12 – Example of Cloud Run services

Service A has had two updates (in the first update, a new container image was created; in the second update, an environment variable was updated). Therefore, it now has three revisions. The first revision is created when you deploy a container image to a new Cloud Run service for the first time. In **Service B**, which has recently been deployed and still has no incoming requests, there is only a single revision and no container instances since there are no service requests. The first server has three container instances; that is, the calculated amount of instances to handle the current number of requests (while taking into account the concurrency settings).

In summary, Cloud Run is a platform for deploying containerized applications (services) with high availability and autoscaling. While Cloud Function was more geared toward event-based, on-demand computing power for lightweight code execution, Cloud Run offers a way for us to deploy and continuously run container-based applications and is especially well-suited for microservices architectures. We will look into microservices more deeply in *Part 3, Designing for the Modern Enterprise*. If you are interested in getting some hands-on practice with Cloud Run, I encourage you to check out a *quickstart* guide for your language of choice at `https://cloud.google.com/run/docs/quickstarts/build-and-deploy`. When you're done experimenting, run the following command to delete the project and all the resources within it as a clean-up step (replace `PROJECT_ID` with your project ID for this chapter's project):

```
$ gcloud projects delete PROJECT_ID
```

We're now going to explore one of Google Cloud's major strengths: Kubernetes.

Understanding when to use Kubernetes

Kubernetes has been around for a while now as a container orchestration platform that adds several automation capabilities to container-based deployments. It was initially designed by Google and then released to the open source world in 2014. It is a powerful system that's capable of autoscaling (horizontally), auto-repairing, and automating how containers are managed and deployed while providing controlled rollouts and rollbacks. A useful introduction to Kubernetes is available at `https://kubernetes.io/docs/concepts/overview/what-is-kubernetes/`. It's a beast of a system and, for that reason, not the easiest thing to work with and set up on your own infrastructure (although this has been gradually changing). Kubernetes is complex enough to deserve its own book (in fact, there are several books out there on this subject exclusively). Therefore, it is outside the scope of this book to offer a comprehensive understanding of Kubernetes and its underlying components. However, we will explore it through the lens of a Cloud or Solutions Architect and help you understand what problems it solves, where it fits into the overall picture, and when you should consider it.

The core purpose of Kubernetes is to containerize applications. When you run multiple application components on a single monolithic VM, you might get conflicting library versions and application dependencies on the same **operating system** (**OS**). Different services sharing the same OS and kernel space can conflict with one another and, even when they don't, they likely have different performance requirements, which makes it difficult to host them efficiently. Containers have changed this paradigm by allowing applications to run in their own self-contained environments, with their own libraries and settings baked in. Due to this, container-based application architectures allow for more portability, reproducibility, and independent scalability of applications.

The caveat, however, is that it creates management and operational overhead by having you handle multiple "lightweight" instances as opposed to one single VM. This is where Kubernetes comes in, as a platform that offers orchestration capabilities that facilitate the management of multiple containers, therefore allowing you to have the best of both worlds.

Over the last few years, cloud providers have gone out of their way to offer Kubernetes as a managed service, taking care of all the infrastructure and platform setup hassle to give you something ready to use and host production workloads. Of course, as the creators of Kubernetes, Google Cloud led the way.

Google Kubernetes Engine (**GKE**) is Google Cloud's managed Kubernetes environment that's used to deploy, manage, and scale containerized applications on top of Google infrastructure. The GKE environment is backed by Compute Engine instances that have been grouped into a cluster (and operated by Google) and are hosting your application containers (more or less fully managed by you). It's not very straightforward to place GKE on the spectrum of delivery models: it can be thought of as IaaS, but also as PaaS. The truth is, it lies somewhere in the middle. It has IaaS characteristics, since you are essentially deploying containers, which you could think of as "lightweight VMs" that you can fully configure, but it has PaaS characteristics due to Google taking up responsibility for managing Kubernetes' control plane and its underlying node clusters. You can even opt to have some manual control over the latter, to make it even more complicated to put Kubernetes into a category. Kubernetes' software itself provides a lot in terms of platform abstraction just by the way it has been designed, even if it's not running as a managed service in the cloud.

One key selling point of Kubernetes is that it enables **platform independence**. Since Kubernetes is agnostic to the actual underlying platform that runs it, once you build applications on Kubernetes, you can run these applications anywhere – be it on GCP, on an on-premises data center, or somewhere else. Granted, when the cloud provider handles certain aspects of the Kubernetes platform to provide you a more comfortable to consume system, to some extent, it is locking you in. It wouldn't be as easy to move from GKE to, say, **Azure Kubernetes Service (AKS)** – Microsoft Azure's managed Kubernetes platform service – as it would be to move a "raw" Kubernetes deployment that you've set up from the ground up from one hosting platform to another. There are peculiarities in how each cloud provider approaches their Kubernetes services and the features provided. Therefore, you should consider this when you hear someone arguing in favor of a managed Kubernetes service (such as GKE or AKS) because it would give them platform independence. You might want to offer the counterargument that, well, it might not be as simple as it seems (though there is some truth in it). That being said, there are many *other reasons* why a platform such as GKE is excellent, and why you should consider it for hosting your workloads.

When you run a GKE cluster, Google Cloud provides certain advanced cluster management features, such as the following:

- Load balancing via Google Cloud's load balancing service
- Node pools
- Autoscaling at the node level
- Automatic upgrades for your cluster's node software
- Autohealing for your nodes
- Logging and monitoring integration with Google Cloud's operations suite

The control plane's life cycle is managed by GKE, including the Kubernetes API server, scheduler, and core resource controllers. Upgrades to the Kubernetes version are also performed automatically. The control plane is the "heavy machinery" behind Kubernetes and the intelligence delivering its most appealing features (such as autoscaling and autohealing).

In Kubernetes, workloads run in **Pods**, which are the smallest deployable objects available. A Pod represents a single instance of a running process in your cluster, and it contains one or more containers (such as **Docker containers** – the kind you'd run with Cloud Run). Generally, however, it's most commonly the case that a Pod maps to a single container, so they can often be thought of as such. Pods are the units that are assigned unique IP addresses and, if a Pod has multiple containers, they will all share the same network namespace, including the IP address and the network ports. Pods can therefore be thought of as self-contained, isolated logical *hosts* for running a single instance of an application. The availability and scalability components are handled by the controller and based on your custom configurations. For example, you would typically create not a single Pod, but a set of identical Pods called replicas (the minimum number of which you would specify). Individual Pods within a set of replicated Pods are created and managed by the controller, which will then perform horizontal scaling as needed and ensure the right number of Pods are running as defined in the replica set configuration. Since Pods run on nodes (which are actual Compute instances comprising, therefore, a failure domain), the controller will also ensure that the Pods are replicated across different nodes. If a node fails, its Pods are recreated somewhere else. With node auto-repair enabled, nodes deemed unhealthy (via periodic health checks) will be repaired by GKE. The repair process involves draining the unhealthy node and recreating it.

The following diagram illustrates the architecture of a Kubernetes cluster in GKE. GKE completely manages the components on the left-hand side, since they belong to the Control Plane. In nodes, agents such as **kubelet** and **k-proxy** are automatically set up to ensure that containers are running in a Pod and to handle network proxying. Then, inside the nodes, you have one or more Pods, each containing one or more containers. You declaratively define their configurations while their life cycles are mostly managed by the controller. There are, however, many control operations that you can run yourself via **kubectl**, a command-line tool for controlling Kubernetes clusters, as shown on the left-hand side of the following diagram:

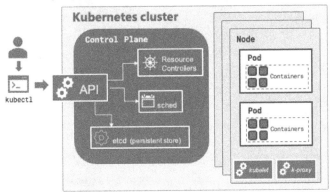

Figure 4.13 – GKE cluster architecture

It's important to understand that *Pods are ephemeral* and disposable units of deployment. They should never be expected to run for long periods of time unaffected, and certainly not forever. And when a Pod is terminated, it cannot be brought back. This has significant implications for networking in Kubernetes. You should never reference a Pod by its IP address since they're ephemeral and likely to change often. Manually handling IP-based firewall rules or routing is certainly unfeasible. Luckily, however, GKE will dynamically configure IP filtering rules, routing tables, and firewall rules on each node, based on the declarative model of your Kubernetes deployments and the cluster configuration. Service discovery and DNS services are also provided and managed by GKE so that service names can be referenced reliably while following a standard specification. This is the power of GKE: *you can define things in code using a high-level, human-readable language, and the platform will take care of nearly everything related to the infrastructure required to run the workloads.* That even includes load balancing and exposing sets of workloads as services.

Services are another crucial design component in Kubernetes deployments. A Service is essentially a set of Pods that have been grouped into one exposed resource, characterized by an endpoint that can be consumed either internally or externally. You can assign Pods as members of a Service by setting labels for them, which are then specified in the selector that defines the Service. This and all of the declarative configurations that are done in GKE are defined in manifest YAML files; an example of a service definition is as follows:

```yaml
apiVersion: v1
kind: Service
metadata:
  name: dinner-recommendation-service
spec:
  selector:
    app: dinnerapp
    department: it
  type: ClusterIP
  ports:
  - protocol: TCP
    port: 80
    targetPort: 8080
```

In the preceding configuration, the `dinner-recommendation-service` Service includes all the Pods that have been configured with the `dinnerapp` and `it` values for their `app` and `department` labels, respectively. A Service can be internal or external and backed by GCP load balancing. The type defined here, `ClusterIP`, is the default type and it's a Service with a stable internal frontend IP address. Once this Service has been created, a cluster IP address will be set and visible to you. You can then use this IP address to send requests to the Service on port `80`, which will, in turn, be forwarded to one of the member Pods on TCP port `8080` (defined in the `targetPort` field). Different types of Services and examples of how to use them can be found at `https://cloud.google.com/kubernetes-engine/docs/concepts/service`.

So, why would you choose GKE over other Compute platforms or, for that matter, IaaS VMs? GKE offers something unique in that it combines the best of both worlds. It gives you the flexibility to package your application on your terms, using your own language and libraries, and, to the extent that you wish, a certain amount of control over the nodes and clusters' setup. On the other hand, it offers you a fully managed control plane and other managed infrastructure services around your deployments, such as networking, storage, and computing. You can also define all your configurations in declarative YAML format, making it a very developer-friendly solution (and facilitating **Infrastructure as Code**). You might have noticed similarities between Cloud Run and GKE. Still, GKE offers a lot more on top of what Cloud Run provides in terms of service orchestration, auto-repairing, and flexibility through the myriad of ways you can define how and where your workloads run and how they're brought together as services. GKE is an ideal solution for modern, robust microservices design that gives you – and take this with a grain of salt – a platform-independent and overall vendor-agnostic solution.

Summary

In this chapter, you learned in what cases you would use IaaS VMs and how to design them for high availability and scalability. You then learned about managed instance groups and deployed a regional group for resiliency against zonal failures. Following that, we discussed Compute platform options such as App Engine, Cloud Functions, and Cloud Run. You learned when to consider these as an option in your design, and got some hands-on practice with them. Finally, we discussed Kubernetes and what you need to know as a Cloud Architect: where it fits in the delivery model spectrum, how it works at a high-level, and why you may choose to use it in your solutions.

You should now have the foundational knowledge to design and architect a Compute-based infrastructure on GCP with VPC networks and either IaaS VMs or Compute platforms (or a combination of both). Of course, applications still need to store and retrieve data from somewhere. Ideally, as you learned in this chapter, this shouldn't be on the instance where the application itself is running – that is not a good practice and may not allow your application to scale horizontally to meet demand. Due to this, in the next chapter, we will explore how to architect a storage and data infrastructure that meets your applications' requirements.

5

Architecting Storage and Data Infrastructure

Virtually every application relies on **data,** and in data is where the real business value lies for most organizations. Knowing how to design a storage solution that best fits your data requirements for **durability**, **availability**, **consistency**, **latency**, **security**, and **compliance** is an essential infrastructure architecture skill.

In this chapter, you will learn how to choose a storage solution based on the type of data and application requirements. You will learn about different storage services within Google Cloud for relational and structured data and non-relational and unstructured data, and how to design those services for high availability and scalability. You will then learn how to approach backups, replication, and data consistency with the different services. Finally, you will get some hands-on assignments to familiarize yourself with two of the most popular GCP database offerings: **Cloud Spanner** and **Cloud Bigtable**.

In this chapter, we're going to cover the following main topics:

- Choosing the right storage solution
- Using relational and structured data stores
- Using non-relational and unstructured datastores

Technical requirements

For the hands-on activities in this chapter, you will need a billing-enabled Google Cloud account and optionally the Google Cloud SDK installed (if you don't have it, you can use Cloud Shell from a browser). Helper scripts and code for this chapter can be found at `https://github.com/PacktPublishing/Architecting-Google-Cloud-Solutions/tree/master/ch5`.

Check out the following link to see the Code in Action video: `https://bit.ly/3e94zpE`

Choosing the right storage solution

A fundamental skill for any cloud architect is to know how to choose the right storage solution for the various types of data an organization possesses. In this section, you will start by learning a mental framework that will make it easier for you to make the right choice of data solution. Let's start by understanding and identifying the different types of data that exist.

Types of data

Data can be categorized in a few different "dimensions," so let's look at each one of them separately.

Relational versus non-relational

This first distinction applies to whether or not datasets are organized according to the **relational model** for databases. A collection of tables of data is considered relational when the relationship between the different tables is important. For example, suppose you have a table containing employees' data, such as their name, department, and salary, and you have another table containing department information, such as its name, its manager, and its yearly budget. Suppose you want to answer the question "who's the (department) manager of employee X?". In that case, you will need to look at the first table to find out which department the employee belongs to, and then at the second table to see who is the department manager for that department, provided departments are identified identically in both tables. You can look at two separate tables to obtain a data point, because those two tables are related (in this example, by the department name or ID). In a relational database, a record is often split (or "normalized") and stored in separate tables, and relationships are defined through the use of *primary* and *foreign* keys.

> **Important note**
>
> **Normalization** is a process defined in the relational model for databases that refers to the organization of data. The goal of this organization is to eliminate data redundancy and undesirable inconsistencies when inserting, updating, or deleting records. There are a few rules (referred to as "normal forms") that dictate ways in which to organize data in order to achieve these goals.

So, when you think relational data, think organized tables. Applications handling relational data rely on a **schema** that defines the **data structure**. The schema defines in a formal language how the data is organized and what kinds of data there are. Specifically, it defines the data entities with their precise data types as well as the relationships between them. The schema imposes integrity constraints on the database, which makes relational databases reliable for querying and processing data but somewhat inflexible when it comes to expanding or modifying its structure (schema). **Structured Query Language (SQL)** is the standard language associated with relational databases for data management, which is why they're often also referred to as SQL databases. With SQL, you can access and manipulate data in databases. For example, you can execute statements to perform tasks such as inserting or updating data in a database, or retrieving data from it.

On the other hand, non-relational data refers to pretty much any other type of data, for example, a JSON file, an image, or a time series record of a device's temperature reading. These are often (though not always) non-tabular data, where each entity is "self-contained" and doesn't hold data that is related (from a data management perspective) to any other data record. Non-relational databases, which are often also referred to as **NoSQL** databases, are typically more flexible, the reason being they don't require a schema to be enforced, and they can more easily be partitioned, which facilitates **horizontal scalability** and their ability to grow (more on that shortly).

Non-relational databases are less complicated and easier to manage in general. This means they are, in a way, more developer-friendly as they can accommodate a complexity of data inputs without having you enforce a schema or structure and without requiring you to run complex *join* and other such (SQL) queries typical in the management of relational databases. IT teams that work with large and complex relational databases will typically have at least one **Database Administrator** (**DBA**) member of staff who is solely responsible for managing the databases and ensuring that they meet capacity and performance requirements at all times.

Teams working with non-relational databases, on the other hand, will typically have an easier time managing them and, in most cases, not require intervention for scaling the databases to meet demand or to fine-tune them for better performance. Part of the reason why they generally perform better is that non-relational databases are optimized for specific data models. They are therefore further categorized based on the particular data model they work with. These categories are as follows:

- **Key-value Store**: For data that is stored as a set of key-value pairs. A record is uniquely identified by its key. As with any of the NoSQL datastores, there is no enforced schema. In addition, in key-value stores, each data entity is treated as a single opaque collection, which may have different fields for different records.

- **Document Store**: For document-oriented information, often referred to as semi-structured data. Document stores are a subclass of key-value stores, the difference being that instead of treating data as opaque objects, a document database can use the underlying structure of the document (a "document" here referring to text-based content with a recognizable hierarchical syntax, such as JSON or XML) to extract metadata that the database engine can use for optimizing data queries and processing. Documents in a document store are somewhat equivalent to the concept of an object in software programming. An object can be an instance of a particular class (with a defined "schema" or set of attributes), but can also have the flexibility to have its own set of attributes and differentiate itself from other objects of the same class. Storing information from an application object into a document is usually very straightforward, as long as that object is serializable into JSON content, for example.

- **Column-oriented Database**: For tabular data where records are stored by columns rather than by row. These types of databases are typically designed to support SQL language for queries and data operations, but they differ from traditional relational databases in that, by storing data in columns rather than rows, it can achieve better performance when finding and filtering through data. In practice, these databases are well-suited for analytics workloads (for example, data warehousing), which typically rely on many complex queries over the entire database. Also, because this increase in query efficiency comes at a slight cost for data insertion, it is not very well suited to transaction-heavy workloads.

- **Graph Database**: For data that contains relationships between the different data points ("nodes") in a graph-like structure. Graph databases are more concerned with the relationship between entities than the entities themselves. The most common use case for this is social networks. A graph database would be well suited to store the relationship between social media members (in other words, who is friends with whom), though not necessarily suited to store information relating to the members themselves (other than their identifiers). Relationships are a first-class citizen in a graph database and can be given several properties (label, weight, direction, and so on). Graph search and other graph operations are optimized for these databases.

- **In-memory**: For data that benefits from memory storage (as opposed to disk storage) for faster access. Memory access is generally significantly faster and with more predictable performance than disk access, which makes query times and overall performance better. This is especially useful for applications that are latency-critical in data retrieval and require fast response times. The price to pay is RAM's volatile nature, which makes this a slightly less reliable form of data storage that comes at a risk of data loss should a power loss event occur. In-memory data systems can be designed to continuously replicate data to separate instances to preserve data durability in the event of the failure of the primary instance.

It's not uncommon in modern cloud design to include not one but a combination of these solutions, so that different types of data are placed in different database services based on what fits them best. This approach of using mixed data storage technologies for varying storage needs is often referred to as **polyglot persistence**.

You should now understand how to identify whether data is relational or non-relational in nature, based on all the concepts you just learned. Next, let's look at a few other ways to categorize data.

Structured versus unstructured

The second distinction to draw is between **structured** and **unstructured** data. Structured data will have an identifiable and repeatable structure for all data points. For example, a table consists of structured data. An HTML file where there is a placeholder for the headers, the body, the paragraphs, and suchlike consists of structured data (or, to be a little more strict with the definition, semi-structured data in this case). So does a JSON file, with a schema that defines what the keys and their value types are. For example, the following screenshot shows what a JSON schema could look like:

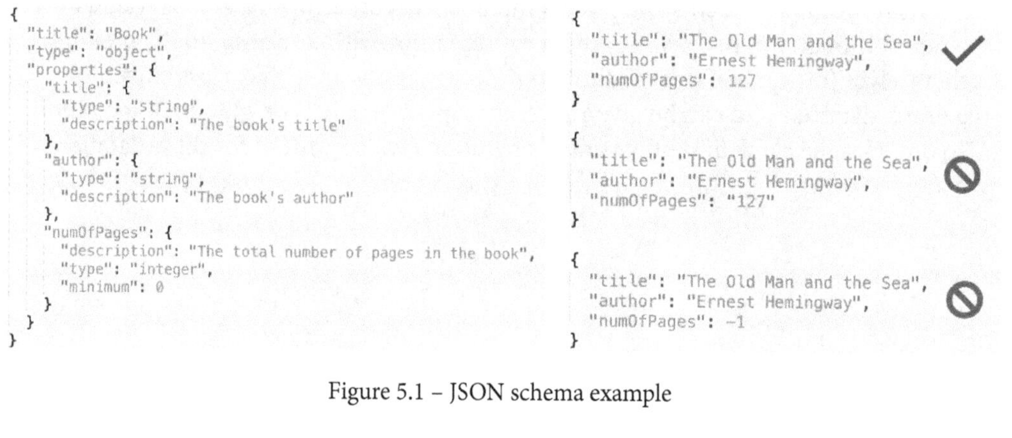

```
{
    "title": "Book",
    "type": "object",
    "properties": {
        "title": {
            "type": "string",
            "description": "The book's title"
        },
        "author": {
            "type": "string",
            "description": "The book's author"
        },
        "numOfPages": {
            "description": "The total number of pages in the book",
            "type": "integer",
            "minimum": 0
        }
    }
}
```

```
{
    "title": "The Old Man and the Sea",
    "author": "Ernest Hemingway",
    "numOfPages": 127
}                                               ✓

{
    "title": "The Old Man and the Sea",
    "author": "Ernest Hemingway",
    "numOfPages": "127"
}                                               🚫

{
    "title": "The Old Man and the Sea",
    "author": "Ernest Hemingway",
    "numOfPages": -1
}                                               🚫
```

Figure 5.1 – JSON schema example

On the left-hand side, a schema for a book object is defined. On the right-hand side, three instances of a book are shown: the one on top is a valid book object according to the schema, while the other two have badly defined values for the numOfPages property.

In other words, structured or semi-structured data is organized and easier to query and process. In the preceding example, you could confidently query a value for the numOfPages property of a book and, for example, do a math operation on it since you know that value is supposed to be an integer. As a data consumer, you know what to expect.

Unstructured data follows no pre-defined structure. Images, videos, and other "binary" contents are unstructured data. Texts and documents are generally unstructured as well. You can't easily query, process, or mine data from unstructured data sources. On the other hand, machine learning applications can often leverage these types of data for predictive analytics.

Transactional versus non-transactional

This next distinction concerns the transactional nature of data. Transactional data means that information is recorded from a transaction, in other words, a sequence of related information exchange that is treated as a data request unit. The most common examples of this are data related to product purchases or financial transactions in general (such as money transfers or payments).

When, for example, a customer buys a product, a few different things happen in the seller's database(s): the product's quantity is decreased in the product catalogue table, the cash money is increased by a certain amount, a purchase event is added to that customer's purchase history table, and so on. In this same example, suppose both buyer and seller are customers of the same bank. In the bank's database, the buyer's balance will decrease by a certain amount, while the seller's balance will increase by the same amount, both operations contained within a single transaction. If those data updates were carried out separately, problems could occur. Imagine that, after updating the balance record for the buyer, the bank's system proceeds to update the balance for the seller, and right at that moment, the database goes down or there's a system failure that prevents it from completing the second part of the transaction, and that operation is lost. Or, even if the application is designed to recover from that, there's an unnecessary risk due to a period of time during which the bank's overall money balance is below what it should be. For banks handling millions of such transactions daily, that could quickly become an issue. That is why systems that deal with transactional records have an "all or nothing" principle, where either the entire transaction is recorded successfully, or it will all fail completely, and the database state will be the same as it was before the attempt.

Tied to the concept of transactions is a set of properties referred to as **ACID: Atomicity, Consistency, Isolation,** and **Durability**. These properties are what guarantee data validity for transactional databases even in the event of system failures (such as power loss and hardware failures).

Atomicity refers to the fact that all statements that compose a transaction are treated as a single "unit," and that they all either fail together or succeed together (the "all or nothing" approach). A database that has the atomicity property will always prevent updates from occurring only partially.

Consistency ensures that a transaction will always bring the database from a valid state to another. A valid state is characterized by having data observing all constraints and integrity (as well as referential integrity through the primary key-foreign key relationship), and so that every database client will read the same data on the same query. We will discuss consistency a little bit more shortly in the context of distributed database systems.

The isolation property refers to the isolation between transactions, in other words, it is the guarantee that the concurrent execution of transactions will still leave the database in the same state as if they had been executed sequentially (in other words, one does not affect the other).

Finally, a database that has durability guarantees that once a transaction has been committed and data has been recorded, it will remain so even in the case of a system failure. This usually simply means that data is recorded in non-volatile storage. When we're talking about transactions on an **ACID-compliant** database, we're therefore talking about a sequence of database operations that satisfies all those properties.

Non-transactional data covers everything else. Updating your social media profile or uploading a video to YouTube are non-transactional requests. If you're playing a mobile game and raising your score, your new score will likely be recorded as a non-transactional event on the game server's database.

Sensitive versus non-sensitive and other data classifications

One last aspect to mention about data is related to data classification. Data is most commonly classified according to confidentiality (in other words, is the data sensitive? Does it contain **personable identifiable information** (PII), or a company's intellectual property? Does it contain credit card numbers or private information?). It can also be classified based on whether it's business-critical (used by line-of-business applications) or non-critical data. For companies dealing with compliance obligations, data can be classified, for example, as falling under the protection of the **General Data Protection Regulation** (GDPR), the **Health Insurance Portability and Accountability Act** (HIPAA), or other such compliance regulations.

Data can also be classified based on its availability (or accessibility) requirements. For example, is the data *hot* and needs to be accessed frequently by applications, or is the data *cold* and can be stored away or archived and only retrieved when needed? All such classifications will impact how the data must be stored and transmitted, as well as its durability and retention requirements, which ultimately help you determine which data storage solution and access tier (when applicable) to adopt.

Now that we've explored the different ways in which we can categorize and classify data, we need to look at one more important bit of theory before exploring storage services in Google Cloud. That is the **CAP theorem.**

The CAP theorem

What really determines the ability to grow and scale in the cloud world (or in any IT system, for that matter) is the capacity to scale *horizontally*. This certainly doesn't apply only to compute systems, but also data systems. However, one crucial thing to understand and keep in mind when working with horizontally scalable, distributed database systems, is the CAP theorem. CAP stands for **Consistency**, **Availability**, and **Partition tolerance**, three properties of database systems. The theorem basically states that you can only have two out of the three. In other words, looking at the following diagram, you can only be in one of the shaded areas at the intersections:

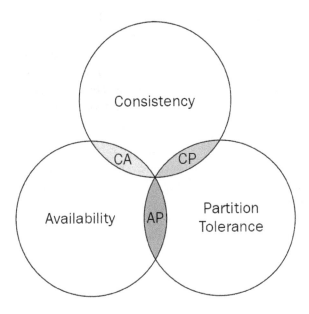

Figure 5.2 – CAP theorem

The partition tolerance property means that the system is tolerant against network partitioning. In other words, it continues to run even in the event of network failures (network nodes or links) that don't result in a general failure of the entire network. For this to work, data records must be sufficiently replicated across combinations of individual database instances to keep everything running without data loss. No network in this world (or any complex system in general) is failure-proof and, therefore, *any distributed database system must be partition tolerant as a design constraint*. This means that the *P* in *CAP* is not an option; it's a must. Something else has to give.

The *Consistency* property means that any *read* operation will return the same value, that of the most recent write operation *across the system*. A system is considered to have consistency if a database transaction starts with the system in a consistent state and ends with the system in a consistent state. During the transaction, there will be a temporary shift into a state of inconsistency. However, as discussed previously, because a transactional database will either apply the entire transaction or rollback entirely if there is an error at any stage, the system will never get "stuck" in an inconsistent state. From this, it can also be concluded that non-transactional databases cannot guarantee consistency, at least not strict, "strong" consistency, as it's often referred to, as opposed to "weak" consistency (usually synonymous with eventual consistency – a specific form of it). To understand the difference between strong and weak consistency, first, we need to understand the *Availability* property (the *A* in *CAP*).

The *Availability* property of distributed databases states that every request from every client will get a response, regardless of the state of any individual server node in the system. If anyone is writing something somewhere to the same database record you're reading and at the same time, the database system will not wait and will not guarantee that you will be reading that latest input (or that you will be reading the same value as someone else reading it closer to the data input node). In other words, to achieve high availability in a partition-tolerant system, strong consistency must be sacrificed.

So, transactional databases typically offer consistency at the expense of availability. This is especially the case for financial institutions, where you cannot possibly afford inconsistency (imagine someone withdrawing money from an account that just went below the required balance due to a transfer operation that happened half a second ago, from another server). Non-transactional databases (or possibly transactional databases as well) that are willing to sacrifice consistency in favor of high availability can do so, as long as the data model (and the business model around that) is such that high availability is really more important than consistency. In fact, in quite a few cases, strong consistency is not required at all, and it's much preferable to have high availability with an eventually consistent system.

Eventual consistency means that the system doesn't meet the consistency property we just discussed ("strong" consistency), but it guarantees that the system as a whole will eventually achieve a state of consistency. The inconsistency window duration will depend on factors such as communication delays and the system load. In other words, it allows itself some time to propagate data inputs across all nodes in the distributed system, knowing that if a few clients are reading slightly outdated records, while other clients are already getting the newest record, is not a big deal. For example, suppose you make an update to your social media profile. In that case, it's not that important that everyone in the world either all collectively see the updated version or the old version. It's fine if it takes a little longer for some readers to see the newest input. This applies to many other types of data as well.

In general, relational databases such as *MySQL* and *PostgreSQL* will aim for strong consistency. Therefore, if you're trying to build a *distributed* relational database system, you will need to sacrifice high availability to some extent. On the other hand, non-relational, NoSQL databases will most often aim for high availability and some will deliver eventual (weak) consistency.

Now that you have the conceptual foundation surrounding data and data types, you should be able to make more informed decisions when designing data solutions. You should now understand how the nature of the data and its specific requirements translate into design constraints that you need to be aware of, particularly regarding what type of databases you must use and the retention and availability configurations to apply.

Let's now explore the data services available on GCP. For each option, we will look into what use cases they would be best suited for, what is offered in terms of availability and backup, as well as things such as data durability and consistency. We will start with relational and structured datastores, and then we're going to discuss non-relational and unstructured options.

Using relational and structured datastores

In Google Cloud, there are two main options for managed relational database services: **Cloud SQL** and **Cloud Spanner**. From what you've learned in the previous section, you should be able to make an informed decision about when to consider a cloud relational database. In short, they would be well suited for compatibility with existing relational data (for example, if you're migrating from an on-premises **MySQL**, **PostgreSQL**, or **SQL server**), or if you're dealing with transactional data or data that needs to preserve a relational structure over which complex queries and JOIN statements are expected. We will explore the capabilities of the managed relational databases on GCP and when you would choose one over the other.

Cloud SQL

Cloud SQL is a fully managed database hosting service for *Microsoft SQL Server*, *MySQL*, or *PostgreSQL*. The platform provides security at rest and in transit by default, with customer data encrypted on Google's internal networks and in database tables, temporary files, and backups. For increased availability, you can configure replication and enable automatic failover. Data is backed up automatically every day, and you can also configure a backup policy for the data you store in the database, as well as **point-in-time recovery** settings. Cloud SQL is SSAE 16-, ISO 27001-, and PCI DSS-compliant and supports HIPAA compliance.

High availability (HA) and failover

For a high-availability configuration, you can deploy Cloud SQL as a regional instance. It will then be located in a primary zone within the configured region and replicated to a secondary zone (as a **Standby** instance) within the same region. The replication is set up as **Synchronous replication**, so that all writes made to the primary instance are also immediately applied to the standby instance. This setup is illustrated in the following diagram:

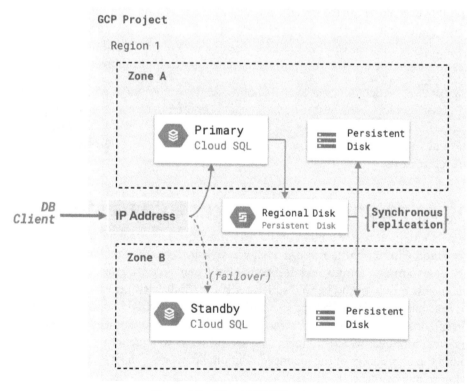

Figure 5.3 – Cloud SQL HA setup

If the primary instance or the entire zone becomes unresponsive (for approximately 60 seconds), the platform will automatically switch to serving data from the **Standby** instance (**automatic failover**). Thanks to a shared static IP address, the **Standby** instance will serve data behind the same IP from the secondary zone, which means connection strings won't need to be updated from client applications. Although the *failover* is automatic, if the **Primary** instance (or zone) recovers, there will not be an automatic *failback*: you will need to perform it manually.

In addition to leveraging backup and point-in-time restore capabilities, consider designing a Cloud SQL solution with the high-availability setup and automatic failover enabled, certainly in production environments. It will save you time, effort, and considerable downtime in the event of a zonal or instance failure, not to mention the fact that it reduces the risk of data loss in case of a zonal disaster that would cause the zone to be deemed unrecoverable.

Replication

Replication of a SQL database can serve a few different purposes. For example, it can be used for scaling out read operations (and offloading the main server), migrating data between regions or even platforms, and also for increased availability and durability in case data in the original instance becomes corrupted or inaccessible. Replicas can only be used for *read* operations (not *writes*) and are therefore referred to as **read replicas**. They process queries, read requests, and analytics workloads.

In Cloud SQL, you can create an **in-region read replica** (where a read replica is created in the same region, but different zone) or a **cross-region read replica** (where a read replica is created in a separate region) for MySQL and PostgreSQL databases. With MySQL, you can also configure replication as an **external read replica**, when the database instance is replicated to another that is hosted by another cloud platform or on-premises environments. Although not "natively" supported, you would also be able to set up Microsoft SQL Server replication using Microsoft SQL management tools.

Consider creating a read replica if the main server is at heavy load. You can then point some of the clients (in particular, the ones that perform analytics and heavy read operations) to the replica (which has its own connection strings). This is essentially a read scale-out operation. Other reasons to consider it include the following:

- Reducing latency for clients in different regions (consider the cross-region read replica)
- Kicking off the migration of data to another region or platform
- Increase overall read capacity in anticipation of heavy read events

Backups and point-in-time recovery

Backups protect your data from unexpected loss or corruption. With Cloud SQL, you can enable automated backups, which, along with binary logging, is a requirement for some operations (such as clone and replica creation). Cloud SQL retains up to 7 backups for an instance, but the backup storage is priced at a lower rate than regular storage. In addition, only the oldest stored backup will be as large as your database instance, since the first backup is a full backup while subsequent backups are incremental. An incremental backup includes only data that changed after the previous backup, not the full dataset. For example, if a database holds a collection of employee records with 500 employees, a full backup is taken to include all 500 employees. If 2 new employees were added to the table since the full backup was taken, a subsequent, incremental backup will hold only those 2 new employees. Should you need to restore all data at this point, your SQL server would apply the full backup first, followed by the incremental backups, meaning that you would have a total of 502 records. If there were multiple incremental backups, they would have been applied sequentially. When the oldest backup is removed (which was your only full backup), the next oldest backup becomes a full backup by taking in all the data.

Backups can be performed on demand or in an automated way. An on-demand backup can be created at any time (regardless of whether the instance has automated backups). For example, if you're about to make a risky change to your system (this may not necessarily be directly on the database itself, but something that may impact it), it's a good practice to create a backup. On-demand backups will persist until you manually delete them (or until the instance is deleted), which is something to keep in mind from a cost management perspective. Manual backups lingering around can quickly become a source of unnecessary high storage costs. When enabled, automated backups happen every day during a customizable 4-hour window, at the start of which the backup operation will begin. When possible, you should make sure that the window fits into a window of least activity on your database to prevent performance degradation from occurring at a moment of high usage.

By default, Cloud SQL stores backup data in two regions (chosen automatically by the platform) for redundancy and resiliency against regional failure. One region can be the same as the region the instance is in. The other is guaranteed to be a different region. You can, however, also define custom backup locations. This is useful if there are compliance and data residency regulations you need to observe in the organization you're working with. For example, if data needs to be kept within a geographic boundary, you will need to customize the backup locations to satisfy that requirement.

Related to backups, *Point-in-time recovery* is a feature that is enabled by default with MySQL and PostgreSQL options and which allows you to recover a database instance back to the state it was at a specific point in time. This is useful when an error causes a loss or corruption of data, in which case you can just restore the database to a moment right before when the error occurred. A point-in-time recovery always creates a new database instance (it's not an in-place restore), similarly to a clone operation, so that instance settings are inherited. If you're running Microsoft SQL Server, this is not a "native" platform feature in Cloud SQL. Instead, you need to set up backups for point-in-time recovery yourself using Microsoft **SQL Server Management Studio** (**SSMS**) (and, for example, uploading them to a storage account). Specific guidance on how to set this up can be found at `https://cloud.google.com/solutions/backup-and-archival-of-sql-with-point-in-time-recovery`.

Maintenance

There is no server for you to manage when you provision a Cloud SQL service. However, there is still a server for Google Cloud to operate, and, for that reason, you need to be aware of maintenance events. Instances will need occasional updates for patching, fixing bugs, and performing general upgrades. All these events generally require a restart of the instance, which can disrupt your service (maintenance events do not trigger a failover to standby instances). In Google Cloud, you can set your preferred maintenance windows and options on instances. You can control, for example, the day of the week and time when an instance should receive updates if there are any. If you don't specify a preferred window, disruptive updates can happen at any time. Even if you do specify a preferred window, however, some high-priority maintenance events (such as critical service updates or patches for vulnerabilities) will likely be rolled out without waiting for your specified window. These disruptions count as downtime against the platform's SLA, but to prevent serious disruptions to your applications, there are some general design recommendations that you can apply to applications communicating with the databases. These include *connection pooling, short-lived connections*, and *exponential back-off for connection retries*. More details and guidance for specific programming languages and SQL engines can be found at `https://cloud.google.com/sql/docs/mysql/manage-connections`. This is an excellent resource to have bookmarked and shared with the development team when you're designing a Cloud SQL solution for them.

Cloud SQL Proxy

The Cloud SQL Proxy provides secure access to Cloud SQL database instances without the need to configure SSL and or network whitelisting. Database clients can access instances via the Cloud SQL Proxy with secure, automatically encrypted traffic (using TLS 1.2) and managed SSL certificates. The way Cloud SQL Proxy works is illustrated in the following diagram:

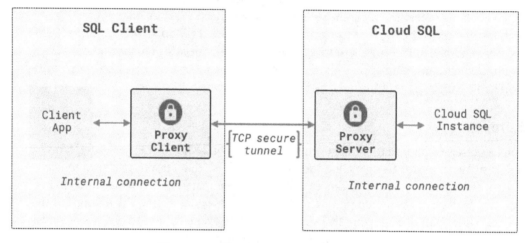

Figure 5.4 – Cloud SQL Proxy architecture

The proxy handles authentication with Cloud SQL and network connectivity without the need for you to set up static IP addresses (the instance still needs to have either a public IPv4 address or a private IP). The applications then communicate with the proxy using the standard database protocol used by the database (in other words, the proxy "impersonates" the database). This communication is represented by the bi-directional arrow between **Client App** and **Proxy Client** in the preceding diagram. The proxy itself can authenticate against the database with a service account associated with a credential file, permanently linked to the proxy as long as it is running.

Access control

Access control can be configured at the instance level and at the database level. The instance-level access configuration method depends on the connection source, but generally, it involves a Cloud SQL Proxy that is either set up by you or automatically by a serverless application service (for example, App Engine, Cloud Functions, or Cloud Run). Once a connection to an instance has been established, the user or application can log in to specific databases with a user account that has been created as part of managing your Cloud SQL instance. The default user (root) must always be set up when creating a new instance, but additional users with fine-grained permissions can be created.

We will discuss audit logs and other security considerations in *Chapter 7, Designing for Security and Compliance*. Let's now look at one final aspect within Cloud SQL that can't be overlooked by a cloud architect: *scalability*.

Scalability

As we've discussed a few times in this book, there are two ways in which you can scale a service: scaling up (increasing the capacity of the current serving instance or platform), also referred to as vertical scaling; and scaling out (increasing the number of serving instances), also referred to as horizontal scaling. Scaling up is the easiest operation as it doesn't impose any requirements on the applications running inside the instance, but it's the option with which you will hit a limit much quicker – after all, you can only increase the capacity of any instance up to the available capacity of the underlying hardware (and the available capacity to *you*, specifically, since we're talking about a shared, multi-tenant infrastructure). In addition, a performance bottleneck may arise not from the lack of compute, memory, or storage power, but from the application's inability to handle any more requests. This is not to mention the fact that an instance may fail in many ways and require a restart or a downtime period. For all those reasons, being able to *scale out* is a crucial goal that we should strive to achieve when architecting cloud infrastructure.

If you need to scale up your Cloud SQL instance, that is easy enough to achieve. Update its machine type to a larger type. This will increase memory and the number of virtual cores, as well as the storage and IOPS capacities of the instance as a whole. As of the time of writing, the largest database-optimized machine type for Cloud SQL on GCP comes with 96 vCPUs and roughly 368 GB of memory. This is a powerful machine indeed, but should you need to scale out your database, let's look at how we can achieve this with Cloud SQL.

We have already mentioned the strategy of using read replicas to scale out read operations for Cloud SQL instances. This is an easy way to scale out, since there's still a single "source of truth," so to speak, or a single database where all the writes happen (and therefore all and any modifications to the existing data are performed at one location). This removes concurrency concerns (concurrent *read* operations are much less of a concern) and is a more or less a frictionless way to scale out. It comes, however, with the obvious limitation of not allowing for the scaling out of *write* operations. For reasons you're now already familiar with from the previous section (remember the CAP theorem in particular), it is not as straightforward to scale out relational databases as it is with non-relational databases, at least not in a way that preserves ACID properties and strong consistency.

There is one strategy, however, that accomplishes a level of horizontal scaling relatively well while somewhat preserving ACID properties. That is **sharding**. Sharding involves partitioning the database into smaller parts (shards, or partitions), and then distributing the shards across a cluster of machines. However, it usually does so at the expense of no ACID guarantees or referential integrity when performing queries and transactions across shards. Data queries are automatically routed to the corresponding server based on either application logic or a query router. One common and simple example of how you can apply this is on a database of users: you can create a shard for each letter of the alphabet (or a grouping of letters, such as *A-E*, if you don't need that many shards). That way, when running queries against the database, you know based on the first letter of the user's name from which particular shard that should be retrieved (or written to).

Sharding is performed particularly well with **MySQL Cluster**, a feature in MySQL that automatically shards tables across nodes. It does so in order to not lose the ability to perform "join" operations (cross-shard queries) without sacrificing ACID guarantees. However, this is a complex problem, and some argue that there can't ever be true horizontal scalability with transactional databases. But we will see shortly that we still can do it if we're willing to make just a little compromise.

You have now learned the most fundamental tenets of a well-designed relational database solution using Cloud SQL. We looked into the high-availability setup you should aim for and features such as backup, point-in-time recovery, and automatic failover, which you can leverage with this service. We then discussed the use of replication and things you need to be aware of in terms of maintenance and access control. Finally, we addressed the elephant in the room of relational databases: horizontal scalability, and how it can become a very complex, borderline impossible problem. Google challenges this notion with its managed relational database service, which we're going to look into next: Cloud Spanner.

Cloud Spanner

Cloud Spanner is Google Cloud's fully managed and *horizontally scalable* relational database service, with *strong consistency* and up to 99.999% availability. This service was designed from the ground up to deliver ACID-compliant, high-performance transactions globally with automatic handling of replicas, sharding, and transaction processing. It's a service built initially for Google's own critical business applications, but made available on GCP.

In a nutshell, the way Cloud Spanner works is by partitioning the database tables into contiguous key ranges called *splits*, with a fast lookup service for determining the machine(s) that serve a key range. Splits are replicated to multiple machines in distinct failure domains to prevent data from becoming inaccessible due to server failures. This is similar to an automatic sharding mechanism that ensures availability. Consistent replication is managed by a **Paxos algorithm**, which implements a voting system to elect a *leader* among replicas to process writes, while all other replicas serve reads.

> **Important note**
>
> **Paxos** is a family of protocols created to solve consensus in unreliable networks (which real networks are), and the use of a Paxos algorithm is a core design choice in Cloud Spanner. If you want a more in-depth look at the problem of consensus in distributed systems and how Paxos is applied, check out this chapter from the Google SRE book: `https://sre.google/sre-book/managing-critical-state/`.

Read transactions will always read the latest copy of data, and write transactions introduce locking on the database in a way that is orchestrated by *Paxos leaders* and involve (very complex) cross-machine communications. With a Google-developed technology called *TrueTime*, every machine in Google data centers knows the exact global time with a high degree of accuracy – this is what allows different Spanner machines to reason about the ordering of transactional operations, and this is one of the things that make Spanner possible. Most importantly, however, all of the details just mentioned are transparent to Spanner clients. The protocols and technologies to ensure data consistency despite the globally distributed nature of the database are much more complicated than that and, if you're curious to know (or a skeptic about the whole thing), they're described in a research paper available at `https://research.google/pubs/pub45855/`.

If you're wondering about the CAP theorem and whether Cloud Spanner "breaks" it, it doesn't, at least not from a technical, purist perspective, but indeed it effectively does (in other words, the users *perceive* it as a CAP system). What is happening is that, in the event of network partitions, Spanner chooses consistency and forfeits availability. Strictly speaking, it's a CP system. However, if its actual availability is so high (given the well-engineered redundancy in the solution) that users can ignore outages, then Spanner can justify an effectively CAP claim. After all, the fact that a database system is not 100% but 99.999% available (one failure in 100,000) is barely noticeable when the applications themselves (and other infrastructure components) have even lower availability SLAs.

From the clients' perspective, Cloud Spanner works in much the same way as any other SQL-based relational database. When executing transactions, however, there are a few things to keep in mind to ensure that the system delivers on its consistency promises:

- If you need to write data to the database, depending on the value of one or more reads, then you should execute the read as part of a **read-write** transaction.

- If you need to make multiple read calls that require a consistent view of your data, those should be executed as **read-only transactions**.

Cloud Spanner differentiates transactions by one of three types it supports: a *locking read-write transaction*, which is the only type that supports writing data; a *read-only transaction*, which provides guaranteed consistency across several reads; and partitioned **Data Manipulation Language** (**DML**), which is designed for bulk updates and deletes. Even though read-write transactions can also read data, you should only use this type of transaction for reading when actually making a subsequent write as part of the same atomic transaction (or even if you just *might* do a transaction depending on a read's value, this can also be used).

When it comes to reading data, Cloud Spanner offers two types of reads: a *strong read*, in which data is read at a current timestamp and is guaranteed to see all data that has been committed up until the start of the read; and a *stale read*, in which data is read at a timestamp in the past.

You may want to consider bookmarking the following references to share with developers and database administrators regarding reads, transactions, and best practices for constructing SQL statements that will help Cloud Spanner optimize execution performance:

- `https://cloud.google.com/spanner/docs/reads`
- `https://cloud.google.com/spanner/docs/transactions`
- `https://cloud.google.com/spanner/docs/sql-best-practices`

In Cloud Spanner, backups are not created automatically but on demand, and they can be retained for up to one year. Longer retention times can be achieved by exporting the database (to a storage account, for example), and if you need periodic backups, you can certainly automate the process.

To get you familiarized with Cloud Spanner, we will create an instance in two geographic regions, create a database, run some simple SQL queries using **gcloud**, and then create a backup. It may sound like only a simplistic "hello-world" type of deployment (and indeed it is), but it is effectively delivering a *multi-regional, scalable, and highly available relational database service* from only these steps – about all you need when you're designing a production relational database solution for organizations, minus the IAM policies, audit logs, as well as other security and compliance components, which we will get back to in a future chapter.

Creating a scalable and highly available SQL database with Cloud Spanner

Let's follow these steps to create the database:

1. Go to the GCP console (`console.cloud.google.com`) and then click on the shell icon in the top-right corner of the screen to activate Cloud Shell:

Figure 5.5 – Activating Cloud Shell

2. In the Cloud Shell terminal, run the following command:

```
$ gcloud projects create --name chapter-5 --set-as-
default
```

3. In the console, click on the down arrow next to where it says **Select a project** (or your current project's name) to open the project selection menu. Click on the **All** tab to see all projects, and then click on the newly created project (**chapter-5**), as shown in the following screenshot:

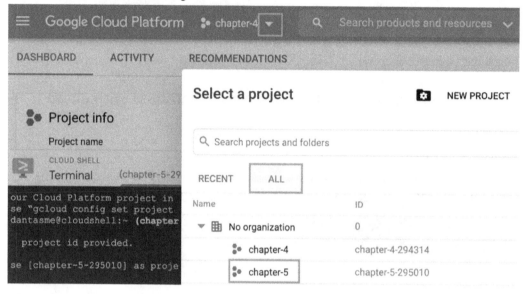

Figure 5.6 – Project selection menu in the console

4. Still in the console, click on the stacked lines icon in the top-left corner of the screen to expand the left-side menu (if not already expanded), as shown on the left-hand side of the next screenshot, and then search for and click on **Spanner**. You will be prompted to enable the Cloud Spanner API. Do so by clicking on **Enable**, as shown on the right-hand side of the following screenshot:

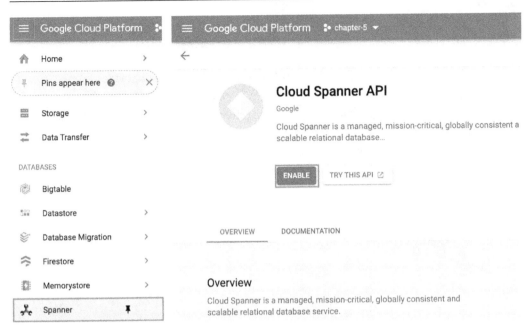

Figure 5.7 – Enabling Cloud Spanner API

5. You will be prompted to enable billing on your project. Click on **Enable Billing**, and then, in the billing account selection menu, expand the **Billing account** drop-down field and click on your existing billing account. Finally, click on **Set Account**.

6. On the **Spanner** page, click on **Create Instance**. Fill in the creation form as follows:

    a) **Instance name**: `spanner-instance`

    b) **Choose a configuration**: **Multi-region**

    c) **Select a configuration**: Choose either one of the available multi-region configurations, for example, **eur3 (Belgium/Netherlands)**.

    d) **Nodes**: 1

7. Click on **Create**. Next, click on **Create Database**.

8. In the database creation form, type `testdb` in the **Name** field, and then click on **Continue**. In the **Define your database schema** field, make sure that the **Edit as text** option is selected and paste in the following under **DDL statements**:

```
CREATE TABLE Customers (
   CustomerId   INT64 NOT NULL,
   FirstName   STRING(1024),
   LastName   STRING(1024),
```

```
    BirthDate  DATE,
) PRIMARY KEY(CustomerId);
```

9. In the left pane of the console, click on **Customers** under the database's name
    (**testdb**). Next, click on the **Data** tab. Finally, click on **Insert**. This is a way to insert
    data easily through a graphical user interface. Just add two rows to this table by
    entering some fake customer information (making sure **CustomerId** is unique),
    as shown in the following screenshot, for example:

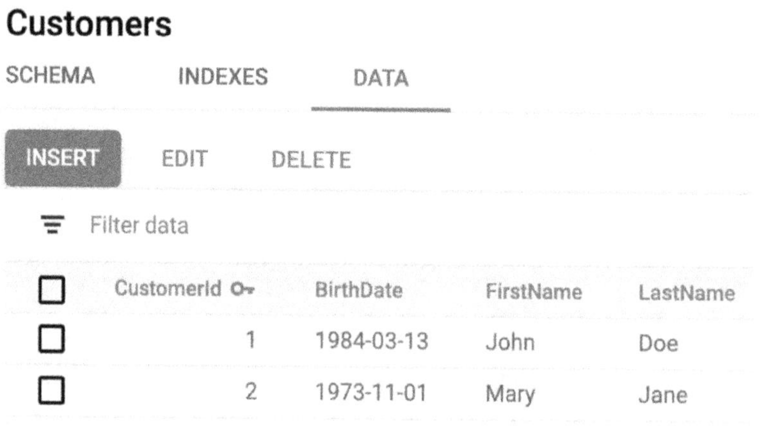

Customers

	SCHEMA	INDEXES	DATA		

INSERT	EDIT	DELETE		

≡   Filter data

	CustomerId	BirthDate	FirstName	LastName
☐	1	1984-03-13	John	Doe
☐	2	1973-11-01	Mary	Jane

Figure 5.8 – Customers' table

10. Now, click on **Query** in the left pane, under the database's name (**testdb**). Then,
    paste the following into the textbox:

```
SELECT * FROM Customers
```

You should see the two users you created in the **Results table** section at the bottom
of the page.

11. Finally, click on the name of the instance (**spanner-instance**) on the left. Next,
    click on **Backup/Restore**. Under **Backups**, click on **Create**. Then, fill in the form as
    follows:

    a) **Database name**: testdb

    b) **Backup name**: testdb-backup1

    c) **Set an expiration date**: **1 day**

12. Click on **Create**. You will be taken back to the instance details page. Scroll down
    until you see **Backup operations** and notice the on-going backup operation.

To ensure external consistency of the backup, Cloud Spanner is now pinning the contents of the database to prevent the garbage collection system from removing relevant data values for the duration of the backup operation. A backup operation happens in parallel on the different zones the instance is replicated to. The database is restorable as soon as the backup operation has been completed.

13. As a final step, go to Cloud Shell (if you don't still have it open, open a new one, making sure you've selected the right project by running `gcloud config set project` and pasting in your project ID). To illustrate how you can run a SQL query using `gcloud`, run the following in the terminal:

```
$ gcloud spanner databases execute-sql testdb
--instance=spanner-instance --sql='SELECT * FROM
Customers WHERE CustomerId = 1'
```

14. You should see the *John Doe* customer as a result (make sure you modify the `CustomerId` value if you've set your own values).

Cloud Spanner has several client libraries for different languages and frameworks. If you wish to continue exploring it with your preferred client, check out the various available libraries and usage instructions at `https://cloud.google.com/spanner/docs/reference/libraries`.

15. To remove the database and clean up all resources, first, we need to remove the backup. Back in the console and on the Spanner page, first click on the instance name (**spanner-instance**) and then click on **Backup/Restore**. Select the backup, **testdb-backup1**, and then click on **Delete**. When prompted, confirm the deletion by typing in the backup's ID (`testdb-backup1`), and then click on **Delete**. Finally, still in the instance details page, click on **Delete Instance**. Once again, confirm by typing in the instance's ID (`spanner-instance`) and then clicking on **Delete**.

You have now learned and explored the relational database options in Google Cloud, their features and capabilities, and how to design them for availability and scalability. Also, you now know what situations they are well-suited for. Generally speaking, if you don't have any of the requirements that call for relational databases (such as ACID compliance and schema enforcement), then a non-relational database is what you should aim for. They're fast, easily scalable, and developers will usually find them easier to work with. We will now explore what the non-relational database options are on GCP.

Using non-relational and unstructured datastores

In general, non-relational data falls under the category of semi-structured or unstructured data. This means that they don't follow any strict tabular structure of data models (as is the case for relational databases), but, in the case of semi-structured data, they do contain elements that enforce a hierarchy of records and fields within the data. The most notable example is **JSON**, short for **JavaScript Object Notation**, which uses attribute-values pairs to describe objects and in which values can potentially be another JSON block, thus allowing for a nested data structure that enables data models to represent complex relationships between entities. The way objects (or entities) are described in JSON is akin to how objects are described in object-oriented programming languages. In addition, the support for lists of objects simplifies data models by avoiding complex translations from lists to a corresponding object in a relational data model.

Non-relational databases have their critics, too. Many argue that the lack of a standard query language such as SQL, and the lack of restraints and schema enforcement, make these types of databases prone to "garbage in, garbage out." That is, they can wind up becoming a dumping ground for inconsistently defined data, making data analytics a difficult, if not downright impossible, task. Furthermore, some argue that even though there are no schemas being enforced, there's still an "implied" schema, in other words, all database clients still need to know what the data is about, how it is structured, and what data types the values are in order to efficiently interact with the data anyway. This brings up the question as to whether they really deliver flexibility, and whether the little flexibility you do get is worth the potential nightmare of running analytics workloads on these systems. Opinionated discussions aside, it all comes down to the fact that applications must be well designed and their data models well architected for non-relational databases to have real value. With best practices and a shared understanding in place, non-relational databases will deliver on their promises.

So, what does GCP have to offer? Let's start big with Cloud Bigtable.

Cloud Bigtable

Cloud Bigtable is a fully managed, scalable NoSQL database service on GCP. It is a *key-value store with high throughput at low latency* and is especially geared toward *large analytical and operational workloads*. It is also well suited for machine learning applications, with a storage engine designed with them in mind. Data is automatically replicated with *eventual consistency,* and the service comes with 99.99% availability (when multi-cluster routing is set up, otherwise 99.9% for single-cluster instances).

It is also an ideal source for **MapReduce** operations, a programming model used for distributed computing, which you will learn more about in *Chapter 8, Approaching Big Data and Data Pipelines*. Cloud Bigtable integrates easily with the existing *Apache* ecosystem of open source big data software. For teams that already work with *Apache HBase*, Cloud Bigtable will feel familiar and will offer a few key advantages over a self-managed HBase setup, namely:

- **Scale**: Self-managed Hbase installations have a design bottleneck that limits the system's performance after a certain threshold is reached. Cloud Bigtable does not have this bottleneck and can scale in proportion to the number of machines in the cluster.

- **Simplicity**: Cloud Bigtable handles aspects of the underlying platform (such as upgrades, restarts, and replication) transparently. In addition, it automatically maintains high data durability.

- **Cluster resizing without downtime**: You can increase a cluster's size (or reduce it) without any downtime. Scaling events won't affect running workloads.

Ideal use cases for Cloud Bigtable include **ad tech** (for marketing data, such as purchase histories and customer preferences), **fintech** (for financial data, such as transactions, stock prices, and exchange rates), **social/digital media** (for graph data, such as information about relationships between users), and **Internet of Things** (**IoT**) (for time series or IoT data, such as CPU usage over time or telemetry from sensors and appliances). Generally, these applications need high throughput and scalability for reads and writes of key-value data (with values not typically being of a large size). Cloud Bigtable also excels in MapReduce operations and machine learning applications. In fact, Cloud Bigtable powers many of Google's own core services, such as *Search* and *Maps*, and is, therefore, battle-tested for scale and heavy analytics.

So how is data stored in Cloud Bigtable? This database uses a proprietary storage system built on a few Google technologies, such as *Google File System*, *Chubby Lock Service*, and *SSTable*. Data is stored in tables, each of which is a sorted key-value map. Each row of the table defines a single entity and is indexed by a single row key, while the columns contain the values for each row. So far, not very different from a tabular, relational database. The main differentiating characteristic is that columns that are related to one another are typically grouped together into a column family, and each row/column intersection can contain multiple cells (or data versions) at different timestamps, providing a record history of how the stored data has been altered over time. Unlike a relational database, the names and data types of the columns can vary from row to row. In addition, tables are sparse; in other words, if a cell does not contain any data, it does not take up any storage space. Because of these characteristics, Cloud Bigtable falls under the category of column-oriented stores, or, to be a little more accurate, **wide-column stores**. Another such database is *Apache Cassandra*.

With Cloud Bigtable, you can create backups for tables' schemas and data, and then eventually restore them to a new table.

Understanding and setting up instances, clusters, and nodes

To use Cloud Bigtable for your storage needs, you first create an *instance*, which is the container for your data. An instance contains one or more (up to four) *clusters*, spread across different zones. Applications will eventually connect to clusters, each of which comprises nodes (or at least one node), which are units of compute that will perform data management and maintenance tasks. When you create a table, you create it on an instance, which is where the table belongs, and not on a specific cluster or node. If you have more than one cluster within the instance, then tables are going to be replicated.

When you create an instance, there are a few properties that need to be defined, most importantly:

- **The storage type**: This determines whether data will be stored on **solid-state drives (SSDs)** or **hard disk drives (HDDs)**.

- **Application profile**: Especially important when setting up more than one cluster, an application profile (or app profile) will store settings that determine how incoming requests from an application should be handled. This includes routing policy (single- or multi-cluster routing) and whether single-row transactions are allowed.

After creating an instance, you can then create one or up to four clusters, which will belong to the instance. Each cluster must be located in a single and different zone from other clusters. The different zones you choose don't need to be within the same region. With a single cluster setup, your instance will not use replication. If you add a second cluster to the instance, *replication will automatically start* with separate copies of your data placed in each of the clusters and updates being synchronized between copies. You can then either choose to connect different applications to different clusters or have Bigtable balance traffic between clusters. If a cluster becomes unavailable, you can fail over to another, which means that a multi-cluster setup provides you with extra availability.

Finally, each cluster in the instance will be assigned one or more nodes, which are compute resources used by Bigtable. The number of nodes dictates the cluster's capacity to handle income requests and store data, and therefore you must think of monitoring your clusters' CPU and disk usage to add nodes when the metrics exceed a certain threshold. Google Cloud offers the following recommendations on what CPU utilization thresholds to use:

Configuration	Recommended maximum values
Single cluster	70% average CPU utilization 90% CPU utilization of the hottest node
Any number of clusters with single-cluster routing	70% average CPU utilization 90% CPU utilization of hottest node
2 clusters with multi-cluster routing	35% average CPU utilization 45% CPU utilization of hottest node
3 or more clusters with multi-cluster routing	Depends on your configuration

For storage utilization, the general recommendation is to not exceed 70% of the storage capacity.

It is now time to get hands-on and go through a quick example that will illustrate how to create an instance, a cluster, and nodes, and how to write some data to the database that uses a column family structure. For this, we will use the **cbt** command-line tool, which is designed specifically for interacting with Cloud Bigtable. It's possible to use **gcloud** for that (or the console, or any of the available APIs, for that matter), but this tool really simplifies the interactions with Bigtable. This tool is available natively within Cloud Shell, so let's go ahead and open a Cloud Shell session from within the console. Refer to *steps 1 and 2* under the *Cloud Spanner* section header, the *Creating a scalable and highly available SQL database with Cloud Spanner* sub-section, for instructions on how to open Cloud Shell and create a new project (if you haven't already done so):

1. Run the following command in Cloud Shell:

   ```
   $ cbt createinstance cbt-instance1 Instance1 cbt-cluster1
   us-east1-d 2 SSD
   ```

2. You may be asked to authorize Cloud Shell to use your credentials to make a GCP API call. Click on **Authorize** if that happens.

   You will notice that this command will run very quickly. The instance, cluster, and two nodes you've just created are already being spun up in the background, and they'll be ready quite soon. The command has a few positional arguments according to the following syntax:

   ```
   cbt createinstance INSTANCE_ID DISPLAY_NAME CLUSTER_ID
   CLUSTER_ZONE CLUSTER_NUM_NODES CLUSTER_STORAGE_TYPE
   ```

   With that command, we have therefore created one instance with the ID of cbt-instance1, a display name of Instance1, then, a cluster with the ID cbt-cluster1, located in zone us-east1-d, with 2 nodes containing SSD storage.

3. To add a new cluster and enable replication, run the following command next:

   ```
   $ cbt -instance=cbt-instance1 createcluster cbt-cluster2
   us-west1-a 1 SSD
   ```

   We now have a highly scalable, highly available, wide-column NoSQL database ready to use. In the console, if you expand the left-side menu and search for and click on **Bigtable**, you should be able to see the following:

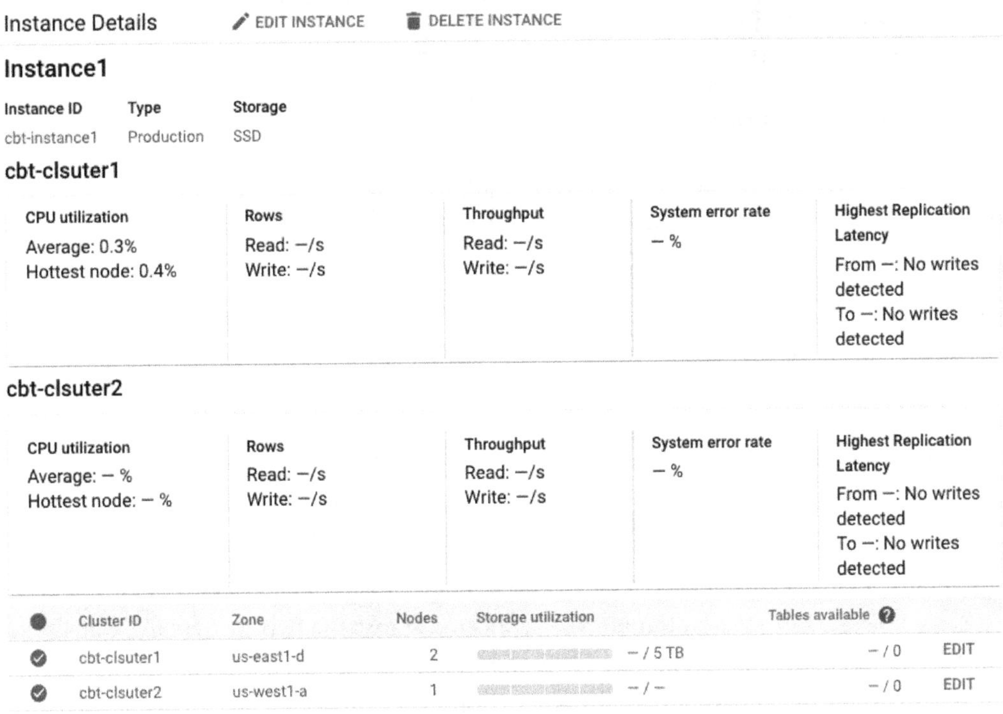

Instance Details   ✏ EDIT INSTANCE   🗑 DELETE INSTANCE

Instance1

Instance ID	Type	Storage
cbt-instance1	Production	SSD

cbt-clsuter1

CPU utilization	Rows	Throughput	System error rate	Highest Replication Latency
Average: 0.3% Hottest node: 0.4%	Read: —/s Write: —/s	Read: —/s Write: —/s	— %	From —: No writes detected To —: No writes detected

cbt-clsuter2

CPU utilization	Rows	Throughput	System error rate	Highest Replication Latency
Average: — % Hottest node: — %	Read: —/s Write: —/s	Read: —/s Write: —/s	— %	From —: No writes detected To —: No writes detected

	Cluster ID	Zone	Nodes	Storage utilization	Tables available ❓	
✔	cbt-clsuter1	us-east1-d	2	— / 5 TB	— / 0	EDIT
✔	cbt-clsuter2	us-west1-a	1	— / —	— / 0	EDIT

Figure 5.9 – Bigtable Instance Details page

4. Still in the **Bigtable** page, you can click on **Application profiles** to see what the app profile is for this instance. Because we didn't specify any, we should have the default profile, which applies *single-cluster routing* and enables *single-row transactions*.

5. Let's now create a table. Back in Cloud Shell, run the following command to set the default project ID and instance name for **cbt** (replace PROJECT_ID with your unique project ID, remembering it's not the same as the project name – **chapter-5**):

```
$ echo -e "project = [PROJECT_ID]\ninstance =
cbt-instance1" > ~/.cbtrc
```

6. Then, run the following two commands to create the table and a column family, which we will call sensors_summary:

```
$ cbt createtable iot-table
$ cbt createfamily iot-table sensors_summary
```

7. After running the preceding command, you can go back to the console and navigate to **Tables** from within the Bigtable page. You should see the following page:

Figure 5.10 – Bigtable table in multi-cluster setup

Note how the table was automatically replicated across the two clusters. Next, let's insert some data. We will do this using the Python client library.

8. Back in the Cloud Shell, download the repository for this book and navigate to the **chapter 5** files by running the following command:

```
$ git clone https://github.com/PacktPublishing/
Architecting-Google-Cloud-Solutions
$ cd Architecting-Google-Cloud-Solutions/ch5
```

9. In the Cloud Shell window, click on the **Open Editor** button located on the top bar:

Figure 5.11 – Cloud Shell Editor

10. In the editor, expand the repository directory, then the ch5 directory, and the open the cbt_ingest.py file. Scroll down in the text editor pane until you see the line that contains PROJECT_ID. Replace that with your own project ID. Do the same for the cbt_read.py file, which also has a line in the end with PROJECT_ID, which you need to edit:

Figure 5.12 – Editing code in Cloud Shell Editor

11. In the Python terminal window on the bottom (if the terminal is not displayed. click on **Terminal** on top of the editor, then **New Terminal**), run the following command to install the Python Cloud Bigtable library:

```
$ pip3 install google-cloud-bigtable
```

12. Now, go back to the cbt_ingest.py file. Click on the *run* icon in the top-right corner of the editor to run this file. You should see an output text in the terminal window below that says, *Successfully wrote row iotdevice#10401*. Next, open the cbt_read.py file and then click on the *run* icon. This time, you should see the row you just wrote, which contains some fake IoT device information (temperature, humidity, and location). A timestamp of the record will also be included. Run these two files a few more times (the ingest application followed by the read one) and see how you're not simply getting additional rows (the cbt_ingest.py application doesn't add a row; it directly creates one with a specified row key), but you get additional timestamped *versions* of the row.

Feel free to explore these Python files to see what they're doing. In short, we wrote a row with a column family of three columns, and then we've read it by querying the table using the row key.

13. When you're done exploring, clean up all resources for this chapter by deleting the project (and everything in it):

```
$ gcloud projects delete PROJECT_ID
```

You've now gotten some hands-on experience with Bigtable, a service you will be likely to work with if you're working with data-driven organizations in Google Cloud. Because so many aspects of such a complex service are taken care of, you should regard it as a great option in your toolbox of data solutions as an architect. Remember the well-fit use cases mentioned at the beginning of this section and analyze your workload requirements against other options.

Let's now briefly look into a few of the other non-relational services and what they're best used for.

Cloud Firestore and Firebase Realtime Database

Cloud Firestore is a database option to consider if you need to store highly structured objects (not necessarily with an enforced schema) in a document database, supporting ACID transactions and SQL-like queries. This is for cases when your data is not necessarily relational, but it may require transactions over at least a subset of the data. In addition, it is especially well suited for **mobile applications**, with features such as **real-time updates** that allow you to synchronize and update data on any connected device. Cloud Firestore is the next generation of a service formerly known as *Cloud Datastore*.

Cloud Firestore is a *document-oriented* database where you store data in documents that contain fields that map to values (and may have nested structures). Documents are stored in collections, which are used to organize documents and over which you can build queries. For example, you can have a collection called *books*. Then, inside that collection, you can have several *documents*, each representing a book. These would have fields such as *Title* and *Category*. Since there are no schemas to follow, fields and data types can differ between entities. You can also have sub-collections. Using the same example, we can organize the *book* collection by sub-collections representing publishers: a sub-collection named *Packt* under the *books* collection holds books published by Packt, whereas other publishers would have their own books grouped under their own sub-collections.

This service has mobile SDKs (for Android and iOS) in addition to web SDKs in several languages and frameworks. Cloud Firestore is a serverless service, in that you don't have to deploy a database server or any intermediary server between clients and the database. Clients can connect directly through the SDKs and APIs. Security rules can be defined declaratively (in code) to control access to the database.

Data can be stored in a multi-regional setting (spread across different regions) or in a regional setting (stored within a region). A multi-regional deployment will deliver a higher availability SLA of 99.999%, whereas a regional deployment delivers a 99.99% availability SLA. Data is automatically replicated across multiple regions (in multi-regional deployments) or multiple zones (in regional deployments). In Cloud Firestore, backups are handled by the managed export and import service, with which you can programmatically export all data into a Cloud Storage account, and later retrieve it through an import operation.

Firebase's Realtime Database is a similar service to Firestore. Both come from Firebase, Google's platform for mobile and web application development, but Firestore is newer and has a richer feature set than Realtime Database. Firestore also scales better and has faster queries. However, for simpler solutions and for specific ways of working with this type of database, you might find Realtime Database to be a better solution. Comprehensive details regarding the differences and a great comparison survey to help you decide which option to use is available at `https://firebase.google.com/docs/firestore/rtdb-vs-firestore`.

Cloud Memorystore

This is Google Cloud's offering for an in-memory data store service for **Redis** and **Memcached**. Tasks including provisioning, replication, failover, and monitoring are all automated and packaged into this PaaS offering, in contrast to a self-hosted Redis solution, for example.

Cloud Memorystore is a fast, in-memory store, and therefore well suited for applications that require fast, real-time processing of data. Common examples of what could benefit from this storage service include user session management, frequently accessed queries and pages, and scripts. Gaming and other such real-time applications can leverage Cloud Memorystore to store, for example, an in-game leaderboard or player profiles. A stream of data such as Twitter feeds or telemetry data from IoT devices can also fit nicely into a Memorystore solution to deliver fast and low latency data access.

Memorystore has two service tiers: **Basic** and **Standard**. The Basic tier can be a good fit for applications that can sustain some loss of data through a cold restart and full data flush. This would most often be the case for applications that use caching, mostly for reading data already stored somewhere else (and reading it faster), or data that is not crucially important to keep.

The Standard tier provides high availability using replication and automatic failover and is well indicated when data durability is of importance. You should remember, however, that this type of in-memory data storage still comes with a trade-off of speed over durability, so even the Standard tier should not be considered if your data requirements set durability as the highest priority.

In terms of technical differences, there aren't many. Both tiers provide instances with up to 300 GB storage size, and a maximum network bandwidth of 12 Gbps. In the Standard tier, each Memorystore instance is configured automatically as a primary and replica pair in an active-standby setup. The replica is always in a different zone than the primary, and data changes made on the primary instance are copied to the standby instance using the *Redis asynchronous replication protocol*. If the primary node fails, the platform will trigger a failover automatically, at which point the replica is promoted to be the new primary and, after recovery of the failure, the former primary becomes the new replica.

When it comes to backups, Memorystore data can be exported to Cloud Storage and restored at a later point. It is possible to automate this process by using Cloud Scheduler (a service we will discuss in *Part 3, Designing for the Modern Enterprise*, of this book) and Cloud Functions. A tutorial on how to do that is available at `https://cloud.google.com/solutions/scheduling-memorystore-for-redis-database-exports-using-cloud-scheduler`.

Cloud Storage for unstructured data

Cloud Storage is a service we have already mentioned a few times in this book. It's a highly durable object storage service where you can store just about any type of data, including binaries such as image and video files or scripts and executable files. Indeed, you can host a static website on Cloud Storage by simply placing HTML and accompanying CSS and/or JavaScript files in there and making it publicly accessible.

This service provides different access tiers, or *storage classes*, based on how often data is accessed. Frequently accessed data should use the standard storage class, whereas nearline, coldline, and archive storage classes offer progressively lower storage prices with correspondingly higher retrieval costs (as discussed in more detail in *Chapter 2, Mastering the Basics of Google Cloud*, in the section relating to cost effectiveness).

Data in Cloud Storage is contained in **buckets**. Buckets organize data and centralize access control and some settings for data **objects** in them. Buckets cannot be nested and, because there are limits to bucket creation and deletion, your applications should be designed to *mostly work with object-level operations and not many bucket operations*. A bucket is created in a geographic location you specify, and with a default storage class for objects stored in the bucket (for when objects don't have a specified storage class themselves). Objects are the individual *blobs* or units of data that you store in Cloud Storage. The service is highly scalable and there is no limit on the number of objects that you can create in a bucket. You pay for the amount of storage consumed.

The geographical location of a bucket can be configured to be a single GCP region, a pair of regions (dual-region setup), or several regions within a broad geographical area (multi-region setup). As of the time of writing, Asia, Europe, and US are the multi-region locations available. Irrespective of the storage class, objects stored in dual- or multi-region buckets will have *geo-redundancy*. Geo-redundancy occurs asynchronously, but all Cloud Storage data is replicated within at least one geographic location as soon as you upload it.

An attractive feature of Cloud Storage is *object versioning*. When enabled, an object will have different versions as you modify it (a *modification* being a new object added with the same name and in the same place. In fact, objects in Cloud Storage are immutable and cannot change throughout its lifetime). This allows you to restore an object that was accidentally replaced, for example, or restore it to a previous *state*. Older versions can be permanently deleted if you no longer need them (the presence of multiple versions will increase the storage costs). The **Object Lifecycle Management** feature allows you to set a **time to live** (TTL) for objects and also things such as the number of non-current versions to maintain. You can set a policy to downgrade storage classes and save costs on infrequently accessed data. This feature is very useful for automating clean-up and housekeeping processes that very often get forgotten and, as a result, incur unnecessary storage costs. Life cycle management configurations can be assigned to a bucket, thus applying to all current and future objects in the bucket. Here are examples of rules that you can define as life cycle management policies:

- Delete objects created before January 1, 2018.
- Keep only the two most recent versions of each object that has versioning enabled.
- Downgrade the storage class of objects older than 90 days to nearline storage.

Cloud Storage data (in other words, objects) are generally unstructured, although you could add any type of structured or semi-structured data as well, for example, tables or JSON documents. In any case, an object's data is *opaque* to Cloud Storage, in other words, it's just a chunk of data into which the platform has no visibility. This means you can't run queries or analyze data that is in Cloud Storage, therefore making it a *storage* service to be used for this exact purpose: storage. It's not a non-relational database, it's an opaque, unstructured object store. To secure your data, server-side encryption is used to encrypt the data by default, but you can also use your own encryption keys. Authentication and access controls can be applied to further secure access. Data security will be a topic revisited in *Chapter 7, Designing for Security and Compliance*.

Cloud Storage has a command-line utility called gsutil, with which you can interact with the service's API. With gsutil, you can perform a range of bucket and object management tasks, such as create or delete buckets, upload or download objects, copy and move objects, and edit a bucket's ACLs. It also supports running *resumable uploads* for more reliable data transfers from, for example, on-premises data storage. Some example commands that you can run include the following:

```
# Create a bucket
gsutil mb gs://BUCKET_NAME
# Upload an object
gsutil cp OBJECT_LOCATION gs://DESTINATION_BUCKET_NAME
# Upload an entire directory tree
gsutil cp -r dir gs://DESTINATION_BUCKET_NAME
# Enable object versioning on a bucket
gsutil versioning set on gs://BUCKET_NAME
# Make all objects in Bucket publicly readable
gsutil iam ch allUsers:objectViewer gs://BUCKET_NAME
```

Can you guess how you could use the commands listed previously to host a static website on GCP? If you're up for a challenge, try to host a static website on Cloud Storage by uploading files to a bucket and making them publicly readable. The `gsutil` command-line utility should be available on your local computer if you've installed the Cloud SDK, but it is also available on Cloud Shell. You can get static website templates for free from `https://html5up.net/`. Once you download one, create a bucket and upload the local directory tree to it, and then set an IAM policy at the bucket level so that all users can view its objects. You won't need to run any additional commands other than the ones listed previously. Once you've finished, you can navigate via your browser to `https://storage.googleapis.com/BUCKET_NAME/DIR_NAME/index.html` (replacing `BUCKET_NAME` and `DIR_NAME` with the name of your Cloud Storage bucket and the directory you've uploaded, respectively). To delete a bucket, you can run the following command:

```
gsutil rm -r gs://BUCKET_NAME
```

If you're familiar with Linux and Bash commands, you may have noticed that `gsutil` commands are built with very similar syntax. That makes it easy to guess how to run a command based on how you would perform the same object manipulation on a local, Linux-based filesystem.

Consider Cloud Storage for your unstructured object storage needs, as well as a place for database backups, or data that is to be archived or accessed infrequently (in which case, you can leverage cost savings with storage classes). If you're hosting websites on GCP, you can place some of the static contents in Cloud Storage, such as JavaScript and CSS files. If the website is entirely static, you can place all of it in there and make it publicly accessible, effectively delivering a highly available and scalable website in a cost-effective manner. Choose at least a dual-region setting for higher availability and durability, but leverage a multi-region deployment when your service and your users are globally distributed or if you need very high durability. Finally, consider enabling object versioning as insurance against accidental object replacement, and don't forget the Object Lifecycle Management feature as a way to save costs and automate housekeeping of your objects.

Choosing the right solution for each piece of data

As mentioned previously, a cloud design that incorporates polyglot persistence, where different data services and technologies are used to meet each specific data type and its requirements, is ideal for modern applications with even modest levels of data complexity. Therefore, you will likely find yourself having to make several decisions when designing the data architecture for your solutions. The following diagram summarizes what you've learned in this chapter into a decision tree to guide you in choosing the best storage solution according to the characteristics of the data:

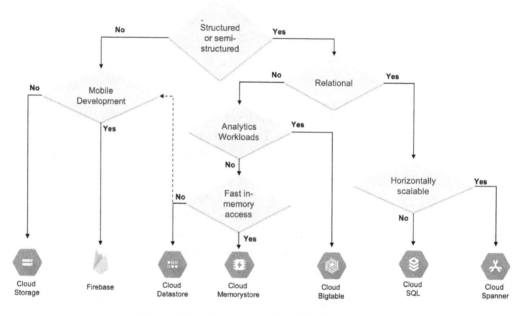

Figure 5.13 – Decision tree for GCP data services

By asking yourself just a few questions about the qualities and the needs of your data, you should be able to find a suitable datastore on GCP, at least as a starting point. There is one data service that was left out of this chapter, and that was Cloud BigQuery. This service, as well as big data concepts such as data lake, data warehouse, and data pipelines, will be discussed in *Chapter 8, Approaching Big Data and Data Pipelines*.

Summary

In this chapter, we covered several foundational concepts regarding data and storage solutions. We then explored relational and structured data services in Google Cloud, and how to design those services for high availability and scalability, and how to handle backups and approach data durability and consistency. You got some hands-on experience with Cloud Spanner, a horizontally scalable relational database service that is also highly available. Finally, you learned about different services for non-relational or unstructured data in Google Cloud. In most modern solutions, a cloud architect will need to be prepared for *polyglot persistence*, a mix of different types of databases for different types of data. Therefore, having learned about all those services will help you design robust cloud-based data architectures that leverage polyglot persistence to obtain optimal solutions.

In the next chapter, we're going to look into one of the strong pillars of a well-architected cloud solution: *observability*.

6

Configuring Services for Observability

You cannot fix what you don't know is broken. And you don't want to find out your system is broken or underperforming when issues are being flagged by users, at which point it's already too late to prevent an impact on the business. Even worse, you don't want to learn your environment has been compromised when an attacker has already gotten hold of important information or done critical damage to your system. For these and many other reasons, which you will learn in this chapter, **observability** is a crucial pillar of great cloud solutions.

In this chapter, you will learn how to design a monitoring solution with Google Cloud, apply logging and debugging tools to applications and services, and analyze logs and metrics from a single pane of glass. You will familiarize yourself with **Cloud Monitoring** and **Cloud Logging**, Google Cloud's primary monitoring and logging services, and learn how to set up actionable alerts and approach incident management. By the end of this chapter, you should feel confident to design a Google Cloud solution for **observability** and implement monitoring best practices.

In this chapter, we're going to cover the following main topics:

- Learning the monitoring basics
- Monitoring cloud services and analyzing logs

- Investigating application performance issues
- Designing for observability with best practices

Technical requirements

For the hands-on activities in this chapter, you will need a billing-enabled Google Cloud account and optionally the Google Cloud SDK installed (if you don't have it, you can use Cloud Shell from a browser). Helper scripts and code for this chapter can be found at `https://github.com/PacktPublishing/Architecting-Google-Cloud-Solutions/tree/master/ch6`.

Check out the following link to see the Code in Action video: `https://bit.ly/3uRYUKq`

Learning the monitoring basics

Monitoring has a few important purposes. It helps you achieve business continuity, carry out **forecasting** and trend analysis, test changes, build **dashboards** with your system's most crucial **metrics**, **alert** on-call personnel to potentially violated **Service-Level Agreements** (**SLAs**), and, in general, provide data for **analytics**, **troubleshooting**, and improved **incident response**. A well-monitored infrastructure will, for example, enable you to get the answers to the following questions:

- Will my system be able to handle the holiday rush? (**Forecasting**)
- What is my database growth rate so that I can plan for capacity in the near future? (**Trend analysis**)
- Did the latest software update affect performance? (**Testing changes**)
- How are customer needs evolving? (**Business analytics and intelligence**)
- Is there an on-going attack on the network? (**Security analytics**)

This level of observability relies on logging and metrics data sent by the various Google Cloud services and **Virtual Machine** (**VM**) instances you provision (through an *agent*), as well as custom logs and metrics you may potentially define. However, monitoring doesn't only apply to the infrastructure and its logs. *Application monitoring* provides further insights into applications' behavior, down to the software state at a particular line of code. In Google Cloud, the following application monitoring capabilities are available:

- **Debugger**: Inspects the code state when a particular line gets executed. It helps with debugging and code troubleshooting, and it works without stopping the application or slowing it down.

- **Profiler**: Examines CPU and memory usage by the application and can be used to spot performance bottlenecks.

- **Trace**: Analyzes latency between application components, especially useful with microservices-based applications.

- **Logs API**: Developers can use it to write directly to Google Cloud logs and include custom application state information.

Well-monitored applications will help you answer some more in-depth questions about the applications' behavior and the quality of the service you provide. It will also likely reduce the time it takes to find and resolve performance issues.

It is important to understand that monitoring is not just about *tooling*. It is not a job role either. Monitoring is a skill that must be honed by every team member, from development to operations. Observability should be a common goal and part of the culture. You should not expect monitoring tools to do it all for you or aspire to obtain a "magic" system that automatically learns thresholds, automatically alerts the right personnel (without false positives), and automatically detects root causes. This is an unrealistic goal. Cloud services indeed facilitate the "single pane of glass" approach to monitoring, but that doesn't mean you will be able to get every single metric, log, and piece of information from your systems on a single view that someone can stare at to spot any and every issue. Monitoring is instead a *process* to be continually improved and fine-tuned. As long as you focus on the important things, you will be moving in the right direction toward maintaining your SLAs. Speaking of "important things" and "SLAs," let's qualify these terms according to Google's **Site Reliability Engineering** (**SRE**) concepts. SRE is a topic covered in *Part 3, Designing for the Modern Enterprise*, but in this chapter, it will be useful to draw on some of its monitoring-related concepts, namely *the four golden signals* and the definitions of **Service-Level Indicators** (**SLIs**), **Service-Level Objectives** (**SLOs**), and SLAs. Let's understand what they mean.

The SRE approach to monitoring

In the book *Site Reliability Engineering* (available at `https://landing.google.com/sre/books/`), the following are defined as "the four golden signals" of monitoring:

- **Latency**: The time it takes to service a request. Common metrics include the following:

    — Page load time

    — Query duration

— Service response time

— Transaction duration

- **Traffic**: A measure of how much demand is being placed on your system, measured in a high-level and system-specific metric. Example metrics include the following:

— HTTP requests per second

— Network I/O rate

— Transactions per second

— Number of concurrent sessions

- **Errors**: The rate of requests that fail, which could be explicitly defined by, for example, HTTP status codes, or implicitly derived from the overall behavior of the application (for example, even if there's a successful response, the response's content may be wrong). Common metrics include the following:

— The number of failed requests

— The number of exceptions

— The number of HTTP 4xx/5xx error codes

— The number of dropped connections

- **Saturation**: A measure of how "full" the service is, with 100% saturation representing the point at which the service cannot take any more load without producing errors or noticeable performance degradation. Examples of metrics are the following:

— CPU utilization

— Memory utilization

— Disk/cache utilization

— The number of connected users

If you measure all of the preceding signals (the listed metrics for each being non-exhaustive and just examples) and have a good, actionable set of alerts configured for them, your service will be "at least decently covered by monitoring," according to the book – which is based on Google's own experience over many years of managing complex distributed systems. From my own personal experience, I can attest that the preceding signals will have you well covered in most cases. You should keep in mind that monitoring systems are prone to becoming unnecessarily complex, so you should aim for simplicity. If you're collecting information but not using it in any way (that is, exposing it on a dashboard or using it for alerts and/or analytics), then it is a good candidate for removal. Signals and alerts must be simple, understood, and reliable. They must not become *noise*.

SRE also lays out the following conceptual foundations around service reliability:

- **SLI**: It's a *quantifiable measure* of service reliability. It should be closely related to the real user's experience. It is generally recommended that this quantity should be a ratio of two numbers: the number of *good* events divided by the total number of events. For example, the number of successful HTTP responses divided by the total count of all valid HTTP responses.

- **SLO**: It's a *reliability target* for an SLI, representing the *desired* experience for end users. It's an attainable goal to aim for based on how high the SLI can realistically and consistently be given the system's design. It provides a common language and shared understanding and forms a basis for decision-making.

- **SLA**: It's the agreed-upon reliability target *committed to for paying customers*. It's the reliability metric that, if violated, will usually incur monetary compensation from the service provider to the customer (service consumer).

Your SLO should be higher than your SLA. The SLO is the objective, the goal to strive for, and should be decided together by engineering and product teams. It should represent the threshold below which the customer would not feel fully satisfied with the service. *You should not aim for an SLO of 100%.* In most cases, the costs will outweigh the benefits. Frankly, 100% reliability is unnecessarily high anyway, as most people tolerate a little bit of downtime, and if downtime is infrequent enough, most people won't even perceive it. The SLO must capture that "sweet spot" where increasing the reliability won't make users happier than they currently are. This also means that an SLO implies an *acceptable level of unreliability*. As a principle highlighted in SRE, it should be treated as a *budget* to be allocated (ideally toward the end of the measuring SLO window rather than at the beginning). This is referred to as an *error budget*. It can be used to motivate the deployment of high-risk changes such as implementing new innovative features or merely *trying things out*, knowing that, if there's a small impact on the infrastructure, the SLO will still be met. It's a useful mental framework to drive innovation and change while keeping reliability metrics within acceptable levels.

On the other hand, the SLA is a binding agreement that usually involves monetary compensation and, for that reason, it should be defined more conservatively. The following figure illustrates a typical set of SLI, SLO, and SLA values based on application availability:

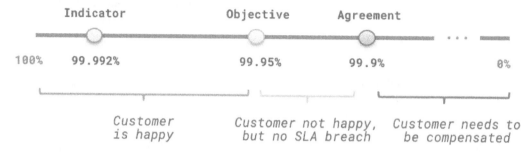

Figure 6.1 – SLI, SLO, and SLA examples

In this example, the current application uptime measure is **99.992%**, above the target value defined by the SLO (**99.95%**). Currently, the customer should be satisfied with the service. Dipping below the SLO may make customers unsatisfied with the service reliability, but depending on how low the SLA is compared to the SLO, you will have a "comfort" margin in which you're still not breaching the set agreement. Within that margin, the customer can't base any complaints on contractual agreements. However, going below the SLA target means some compensation will be involved, not to mention reputation damage and other potential indirect impacts on your business.

Now that we've laid out the basic concepts for monitoring, we're going to look at how to approach it all on **Google Cloud Platform (GCP)**.

Monitoring cloud services and analyzing logs

The primary components of a monitoring solution on GCP are **Workspaces** and **the Cloud Monitoring** and **Cloud Logging** services. In this section, we will explore these services and also the monitoring and logging capabilities within Google Cloud.

The monitoring landscape in Google Cloud

Workspaces are where monitoring information is organized and can be created at no charge. The monitored resources can be in one or more Google Cloud projects and one or more AWS accounts. Every Workspace has a host project, which is the GCP project in which it is created. A Workspace can monitor up to 100 Google Cloud projects and AWS accounts, but it is the host project that has all the configurations related to dashboards, alerting policies, uptime checks, notification channels, and other group definitions that you configure.

In other words, the host project is where monitoring is centralized from a governance perspective. It is not uncommon for host projects to be empty of any resources and solely dedicated to hosting the Workspace. Logging and metric data ingested by the monitored projects are associated with their respective project's billing account (for AWS accounts, that would be the billing accounts of the AWS connector projects in Google Cloud).

Cloud Monitoring is a collection of tools that help realize the purposes of monitoring that we highlighted in the previous section. It measures key aspects of Google Cloud services, and gives you the ability to graph the measurements and answer some of the questions we mentioned previously. A collection of these measurements is generically defined as a *metric*, of which there are over 1,500 types of in Monitoring (which include metrics for Google Cloud, AWS, and supported third-party software). Cloud Monitoring is also where you can set up notification alerts when measurements deviate from what you define as normal and acceptable. Monitoring capabilities can be categorized into four kinds:

- **Black-box monitoring**: This is the type of monitoring concerned only with "how it looks from the outside." This means probing the service in the same way that an end user would be able to, and it tries to reflect the current user experience of the service. The service itself is treated as an opaque entity, that is, the internals of the service are not monitored. In Cloud Monitoring, this type of monitoring is provided with *uptime checks*, which validate whether the service is up or down by trying to reach (from at least three different locations) its exposed URL, IP address, or DNS name. These checks also measure and display the latency associated with the responses.

- **White-box monitoring**: This enables you to monitor the internals of the service, and specifically those aspects of the service that are important from the perspective of its quality and health. This type of monitoring requires instrumentation of the service by including programming libraries such as *OpenCensus*, or by writing custom time-series data using the **Cloud Monitoring API** from within your code. We will discuss code instrumentation in more detail later in this chapter, in the *Investigating application performance issues* section.

- **Gray-box monitoring**: As the name implies, this type of monitoring is somewhere in the middle between the black- and white-box types. It's about collecting information on the state of the *environment* in which services are running. It includes things such as the CPU usage of the underlying VM instances or metrics related to storage and network usage. It's not something that requires the application to be instrumented, but it requires *agents* to be installed in the underlying instances. There are also third-party plugins that can provide more in-depth service-level data on Linux VMs running certain common applications such as Apache, NGINX, or MongoDB.

- **Logs-based metrics monitoring**: Logs-based metrics are collected from the content of *logs* (rather than direct measurements) written to Cloud Logging. Predefined system logs-based metrics include values such as detected service errors or the total number of log entries received. You can define custom logs-based metrics, such as the count of log entries that match a given query, indicating a specific system behavior.

Cloud Logging is the service that allows you to store, search, analyze, and alert on logging data and events from both Google Cloud and AWS platforms. Cloud Logging also includes access to the partner service *BindPlane* (`https://bluemedora.com/products/bindplane/bindplane-for-stackdriver/`), which can be used to collect logs from over 150 common application components, in Google Cloud or elsewhere. The Logging service encompasses the following four capabilities:

- **Collection**: The automatic collection of logs from Google Cloud services.

- **Analysis**: Real-time log data analysis with tools such as **Logs Explorer**, Dataflow, and BigQuery. Archived logs from Cloud Storage can also be analyzed.

- **Export**: Export logs to Cloud Storage or stream to Cloud Pub/Sub or BigQuery. Logs-based metrics can be exported to the Monitoring service.

- **Retention**: Access logs can be retained for up to 3,650 days (in logs buckets with a configurable retention period) and admin logs for 400 days. Logs exported to Cloud Storage or BigQuery can have a longer retention period configured in those services.

Cloud Logging handles the following main types of logs:

- **Audit logs**: Data access logs, admin activity logs, and essentially anything that answers the question "*who* did *what, where* and *when*"?

- **Agent logs**: Logs collected by the logging agents and common third-party applications.

- **Network Logs**: Logs related to firewall rules, VPC network traffic, and other networking services.

The Monitoring and Logging agents play an essential role in the observability and monitoring of the environment (gray-box monitoring in particular), so let's better understand how they work.

Monitoring and Logging agents

The **OS Monitoring agent** is a software agent based on the open source tool **collectd** and is responsible for gathering system and application metrics from compute instances. The agent can be configured to monitor third-party applications, such as *Apache, NGINX,* and *MySQL.* All metrics collected by the agent are sent to Cloud Monitoring.

The **OS Logging agent**, on the other hand, is based on the open source log data collector **fluentd** and can stream logs from third-party applications and system software to Cloud Logging. It supports common applications such as *Apache, Tomcat, NGINX, Chef, Jenkins,* and *Puppet,* as well as database applications such as *Cassandra, MongoDB,* and *MySQL.* Custom fluentd configuration files can be added to configure the agent and apply custom log parsing. All logs are sent to Cloud Logging.

For OS-specific instructions on how to install the agents on a VM, go to `https://cloud.google.com/monitoring/agent/installation` (for the Monitoring agent) or `https://cloud.google.com/logging/docs/agent/installation` (for the Logging agent).

To automate the setup of Monitoring and Logging agents in IaaS VMs, you can either define startup scripts that install the agents at VM creation or bake the agent into a base OS image that you use to create VM instances. In fact, there are a few other reasons why you should consider working with base "golden images," if you deploy IaaS VMs. For instance, this allows you to centrally perform security hardening of the operating system, apply custom configurations, and include patches, custom software, and other things that you may wish all your VMs to have (such as Monitoring agents). By building an automation pipeline to set up your images through scripts and configuration files, they can also be treated as code and their lifecycle can be managed in an **Infrastructure-as-Code (IaC)** fashion along with the VMs themselves and other resources.

Compute platform services, such as App Engine (both Flexible and Standard environments), have monitoring and logging built in with pre-installed and pre-configured agents. You can create logs from applications by simply writing them to **standard output (stdout)** or **standard error (stderr)** streams from your code, and you may also use the Cloud Logging API (or other supported APIs, such as Winston on Node.js). **Google App Engine (GAE)** logs are viewable under the GAE application resource in the console.

Serverless compute services such as Cloud Run and Cloud Functions provide integrated monitoring and logging, with the platform handling the collection and the "plumbing" for you. Metrics and graphs are also viewable under the resources themselves in the console.

In **Google Kubernetes Engine (GKE)** nodes, monitoring and/or logging can be configured and are enabled by default. Furthermore, **Prometheus** is an open source monitoring tool available on GCP, used to extend Kubernetes monitoring capabilities. With Standard GKE monitoring enabled, you can add Prometheus support by setting up a Prometheus server and collector. Metrics collected by Prometheus can be made visible in Cloud Monitoring.

Cloud Monitoring metric model

A *metric* is a set of related measurements of some attribute of a resource. Therefore, measures can consist of many different things, such as the request latency of a service, the available disk space on a machine, the number of tables in a SQL database, the percentage of CPU utilization of an instance, and so on. To establish a standard structured model for metrics, Cloud Monitoring defines three primary components:

- Information about the *source*, that is, the *monitored resource*
- A set of *time-stamped measurements*
- Information about the *values* of the property being measured

The information about the source must simply provide a way to uniquely identify the source of the measurements. Because metrics can be custom-defined and represent high-level business concepts such as the number of products sold, the monitored resource doesn't always correspond to a GCP resource. In this example, the monitored resources could be physical stores, with their unique location and ID. The measurements themselves must always be defined as a set of data points, consisting of timestamp-value pairs. This is because a property's value provides very little information without the precise time it was measured. Finally, the information about the values provides a means to interpret the data by including, for example, the data type (integer, string, and so on), the data unit (requests per second, gigabits, and so on), and the kind of each measurement (total, cumulative, change since previous, and so on). In Cloud Monitoring, all three components of the metric model are combined together into a *time series*.

Both monitored resources and metrics support *labels*, which allow data to be classified during analysis. For example, a VM (a monitored resource) might include labels for the project ID and location, or Google Cloud zone, of the machine. It may, however, also include system- or user-provided metadata labels, with which you can further classify VMs.

A comprehensive list of all the Google Cloud metrics (including their set of labels) you can work with is available at `https://cloud.google.com/monitoring/api/metrics`. In particular, the metrics generated from the Monitoring agent and the Logging agent running on VM instances are available at `https://cloud.google.com/monitoring/api/metrics_agent#agent`. You might also want to bookmark this list of all monitored resources and their labels in *Monitoring* (including both Google Cloud and AWS resources): `https://cloud.google.com/monitoring/api/resources`, and the slightly different list of monitored resources in *Logging*: `https://cloud.google.com/logging/docs/api/v2/resource-list#resource-types`. That's a lot of URLs to keep track of, but these are not only extensive lists that would hardly fit in the chapter of a book but also constantly evolving lists. It's useful to have those up-to-date references whenever you need to check on a particular metric or resource, especially if you're looking into creating your own custom metric since it might already exist. Don't reinvent the wheel.

Network and audit logs

Network logging encompasses **Cloud NAT Logs, VPC Flow Logs, Firewall Rules Logs,** and **Packet Mirroring**.

Cloud NAT provides logs of **Network Address Translation** (**NAT**) connections and/or errors (specifically related to packets being dropped due to there not being available ports for address translation). A log entry will contain fields such as a 7-tuple connection object, allocation status, endpoint, destination, and details about the affected VPC and NAT gateway. Cloud NAT logs can be enabled or disabled within the settings of a Cloud NAT resource.

VPC Flow Logs are records of sampled network packets flowing through your VPC network. They can be used for network monitoring, traffic analysis, forensics, real-time security analysis, or network troubleshooting. It is enabled (or disabled) at the subnetwork level. VPC Flow Logs entries contain a 5-tuple object consisting of source and destination IP addresses, source and destination ports, and a protocol. Other present fields are start/end time, bytes/packets sent, and details about instance, VPC, and geographic location for the flow. For example, the following is a snippet of a real log entry:

```
...
src_instance: {
  region: "us-central1"
  project_id: "robotic-tract-298430"
  zone: "us-central1-a"
  vm_name: "peinstance-01"
```

```
}
...
connection: {
  protocol: 6
  dest_port: 443
  src_ip: "10.128.0.2"
  src_port: 56342
  dest_ip: "172.217.214.95"
}
...
start_time: "2020-12-17T14:08:12.263046604Z"
end_time: "2020-12-17T14:08:12.263046604Z"
```

Firewall Rules Logging, on the other hand, provides further insights into the way traffic flows in the network by helping to identify which connections hit which firewall rule. For example, if you need to investigate whether firewall rules are causing an application outage by blocking legitimate traffic, or whether firewall rules are indeed stopping undesired traffic, then this type of logging will help answer such questions. A snippet of an example log entry is shown as follows:

```
disposition: "DENIED"
vpc: {
  subnetwork_name: "default"
  vpc_name: "default"
  project_id: "robotic-tract-298430"
}
remote_vpc: {
  vpc_name: "default"
  subnetwork_name: "default"
  project_id: "robotic-tract-298430"
}
remote_instance: {...}
instance: {...}
connection: {
  dest_ip: "10.128.0.2"
  src_port: 37656
  protocol: 6
  dest_port: 3389
```

```
    src_ip: "10.166.0.2"
}
...
```

By default, Firewall Rules Logs is disabled, since it tends to generate voluminous amounts of log entries, which can increase ingestion costs. You can enable it on a per-rule and as-needed basis by updating an existing firewall rule or upon its creation. You can disable it when no longer needed.

Packet Mirroring is a feature that allows you to capture and examine all ingress and egress network traffic and packet data, such as payloads and headers, for specified compute instances. It does so by cloning the traffic of the instances you specify, hence the name Packet Mirroring. It is a useful feature for a more in-depth analysis of your network security. Instead of taking a sample of packets, as the VPC Flow Logs service does, it exports *all traffic* for examination. You can use specialized threat and anomaly detection software to analyze the mirrored traffic or inspect the full traffic flow to detect performance issues affecting your applications. To set up Packet Mirroring, you create a Packet Mirroring policy that specifies the *source* (one or more Compute Engine instances) and a *collector destination*. The collector destination must be an instance group (managed or unmanaged) behind a load balancer, running the software of your choice for data inspection and analysis. Examples include **Intrusion Detection System (IDS)** tools, **Deep Packet Inspection** (DPI) engines, or network forensics software for compliance and other regulatory use cases.

Beyond network-related logs, certain events in the platform are important *auditable* information you don't want to miss logs for. Cloud Audit Logs is a crucial logging service component that maintains audit logs for *Admin Activity*, *Data Access*, *System Event*, and *Policy Denied* events. These types of logs help you answer the question "*who* did *what*, *where*, and *when?*", which allows you to have control over the activities carried out by users in the organization. Google Cloud is continuously working toward having all its services provide audit logs, but as of this writing that is not yet the case. For a list of all services that provide audit logs, go to `https://cloud.google.com/logging/docs/audit/services`.

If you use **Google Workspace** in your organization, you will also see audit logs related to certain activities within Google Workspace. These are **Enterprise Groups Audit** and **Admin Audit** (both are of type **Admin Activity**), and **Login Audit** (of type **Data Access**).

You can view abbreviated, simplified audit log entries for a project or organization from the **ACTIVITY** page in the console, as shown in the following figure. The actual log entries available in the Logs Explorer contain more detailed information:

Figure 6.2 – Activity logs in the console

In the screenshot, the first log entry shown (**Completed:google.api.servicemanagement. v1.ServiceManager.ActivateServices**) was expanded to show more information. Otherwise, you're able to see an abbreviated entry containing the activity (for example, **Set IAM policy on project**, as shown in the screenshot) and the user or service account that did it. The expanded context pane shows the affected resource, project, and additional information depending on the type of activity. The **ACTIVITY** page provides a quick, bird's-eye view of the activities going on the platform.

Complete log entries are sent to Cloud Logging, like most other types of logs. For a sample of a full *raw* audit log entry and explanations on how to interpret its contents, go to https://cloud.google.com/logging/docs/audit/understanding-audit-logs.

The following table summarizes the characteristics of each of the audit log types:

Audit Log Type	Description	Required IAM role to view	Enabled by Default
Admin Activity	All API calls and administrative actions that modify the configuration or metadata of resources.	Logging/Logs Viewer or Project/Viewer	Yes. Can't be disabled.
Data Access	All API calls that read the configuration or metadata of resources, as well as API calls that create, modify, or read user-provided resource data. Does not record data-access operations on resources that are publicly shared.	Logging/ Private Logs Viewer or Project/Owner	No
System Event	All administrative actions driven by Google systems that modify the configuration of resources.	Logging/Logs Viewer or Project/Viewer	Yes. Can't be disabled.
Policy Denied	All access denied events to users or service accounts due to security policy violations.	Logging/Logs Viewer or Project/Viewer	Yes. Logs exclusions can be used to remove these from ingestion into Logging.

User-driven Admin Activity audit logs and system-driven System Event audit logs are so crucial to observability and transparency that the platform will not give you the option to disable them. It's effectively the only way to ensure transparency on administrative activities in the platform. They help maintain audit trails in Google Cloud and provide valuable information to answer several governance-related questions that may surface; for example:

- Is the segregation of duties principle enforced in the environment? That is, is any one individual performing too many highly privileged operations?

- Is the **Infrastructure-as-Code** (**IaC**) principle enforced in the environment? That is, are there resources being created or modified by users as opposed to pipeline service accounts?

- Has an identity been potentially compromised? That is, are there users performing activities that seem to indicate the behavior of an attacker?

- Has an infrastructure change caused an outage? That is, are there administrative actions that occurred right before an incident was reported?

The list is non-exhaustive, but hopefully, you get the idea of how important it is to not only maintain audit logs (at least in Google Cloud, you certainly won't have the option not to) but to review them regularly.

> **Important note**
>
> Consider having organizational policies or processes in place that dictate when and how audit logs shall be reviewed, taking into account the pricing considerations for enabling the ingestion of Data Access and/or Policy Denied logs. Define and configure alerts to distinguish between events that require immediate investigation and those that do not. As a security best practice, two overarching principles guiding your decisions should be the principles of least privilege and segregation of duties.

Regardless of options to see service-related logs, abbreviated or otherwise, from within a service itself, all the types of logs mentioned so far in this book can be visualized in the **Logs Explorer** (formerly Logs Viewer). In fact, monitoring and log analysis are much more efficient when they can be visualized from a single location. Next, we will explore the visualization capabilities in Google Cloud, including charts and dashboards for metrics.

The Logs Explorer and Logs Dashboard

The main graphic interface for Cloud Logging is the Logs Explorer. It allows you to quickly retrieve, view, and analyze logs through search queries. There are several additional features that you can also leverage in Logs Explorer, such as the following:

- The ability to select a time range.
- Download logs in CSV or JSON format.
- Use saved queries.
- Copy log entries to the clipboard.

Contrary to Monitoring, Logging doesn't require you to have a Workspace, unless you're receiving logs from AWS. And you also don't get a combined view from multiple projects; you need instead to select a specific project to view its logs.

You can further refine the scope of the logs displayed in the Logs Explorer by storage view, that is, by specific storage buckets where logs are stored. These may be the default ones used for the project or others you create. The interface provides a query builder, with which you can build queries by selecting filters from the drop-down fields **Resource, Log name**, and **Severity**. Add the **Time range** selection, and you have the four dimensions on which you can query logs in Logs Explorer. Using the query builder, you don't need to know the syntax of queries; you can just use the graphical interface to build the exact query you need. For more complex queries, however, you may want to learn the Logs Explorer's query syntax, explained in detail at `https://cloud.google.com/logging/docs/view/logging-query-language`.

In addition to querying and browsing through logs, you can visualize the health of the systems in the **Logs Dashboard** tool within Cloud Logging. It provides a high-level overview of resources currently providing log data in the selected project. This overview is organized in pairs of charts for each resource type: the first containing a breakdown of logs by severity, the second displaying only the error logs for that resource type. The following resource types are scoped and will automatically generate charts if deployed in the project:

- GKE
- GCE
- App Engine
- Cloud Load Balancing
- Cloud SQL
- BigQuery

The following figure shows an example of a pair of charts for Cloud SQL resources. In this simple example, there are many log entries of **INFO** severity level and a few of **WARNING** severity:

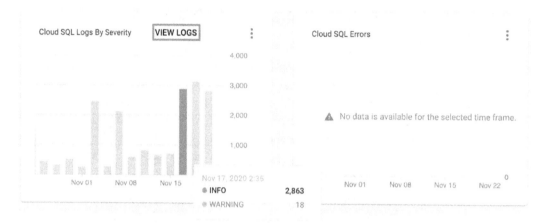

Figure 6.3 – Logs Dashboard

You can explore the logs represented in a chart by clicking on it and then on the **VIEW LOGS** button above the chart, as shown in the preceding screenshot. You will then be taken to the **Logs Explorer**, where you can investigate them further.

In the hands-on activity we will do at the end of this section, you will get to use the Logs Explorer to delve into some of the log analysis capabilities on GCP. Let's now look at how we can visualize *metrics*.

Monitoring charts and dashboards

Dashboards offer a way for you to view and analyze data that is *important* to you. For even moderately sized environments, you can't fit every metric into a dashboard, or at least not one a human being could make sense of at a glance. A dashboard combines graphical representations of key signal data to help you make quick judgments on the health, performance, and trends of your services. Similar to how Logs Dashboard works, Monitoring dashboards will automatically show charts for resource types that are deployed in the environment. As you add resources, charts are automatically added to the resource type's default dashboard. However, you can still create your own dashboard and customize it to your preferences, should you decide to add other signals that are more relevant and remove any of the suggested ones. The default dashboard serves as a good starting point.

A chart displays one or more metrics over a specified window of time. It does the necessary math to take timestamped values and group them into plottable values depending on the chart type and configurations. Ultimately, you get a picture that represents how that metric is evolving over time. For example, there are metric charts for queries, network connections, CPU utilization, memory utilization, and a few others in the default Cloud SQL dashboard. The following figure shows what the **queries** chart looks like and a snippet from the metrics list documentation that gives details about this particular metric:

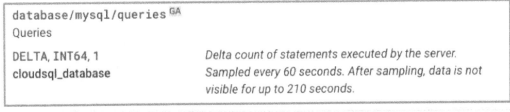

From the metric description, we can infer that at each data point, we are looking at the **delta count** of queries executed against the database from the last 60 seconds.

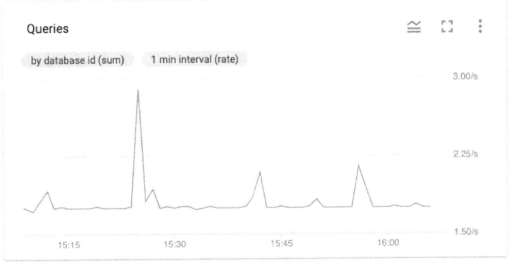

Figure 6.4 – Metric chart for Cloud SQL queries

From the metric description, we can infer that at each data point, we are looking at the **delta count** of queries executed against the database from the last 60 seconds.

You can build your own metric charts using the **Metrics explorer** feature in **Monitoring**. After defining what metric(s) to show, along with filters and/or labels, the aggregator type (sum, average, count, and so on), and the period over which to aggregate data, you can save a chart to a dashboard and/or generate a shareable URL for it. You can also simply use the **Metrics explorer** for ad hoc analysis and not save the resulting chart. The following figure displays an example custom chart for the **Memory utilization** metric of a **Cloud SQL Database** resource:

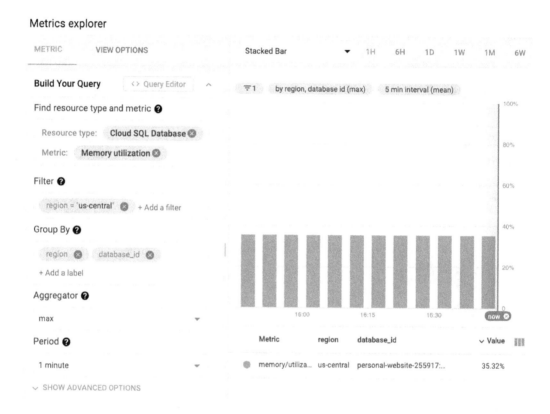

Figure 6.5 – Using the Metrics explorer

This chart is only selecting metrics for Cloud SQL databases in the **us-central** region and grouping them in the chart by **region** and **database_id**. The aggregation function used is **max** and the period is **1 minute**, which means the maximum memory utilization values measured over 1 minute are displayed in a timeline. The chart type selected was **Stacked Bar**. Only one database resource is providing this metric in this example, hence the single bar color and legend. A **Save Chart** button (not shown in the screenshot) will give the option to save this chart to an existing custom dashboard or to a new dashboard that gets created with the saved chart.

Monitoring alerts

In Cloud Monitoring, you can create alerts to notify you via some notification channel you define that something requires attention. In practical terms, an alert indicates that the value for a specific metric has deviated from what you consider to be acceptable from a quality of service and reliability perspective. On the **Alerting** page of the Cloud Monitoring service, you can create an alerting policy, which will include the following:

- **A condition**: A combination of target metric and threshold configuration

- **A notification target**: Who should be notified via what means

- **Steps to fix the issue**: Optional troubleshooting documentation with instructions on how to act on the alert

Alerts set the foundation upon which an incident response strategy is built. Ideally, you should create alerts that are *actionable*, that is, indicating something needs to be acted on; for example:

- An application is down.

- An application's response time is too long.

- A user's identity is presenting signs of anomalous behavior.

In contrast, an alert that says that a managed instance group's CPU utilization is high when autoscaling is already configured for the group on a CPU threshold is not useful. If that group fails to scale in time to prevent availability and response time SLOs from not being met, then you'd want an alert defined to capture those outcomes specifically, not the fact that the underlying CPU utilization was high for a moment.

When creating alerts, it's safer to err on the side of caution by having alerts generate more false positives (alerts on events that didn't quite require attention) than false negatives (alerts *not* generated when things did indeed require attention). However, too many alerts may put you in a situation where there is a lot of *noise* and very few *signals*, which can create "alert fatigue" in operations personnel handling them. In any case, alerts must not be ignored, which is why they must be constructed to be actionable and useful.

The last section of this chapter will discuss best practices around defining an alerting and incident management strategy.

A word on SIEM and exporting logs

A **Security Information and Event Management (SIEM)** is an integral part of an enterprise's monitoring landscape, especially for larger enterprises that need a dedicated system for a security management system. Google Cloud has the **Security Command Center** service, which offers some SIEM capabilities. Still, you can have any third-party SIEM solution that supports the ingestion of logs and events from Google Cloud (most solutions have "connectors" or "modules" for each public cloud platform to facilitate the integration). You can configure log exports in Google Cloud to send logs to, for example, the Cloud Pub/Sub service, from where it can be streamed to SIEM log collector software. You can also configure the export of logs to Splunk, a SIEM solution for which Google Cloud offers native integration. Logs exports are managed in the Logs Router tool within Cloud Logging. You set up exports by defining a *logs sink* destination and which logs to include, plus an optional exclusion filter.

For an overview of how log exports work and common logging export and integration scenarios, go to `https://cloud.google.com/logging/docs/export`. We will revisit Google Cloud's Security Command Center in the next chapter.

Now that we have covered the monitoring landscape in Google Cloud with the main services, tools, and capabilities, let's now get hands-on to better internalize some of the concepts we've discussed so far.

Hands-on with Cloud Monitoring

We will deploy an App Engine application and an uptime check and observe its metrics and logs. We will then deploy a second version of the same application, which now contains a custom metric that we'll add using the Cloud Monitoring API. Finally, we will visualize it all using charts and dashboards:

1. Go to the GCP console (`console.cloud.google.com`), then click on the shell icon in the top-right corner of the screen to activate Cloud Shell. Alternatively, you can use your own local shell if you have installed the Google Cloud SDK:

Figure 6.6 – Activating Cloud Shell

2. In the Cloud Shell terminal, run the following command to authenticate:

```
$ gcloud auth login
```

Then follow the onscreen instructions to log in to the right account.

3. Now, run the following to create a new project:

```
$ gcloud projects create --name chapter-6 --set-as-
default
```

When prompted, press *Y* to confirm the autogenerated project ID.

4. Next, we need to associate a billing account with this project. First, if you don't know what your billing account ID is, run the following:

```
$ gcloud beta billing accounts list
```

Then, run the following command, replacing PROJECT_ID and ACCOUNT_ID with your project ID and the account ID copied from the last command's output:

```
$ gcloud beta billing projects link [PROJECT_ID]
--billing-account [ACCOUNT_ID]
```

5. Now run the following to download files for this chapter:

```
$ git clone https://github.com/PacktPublishing/
Architecting-Google-Cloud-Solutions
$ cd Architecting-Google-Cloud-Solutions/ch6/
app-monitoring
```

Note: If you have previously done this in Cloud Shell, the directory will already exist, and you won't need to clone the repository again. Your Cloud Shell files persist across sessions.

6. Next, from the ch6/app-monitoring directory, deploy the application by running the following:

```
$ gcloud app deploy
```

Choose a region to deploy App Engine to when prompted, and type *Y* and hit *Enter* to confirm the deployment.

7. After a few minutes, the deployment will be ready. Copy the website URL displayed in the output and paste it into your browser. You should see a simple web page, as follows:

Hello There!

This is the main page

Figure 6.7 – Web app front page

8. Still in the browser, append /cat to the URL and press *Enter*. The website should display a cat picture. Then, replace /cat with /dog, and press *Enter* again to reload the page. The website should now show a dog picture.

9. Open the console in your browser, make sure you select the **chapter-6** project from the project selection dropdown in the top-left corner (look under the **All** tab if it doesn't show up under the **Recent** tab). Now, expand the navigation menu on the left, scroll down until you see the **Operations** menu sub-group, and click on **Monitoring**.

   Because we haven't created a Workspace, the platform will create one automatically in the same project. This project will be the Workspace host project.

10. On the left-side menu, click on **Uptime checks**. Then, click on **Create Uptime Check**.

11. Fill in the **Create Uptime Check** form as follows, clicking **Next** each time to go to the next configuration group:

    Title: webapp-upcheck

    Target

    -- **Protocol**: HTTPS

    -- **Resource Type**: App Engine

    -- **Service**: Select your App Engine service from the dropdown

    -- **Path**: Leave empty

    -- **Check Frequency**: 1 minute

Response Validation

-- **Response Timeout**: **5 seconds**

-- **Log check failures** Should be checked

Alert & Notification

-- **Create an alert** Should be checked

-- **Name**: Leave as the default suggested

-- **Duration**: **1 minute**

-- **Notification Channels**: Click on **Notification Channels**, then **Manage Notification Channels**. A new tab or window will open. On the new page, search for **Email** and click on the **Add New** button next to it. Fill in your personal email in the **Email address** field. Finally, fill in the **Display Name** field with a friendly display name of your choice, then click on **Save**. Go back to the page you were previously on. Click on **Notification Channels** again and on the refresh icon to refresh the list. Your email should show up as an option listed with the display name you chose. Select it, then click **OK**.

Finally, click on **Create**.

12. Click on **Overview** in the left-side menu to navigate back to the Cloud Monitoring overview page. Explore the interface – note your newly created uptime check and some charts automatically generated for you. There won't be much data yet, as we just created the app. After a minute or two, your recently completed uptime check should be displayed with a green icon next to it, indicating a healthy service.

13. Still on the **Overview** page, click on **Go To Logging**. If you don't see this option, expand the navigation menu, and click on **Logging** under the **Operations** menu sub-group.

    You will be taken to the **Logs Explorer** page. At the bottom, you will see the query results pane, which should be showing all the logs you've received so far, in the last hour, which is the default time range. Take some time to explore this interface. Find the time range selector in the top-right corner, and feel free to change it. Expand some of the log entries and see their details. Note that you can further expand log entry fields.

14. On the **Query builder** page, paste the following inside the query text editor:

```
resource.type="gae_app" AND
protoPayload.status >= 400
```

15. Then, click on **Run Query**. The preceding query looks for HTTP error codes in App Engine applications (specifically, searching for HTTP status codes that are equal to or greater than 400). The result shouldn't display anything since there shouldn't have been any errors at this point.

16. In a new browser tab, paste in the app URL you got previously but, this time, append a dummy URL path such as /dummy. Hit *Enter* a few times. You should be getting HTTP 404 errors since this path was not implemented in the application.

17. Wait a few seconds, then repeat *step 14*. You should now see log results for those HTTP 404 events as shown in the following figure:

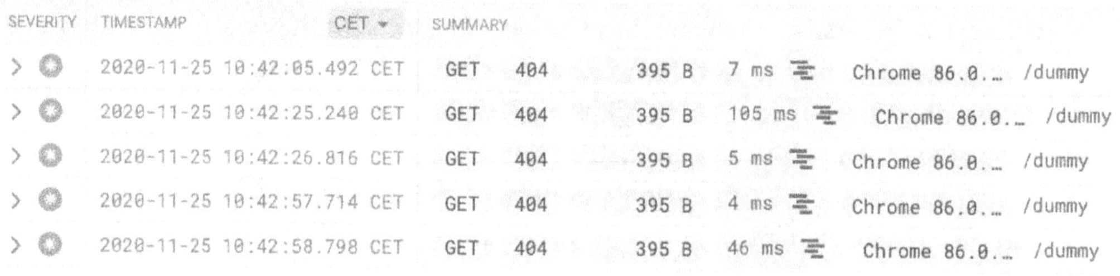

SEVERITY	TIMESTAMP	CET ▼	SUMMARY						
> ⊙	2020-11-25 10:42:05.492 CET		GET	404	395 B	7 ms ≋	Chrome 86.0.…	/dummy
> ⊙	2020-11-25 10:42:25.240 CET		GET	404	395 B	105 ms ≋	Chrome 86.0.…	/dummy
> ⊙	2020-11-25 10:42:26.816 CET		GET	404	395 B	5 ms ≋	Chrome 86.0.…	/dummy
> ⊙	2020-11-25 10:42:57.714 CET		GET	404	395 B	4 ms ≋	Chrome 86.0.…	/dummy
> ⊙	2020-11-25 10:42:58.798 CET		GET	404	395 B	46 ms ≋	Chrome 86.0.…	/dummy

Figure 6.8 – Query results for GAE HTTP errors

Note how you can see, from the log entry, the exact URL path that originated the error. You can also see the payload size (**395 B** in this example) and the response latency indicated next to it.

18. To see all logs related to Google App Engine apps, run the following query:

```
resource.type="gae_app"
```

Take some time to explore the log entries you get. Can you spot the ones corresponding to your previous /cat and /dog path requests? Can you guess how you would build a query to filter by URL path?

> **Tip**
> It will be very similar to the query in *step 14*, except instead of **status**, it will be a different field.

So far, you've created an uptime check and observed some of the logs generated by App Engine, including logs for HTTP error events. Let's continue to build our monitoring solution by setting up charts, dashboards, and metrics:

1. Expand the navigation menu, then search for and click on **Monitoring**. You should now have more information displayed on the default charts. Click on **Dashboards**, then click on **App Engine**. Click on your project ID.

   This is the default dashboard for App Engine apps. Google automatically selects some metrics that are commonly used to monitor this type of resource. Have a look around.

2. Click on the **System** tab to display system metrics. Search for the **CPU Usage (megacycles)** chart, then click on the triple dots icon in the top-right corner of the chart, and click on **View in Metrics Explorer**, as shown in the following figure:

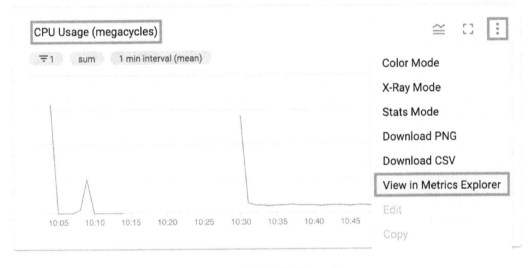

Figure 6.9 – GAE CPU Usage chart

3. On the **Metrics explorer** page, change the **Aggregator** field to **max**. Keep this window open. Now, open a new tab or window and paste in the URL of the app, this time with the path suffix /gowild. This will make the app run a CPU-intensive process. Switch back to the tab with the **Metrics explorer** and observe the graph for a few minutes. You will notice a high peak in the CPU megacycles metric. Note it may take about 5 minutes for you to see the change.

4. Navigate back to **Dashboards**. In the **HTTP** tab, note the **Response Latency** chart. There should be a noticeable peak there as well, corresponding to the CPU-intensive request.

5. Back to Cloud Shell, navigate to the ch6/app-monitoring-custom-metric directory, and edit the content of the app.yaml file to replace YOUR_PROJECT_ID with your project ID. You can edit it using nano, vim, or by clicking on **Open Editor** in the top-right corner of Cloud Shell to open the graphical editor (click on **Open Terminal** once done to go back to the terminal). Now, run the following to re-deploy the app – this time, a different version of it that includes a custom metric:

```
$ gcloud app deploy
```

6. Type *Y* and hit *Enter* to confirm and wait a few minutes for the deployment to complete. When done, paste the URL in the browser to verify that the application works. You should see the same front page as before.

7. Reload the web app by appending the /cat path to the URL. Once you see a cat picture, hit *Enter* a couple of times. Then, replace /cat with /dog and hit *Enter* a few times once the page has loaded.

8. Back in the console, on the **Monitoring** page, click on **Metrics explorer**. Under **Build Your Query**, in the **Find Resource type and metric** field, type gae_instance, and then select **GAE Instance**. Then, in **Select a metric**, type in pets. Then, select custom/pets_requests_PROJECT_ID where PROJECT_ID is your project's ID. That's our custom metric. If it says **No results**, wait a few minutes and then retry (it may take about 5 minutes and you may need to refresh the page before retrying – maybe get coffee?). For **Aggregator**, select **sum**. You should then see a chart for our custom metric that measures the number of pets requested (this metric is incremented each time the /cat or the /dog URL paths are called). The resulting chart should look similar to the one in the following figure:

Figure 6.10 – Custom metric chart

Run a few more requests on either the /cat or /dog URL path, and you should see the chart update with new values.

Feel free to explore Cloud Monitoring and Cloud Logging a little further. In the next steps, we're going to disable the application and test the **Uptime check** feature.

9. Expand the navigation menu, then search for and click on **App Engine**. Click on **Settings**, then on **Disable application**. Confirm by typing your project ID, then click on **Disable**.

10. Navigate back to the **Monitoring** page. Click on **Uptime checks**. You should see that it now indicates the application is down, and you should also receive an email soon to alert you about it. Click on **Delete** and then **Confirm** to delete the uptime check (otherwise, you will receive many alert emails!).

Congratulations, you now have some hands-on experience with implementing monitoring in Google Cloud!

Clean-up

To delete the project for this chapter and all resources in it, run the following command:

```
$ gcloud projects delete [PROJECT_ID]
```

> **Important note**
>
> In the next section, when we explore how to investigate application performance issues, there will be implementation challenges for you. If you wish to do them, then keep your resources to reuse the same application for the challenges. You can then execute the clean-up step when you're done, at the end of the chapter.

Being able to generate and visualize metrics and logs is not enough for a good monitoring foundation. In the next section, we will explore how to define a strategy for reacting when things go awry.

Investigating application performance issues

Observability doesn't only apply to the systems and the environment where the applications run. It is also useful to observe what is going on *inside* your applications, down to a specific line of code. In Google Cloud, the suite of tools that allow you to perform these tasks includes: Cloud Debugger, Cloud Trace, and Cloud Profiler. In this section, we're going to learn what we can do with each of them.

Cloud Debugger

Cloud Debugger allows you to inspect the state of an application in real time by capturing its *call stack* and variables at any point in your source code using non-intrusive *snapshots*. The service is not impacted while you do this, so you can run it in production code. You can run Debugger on any compute service and against code written in several languages, namely: Java, Python, Go, Node.js, Ruby, .NET, and PHP. However, not all features are available in all combinations of language and runtime. You provide Debugger with access to your source code either from the local filesystem in the compute node where it is running or from the code repository where it was pulled from. To use it, you need first to enable the Cloud Debugger API in your project and then enable it in your code. The exact instructions for enabling it in your code are language- and environment-specific, and you can check them at https://cloud.google.com/debugger/docs/how-to.

The underlying compute resource will need permission to upload Debugger telemetry. App Engine and Cloud Run platforms have this access by default. For other runtimes, such as GCE, GKE, or VMs running elsewhere, you will need a service account that has been assigned the *Cloud Debugger Agent* role to run your code. While the GAE standard environment will automatically select your source code, other platforms such as GAE flexible environment, GCE, GKE, and Cloud Run require a `source-context.json` file in the application's root folder. This file can be generated with the `gcloud` command `gcloud debug source gen-repo-info-file`. Or, from the **Debugger** page in the console, you can also use the *Alternative source code* option to manually select the source code location.

As an example, to instrument Python code running on GAE standard environment to use Cloud Debugger, you would do the following (after enabling the Cloud Debugger API in your project):

1. Add `google-python-cloud-debugger` to your `requirements.txt` file. This is the Python library for Cloud Debugger.

2. Add the following code snippet to be initialized early on, for example, in the main function toward the top:

```
try:
    import googleclouddebugger
    googleclouddebugger.enable(
        breakpoint_enable_canary=False
    )
except ImportError:
    pass
```

Optionally, you can set the `breakpoint_enable_canary` value to `True` in the preceding code snippet. This will enable the **Canary snapshots** feature, in which case Debugger will "canary" snapshots of your code by creating them on a subset of your running instances (if there is more than one) each time they are set. After Debugger verifies that the snapshot does not adversely affect any of the instances, it then applies the snapshot to all of them. If you want to be on the safe side in production environments, you should enable this.

Because the preceding example refers to GAE's standard environment, there's no need to set up permissions or define a source code location. You can already use the Debugger page in the console to dynamically add breakpoints (referred to as "log points") to your code and inspect it in real time.

As a challenge to you, try to implement Debugger in the application code for this chapter's hands-on activity.

Trace

Cloud Trace is a distributed tracing system that collects request response latency data from your applications. It displays near real-time performance insights and provides in-depth reports for service performance degradations. Cloud Trace is a useful tool for troubleshooting performance issues or spotting performance optimization opportunities.

Cloud Trace supports several mainstream languages, and you can instrument your code using either the Cloud Trace API or **OpenCensus** (now merged into **OpenTelemetry**), an open source set of libraries for telemetry collection. Cloud Trace creates a timeline for each *trace* to show you how the latency of a request is broken down into downstream requests (referred to as *spans*), showing the latency contribution from each. The **Trace Overview** page in the console provides useful high-level information such as a list of the most frequent URI and RPC calls, recent traces, autogenerated performance insights, and a daily analysis report.

Cloud Trace runs on Linux and supports GCE, GKE, GAE flexible, and the standard environment, as well as VM instances running outside of Google Cloud. In the GAE standard environment, applications coded in certain languages don't need to use the Cloud Trace libraries, as they are built into the runtimes. For an up-to-date list of supported languages and whether they support the OpenCensus library or not, go to `https://cloud.google.com/trace/docs/overview#language_support`.

Google Cloud recommends using OpenCensus (or OpenTelemetry) to instrument your application, if the option is available, as opposed to Google's native client libraries. OpenTelemetry is actively in development and is the recommended package. Based on availability for each runtime and order of preference, a list of recommended client libraries is documented at `https://cloud.google.com/trace/docs/setup#recommended_client_libraries`. You will find links to specific instructions for instrumenting code based on the language and runtime from this same URL.

With the GAE standard environment and the Python runtime, Cloud Trace is enabled by default. If you did the hands-on activity in the previous section, you can go to the **Trace** page in the console and you should be able to visualize traces for the various requests that you performed during that assignment. You will see something similar to the following screenshot:

Figure 6.11 – Cloud Trace for the GAE standard environment application

Profiler

Cloud Profiler is a low-overhead profiling service that continuously gathers CPU usage and memory allocation information from applications. This is different from regular monitoring metrics for CPU and memory resources in that it attributes the values it reads to the source code that generated them. Therefore, it helps you identify how the specific components of your application consume resources, and potentially components that may be responsible for performance bottlenecks. In addition, Cloud Profiler doesn't simply provide an aggregate CPU and memory utilization value, but the more insightful profile metrics:

- CPU time

- Heap

- Allocated heap

- Contention

- Threads

- Wall time

The supported languages are Python, Go, Java, and Node.js. Not all languages support all the aforementioned profile types, however. Similar to the Cloud Debugger and Cloud Trace services, all compute services in Google Cloud are supported, as well as VM instances running outside of GCP.

Cloud Profiler collects data for about 10 seconds every minute for each instance where the service is configured. According to Google, the overhead of the CPU and heap allocation profiling at the time of the data collection is less than 5 percent. Amortized over the execution time and across replicas of services, that comes down to less than 0.5 percent on average.

Language-specific instructions to set up Cloud Profiler are available at `https://cloud.google.com/profiler/docs/how-to`. As an example, to instrument Python code running on the GAE standard environment to use Cloud Profiler, you would do the following (after enabling the Cloud Profiler API in your project):

1. Add `google-cloud-profiler` to the `requirements.txt` file.

2. Add the following code snippet to be initialized early on, for example, in the main function toward the top:

```
import googlecloudprofiler

try:
    googlecloudprofiler.start(verbose=3)
except (ValueError, NotImplementedError) as exc:
    print(exc)   # Handle errors here
```

As a challenge to you, try to implement Cloud Profiler in the application code for this chapter and test it out.

You should now have a strong foundation for designing for observability using Google Cloud. You've learned about the many tools, features, and capabilities available on the platform. Next, we will look at some best practices.

Designing for observability with best practices

In this section, we will discuss some common observability architectures, how to build a cost-effective monitoring solution, and how to define an alerting and incident management strategy.

Choosing the right observability architecture

As mentioned previously, a Workspace can monitor up to 100 projects. It doesn't mean that you should always have a single Workspace for all your projects if you have less than 100 of them. Let's look into some of the common observability architectures and their pros and cons. However, before we get into these design patterns, it's useful to understand the three IAM roles related to monitoring:

- **Monitoring Viewer**: Gives the user read-only access to the Cloud Monitoring console and APIs

- **Monitoring Editor**: Gives the user read and write access to the Cloud Monitoring console and APIs, including writing monitoring data to a Workspace.

- **Monitoring Admin**: Gives the user full access to Cloud Monitoring.

Because a Workspace can monitor multiple projects, these roles are assigned in the Workspace's host project. Their permissions will also apply to all monitored data provided by the service projects. With that in mind, let's look at different ways to architect your monitoring solution.

One Workspace, multiple projects

This design pattern is about having a single Workspace to manage all your projects. For example, if you have one project per development environment, you may have an additional host project for your Workspace, responsible for monitoring all environments (for example, development, test, and production). While this has benefits from the perspective of providing a centralized, single pane of glass through which to monitor all your environments, it has some security implications. Whomever you assign the role of Monitoring Viewer to in this project will have access to read monitoring data from all environments, development, and production included. This may or may not be desirable in your organization. This architecture is illustrated in the following figure:

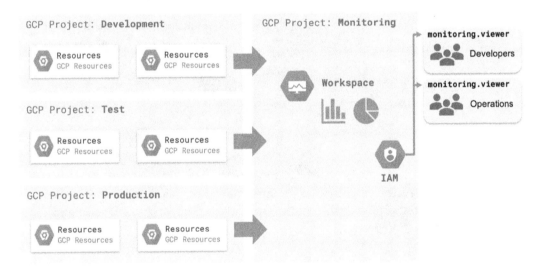

Figure 6.12 – One Workspace, multiple projects

In this example, two groups of users (**Developers** and **Operations**) *both* have access to live monitoring data from resources in all environments.

Multiple Workspaces, multiple projects

In this design pattern, you can create more than one Workspace to provide some isolation between different projects' monitoring data. A typical example would be to have one Workspace for non-production environments (for example, dev, test) and another Workspace for production and QA/staging environments. This way, only a restricted list of individuals will have access to live production monitoring data. An example of such architecture is shown in the following figure:

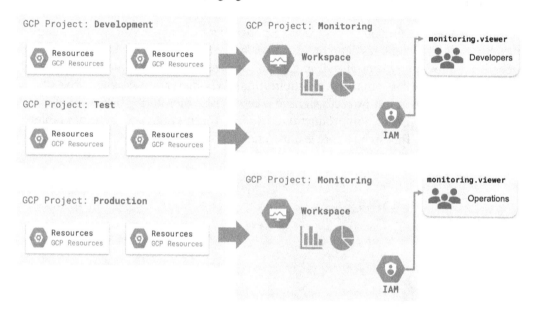

Figure 6.13 – Multiple Workspaces, multiple projects

In this example, the **Developers** group has permissions to view monitored resources in the development and test projects, whereas the **Operations** group can view monitored resources in the production project.

One Workspace per project

This architecture provides maximum isolation by setting up one Workspace per project (each project being the Workspace host project itself). If you have strict IAM policies with different user groups for each project, this may be the ideal choice from an identity governance perspective. This may also be the case if you have various projects for different departments or divisions within the organization, with complete segregation of monitoring responsibilities between them.

Defining an alerting and incident response strategy

When things go wrong, you don't simply want the responsible team to "do their best" and come up with a solution. You want a formal and structured incident response methodology. As a cloud architect, you will often be involved in determining one.

User trust depends largely on the consistency and reliability of a service. Therefore, your incident response matters for maintaining user trust and, as a consequence, user retention. In particular, users appreciate transparency. If you provide detailed information about an ongoing incident and reassure users that steps are being taken to mitigate it, they will be more tolerant and understanding.

According to the SRE book, the basic principles of incident response are identified as the following:

- Maintain a clear chain of command.

- Designate clearly defined roles.

- Keep a working record of debugging and mitigation as you go.

- Declare incidents early and often.

These principles have the common goal of enforcing consistency in the incident response strategy by reducing duplication of effort, clarifying who is doing what, and to whom everyone reports. Keeping a record of mitigation steps will help prevent similar incidents from re-occurring, or, at the very least, help speed up their resolution. Waiting until everything is over to document steps is not recommended, as the motivation to do so and the ability to recall actions taken precisely will quickly fade.

Before incidents happen, there are a few best practices to have in place. Firstly, establish clear criteria for what constitutes an incident and when one should be declared. It's often better to err on the side of caution, that is, set criteria that generate more false positives than false negatives.

Secondly, establish the default communication channel in advance for incident updates (email, Slack channel, and so on). To save time, create templates that are easy to fill in for those responsible for communications.

Finally, train the team on incident response and conduct drills and practices to help reinforce the knowledge.

When an incident happens, appoint one person to be in charge of the incident. They shall delegate the necessary tasks to others and coordinate their execution. They shall also maintain a log of the incident state and response. Communication is crucial, so let those affected know you're responding, and make it clear who they can contact. Finally, once everything is over, prepare a **postmortem** report. Determine the root cause(s), and update playbooks and checklists. In short, document everything learned in a way that makes everyone's life easier next time something similar happens. It's important to maintain a *blameless culture* and avoid pointing fingers at individuals if the incident was caused by human error. Blaming doesn't benefit anyone and is counterproductive. For a postmortem example that you can use as a reference template, go to `https://sre.google/sre-book/example-postmortem/`.

When should an incident be declared? There's no short and simple answer to this question. It will depend on the criticality of different applications to your organization and on thresholds you define based on what reliability levels your organization wants to ensure for them. What triggers an incident will typically be an alert, a combination of different alerts, or even the duration of an active alert. Once an initial triage is carried out and it is confirmed that an incident should be declared, the incident response process starts. The following figure illustrates the full lifecycle of an incident:

Figure 6.14 – Incident response workflow

It is not uncommon for an incident to be caused by an infrastructure or application change. In this case, if your team works with Infrastructure-as-Code and DevOps practices, you will likely be able to respond quickly by rolling back the latest code change(s). In fact, a DevOps (or SRE) culture of communication and shared responsibilities is crucial to prevent the disconnect from development and operations that is often the reason issues go unsolved for too long. The SRE culture, as we shall learn more about in *Part 3, Designing for the Modern Enterprise*, revolves around collaboration, communication, and sharing. Reliability will be improved in the long run when you and your team are able to respond to and learn quickly from mistakes and are able to share the lessons learned.

Optimizing the costs of monitoring

There are many components of the monitoring landscape in Google Cloud that cost nothing. For example, Cloud Audit logs, metrics, dashboards, uptime checks, Debugger, and Profiler services. These are all free. However, where monitoring starts to incur costs is typically in heavy network traffic for monitoring data (for example, streaming logs) and storage (for example, the retention of log exports). Or, when you use services beyond their free quotas, such as the Cloud Monitoring API and Trace. Just like pricing, quotas can change over time, but here are some numbers to give you an idea of the current free allotments in Google Cloud:

- **Logging**: 50 GB per project
- **Monitoring**: 150 MB per billing account
- **Monitoring API calls**: 1 million per project
- **Trace ingestion**: The first 2.5 million spans per project
- **Trace spans scanned**: The first 25 million spans per project

In general, logs sent to Cloud Logging are free to generate but billed for storage. Exporting logs to external services is also something you pay for, based on storage size.

You can estimate costs from the **Billing** page in the cloud console. By going to **Reports** and filtering resource usage by SKU to include, for example, *Log Volume* and *Metric Volume*, you will be able to check current usage and cost, as well as cost forecasts based on current trends. If you, for example, determine that you have been paying more for log volume than expected, you can navigate to the **Metrics Explorer** in Cloud Monitoring and run a query on all resource types (choose **Global** for resource type) and the metric **Monthly logs bytes ingested**. You will then be able to identify in the resulting chart which resource types are ingesting the most logs. With that same logic, you can search for **Metric bytes ingested**, to identify metrics' biggest cost generators. On the **Monitoring** page in the console, you can see a breakdown of the overall metrics ingested by the project (if you have more than one project monitored from the same Workspace) and/or AWS accounts by going to **Settings**.

Cost control best practices are no different for Cloud Monitoring than for other consumed resources in Google Cloud. In short, you need cost visibility first and foremost: know your costs and exactly where they're coming from. Use alerts on metrics related to monitoring ingestion so that you can be notified if things get out of hand. Pay special attention to resources that can generate a high volume of logging data: Cloud Load Balancing, Compute Engine resources with the Logging agent, and resources with many write operations to the Cloud Logging API. Exclude from ingestion configuration log entries you don't need. For example, you may want to exclude *HTTP 200 OK* responses from application request logs, as these may not provide much value but may be generated very often. Finally, when creating custom metrics, choose a reasonable sampling period so that services don't generate large volumes of metric values unnecessarily.

Summary

In this chapter, you learned the basics of monitoring and observability and, in particular, the monitoring principles of SRE. You learned about and explored the monitoring landscape in Google Cloud, with its many tools and features. You learned how to configure services for observability, set up logs and metrics, and visualize them in charts and dashboards. You also got some hands-on experience involving several of the monitoring and logging capabilities on GCP. Finally, you learned how to choose the right observability architecture, the right alerting and incident response strategy, and some best practices for keeping monitoring costs under control.

In the next chapter, we will have an in-depth look at security and compliance in Google Cloud, yet another crucial pillar of great cloud solutions.

7
Designing for Security and Compliance

If you start building your infrastructure thinking of making it secure after the fact, it's a bad start. **Security** is fundamental in any cloud solution design; it's not an afterthought. Integrating security and **compliance** requirements from the ground up will provide you with a robust foundation on which to deploy your applications, with much less effort than trying to do it afterward. In this chapter, you will learn how to design Google Cloud solutions for security and compliance. You will learn how to protect identities, networks, applications, and data. You will also learn how to enforce security and compliance and what tools and services are available on **Google Cloud Platform** (**GCP**) to improve your **security posture**.

In this chapter, we're going to cover the following main topics:

- Understanding cloud security
- Securing identities and access to resources
- Securing networks

- Securing data and ensuring compliance
- Detecting vulnerabilities and malicious activities

Understanding cloud security

In *Chapter 1, An Introduction to Google Cloud for Architects*, we discussed the measures taken by Google to secure their infrastructure and their approach to cloud platform security. We also highlighted the importance of understanding that security is a *shared responsibility*, even in **Platform-as-a-Service (PaaS)** or **Software-as-a-Service (SaaS)** delivery models. Throughout this chapter, we will explore the things that fall under your responsibility, as a cloud architect, to ensure your solutions are secure and aligned with enterprise best practices. We will start by understanding how security is different in modern cloud systems compared to what it used to be in traditional on-premises IT systems, and some of the basic concepts and best practices surrounding cloud security.

Security in the cloud world

There are significant differences in visibility and control points across the layers of the infrastructure in the cloud. With the variety of new cloud services and the velocity with which they can be consumed come new security challenges for cloud-based environments. With new ways for organizations to deploy, manage, and operate systems come new considerations and tools for applying security. In the cloud, there's a balance to be struck between agility and security. Your cloud **security model** will likely differ to some degree from those of on-premises systems. The differences mostly stem from the shared responsibility model and the programmatic capabilities of the cloud. The physical hardware components can be removed altogether from your model, while Google constantly takes measures to ensure that the security of hardware layers meet industry standards and several compliance requirements. From your side, you need to ensure your teams can be empowered to deliver applications and products with the agility that the cloud offers, without jeopardizing the security of your assets.

For a robust foundational security model in the cloud, you need a combination of **preventive** and **detective** controls, with an emphasis on automation. Preventive controls are realized primarily through *policy* and *architecture* and may also include supporting tools such as a *change management system*. On the other hand, detective controls are realized through *monitoring* capabilities that look for vulnerabilities or malicious behavior. In tandem with detective controls are also the *corrective controls* that aim at reducing the consequences and limiting the damage of an incident. This is related to the subject of incident response, which we will revisit later in this chapter.

Policy controls on GCP are *programmatic* constraints that protect your organization from one or more specific threats and their associated business risks. The architecture refers to how the infrastructure is constructed, and it influences the exposed attack surface areas and the protective layers of your digital estate.

A basic security model for organizations working in the cloud is depicted in the following diagram:

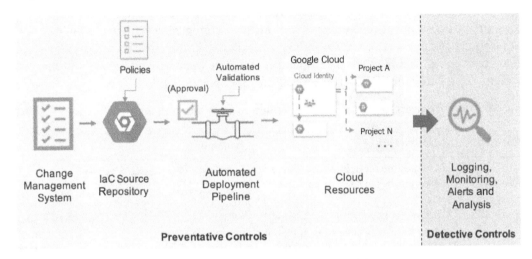

Figure 7.1 – An example security model

This model includes a source-controlled codified infrastructure (Infrastructure-as-Code), which presents opportunities for built-in security. Deploying code through an automated pipeline that has policy validation and approval stages will help bring security to the early stages of development. This approach, in conjunction with the collaborative framework of DevOps, is often referred to as **DevSecOps**. It emphasizes the need to "shift left" and build a security foundation and shared responsibility mindset into DevOps practices. The architecture component encompasses all GCP resources and their configurations, including network connectivity, firewalls, and **Identity and Access Management** (**IAM**) policies. Finally, the detective controls encompass monitoring functions and capabilities to detect vulnerabilities, threats, or anomalous behavior.

Your cloud estate's overall security status, including all security controls and measures in place at each layer of the security model, is referred to as your organization's *security posture*. All the capabilities, recommendations, and best practices that you will learn throughout this chapter are ways for you to achieve a robust enterprise-grade security posture. However, it's important to understand that at the same pace at which your organization incorporates innovation and evolves its business, you need to develop your security posture. It's a continuous process, not a one-off activity.

One of the most significant advantages that the cloud offers for securing your infrastructure from the ground up is the ability to define policies programmatically. Let's learn some of the policy-based controls you can apply as a starting point when building Google Cloud solutions.

Policy controls

In Google Cloud, you can use the **Organization Policy Service** to centrally determine programmatic constraints over the cloud. This includes configuring restrictions on how your resources can be used and establishing guardrails and compliance boundaries for development teams. Ultimately, it helps members do their work with agility without the risk of breaking foundational security and compliance obligations.

Some common use cases for policies are described in the following table:

Constraint	Description	Example
GCP – Resource Location Restriction	Defines the set of locations where location-based GCP resources can be created. A location can be a cloud region (such as us-east1) or a multi-region area (such as asia). A policy applied to a multi-region location doesn't automatically apply to all regions within it. It is to be used for resources that have multi-regional deployment settings.	in: europe, europe-west1
App Engine Service – Disable Source Code Download	Disables code downloads of source code previously uploaded to App Engine.	`disableCodeDownload` is True
Cloud SQL – Restrict Authorized Networks on Cloud SQL instances	A boolean constraint that restricts adding authorized networks for unproxied database access to Cloud SQL instances.	`restrictAuthorizedNetworks` is True
Cloud SQL – Restrict Public IP access on Cloud SQL instances	A boolean constraint that restricts the configuration of public IPs on Cloud SQL instances.	`restrictPublicIp` is True

Compute Engine – Restrict Shared VPC Host Projects	Defines the set of Shared VPC host projects that projects at or below this resource can attach to.	`under:folders/myfolderID`
Compute Engine – Define allowed external IPs for VM instances	Defines the set of Compute Engine VM instances that are allowed to use external IP addresses. VMs not listed in the policy will not be allowed to use external IP addresses.	`is:projects/myprojectID / zones/us-east1-c/instances/ dmzserver1`

Some constraints are not retroactive and will not apply to resources previously deployed, which is why the sooner you apply policy controls, the more effective they will be as preventative measures. You can see a list of all available policies and their documentation at `https://cloud.google.com/resource-manager/docs/organization-policy/org-policy-constraints`. You need an organization node in your resource hierarchy to be able to create and manage policies. You can view, create, and edit policies in the *Organization Policies* page in the console, which is located under *IAM & Admin*. However, a better practice is to define policies in code (using, for example, Terraform templates) and deploy them through a deployment pipeline.

In addition to the organization policies listed in the URL mentioned in the previous paragraph, there are also certain types of policy-based controls that you can apply to tighten the organization's overall security posture. These include the following:

- Limit session and *gcloud* timeouts – from the Admin console
- Disable Cloud Shell – from the Admin console
- Enable Access Transparency and Access Approval – via Google Cloud Support

Limiting session and *gcloud* timeouts can reduce the risk of user accounts being compromised during active authenticated sessions, while disabling Cloud Shell can be a way to prevent resource deployments outside of IaC pipelines. The **Access Transparency** and **Access Approval** controls relate to Google personnel's access to your data and infrastructure. Access Transparency provides you with log data for Google personnel's actions when accessing your content, which may happen for reasons such as fixing an outage or when the Google support team attends to your requests. Those tracked access events can be fed into a **Security Information and Event Management (SIEM)** tool for analysis or kept for meeting compliance and legal obligations.

Access Transparency can be enabled by contacting Google Cloud Support (via `https://console.cloud.google.com/support`, only available for specific customer support levels) and is a prerequisite for enabling the Access Approval feature. The latter enables you to require your explicit approval whenever Google support and engineering teams need access to your content. To enroll in Access Approval, after enabling Access Transparency in your organization, you can follow the guide at `https://cloud.google.com/access-approval/docs/quickstart`.

Now that you've learned about policy controls, you should be able to set up a solid security foundation and set of constraints for your infrastructure. Let's dive a little deeper into the concept of DevSecOps.

Deployment pipelines and DevSecOps

With the technological shift toward "Everything as Code" in the cloud world, it has become possible to define even foundational governance-level entities (such as organizational policies, projects, identities, and role bindings) as code using declarative template languages. When working with infrastructure code and pipelines, you can generally group your resources into one of two categories: *foundation* or *workload* components.

Foundation resources include policies and other security architecture elements and need to be more tightly secured and audited to avoid compliance risks. Infrastructure resources such as Shared VPC networks, subnets, routes, or firewall rules are also included in this category. These resources can be more reliably and consistently deployed across your environments when done through an IaC deployment pipeline.

To "bake" some basic security into your infrastructure deployment pipelines, there are three practices you should consider adopting:

- **Pull request (PR)** workflow: All code needs to be reviewed and approved via a PR workflow before it can be merged into the main branch in the source repository.

- **Automated policy checks**: Security tools should run as part of the build pipeline to validate the code against vulnerabilities and drift from an established baseline. For example, VM images can be scanned for required hardening configurations, and the code can be scanned for clear-text passwords or connection strings. If not successfully validated, the build pipeline must fail, preventing the release pipeline stage from running and deploying an infrastructure that is insecure based on your standards.

- **Approval stage**: A manual approval stage can optionally be incorporated before deployment, so that a human (for example, a security team member) can inspect the code artifacts before they are "released" and deployed. However, having an approval stage is a trade-off of extra security for agility.

These are ways of working that application developers may be used to, but your organization may need to extend existing training and development programs for infrastructure and platform operations staff to include such skills. They may not come naturally to all IT professionals.

A useful tool for applying automated policy checks, if you're using **Terraform** as your template language, is the **Terraform validator** available at `https://github.com/GoogleCloudPlatform/terraform-validator`. It validates Terraform templates against policy rules you define before they are applied. This would be one instance of *Security as Code*, one of the tenets of DevSecOps.

Once you have established your infrastructure pipeline with the foundational elements, you can set up workload pipelines that will include services such as VMs, databases, and **Google App Engine** (**GAE**). The same pipeline (or, optionally, a separate one) may contain application-related elements such as VM images, containers, or application code.

The next step is to define an access control strategy to separate access and management of foundation (infrastructure) pipeline(s) from access and management of workload (services/application) pipeline(s). For example, you may decide to have three deployment pipelines: one for infrastructure, one for services, and one for applications. Then, you can have different teams manage each pipeline, as exemplified in the following table:

Deployment pipeline	Resources	Owner
Infrastructure	Organization policies, IAM policies, projects, folders, VPC networks, subnets, routes, firewall rules	Platform Operations Team
Services	GCE VMs, Cloud SQL, Cloud Pub/Sub	Services Operations/ Automation Team
Applications	VM images, application artifacts	Application Development Team

With this strategy, you impose a clear separation of responsibilities and duties, improving your overall security and reliability status.

Once you have thought through your security model, policies, and resource deployment strategies, you will also need to set up the proper authentication and authorization mechanisms to secure your users' identities and access to cloud resources. We will look next at ways to achieve that, as the first step in defining your security architecture.

Securing identities and access to resources

In *Chapter 2, Mastering the Basics of Google Cloud*, we discussed IAM in Google Cloud and the **principle of least privilege**. You learned that identity is the new *perimeter*, and that it is crucial to protect users' identities first and foremost before thinking of protecting your infrastructure resources. You also learned the resource hierarchy on GCP and how that affects access management. The concepts we laid out in that chapter are fundamental and need to be grasped as a prerequisite for understanding how to secure identities. Therefore, if you haven't done so, I encourage you to read through the *Understanding identity and access management (IAM)* section of *Chapter 2, Mastering the Basics of Google Cloud*, before continuing.

In this section, you will learn about **Cloud Identity** and how to approach authentication and authorization on GCP.

Cloud Identity

Cloud Identity is an **Identity as a Service (IDaaS)** solution used for centrally managing users, groups, and domain-wide security settings. The Identity console page (referred to as the *Admin console*) provides a single pane of glass to manage users' identities and access permissions across your domain. You may remember that some policy controls related to the session and *gcloud* timeout are managed in the Admin console from the previous section. It is not required to be a customer of *Google Workspace* (formerly known as *G Suite*) to be able to use Cloud Identity. If you own a domain (such as `example.com`), but you're not using Workspace, you can simply register your domain as a Cloud Identity domain by following the guide at `https://workspace.google.com/signup/gcpidentity/welcome`. At the end of it, you will also be guided through the process of proving ownership of the domain, which involves adding a DNS record on your domain registrar. Once that is done, the Admin console is ready to use at `https://admin.google.com`. From there, you can manage users and groups, create Identity security policies, view reports, audit logs, and manage devices and apps, including Google Workspace apps if you use them. The Admin console home page is shown in the following screenshot:

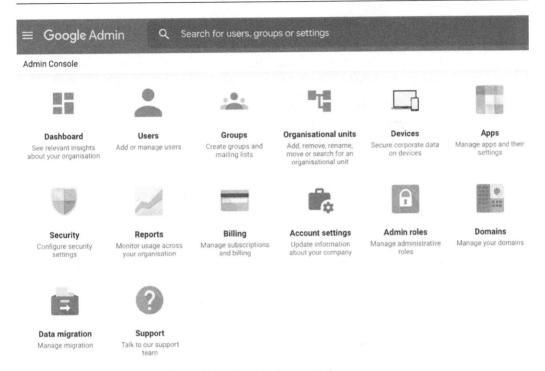

Figure 7.2 – The Admin console home page

The first domain you add will become the primary domain in Cloud Identity, but you can add up to 600 domains as long as you prove ownership for any you add.

The **Google Cloud Directory Sync (GCDS)** tool can help simplify the provisioning and de-provisioning of a large number of user accounts. If your organization already uses a Microsoft Active Directory or LDAP-based identity solution, you can use GCDS to set up one-way synchronization of user accounts to the Cloud Identity domain. To do this, the following steps need to be performed:

1. Set up GCDS locally in your server environment where your LDAP or **Active Directory (AD)** server is.

2. Export data as a list from your LDAP or AD server. You can set up rules to specify how and when the export is generated.

3. Use GCDS to connect to your Cloud Identity domain and generate a list of existing users, groups, and shared contacts; when running the synchronization, GCDS will compare this list with the list exported from LDAP/AD and will update your Cloud Identity domain accordingly to match the source.

GCDS only performs one-way synchronization and, therefore, never writes any data back to the source identity server. You can keep managing your users and groups from your LDAP or AD server, as the "source of truth" for your identities, and periodically synchronize them (using Task Scheduler or a CRON job) to Google's Cloud Identity.

If you wish to extend your AD footprint into the cloud instead and run AD domain controllers on GCP, you can use Google Cloud's *Managed Service for Microsoft Active Directory*. As the name implies, it is a managed service that doesn't require you to provision and manage servers yourself, which are hardened, patched, and provisioned in highly available configurations automatically. It runs AD domain controllers on Windows Server VMs as either a standalone domain or a hybrid cloud domain connected to on-premises. If your organization uses AD-specific tools and features such as Group Policy and **Remote Server Administration Tools** (**RSAT**) in the on-premises AD, these can still be used in the same way to manage cloud-based AD domains on GCP. You can also extend Managed Microsoft AD to multiple regions without requiring VPC peering between them.

To use this service, you start by specifying the name of the Managed Microsoft AD domain and the Google Cloud VPC network(s) where the domain is authorized to be available. VMs deployed in your authorized VPC networks will be able to access and join the managed domain. Managed Microsoft AD provides a *delegated administrator account* to manage your AD domain on GCP, and the *cloud organizational unit*, which can be used to create your AD objects (users, service accounts, additional organizational units, and so on).

As a best practice, you should deploy your managed domain controllers in a Shared VPC to be used across multiple projects, as exemplified in the following architectural diagram:

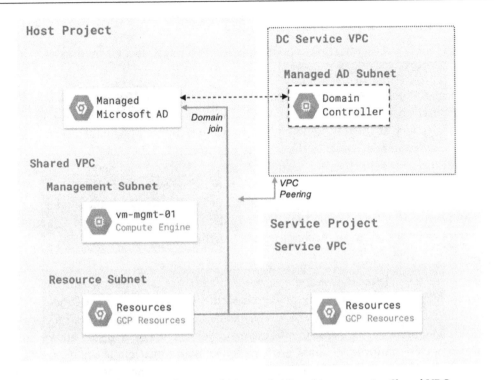

Figure 7.3 – Example of Managed Microsoft AD architecture using Shared VPC

You should set up a dedicated host project for that purpose. When you deploy **Managed Microsoft AD**, the domain controllers are deployed outside of your project and do not appear as VM instances in your project. A VPC peering is set up between the underlying service project used by the managed domain controllers (not controlled by you) and your host project. A Cloud DNS private peered zone is also created in the project to forward DNS queries matching your AD domain to the DNS service run as part of Managed Microsoft AD. One or more resource subnets can be created to host resources that can join your domain. In the preceding reference diagram, a **Management Subnet** is also created to contain VMs to manage the domain controllers.

Your subnets must be properly secured with firewall rules. Also, do not expose domain controllers externally by assigning external IP addresses. Instead, enable Private Google Access on the subnet that you plan to deploy domain controllers in, and ensure that the VM instances can access kms.windows.googlecloud.com, which is required for Windows activation. If internet access is needed, use a Cloud NAT gateway as a more secure approach than a directly attached external IP address. Other managed AD best practices for your specific choice of hybrid and AD forest architectures are documented at https://cloud.google.com/managed-microsoft-ad/docs/best-practices.

Authentication

There are two types of authentication supported by GCP: **Google authentication** and **single sign-on (SSO)**.

Google authentication is the primary mechanism for signing in to GCP. With this approach, the user's password is stored within Google's infrastructure. You can specify password policies such as the minimum and the maximum number of characters and monitor the length and relative strengths of users' passwords. On the other hand, the SSO authentication works with either **Security Assertion Markup Language (SAML)** protocol-based systems, such as **Active Directory Federation Services (ADFS)**, or OpenID-compliant SSO systems. With this approach, Google operates as the service provider and your SSO system as the **Identity Provider (IdP)**. You can manage credentials and use your own authentication mechanisms from within your SSO system.

SSO authentication provides a convenient way for users to use multiple platforms and services with a single username and password. In addition, they don't need to sign in multiple times since there's one single central identity provider to take care of authentication requests. In addition to the convenience, SSO adds some level of security to your users' identities, as managing identities and policies centrally, and also not forcing users to keep track of multiple accounts, are ways to facilitate consistent use of password best practices. You can set up SSO from the Admin console on the **Security Settings** page. Choose between setting up SSO for SAML applications or third-party IdP, and you will get the necessary setup instructions.

Bringing it all together, the following diagram depicts a typical identity architecture, including an Azure AD Domain, GCDS, and Cloud Identity components:

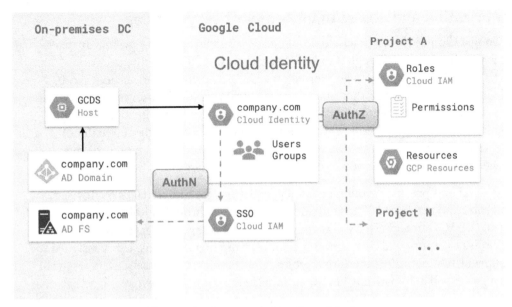

Figure 7.4 – An example identity architecture

In the diagram, **AuthN** refers to authentication and **AuthZ** to authorization. Single sign-on (**SSO**) is set up in this example with **Active Directory Federation Services** (**AD FS**) using SAML. Users and groups are synchronized via a **GCDS** host deployed on-premises.

An important consideration for your authentication strategy is that of **Multi-Factor Authentication** (**MFA**). As a policy set in the identity provider responsible for user authentication, it helps protect identities by requiring one or more extra pieces of evidence (or *factors*) for successful authentication. A **two-factor authentication** (commonly abbreviated as **2FA**) is one instance of it that only requires a second factor (in addition to a password) to confirm users' claimed identities and authenticate them. There are different mechanisms that are standard in the industry for 2FA implementations; the most commonly used ones are those that require a mobile phone (with text messages or app notifications providing the second factor) or a dedicated physical device. Google's **Titan Security Key** is a tamper-resistant 2FA hardware created by Google for that purpose. It is available for purchase on the Google Store and for bulk orders in select countries. More information is available at `https://cloud.google.com/titan-security-key`.

Regardless of your choice of 2FA or MFA implementation, it is a good practice to implement this feature at your identity provider for *all your users*. Privileged identities could benefit from a physical 2FA device, such as Titan Security Key, as they are less vulnerable to sophisticated phishing attacks than mobile phone-based options.

Authorization and access management best practices

The Google Cloud Platform itself does not create or manage users or groups. Instead, a GCP member can be a Google, Google Workspace, or Cloud Identity user or group. Often the easiest way to get started on GCP is by using Gmail accounts and/or Google Groups; however, they offer no centralized method for user management as an unmanaged type of identity. Ideally, you should avoid adding unmanaged Google accounts to your Google Cloud organization. Cloud Identity provides a free tier of the service, which does not include some advanced features such as mobile device management, but still allows you to create and manage users and groups centrally.

As a general best practice, avoid managing permissions for individual users. Instead, assign roles and manage GCP permissions using groups through a Role-Based Access Control (RBAC) strategy. This will reduce operational complexity, as it is much easier to assign roles to groups and then centrally handle group memberships. Users assigned to a group will automatically inherit that group's permissions. Conversely, users removed from a group will automatically have their inherited permissions revoked. For high-risk roles and sets of permissions, you may need to create an exception to this rule and assign permissions to a few individual users instead.

Speaking of high-risk roles, you should have at least two organization admins. This provides some basic "redundancy" and insurance in case one is not available or one of the accounts is lost. However, as a general principle, don't add more than three organization admins. This role is highly privileged and should be limited to very few individuals. In general, the privileged roles you need to pay special attention to are the following:

- Super administrator
- Organization administrator
- Billing account creator
- Billing account administrator
- Folder administrator
- Editor

The **super administrator** role needs special consideration. This role has irrevocable administrative permissions and bypasses the organization's SSO settings to authenticate directly to Cloud Identity. This is to provide access to the Admin console in the event of an SSO outage or misconfiguration. As a best practice, you should configure a super admin email address that is not associated with any particular user. This account is often referred to as the emergency or "break glass" account. It should be further secured with MFA, optionally (and ideally) with a physical authentication device or security key that is kept at a physical location.

The use of this account should be discouraged. It's not for daily administration activities but for particular situations that require it, such as reconfiguring MFA or helping another admin recover their lost account. In fact, access to this account should ideally require the consent of at least two people in the organization. For example, one person may control access to the account's password, while another person controls access to the associated security key or token.

The **Admin audit logs**, which show all tasks performed in the Admin console, should be reviewed frequently as part of a periodic audit process. Optionally, alerts can be set for specific events, such as suspicious sign-in attempts or changes made by an admin. For example, you can set up alerts whenever an API call is made to `SetIamPolicy()`, letting you know when anyone modifies any IAM policy.

It's worth repeating this best practice: *adhere to the principle of least privilege*. If you don't find a predefined role that doesn't include one or a few too many permissions for what is needed, create a custom role and prune it down to only include those permissions required for the job. Remember that, in the context of the GCP resource hierarchy, a less restrictive parent policy will always override a more restrictive child resource policy. For example, suppose you assign a user or group the role of project editor for a project. In that case, you cannot later on restrict their permissions by, for example, assigning them the **viewer** role on specific resource types under that project. The more permissive **project editor** role will prevail because it's been assigned at a parent node. The **Cloud Recommender** service helps hone permissions and enforce the least privilege principle by comparing role assignments with actual permissions used within the last 90 days. If one or more permissions have not been used within that time, Cloud Recommender will potentially *suggest* revoking it based on its machine learning-based intelligence. You can then review and apply the recommendations (they won't be applied automatically). How-to guides for this service are available at `https://cloud.google.com/recommender/docs/how-to`.

Another useful tool in the Google Cloud IAM landscape is the **IAM Policy Troubleshooter**. It helps you examine and troubleshoot IAM policies, to reveal whether a member's roles include permissions related to a specific resource and, if so, which policies bind the member to the role(s). Simply put, given an email, resource, and permission, the Policy Troubleshooter will generate a report. This service can be accessed via the console, *gcloud*, or the REST API. For the maximum effectiveness of this service, the user running it must have the **security reviewer** role.

In *Chapter 6, Configuring Services for Observability*, we highlighted the importance of audit logs as a record of all administrative activities on GCP. Audit logs include permission changes and other IAM-related activities and cannot be disabled. Identities with the Cloud IAM role **logging/logs viewer** or **project/viewer** will be able to view IAM audit logs. As a best practice, review these types of logs regularly and export them to Cloud Storage to store your logs for more extended periods of time.

You've now learned ways to secure your identities, which go a long way toward improving your security posture. Next, you will learn how to secure networks, an important component of infrastructure security.

Securing networks

Networking plays a fundamental role in securing your infrastructure. A network designed to be open and permissive is what allows attackers to move laterally and penetrate further into systems once they get in. In *Chapter 3, Designing the Network*, we discussed the concept of **zero trust security**. The main point to remember is that you should always assume a breach, making design decisions that protect your infrastructure *when* a breach happens. What that means for networks is that you should always ensure traffic is implicitly denied, while only specific IP addresses and network ports are allowed in the firewall on an as-needed basis. Another way to frame this is to assume each network request in the environment is coming from a compromised server or an open, untrusted public network. What can you do to minimize the impact such requests can have? **Isolation** and **firewalling**.

Isolating networks by design

Start by isolating different environments (for example, development, test, production) into their dedicated isolated network. There should not be any link between these networks. If you have services that must be shared across different environments (such as a managed AD domain controllers), you can use a Shared VPC design. In this configuration, network policy and controls for all network resources are managed centrally. This enables a clear separation of responsibilities for different teams in the organization: a team is responsible for ensuring the networks are secure across all projects and environments, and other teams are responsible for deploying and managing resources running on those networks. You can also have different Shared VPCs each contained within a single project. For example, you may have one shared network for most of your workloads and resources and a *restricted* network where the most sensitive data is placed. You can then enforce tighter security controls on the restricted network to mitigate data exfiltration risks. This can be done with, for example, **VPC Service Controls**.

This Google Cloud service allows you to create perimeters that protect the resources and data you specify. Resources within a perimeter are only accessed privately from clients within authorized VPC networks, and data cannot be copied to unauthorized resources outside the perimeter. In addition, clients within a perimeter and with access to resources will not have access to unauthorized resources (even if public) outside the perimeter. This service adds a layer of isolation and security defense that combines network- and access-based restrictions around resources and services within a VPC. The following diagram shows an example Shared VPC design that includes a restricted Shared VPC with a **VPC Service Control perimeter**:

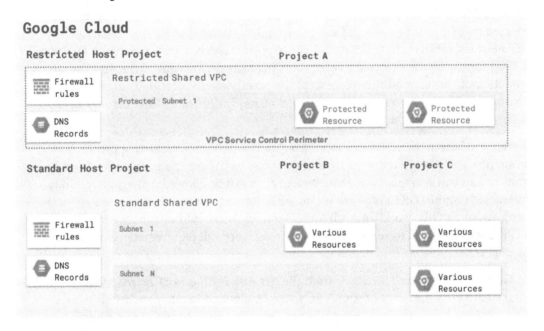

Figure 7.5 – Example Shared VPC design with VPC Service Control

Instructions for creating a service perimeter are available at `https://cloud.google.com/vpc-service-controls/docs/create-service-perimeters`.

For hybrid connectivity scenarios, the **Dedicated Interconnect** service maximizes security and reliability by setting up a direct link between your on-premises network and Google Cloud. This direct connectivity reduces the risk of **man-in-the-middle** attacks that are a potential threat for publicly routed traffic.

Using firewalls

Firewall rules are essential to protect your network. As discussed in *Chapter 3, Designing the Network*, you should avoid using the overly permissive default firewall rules that come with the default and auto mode networks. Make sure communications not explicitly allowed are denied. To facilitate firewall rules management, you can use **network tags** as logical labels that you can apply to VMs and reference from your firewall rules. For example, if you have several VMs in a web server cluster, you can assign them the network tag `webserver` that you then use to create firewall rules, such as one that allows ingress from any source to a `webserver` tag on an HTTPS port. Network tags can be added or removed from VMs by users with **owner**, **editor**, or **compute instance admin** roles. Those are types of roles you should assign carefully to your organization's users, as they entail permissions that can affect your security posture, such as setting network tags. You could optionally create a custom role for users managing VMs with all the permissions of the compute instance admin role, except the permission to set tags. Thus, adding or removing tags can be controlled by a deployment pipeline or another automated mechanism that involves an approval stage.

One thing to keep in mind when adopting a zero trust network security approach is that specific services will require access to certain external dependencies to work, and some services will also require specific ingress access to be allowed. For example, **Google Kubernetes Engine** (**GKE**) requires you to whitelist some cluster control plane services when you have a GKE workload with ingress traffic. You should search for each service's specific documentation to see whether there are any firewall requirements to be aware of and what is the most up-to-date information.

The **Firewall Insights** tool, available from the *Network Intelligence Center* service on GCP, allows you to view the usage of your VPC firewall rules and identify and troubleshoot traffic patterns. It's useful in showing you not only what communications are being blocked and which should potentially be allowed for a service to work, but also the opposite: what communications are happening that were never meant to be allowed. Firewall Insights can be used for live debugging or to analyze firewall rules' action over a specified time period. The following screenshot shows an example of the kind of information it provides:

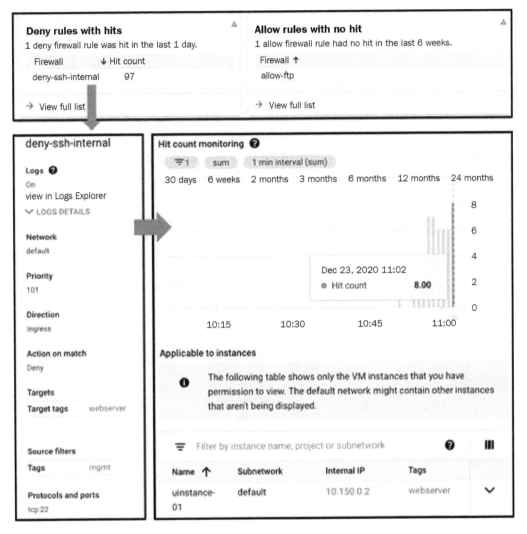

Figure 7.6 – Firewall insights example

Cloud Recommender will also show recommendations based on detected shadowed firewall rules by the firewall insights tool. You can use this feature to remove *allow* rules that have not been used during an observation period, which defaults to 6 weeks but can be set from 1 day to 24 months. It can be a useful way to automate the pruning process of firewall rules in your network, albeit with the risk of removing a legitimate firewall rule.

If your organization requires a **next-generation firewall** (**NGFW**), you may want to consider alternatives to Google Cloud's Firewall service. Luckily, GCP has partnered with several security-centric companies to offer their products from within the Google Cloud Marketplace. These tend to be pre-packaged VM solutions that you can quickly deploy to **Google Compute Engine** (**GCE**) VMs, including a custom image with pre-installed software and, usually, accompanying documentation for installation steps and usage. Although the solution is "packaged", you still get in the end an IaaS solution, which you will have to manage to a larger extent than you would a GCP-native service. However, it's a good way of getting more robust, specialist features. Examples of partners with available NGFW offerings in Google Cloud are Barracuda Networks, Check Point Software Technologies, Fortinet, and Palo Alto Networks.

For web applications, you should consider the advanced protection of a **Web Application Firewall** (**WAF**). **Cloud Armor** is Google Cloud's native offering of a WAF service that works in conjunction with the global HTTP(S) load balancing service to protect your internet-facing applications against the most common web-based attacks, including **Distributed Denial-of-Service** (**DDoS**) attacks. You can customize defense techniques based on your **threat model** and your application's specific technologies and vulnerabilities. Threat modeling is a useful security practice that aims to identify potential threats and define mitigation strategies, preferably early on in the design process. Most threat modeling methodologies will, at a minimum, elicit answers to the following questions:

- What resources are to be protected?

- What can go wrong and what are we going to do about it?

- Are we doing a good job at mitigating threats?

If your organization's IT environment currently doesn't have a threat model, start by creating an application and infrastructure architectural diagram and work to answer the three preceding questions.

In Google Cloud's network Premium Tier, user traffic to an external HTTP(S) load balancer enters the **Point-of-Presence** (**PoP**) closest to the user, which means Cloud Armor prevents unwelcome traffic from consuming your resources or entering your VPC networks. You can also use Cloud Armor in combination with Cloud CDN to keep your origin servers protected on cache-miss events and dynamic requests that bypass the CDN servers. To use Cloud Armor, you can simply enable it as a configuration option within the global HTTP(S) load balancing service. In Google Cloud's partner security ecosystem, you will also find marketplace WAF products from NGINX, F5 Networks, Qualys, and Fortinet.

For extra protection of your website against automated attacks and fraudulent activities such as scraping, credential stuffing, and automated account creation, you may want to consider **reCAPTCHA Enterprise**. This service protects websites from spam and abuse by challenging users and using advanced risk analysis techniques to tell humans and bots apart. The way you implement this service is by embedding a snippet of JavaScript on pages that require protection, enabling signal collection between reCAPTCHA Enterprise servers and the end user's machine. This service also works with mobile apps, and platform-specific instructions are available at `https://cloud.google.com/recaptcha-enterprise/docs/how-to`.

Securing your network communications and keeping malicious bots out will offer a strong level of protection for your infrastructure. However, for the vast majority of organizations, their most crucial asset to be protected and kept away from malicious agents' hands is their data. The security controls we've explored so far certainly offer a degree of protection against data exfiltration, but we will explore next what additional measures you can take to ensure your data is safe.

Securing data and ensuring compliance

The first step toward efficiently securing your data is classifying it. After all, not all data is created equal, and you don't want to spend the same measure of effort and money on protecting every type of data.

Classifying your data

As discussed in *Chapter 5*, *Architecting Storage and Data Infrastructure*, data can be classified according to sensitivity levels. Example levels could be *restricted*, *sensitive*, and *unrestricted*. Alternatively, the levels could be **confidential**, **internal use**, and **public**. A three-tier classification system works well in most cases, but it could be different for your organization. The basis for classification can either be the data's content itself, the context surrounding the data (for example, which application or business function created it?), or a manual classification. A data classification policy could look like the following:

Sensitivity level	Data types
Confidential	Credit card numbers, customer personal data, social security numbers, intellectual property, application keys and secrets
Internal use	Internal correspondence, contracts, IT service management (ITSM) information, system and application logs, architectural diagrams
Public	Public website content, marketing materials

On GCP, the **Cloud Data Loss Prevention** (**Cloud DLP**) service allows you to discover, classify, and apply protection policies to your most sensitive data. It supports structured and unstructured data from several GCP-based sources, such as Cloud Storage, BigQuery, and Datastore, as well as any other sources capable of exporting content to a Cloud DLP streaming content API. Cloud DLP includes **Optical Character Recognition** (**OCR**) technology to recognize text in images before classifying them. Once your data is classified, you can start thinking about whether and how you should secure each data type in your environment.

Securing data at rest

In Google Cloud, data at rest is encrypted by default in all platform products. A data is "at rest" when it's not being transferred over the network but simply stored on a GCP service for eventual retrieval. This includes VM disks, disk snapshots, and data stored in Cloud Storage or any other GCP service. Data at rest is encrypted at the storage level using AES256, with the exception of a smaller number of persistent disks created before 2015 that use AES128.

> **Important note**
>
> The **Advanced Encryption Standard** (**AES**) is a specification for the encryption of electronic data that is used worldwide. AES-encrypted data has an associated key size used for encryption, which can be 128, 192, or 256 bits. The larger the key size, the stronger the encryption. If you wish to learn more about the inner workings of this cryptographic technique, check out the publication at `https://www.nist.gov/publications/advanced-encryption-standard-aes`.

The **data encryption keys** (**DEKs**) are stored near the data and are themselves encrypted with keys, a processed referred to as key wrapping. You can manage the wrapping **key encryption keys** (**KEKs**) using Cloud **Key Management Service** (**KMS**) on GCP. KEKs are further encrypted (wrapped) by an internal master key exclusively stored and used within Google's central KMS, which is redundant and globally distributed. The Master Key is distributed in memory for faster retrieval and backed up on hardware devices. Each Cloud KMS server fetches a copy of the **Master Key** during startup as a hard dependency, and a new copy is retrieved every day. The **Master Key** is refreshed by Google on a monthly basis. The full hierarchy is illustrated in the following diagram:

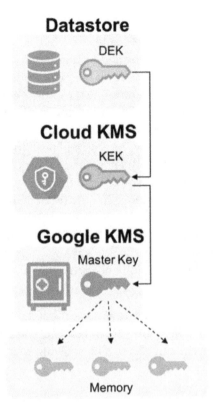

Figure 7.7 – Encryption key hierarchy

When you opt to manage the **KEKs**, they are referred to as **customer-managed encryption keys** (**CMEKs**) and can be used for cloud services such as Cloud Storage, Cloud SQL, Compute Engine, Kubernetes Engine, and several others. A full list of CMEK-integrated services is available at `https://cloud.google.com/kms/docs/using-other-products#cmek_integrations`. You can also optionally choose not to keep your encryption keys in Cloud KMS but elsewhere (on another cloud platform or on your on-premises network), in which case they are referred to as **customer-supplied encryption keys** (**CSEKs**). These can only be applied on Cloud Storage and Compute Engine services.

The objective of encrypting data at rest is to ensure that in the event of data exfiltration, the contents will not be accessible without being in possession of the encryption keys, effectively rendering the data unusable by the attacker. Therefore, properly securing your encryption keys is paramount for making sure that data encryption at rest is effective.

Securing data in transit

It is not enough to keep your data encrypted at rest if, when accessed over the network, it is transmitted unencrypted. A man-in-the-middle attack would, in this case, be successful in obtaining the content without the possession of any encryption keys. To also protect your data in transit, you should consider enforcing the end-to-end use of TLS-encrypted application protocols such as HTTPS or **TDS** (short for **Tabular Data Stream**). Google Cloud already does its part by securing communications between the users and the **Google Front End** (**GFE**) using TLS. However, you still need to do your part to ensure traffic between GFE (at Google's edge POP) and your application components within VPC networks are encrypted. You can more easily achieve this with services such as HTTP(S) load balancing and SSL Proxy load balancing. To fully implement end-to-end encryption, you can also ensure that communication between your frontend load balancer and your backend instances are encrypted with the choice of secure backend protocols. The caveat is that, in this case, you must install private keys and certificates on your backend instances or endpoints (which, however, don't need to match the load balancer's frontend SSL certificates).

Encryption of network traffic with SSL certificates is depicted in the following diagram, with the scenario on the left-hand side showing full end-to-end encryption with backend SSL certificates, and the one on the right-hand side showing encryption only up until your application frontend:

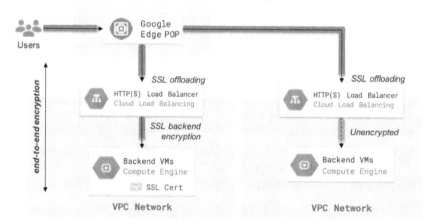

Figure 7.8 – Protecting data in transit with network traffic encryption

For hybrid connectivity, you can encrypt the communication between your on-premises networks and VPC networks with Cloud VPN, which applies IPSec encryption protocols on the connection. Alternatively, you can use Cloud Dedicated Interconnect, in which case traffic is not encrypted by default but it consists of a direct, private connection that effectively reduces the risk of network eavesdropping.

Beyond encryption, there are categories of data exfiltration events that you should be aware of, for example:

- Outbound emails

- Uploads to external services

- Downloads to insecure devices

- Rogue administrators and employee terminations

All of these pose a risk of sensitive data being compromised or intellectual property being stolen. Google's documentation on recommended preventative measures for such events is an excellent reference and is available at `https://cloud.google.com/security/data-loss-prevention/preventing-data-exfiltration`.

Managing secrets, keys, and certificates

Your SSL certificates, keys, and secrets in general should all be stored securely in an appropriate secret management service that keeps them stored safely and offers guardrail features for you to restrict and audit access. On GCP, you can use **Secret Manager**. This service allows you to store, manage, and access secrets as binary blobs or text strings. You can use it to store sensitive information such as database passwords, API keys, or TLS/SSL certificates used by applications. Individuals with the appropriate access will be able to see the contents of secrets. On the other hand, Cloud KMS allows you to manage cryptographic keys and use them to encrypt or decrypt data, but not view, extract, or export the keys.

Access to secrets can be controlled with Cloud IAM. There are five curated IAM roles that create a default separation of duties for secret management:

- **Secret Manager secrets assessor**: Enables examination of the payload

- **Secret version adder**: Enables the addition of new versions to secrets (that is, rotating them)

- **Secrets version manager**: Enables creating and managing versions of secrets

- **Secret Manager viewer**: Allows the viewing of metadata of all Secret Manager resources

- **Secret Manager admin**: Allows access to perform all administrative activities on all Secret Manager resources

You should leverage these roles to incorporate the separation of duties into your secret management processes, and you should also consider having multiple secret repositories. For example, it makes sense to have different repositories for different environments and/ or folders representing different departments/teams. That way, you can more granularly define access control and the separation of responsibilities.

Google Cloud also offers the **Certificate Authority Service**, enabling you to deploy and manage private **certificate authorities** (**CAs**). You can access it via the console, under the *Security* menu group. You can create a root or a subordinate CA and configure its key and cryptographic algorithm from a key stored in Cloud KMS. After you have created one or more CAs, you can request and manage certificates from the same service menu request. Using certificates issued by a privately managed CA on your internal systems can help optimize cost and efficiency in generating and rotating certificates. You should not use this for internet-facing applications since users' web clients won't be able to recognize and trust your private CA. For those applications, you should rely on a public, recognizable CA to issue your certificates. Certificates have an expiration date by design and must therefore be renewed regularly.

As a good practice for improving your security posture, certificates, keys, and secrets must be rotated periodically. You rotate a certificate by issuing a new certificate to replace the previous one. Similarly, you rotate a secret by adding a new secret version to an existing secret. Older certificates can be revoked (if not already expired), and older versions of a secret can be disabled to prevent them from being used. Specific instructions on creating secrets and versions for each available API option are documented at `https://cloud.google.com/secret-manager/docs/creating-and-accessing-secrets`. Keys in Cloud KMS can either be automatically rotated by configuring automatic rotation on an existing key, or manually rotated via the console, `gcloud`, REST API, or a supported programming language API. Specific instructions for each option are available at `https://cloud.google.com/kms/docs/rotating-keys`. You should consider rotating keys automatically and on a regular schedule. Some industry standards, such as **Payment Card Industry Data Security Standard** (**PCI DSS**), require regular rotation of keys.

Standards and compliance regulations set forth a number of obligations and requirements primarily related to security (and the security of specific types of data) that you should be aware of. We will delve next into the subject of compliance.

Compliance

There are several industry-specific regulatory frameworks and guidelines meant to protect sensitive workloads in IT systems, whether they are privately owned or in the public cloud. Because of the shared responsibility model in the public cloud, cloud providers ensure that the infrastructure layers under their responsibility meet several compliance requirements. Google Cloud is no exception, and GCP products regularly undergo independent verification and audits of their security, privacy, and compliance controls. Google maintains an up-to-date list of compliance resources (including third-party issued certificates and reports) in its Compliance Reports Manager at `https://cloud.google.com/security/compliance/compliance-reports-manager`.

Some examples of Google Cloud compliance include the following:

- **International Organization for Standardization (ISO)** 27001
- **Health Insurance Portability and Accountability Act (HIPAA)**
- **Federal Risk and Authorization Management Program (FedRAMP)**
- **System and Organization Controls (SOC)** 01
- PCI DSS
- Several others

If your organization has other specific compliance requirements for IT infrastructure, make sure you check the Compliance Reports Manager to see whether Google Cloud offers any attestations.

However, the fact that Google can demonstrate compliance doesn't mean that you're off the hook. There are still many things you will need to pay attention to when designing Google Cloud solutions to ensure that you remain compliant. After all, you will be handling many aspects of data storage and data access control, which are the primary targets of compliance requirements in most cases. Because there's no one-size-fits-all solution when it comes to compliance, it's hard to give prescriptive guidance on how you can achieve it on GCP. However, you should refer to the **Compliance Reports Manager** as your primary source for obtaining information on your specific compliance regulation. From there, you will also find links to additional resources that can be helpful, including the Google Cloud security best practices center, where you can find industry-specific deployment blueprints and documented security best practices based on standards that apply to your organization.

That being said, some of the common practices for meeting compliance requirements are the following:

- **Logging**: Keeping a record of all administrative logs and network flow logs. Admin activity logs are especially important and should be retained for a longer period of time.

- **Separation of duties**: As mentioned a few times in this book, the principle of least privilege and the separation of duties should be applied to prevent risks associated with identity theft or insider threats.

- **Data protection**: All sensitive data should be encrypted at rest and in transit, and access should be controlled and audited regularly. Keys and secrets associated with data encryption and data access should be stored securely and rotated periodically.

- **Data governance**: Business processes and policies must be in place to enforce a regular cadence in reviewing and applying the data protection controls. These will be very specific to the type of controls that need to be enforced and how and with what frequency they should be reviewed.

- **Network security**: A firewall should restrict network connectivity to networks where protected data resides, and log records of each time a firewall rule allows or denies traffic must be kept for a period of time.

In fact, these are security best practices that you should consider incorporating into your Google Cloud solutions irrespective of compliance obligations. Sometimes you will also face data sovereignty requirements, in which case you may be forced to keep all or a subset of your data within a particular geographical region (such as the United States or the European Union). Organization policies offer a great way to enforce the deployment of all your resources to specific Google Cloud regions.

The last piece of our baseline cloud security model involves the detective controls. Let's explore next how they can be approached on GCP.

Detecting vulnerabilities and malicious activity

The detective controls are the various platform telemetry tools used to detect vulnerabilities and potentially malicious activities in the cloud environment. Many enterprises include a security system in their security tooling, which centralizes many, if not all, of the detective functions. On GCP, you can use the **Security Command Center** for that purpose. As either an alternative or in addition to it, you can also use a SIEM product inside or outside of Google Cloud.

Security operations on GCP with Security Command Center

Security Command Center offers a single platform to aggregate and manage security findings on GCP. It was designed by Google to provide both visibility into how resources are configured as well as the ability to reliably detect threats in real time. Security misconfigurations are often in and of themselves a vulnerability for your systems. Therefore, monitoring for misconfigurations is one of its core capabilities in addition to monitoring for common web application vulnerabilities. Security Command Center offers near-real-time visibility into GCP resources and policies, as well as the detection of threats and compliance violations based on industry standards and benchmarks. You should consider using this service if you want to obtain a centralized view of your security and data attack surface and be able to answer questions such as the following:

- What are all the GCP projects and resource types currently deployed?

- What is the deployment history? In other words, what was deployed and when?

- What are the IP addresses exposed to the public?

- What images are running on VMs?

- What are all my assets, and can they be annotated, categorized, organized, and searched?

You attain visibility into your resources with the asset inventory and tracking capabilities. Security Command Center asset discovery runs at least once each day, but you can manually re-scan on demand. Other features include sensitive data identification (through a native integration to Cloud DLP), application vulnerability detection, access control monitoring, and anomaly detection. In addition to the built-in features, Security Command Center also supports inputs from third-party security tools such as Cloudflare, CrowdStrike, and Qualys to detect events such as DDoS attacks, compromised endpoints, and others. Your own applications can also generate custom findings in Security Command Center through the *Findings* and *Sources* API. The resulting assessments are listed in the *Vulnerabilities* tab of the Security Command Center dashboard (accessible from the console, under the *Security* menu group).

Some examples of detected vulnerabilities related to misconfigurations include open RDP/SSH port, a publicly available Cloud Storage bucket, non-enforced SSL, public SQL instance, and public IP address. You will see the associated compliance benchmarks for each vulnerability category to bring your attention to any potential compliance issues you may be facing. There are many possible findings beyond these examples, however, and a full list is available at `https://cloud.google.com/security-command-center/docs/concepts-vulnerabilities-findings`.

This feature is very useful in finding several infrastructure resource configurations that lead to increased attack surface areas when, in many cases, they were just in place due to it being the default option, or because the team who deployed them wanted a more convenient and low-friction solution. Ideally, most of these misconfigurations should be prevented by programmatic policy controls and validations. However, for configuration categories that are not enforced in some way or another, it is very useful to have one single pane of glass through which to quickly assess your environment setup and security posture.

With built-in *compliance monitoring*, Security Command Center allows you to visualize compliance status reports for a few popular compliance regulations such as CIS 1.0, PCI DSS, and ISO 27001. In addition to vulnerability assessments and compliance monitoring, you should also leverage the bult-in active **threat detection** capabilities. These include **Event Threat Detection** and **Container Threat Detection**. The former detects threats that target your Google Cloud assets, providing near-real-time detection based on platform, network, and compute logs. The latter specifically detects threats that target GKE containers, with near-real-time detection of reverse shell execution, suspicious binary execution, and the linking of suspicious libraries. Threat detection findings are automatically written to the Security Command Center and can be exported to Cloud Logging.

Beyond the ability to detect, it's crucial to respond to and remediate vulnerabilities and threats quickly. You can set up security alerting from the Security Command Center through its built-in *Pub/Sub* integration. You set up one or more *Pub/Sub* topics and use the *Security Command Center API* to send notifications for active findings. You can use the definition and organization of notification topics you set to configure the routing of security alerts to the appropriate teams. You can also connect Pub/Sub topics to an external SIEM software. If you wish to centralize all findings notifications into a single SOC or SIEM system, a common pattern is to create a single topic for active findings and integrate that with your client system. If you instead opt for a more modern, DevSecOps approach where each application team owns the end-to-end security responsibilities related to their application infrastructure, an appropriate pattern would be to set up a Pub/Sub topic for each team and use the selection filter in the notification config to determine the finding categories that should be sent to each topic.

There are several IAM roles associated with Security Command Center. A full list of available roles and their set of permissions is available at `https://cloud.google.com/security-command-center/docs/access-control`. You can leverage these many different roles to create a granular access control strategy that takes the separation of duties into account. Security Command Center creates a service account to scan resources and perform vulnerability assessments on your environment. It requires *Security Center service agent*, *Security Center service usage admin*, and *cloud functions service agent* roles. A *Security Center admin* user must grant these roles during the Security Command Center's initial, guided setup.

As with organization policies, you will need to have an organization set up in Google Cloud to use Security Command Center. This service has a free Standard tier and a paid Premium tier. The Standard tier offers basic analytics and vulnerability assessments. In contrast, the Premium tier offers all the features mentioned previously and should be the preferred option for enterprises with strong security requirements.

Logging and SIEM

For more comprehensive analytics of your security findings, you can leverage specialized security and SIEM products that offer these capabilities. If you have a multi-cloud setup or on-premises systems to manage, you can have multiple security sources' data fed to and correlated in these types of products.

For example, Cloud Logging and Security Command Center events can be exported to *Chronicle*, which is purpose-built for security threat detection and investigation at scale. It is a product that is built on the Google infrastructure and is part of Google Cloud. An enterprise SIEM product can also provide centralized aggregation of analytics of security events. Different SIEM tools can integrate with Google Cloud in different ways, but some common methods you can use are the following:

- Direct ingestion from Security Command Center through Pub/Sub topic

- Direct ingestion from a Pub/Sub log sink

- Flat-file ingestion from Cloud Storage or a file server

- Use of SIEM APIs to pull logs from Google Cloud (using Google APIs), or to push logs using Cloud Functions that can take Pub/Sub events and turn them into API calls

In particular, **Splunk** offers an easier integration experience in Google Cloud with the *Splunk Add-on for GCP*. In Cloud Logging, you can set up logging export to Splunk and, from Security Command Center, you can set up a notification config that sends events to Pub/Sub. Google's template solution for streaming Pub/Sub events to Splunk using *Dataflow* is available at `https://cloud.google.com/dataflow/docs/guides/templates/provided-streaming#cloudpubsubtosplunk`.

An example of detective integration architecture is illustrated in the following diagram:

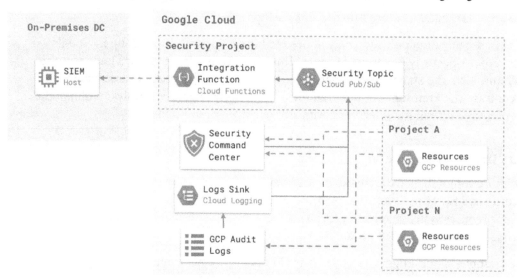

Figure 7.9 – Example of detective architecture

In this example, the SIEM system is located at an on-premises data center, but it could be in another cloud provider or even in a separate GCP project. A single cloud Pub/Sub **Security Topic** aggregates Security Command Center findings and Cloud Logging events such as **GCP Audit Logs**. VPC flow logs can be included as well.

If you have a large environment producing a high volume of logs and events that are too much for a SIEM solution to handle, you can build your own security analysis solutions made up of highly scalable cloud-native tools such as BigQuery, Pub/Sub, Cloud Functions, and Security Command Center. You don't need specific specialized products for building an effective detective system, but you do need to think about a smart alerting strategy. Examples of security risk events to set up alerts for include the following:

- Login events from a super admin or organization admin account
- Privileged Cloud IAM roles granted

- Changes made to Cloud Logging settings
- VPC Flow Logs containing IP addresses outside known and expected ranges
- Changes made on permissions regarding access to sensitive data

If you use BigQuery, you can obtain these and other relevant events by designing SQL queries with appropriate filters to pull the relevant data you want. A non-empty query result can then be used as a trigger for alert notifications.

Ultimately, you must be able to not only detect vulnerabilities and threats, but eventually alert relevant personnel of high-risk events and anything that may potentially indicate a violation of compliance.

Summary

In this chapter, you learned how to design a Google Cloud solution for security and compliance from the ground up. You learned how to apply modern and cloud-based concepts to your security model, such as DevSecOps practices and policy constraints. You then learned how to protect users' identities and access to cloud resources with authorization, authentication, and IAM strategies.

From that foundational level of security, you learned to build a secure infrastructure that protects your networks and your data with access control and encryption, as well as best practices to keep your keys and secrets well protected. Finally, you learned about the security monitoring and operations ecosystem in Google Cloud with Security Command Center and integration options for SIEM products. With all that you've learned in this chapter, you should now be able to confidently take measures to improve the security posture of your organization.

Next, you will start learning design practices for the modern enterprise with big data and data pipelines.

Section 3: Designing for the Modern Enterprise

In this section, you will learn about advanced patterns, technologies, and best practices for designing modern solutions that are robust and highly scalable. You will learn modern application and infrastructure design strategies, including big data pipelines, DevOps and automation, microservices, machine learning, and operations best practices.

The following chapters will be covered in this section:

- *Chapter 8, Approaching Big Data and Data Pipelines*
- *Chapter 9, Jumping on the DevOps Bandwagon with Site Reliability Engineering (SRE)*
- *Chapter 10, Re-Architecting with Microservices*
- *Chapter 11, Applying Machine Learning and AI*
- *Chapter 12, Learning about Operational Excellence and Best Practices*

8
Approaching Big Data and Data Pipelines

Big data plays an essential role in modern enterprise architectures and practices. While traditionally, businesses have been able to store and use their data entirely using relational database management systems, datasets have become too diverse and voluminous to be managed with traditional methods. For data-driven companies, being able to unlock value from data is almost a matter of survival.

In this chapter, you will learn about core big data concepts and services and how to design solutions using **data pipelines** for **ingestion**, **streaming**, **batch processing** and **analytics**. You will also learn about common architectural patterns and get hands-on experience with building a big data solution on GCP. By the end of this chapter, you should have acquired a good understanding of the big data ecosystem on GCP and feel confident with designing solutions that solve real challenges faced by data-driven businesses.

In this chapter, we're going to cover the following main topics:

- Understanding big data services in Google Cloud
- Designing and building data pipelines
- Getting hands-on – a big data case study

Technical requirements

For the hands-on activities in this chapter, you will need a billing-enabled Google Cloud account and, optionally, the Google Cloud SDK installed (if you don't have it, you can use Cloud Shell from a browser). Helper scripts and codes for this chapter can be found at `https://github.com/PacktPublishing/Architecting-Google-Cloud-Solutions/tree/master/ch8`.

Check out the following link to see the Code in Action video: `https://bit.ly/2MONi9U`

Understanding big data services in Google Cloud

As more organizations undergo digital transformation and the number of internet-connected devices entering the market increases, the amount of generated data is growing very rapidly. Traditionally, most businesses have been able to store and use their data entirely using relational database management systems. This is no longer the case. Not only have datasets become so voluminous, but they have also become significantly diversified in their format. Whereas data has traditionally been structured and relational, nowadays, both structured and unstructured data (including images, files, device telemetry data, and so on) has fundamental value for businesses. "Big data" refers to this large, diverse volume of data that is too complex or too big to be managed and processed in a cost-efficient way using traditional methods. In the past few years, however, solutions to this problem have seen mainstream adoption, with technologies such as **NoSQL** database systems and **Apache Hadoop**. Many of these solutions leverage the scale of the cloud to deliver powerful capabilities, and cloud providers have built their own cloud-native services based on these types of solutions.

In *Chapter 5, Architecting Storage and Data Infrastructure*, the differences between relational and non-relational (NoSQL) database systems were explained, with the primary one relating to the consistency versus scalability trade-off. As you may recall, non-transactional data for which strong consistency is not a requirement can be scaled horizontally very efficiently with NoSQL databases. Consequently, these systems can also serve requests much faster and at larger volumes than traditional relational database systems. While this solves the problem of storing and retrieving data to some degree, real business value cannot be derived if there's no intelligence applied to how data is processed, differentiated, and analyzed. This is where data pipelines, which will be a central topic of this chapter, come in. Especially considering how disparate data sources can now be, it is essential to be able to consistently aggregate and extract value from data regardless of where it is coming from and in what format. The ability to do so is a trait of successful organizations across virtually every industry, and this is one of the tenets of the big data paradigm.

Although, by most measures, data is considered *big* only at petabyte-scale volumes, much smaller volumes of data, but which have the same defining big data characteristic, and are expected to grow over time at rapid rates, can still be considered big data. Organizations in this situation will likely be facing some of the same challenges and will need the same solutions. And the sooner they're in place, the better.

In *Chapter 1, An Introduction to Google Cloud for Architects*, the primary strengths of GCP were highlighted, one of which was its big data and **Artificial Intelligence** (**AI**) ecosystem. In addition, as a general characteristic of hyperscale public clouds, you get the capacity to scale to meet the stringent demands of big data systems in a way that would be, for most organizations, prohibitively expensive with privately owned, on-premises data centers. The on-demand availability of storage and processing resources with elastic scaling capabilities is the primary enabling factor for many companies to maximize the value obtained from their data in the cloud. In addition, with the analytics capabilities that were built on Google's extensive developments for their own big data needs, you can leverage some of the best-of-breed technologies in the field as a GCP customer.

In this section, you will learn about some useful big data concepts, and then you will learn about a few different big data services on GCP and what purpose they serve. This should give you an overall picture of the big data ecosystem in Google Cloud before we get more practical.

Big data concepts

If you're not a data engineer or someone who works a lot with data solutions, you may be unfamiliar with some of the concepts surrounding big data. This introductory section will clarify a few important ones.

Data lake

At the beginning of this chapter, we´ve mentioned how one of the main challenges facing data-driven businesses today is the sheer diversity of data formats and their sources. Data can come from anywhere. With the emergence of the **Internet-of-Things (IoT)**, a data source can virtually be any *thing*. That means the first question we need to ask, before even considering using or processing the data, is how to collect and hold all of that data in a single place. This is what a **data lake** is an ideal solution for.

A data lake is a centralized data *repository* where you can collect a vast amount of raw data *in its native formats*. It doesn't matter whether it's structured or unstructured, relational or non-relational; if it's data that you intend to do something with eventually, it can belong in a data lake. A data lake is *not* a filesystem. Instead, it uses a flat architecture to store data, as opposed to a hierarchical file structure, and is often associated with a Hadoop-based object storage architecture. Data lake services also incorporate analytics and data mining functionalities so that you can extract information and derive value from your data. However, the term primarily refers to a storage *strategy* rather than a specific storage *technology*, so different instances and offerings of data lakes will vary in their implementation and capabilities.

The main premise of a data lake is to remove the complexities of ingesting and storing data of different formats and sources while making it possible to efficiently batch, stream, and run analytics processing on the data. *No schema or data requirements are imposed on the source data, and none are defined until the data is used*. The following diagram illustrates the idea of a data lake:

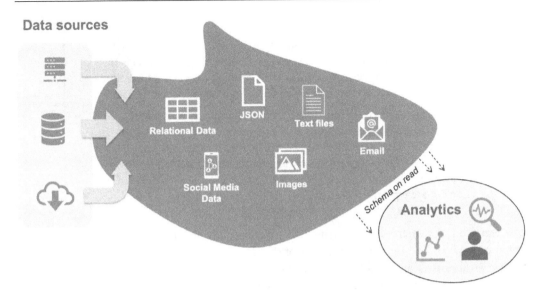

Figure 8.1 – A data lake

By way of an example, a retail company can use a data lake to combine customer data from their **Customer Relationship Management** (**CRM**) platform with their Twitter feed and analytics, incident tickets, marketing campaigns, and other sources from which correlations and insights can be drawn to better understand the customers and sales trends. Other use cases and industries include IoT, smart cities, life sciences research, and cybersecurity.

Data warehouse

A **data warehouse** has similar characteristics to those of a data lake. However, data warehouses are optimized to store and analyze *structured* and *semi-structured* data coming primarily from *relational* database systems. A structure and schema are defined in advance and done in a way to optimize SQL query performance. These systems are meant to be used for **analytics workloads – Online Analytical Processing** (**OLAP**) – and operational reporting of both current and historical data.

> **Important note**
>
> OLAP refers to workloads and tools that are used for data analysis. OLAP systems are characterized by the relatively low volume of queries, which are often complex and involve aggregations. Their primary goal is not to produce data but to produce reports and obtain insights from already existing data.
>
> **Online Transaction Processing (OLTP)** refers to transaction-oriented workloads. OLTP systems emphasize fast query processing, data integrity, and the ACID properties discussed in *Chapter 5, Architecting Storage and Data Infrastructure*. An OLTP system is a critical component that applications rely on to function properly, whereas OLAP systems have an important business function but are typically less critical.

A data warehouse is where data is "cleaned," and eventually also enriched and transformed to enhance analysis and reporting qualities of the data. In contrast to data lakes, the data in a data warehouse is often highly curated for its business value potential. The primary use cases are in the **data science** and **business intelligence (BI)** areas.

The most commonly used data sources are the various structured OLTP data generated internally by enterprises, for example, financial transaction records, and CRM data. The main objective of data warehousing is to provide a *decision support system* for business analysts, allowing them to derive insights from data that can help drive business outcomes. It is common to build dashboards and visualization charts that are regularly updated with the data, shared with stakeholders, and used as basis to make informed business decisions. The following diagram illustrates this idea:

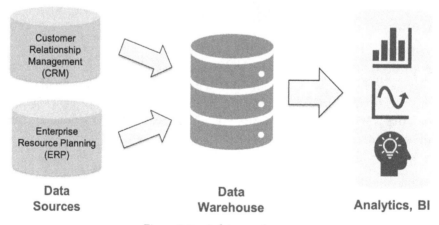

Figure 8.2 – A data warehouse

Data warehouses have been evolving to simplify and improve support for modern big data and analytics workloads. It has been made possible, for example, to integrate Hadoop systems into data warehouses. Because data warehousing is a traditional practice that has been around for some time, *data warehouse modernization* is a common endeavor that aims to bring new paradigms and features to these systems to truly unlock and enable big data capabilities. This typically also entails migrating them to the public cloud, where scale and performance can be leveraged in a cost-effective manner.

Data integration

Regardless of the data storage technologies that are present, **data integration** is one key aspect of big data systems. Data integration is the process of consolidating different types of data from various sources. Data integration services and platforms will generally include tools such as the following:

- **Data ingestion tools**: To import data from various sources.
- **Data cleansing tools**: To clean up "dirty" datasets by modifying them in some way.
- **ETL tools**: To **extract, transform, and load** (ETL) data. This is sometimes the only capability present as it encompasses all the essential integration functions. Depending on the data processing scenario, such a tool may also be referred to as **extract, load, and transform** (ELT).
- **Data governance tools**: To manage data usability and ensure the availability, security, and integrity of data.
- **Data migration tools**: To migrate data between storage systems.

Data integration services can be used, for example, to collect data into a data lake or data warehouse. They can also be used for consolidating data from IoT devices or to replicate databases. Whatever the use case, one of the main problems that a data integration solution aims to solve is the tight coupling between applications (data consumers) and their data. By **decoupling** the data layer from the application layer, a data integration solution can facilitate scalability and performance – two of big data systems' primary concerns. When applications can scale independently from their data, you can also potentially build more cost-effective infrastructure.

Having discussed the most fundamental concepts related to big data, we will now explore the big data ecosystem in Google Cloud.

Big data storage services on GCP

In this section, we will dive into the capabilities available on GCP for scalable data warehousing and data lakes.

BigQuery for data warehousing

One of GCP's main offerings within data analytics services is **Cloud BigQuery**. BigQuery has several features that make it a uniquely good fit for big data solutions. It is a **petabyte-scale** analytics data warehouse service that comprises both a *managed storage* service and a *SQL query engine* component. Therefore, you can load and store data in BigQuery and also query and visualize data in a few different ways. For example, you can run interactive, ad hoc queries or batch queries; you can also create a **view**, which is a dynamic virtual **table** defined by the result of a SQL query; and you can visualize data from BigQuery using **Google Data Studio**, a natively integrated service. We will explore these features briefly in this section and work with them later in this chapter.

Cloud BigQuery is highly available, with a 99.99% uptime availability SLA according to the documentation available on `https://cloud.google.com/bigquery/sla`. Data is automatically replicated and a 7-day history of changes is kept for restoring or comparing data from different times. Beyond the console and regular platform APIs, you can also interact with the service through a command-line tool called **bq**. There are a few different components within BigQuery, and understanding what they are and how they work together is crucial to anyone designing data warehouse solutions with this service. Let's break it down.

Jobs

When you load, export, query, or copy data, BigQuery runs a **job** on your behalf. Jobs are the various actions that you perform on data, except for shorter ones such as listing resources or getting metadata. Job resources are managed by the underlying platform and are automatically created, scheduled, and run. For example, when you programmatically create a data export job, BigQuery schedules and runs the job for you. Jobs execute asynchronously and can be polled for their status.

> **Important note**
>
> When a process runs *asynchronously*, it means that the application that requested it is not actively waiting for the reply (a state that would have been referred to as "*blocked*"). Asynchronous processing is an effective and highly scalable way of performing background tasks, in other words, those for which an immediate response is not needed.

Datasets

The top-level containers that are used to organize and control access to your tables and *views* are called **datasets**. A table or *view* must belong to a dataset, so before moving data into BigQuery, you need to create at least one dataset. A geographic location, which can be a specific or a multi-region area (such as the United States), must be set at creation time and cannot be changed afterward. Also, when a query references multiple tables, all tables must be stored in datasets in the same location. Therefore, when creating a dataset, you need to determine a geographic location with these considerations in mind.

The following screenshot shows one of the example public datasets available in BigQuery:

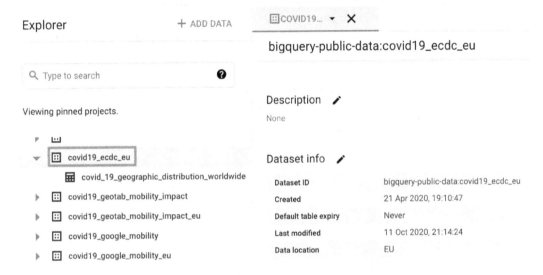

Figure 8.3 – BigQuery dataset

In the preceding screenshot, a publicly available dataset containing the worldwide geographic distribution of Covid-19 cases is shown. Clicking on the dataset exposes information about it, such as **Data location** (**EU** in this case), the date it was created, and the date it was last modified (the **Created** and **Last modified** fields, respectively).

Many other datasets are publicly available on Google Cloud's Marketplace. You can find them at `https://console.cloud.google.com/marketplace/browse?filter=solution-type:dataset`.

Tables and views

Once at least one dataset exists, you can start loading data into it, at which point BigQuery lets you specify a **table's schema**. Alternatively, you can use **schema auto-detection**, as long as data is constituted of known, supported formats. When you load data from self-describing sources such as *Avro*, *Parquet*, *ORC*, or *Firestore* export files, the schema is automatically retrieved from those files. Otherwise, you can manually specify the schema using Cloud Console or inline using the **bq** command-line tool. Alternatively, you can create a schema file in JSON format or provide the schema using BigQuery's API calls for data insertion.

At this point, you 've created a dataset in a geographical location, defined a table schema, or opted for schema auto-detection. Now, you can create a **table** and load it with data. A table, similar to relational database systems, is what contains individual data records organized in rows. In BigQuery, a table can be *native*, backed by its native storage, *external*, backed by storage external to BigQuery, or a *view*, a virtual table defined by a SQL query. You can create them manually via the console or bq tool, or programmatically via the service's API. The following screenshot shows the associated table and schema of the previous Covid-19 dataset example:

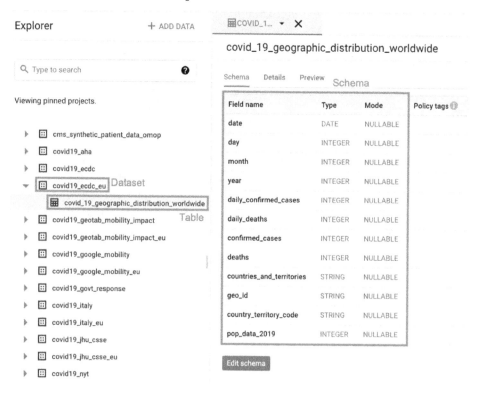

Figure 8.4 – BigQuery table and schema

In this dataset, the table is called **covid_19_geographic_distribution_worldwide**. The schema defines several columns, such as **day**, **month**, **year**, **confirmed_cases**, and **countries_and_territories**. The following screenshot shows an example interactive SQL query against this table that lists the first 1,000 results for Brazil only:

Row	date	day	month	year	daily_confirmed_cases	daily_deaths	confirmed_cases	deaths	countries_and_territories	geo_id	country_territory_code	pop_data_2019
1	2020-03-27	27	3	2020	482	20	2915	77	Brazil	BR	BRA	211049519
2	2020-03-28	28	3	2020	502	15	3417	92	Brazil	BR	BRA	211049519
3	2020-03-29	29	3	2020	487	22	3904	114	Brazil	BR	BRA	211049519
4	2020-03-30	30	3	2020	352	22	4256	136	Brazil	BR	BRA	211049519
5	2020-03-31	31	3	2020	323	23	4579	159	Brazil	BR	BRA	211049519

Figure 8.5 – BigQuery interactive query

Note the excecution details displayed above the results table. They show that, for this particular query, **5.4 MB** of data was processed and it took **0.2** seconds to run it.

BigQuery Table **Access Control List** (**ACL**) lets you set table-level permissions to determine the users, groups, and service accounts that can access a table or view. Therefore, you can give users granular access to specific tables or views without giving them access to the complete dataset. Commonly, read-only permissions are granted to users via the *BigQuery Data Viewer* role assigned at the table level.

The following diagram illustrates the essential components of BigQuery discussed so far:

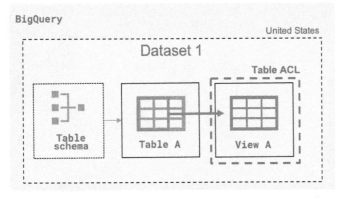

Figure 8.6 – Cloud BigQuery components

In the preceding diagram, **View A** was obtained as a result of a SQL query against **Table A**, therefore containing a subset of its data. A table ACL was applied to that view so that specific team members will be able to access it without having access to **Dataset 1** entirely.

A special type of table is the **partitioned table**. As the name implies, this can be used to divide tables into *partitions*, which is particularly useful for large tables. It can improve query performance in such cases and make it easier to manage and query the data. You can partition BigQuery tables by data ingestion time (in which case BigQuery automatically loads data into *daily* partitions); by either one of the TIMESTAMP, DATE, or DATETIME columns; or by an integer range, based on an integer column within the table.

Another useful capability of tables in BigQuery is **clustering**. When you create a **clustered table**, the data in the table is automatically organized to colocate related data based on content filters you specify on one or more columns. The most typical usage patterns for clustering are when columns have a very high number of distinct values, such as unique identifiers, or when multiple columns are frequently queried together.

Clustering can improve the performance of certain types of queries, such as queries that use *filters* or *aggregation against multiple columns*. Clustering can be applied in conjunction with partitioning, a scenario illustrated in the following diagram:

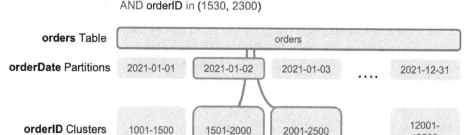

Figure 8.7 – Partioning and clustering in BigQuery

In the example query shown, BigQuery first locates the right partition (in this case, the table is partitioned by **orderDate**, which is a date-type field), and then it looks only at the clusters containing the **orderID** values requested. Because BigQuery's built-in metadata management system stores the range information of columns for each block, it knows what range of values are in each. With the "search space" reduced by combining partioning and clustering, BigQuery can more quickly process queries (especially as the number of blocks become very large). Still, clustering should be preferred over partitioning if the latter results in a small amount of data per partition and/or in a large number of partitions beyond GCP limits on partitioned tables.

Finally, as already mentioned, a table can be defined by a SQL query, in which case it is referred to as a *view*. You can further query the view in the same way you would query any table. Therefore, views are useful as a way to extract a subset of data with specific qualities and use that as a table against which to run further analysis. Thanks to the *granular access control* capabilities of BigQuery, you can grant a Data Viewer role to users and groups at the view level. A **materialized view** is a special precomputed view that periodically caches query results for increased performance and efficiency. Queries that use materialized views are generally faster and less resource-intensive than queries that directly retrieve the same data from the table on which the view is based. They can be useful for workloads that use *common and repeated queries*. A materialized view is always consistent with the base table from a caching perspective. If the table is modified in any way, BigQuery will invalidate the impacted portions of the materialized view and fully re-read the corresponding portion of the base table. It also applies smart tuning to your queries automatically, meaning that if a query against the source table can instead be resolved by querying the materialized view, it will reroute the query to use the materialized view instead for better performance.

To secure tables with sensitive data columns, you can leverage BigQuery's **column-level security** feature by using *policy tags* or type-based classification of data. You can create policies that check, at query time, whether a user has proper access to a column's data. For example, a policy can enforce an access check on a column containing credit card numbers and deny access to those not belonging to a specific IAM group.

BigQuery pricing, reservations, and additional features

Under on-demand pricing, BigQuery charges for queries according to the number of bytes processed, whether the data is stored in BigQuery or an external data source. As of the time of writing, the first 1 TB per month is free, while additional queries are priced at $5.00 per TB in the United States. A useful feature in BigQuery for estimating costs before running a query is the *dry run*. This will not execute the query, but it will estimate the cost of running it based on the query's input.

With flat-rate pricing through the purchase of dedicated resources, BigQuery can be used at a more predictable cost. You can choose flat-rate pricing with **BigQuery Reservations**. Beyond predictability, you get price flexibility by deciding how much capacity to purchase and being billed per second until you delete the capacity commitment. In addition, after you purchase slots, you can allocate them to specific workloads that can then have a dedicated pool of resources available for use. At the same time, any unused slots are shared automatically across other workloads. This gives you better control over the management of resources for your workloads.

Finally, it is worth mentioning that BigQuery also has many additional features for specific use cases, namely the following:

- **BigQuery ML**: For machine learning applications

- **BigQuery GIS**: For **Geographical Information Systems (GISes)**

- **BigQuery BI Engine**: For BI applications

- **Connected Sheets**: For analyzing table rows within Google Sheets

BigQuery is continually evolving to incorporate new features and capabilities. For example, as of the time of writing, *BigQuery Omni* is available in the private alpha stage as a feature that allows you to analyze data across different cloud platforms from within BigQuery. *Data QnA*, also in private alpha, offers the capability to derive data insights from BigQuery through **natural language processing** (**NLP**). BigQuery is such a robust, feature-rich service that discussing each and every one of its capabilities in greater depth would require an entire book. In the hands-on activity for this chapter, you will at least get to familiarize yourself with BigQuery basics and its commonly used features. The most important takeaway of this chapter is that you learn what this service is a great fit for and how you can combine it with other services to build data-driven architectures that can solve big data challenges.

Data visualization and analytics

To make the most out of data, it is useful to have tools that assist in visualizing and running analytics workloads. **Looker** is an enterprise platform for BI, data applications, and embedded analytics. It lets you describe data using a lightweight modeling language called **LookML**. With a model created in LookML, everyone in the organization can create easy-to-read reports and dashboards to explore patterns in the data. Looker works with relational databases such as MySQL, and analytical data stores such as BigQuery. It is a platform-independent service that can be hosted in Google Cloud and easily integrated with data sources such as BigQuery. If your BigQuery use case includes BI, you may want to consider Looker. Data applications and embedded analytics are also two functionalities your BigQuery workloads can benefit from by using Looker.

Google Data Studio is a GCP-native tool for data visualization and analytics. You can use it to turn data into informative, easy-to-read, and shareable dashboards and reports. Google Data Studio connects to a variety of data sources, including BigQuery, MySQL, PostgreSQL, CSV files from Cloud Storage, and even social media platforms such as Facebook and Twitter. A common scenario is to create a view in BigQuery and use it as the data source for visualization in Data Studio, which can be shared with business stakeholders. You can fully customize how you lay out charts to create a dashboard. There is also a report gallery with several samples and templates you can use at `https://datastudio.google.com/gallery`. If you want to have a good idea of what kind of visualizations you can create with Data Studio, I encourage you to check this out.

Apache Hadoop data lake

With **Cloud Dataproc**, you can build fully managed, autoscaling data lake clusters based on **Apache Spark**, **Apache Hadoop**, and other open source frameworks on GCP. You're able to create new clusters quickly and on demand and pay only for the resources you need. Dataproc has built-in integration with other GCP data services, such as BigQuery, Bigtable, and Cloud Storage. You can also connect to Cloud Logging and Cloud Monitoring to use logs and monitoring data. Existing Spark or Hadoop projects can be moved to Dataproc without redevelopment since the APIs and tools are the same as those provided by these open source technologies.

You would use Dataproc for the same real-world use cases as those of, for example, Apache Hadoop. These include the following:

- Analytics and risk assessments for financial services companies
- Customer behavior analytics for retail companies
- Predictive maintenance for IoT devices
- Indexing large-scale data such as log files
- Searching and reporting data

Many of these use cases are made efficient (or possible) thanks to **MapReduce**, a Hadoop component. The MapReduce programming model is one of the core enablers of big data, so let's delve a little bit into what it is and how it works on a high level.

MapReduce

MapReduce is an algorithmic technique for processing large datasets by leveraging distributed computing. A *Map* function processes a key-value pair to generate a set of intermediate key-value pairs, while a *Reduce* function merges all intermediate values and produces outputs. The execution of programs written in this functional style is automatically parallelized to run on a large cluster of commodity machines. The system's runtime takes care of the details, such as the partitioning of the input data, scheduling the program's execution across a set of machines, machine failure handling, and inter-machine communication management. MapReduce originally referred to Google's proprietary technology, which was once used to completely regenerate Google's index of the World Wide Web. It has since become generic and has seen multiple implementations based on different programming languages.

A canonical and straightforward example to illustrate how MapReduce works is the problem of counting the occurrence of each word in a set of documents. This example is illustrated in the following diagram:

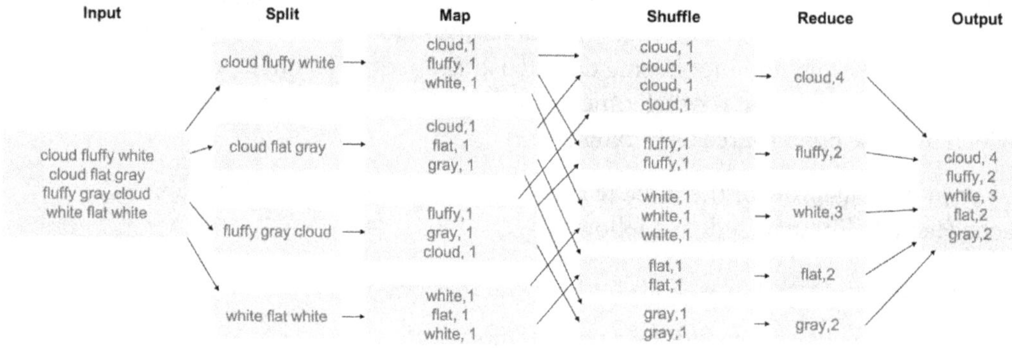

Figure 8.8 – MapReduce example

Note the presence of a **Shuffle** stage, which can be thought of as part of the Reduce function. In this stage, worker nodes redistribute data based on the key produced by the map function. For this example, the keys are the words in the document(s). Evidently, for a small document, a MapReduce program does not give us an advantage over a simpler program that iterates through all the words and accumulates their count. However, for large-scale datasets, such programs may become prohibitively slow to run. MapReduce's ability to distribute computations over potentially hundreds or thousands of worker nodes is what makes it powerful. There is nothing really special about the Map or Reduce functions *per se*, other than they allow a problem to be broken down into parts that can be processed independently. In other words, MapReduce helps us to leverage *horizontal scalability* and parallelism to optimize the solution for a large class of problems.

Because MapReduce relies on distributed computing and data processing, it must be backed by specially designed filesystems to be effective. In Apache Hadoop, the **Hadoop Distributed File System (HDFS)** is the distributed filesystem technology designed to run on commodity hardware and support MapReduce operations. It is the open source version of **Google File System (GFS)**, Google's original filesystem implementation. GFS/HDFS are also capable of storing very large files, potentially of TB or PB sizes, which is an essential prerequisite for big data applications.

When a data lake service is built on Hadoop or other MapReduce-based technology, you know that it is designed to not only handle the storage of large amounts of data, but also to run certain data processing applications much more efficiently than traditional data storage and analytics solutions. Example applications that benefit from the MapReduce model include distributed searching and sorting, log statistics, document clustering, and machine learning.

Using Cloud Storage to build a data lake

A data lake can be built more simply with **Cloud Storage**, when there's no need for MapReduce-based distributed processing. In *Chapter 5, Architecting Storage and Data Infrastructure*, you learned that Cloud Storage is a highly available and durable storage service with high throughput capabilities. Also, you learned that objects in Cloud Storage can be in any format – the service is agnostic to the type of data stored in it. In addition to the extensive integration capabilities with other GCP services and external data sources, these features represent precisely the qualities of a data lake storage service. Cloud Storage also provides filesystem compatibility, allowing objects to be worked with as files in a traditional filesystem.

Data in Cloud Storage is served up with moderate latency and high throughput. Latency can be reduced by placing data in the region closest to where it will be consumed or processed. As a global service, you can have objects replicated across multiple regions for global availability. The archival features of Cloud Storage discussed in *Chapter 5, Architecting Storage and Data Infrastructure*, are also an added benefit since they allow you to reduce the cost of objects that are no longer used or not intended to be accessed frequently.

Consider using Cloud Storage for your data lake solution if you don't require data processing with Apache Hadoop or similar frameworks. Also, if you don't have an immediate use for data and just need a durable and persistent storage location for it, Cloud Storage is your best choice on GCP. Most data-related GCP services support Cloud Storage as a data source, so extending existing data applications to consume Cloud Storage data should be relatively easy. Although you can store any type of data on Cloud Storage, the service is best suited for unstructured data. Structured data, on the other hand, can be stored on services such as Cloud SQL, Cloud Spanner, or Cloud Firestore. Latency-sensitive, non-relational data can be stored on Cloud Bigtable or BigQuery. As mentioned before, a data lake is not a technology or service, but a storage strategy. That means you can have multiple storage technologies comprising your data lake.

Now that you are familiar with big data storage technologies and the related services you can leverage on GCP, we will delve into the data *integration* topic and learn how to design and build *batch* and *streaming* data pipelines.

Designing and building data pipelines

A data pipeline for big data systems must be able to integrate, consolidate, and transform many different types of data from various sources. Other useful supporting capabilities include data discovery, preparation, and management. Let's look at each of these.

Data integration

Google Cloud has a suite of services for data integration functions. **Cloud Dataflow** is a unified stream and batch processing service based on **Apache Beam**. It is a fully managed, serverless service offering with *horizontal autoscaling*. It allows you to create Apache Beam pipelines. These are data integration pipelines that offer functionalities to read, transform, and ingest data. If you're unfamiliar with Apache Beam pipelines and their use cases, one simple example would be a pipeline that writes different data subsets to different data stores based on a filter. Suppose, for instance, that you have a database of books identified by their titles. Your pipeline can extract the books whose title starts with A and output them to a *collection* (referred to as a **PCollection** in Apache Beam), and books whose title starts with B and output those to a separate collection. This pipeline is set out in the following diagram:

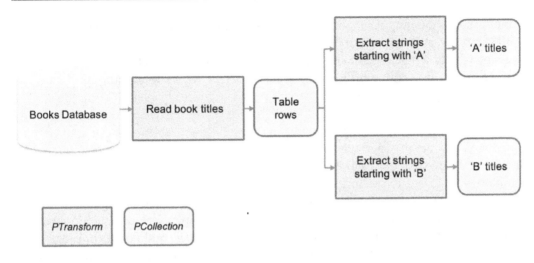

Figure 8.9 – Example Apache Beam pipeline

Each of the actions shown in this example is called a **PTransform** in Apache Beam.

The two different output collections can now be stored separately, for example. You can also eventually transform the data, merge different collections, or join collections from different sources. For example, suppose you had another database of books you wish to merge to the existing one in this pipeline, but one where book titles are written all in lowercase (as opposed to title case, which is how the first database writes them). You could modify the pipeline to read book titles from the second database, transform them to title case, and then merge all titles by applying a *flatten* transform. This pipeline's output would then be a **PCollection** containing book titles from both databases, all in "proper" title case.

A pipeline could also do a more complex operation, such as performing a frequency count on each word in a document (the same MapReduce problem discussed previously). *When you have a standard set of operations that you need to consistently perform on data, you can benefit from using a data pipeline.*

In Cloud Dataflow, you can use the familiar Apache Beam SDKs to build a program that defines a pipeline and then runs it on a highly available and autoscaling service while paying only for resources you use. Thus, you can concentrate on your data processing workload's logical composition rather than the low-level implementation details of distributed parallel processing.

The input source and output sink of a Cloud Dataflow pipeline can be of the same or different types, allowing you to convert data to different formats. Beyond the batch processing of data, a pipeline can also include an unbounded **PCollection**, representing a **data stream** from a continuously updating data source such as **Cloud Pub/Sub**. Cloud Pub/Sub is an asynchronous messaging service mentioned already a few times in this book. It is a useful data integration tool for batching or streaming data from many possible sources into different destinations using the publish-subscribe pattern. It offers *at-least-once*, *in-order* message delivery at scale using either a *pull* or *push* consumption pattern. Multi-region systems can leverage its global message routing for reliable delivery to multiple regions. For the security of your data, the service ensures end-to-end encryption. The main reason to consider Pub/Sub in your data solution design, beyond its scalability potential and rich set of features, is that it decouples services that produce events (messages) from services that process them. It fits into the middleware or event ingestion layer, so it is useful for streaming analytics and modern event-based application architectures. These types of architectures are often referred to as **message-oriented architectures**. The following diagram illustrates an example of such an architecture:

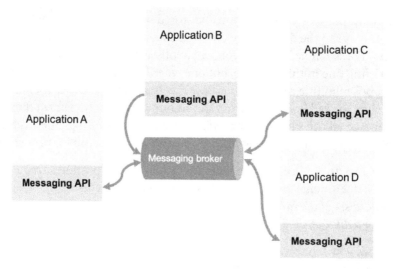

Figure 8.10 – Message-oriented architecture

The core concepts of Cloud Pub/Sub are **topics**, **subscriptions**, and **messages**. A topic is a named resource to which the publishers send messages. A subscription is a named resource representing the stream of messages from one specific topic to the subscribing application. A message is the actual data content being published and consumed, which can optionally include attributes (key-value pairs) added by the publishing application. Communication can be one-to-many (*fan-out*), many-to-one (*fan-in*), and many-to-many. The following diagram illustrates how Pub/Sub works and the relationship between its different components:

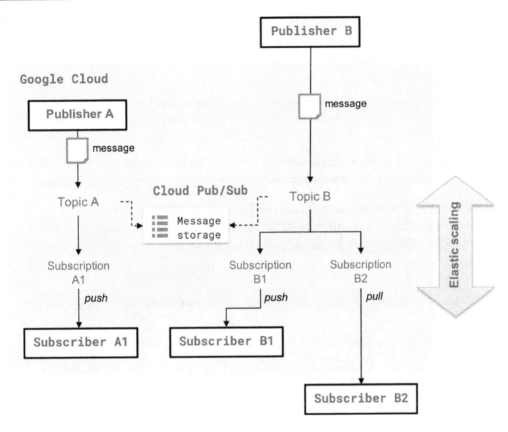

Figure 8.11 – Cloud Pub/Sub example

As you can see, this architectural pattern can facilitate scalability with the decoupling between application components, the asynchronous nature of message delivery, and the elasticity of the messaging layer itself. Cloud Pub/Sub offers durable message storage, which can persist messages for up to 7 days, so even if subscribers are not available for a few days, messages are not lost. Pub/Sub can deliver messages to a **push** endpoint, in which case it sends the message in the body of a POST request; or it can deliver messages via a **pull** endpoint, in which case the subscribing application must pull messages via Pub/Sub APIs (and optionally implement message listeners).

Some common use cases for Pub/Sub are as follows:

- **Balancing workloads in clusters**: Tasks can be queued using Pub/Sub and distributed among multiple workers in a compute cluster.

- **Asynchronous workflows**: For example, an order processing application that places orders on a topic to be processed by one or more workers without blocking or slowing down the main application.

- **Distributing notifications and events**: Event-driven applications and automation systems can subscribe to topics where specific events and notifications are sent. For example, notification of a system component failure can trigger an automated remediation runbook.

- **Distributing logs to multiple systems**: Logs can be written to a topic and be consumed by multiple different systems for different purposes, such as storing and querying.

- **Data streaming from multiple devices**: IoT sensors and devices can stream data to backend processing servers via Pub/Sub.

Cloud Pub/Sub integrates natively with several GCP services that can be either data sources (publishers) or data consumers (subscribers). A real-world scenario that puts together Pub/Sub, Dataflow, and BigQuery as a big data solution could look like the following:

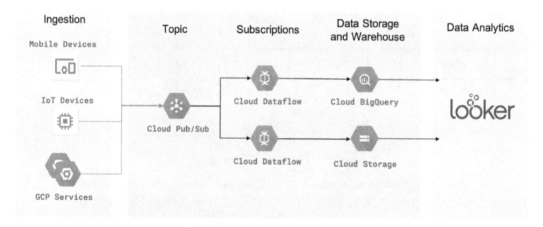

Figure 8.12 – An example big data analytics solution

In this example, **Pub/Sub** has two separate **Dataflow** subscribers. One has a batch subscription and sinks data to **Cloud Storage**, while the other one has a stream subscription and outputs data to **Cloud BigQuery**. The two Cloud Dataflow pipelines perform their own data transformations before outputting the results. **Looker** is used to visualize and analyze data from both places.

Consider using Pub/Sub for your application messaging needs. Whenever a publish-subscribe pattern with asynchronous message delivery suits your messaging requirements, Pub/Sub offers a robust, serverless way of achieving it.

An alternative service for building data pipelines on GCP is **Cloud Data Fusion**, which offers a visual point-and-click interface for *code-free deployment* of ETL data pipelines. It is powered by the open source project **Cask Data Application Platform (CDAP)** (`https://github.com/cdapio/cdap`). It includes a broad library of preconfigured connectors and data transformations that you can apply to your pipelines. For example, suppose you want to fetch compressed data from Amazon S3, decompress it, and store its CSV contents on BigQuery and other types of content from Cloud Storage. You can achieve all of this without any coding by combining *source*, *action*, and *sink* plugin types available in the library to build a pipeline to perform these tasks. CDAP is a layer of software running on top of Apache Hadoop to provide scalable data integration. Indeed, Cloud Data Fusion's service account requires permissions to run Cloud Dataproc jobs because that's what it does under the hood. It automatically provisions ephemeral Dataproc clusters to run pipelines on, and then automatically tears them down once the pipeline run is completed.

The following diagram shows what a Data Fusion pipeline can look like:

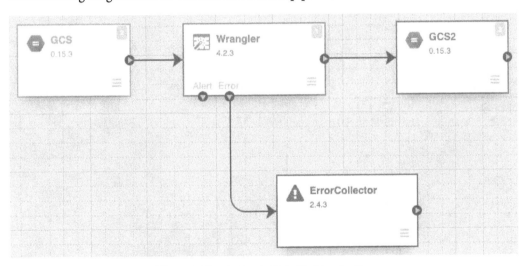

Figure 8.13 – A simple Data Fusion pipeline

The **Wrangler** plugin shown in the diagram can be used to apply data cleansing transformations easily. In this simple example, data is fetched from Cloud Storage, and then cleansed and stored back in Cloud Storage. An **ErrorCollector** node runs on an error to flatten the emitted errors by adding the error message, code, and stage to the record before outputting the result. Each of these plugins can be configured through the UI without any coding. Consider, therefore, incorporating Cloud Data Fusion into your solutions when you have more straightforward data transformation use cases, and you want to leverage its easy-to-consume, code-free interface.

Data integration for IoT

For the specific use case of IoT, Google Cloud offers a fully managed service to connect, manage, and ingest data from globally dispersed devices. This service is called **Cloud IoT Core**. You can securely connect to existing devices using standard MQTT and HTTP protocols with end-to-end asymmetric key authentication over TLS 1.2. The connection can be established as either one-way or two-way communication. A protocol bridge provides endpoints for protocols with automatic load balancing for all device connections, allowing you to scale seamlessly.

All your devices can be centrally managed in Cloud IoT Core, a serverless single pane of glass for your IoT devices. You can easily set up integration with services such as Pub/Sub or Dataflow for downstream analytics of devices' data. IoT Core can therefore be thought of as a messaging hub for IoT data sources, as illustrated in the following architectural diagram:

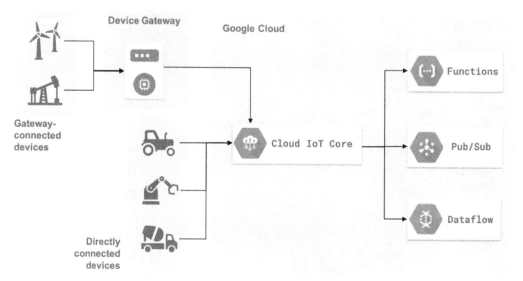

Figure 8.14 – Example IoT architecture with Cloud IoT Core

Devices can be either directly connected or connected via an IoT gateway that brokers connectivity to Google Cloud. Cloud IoT Core consolidates all incoming device messages and can be used as a source for several other GCP services. Cloud IoT Core should belong in your design if you work with IoT solutions using standard MQTT and HTTP protocols.

Data discovery, preparation, and management

This last suite of services includes additional capabilities such as discovering and managing data, preparing data, and workflow orchestration.

Cloud Composer is a fully managed workflow orchestration service built on the **Apache Airflow** open source project. In data analytics, a workflow represents a series of tasks for ingesting, transforming, analyzing, or utilizing data. Therefore, the concept of a workflow is not that different from that of a data pipeline, except workflow tasks are more generic and can represent things not directly related to data manipulation. For example, a task can monitor an API, send an email, or run a pipeline. In Apache Airflow, workflows are created using **Directed Acyclic Graphs** (**DAGs**) defined in Python code. To run workflows in Cloud Composer, you need first to create an *environment*. Cloud Composer then provisions the underlying Google Cloud components comprising your environment to run your workflows. These components are a **Google Kubernetes Engine** (**GKE**) cluster, a web server, a database, and a Cloud Storage bucket. However, because Composer is a fully managed service, you don't need to run and operate these components yourself. The service includes a web interface that you can use to manage workflows' DAGs and the Airflow environment.

So, how and when should you use Cloud Composer? Writing DAGs within Cloud Composer requires Python knowledge, but instructions and examples are available at `https://cloud.google.com/composer/docs/how-to/using/writing-dags`.

Cloud Composer is an obvious service choice if you have a team of data analysts that already works with Apache Airflow to create orchestration workflows. With no infrastructure to provision and manage, your team will be able to achieve greater agility and reliability than they could with a self-hosted solution. Consider using this service if you need complex workflows that can benefit from the flexibility and power of a fully fledged programming language. Refer to `https://airflow.apache.org/use-cases/` for real-world use cases of Apache Airflow, from which you can learn what sort of business and technical problems were solved with the open source tool that Cloud Composer is built on.

Cloud Dataprep is a serverless data service for visually exploring, cleaning, and preparing data for analysis, reporting, and **machine learning**. It is an integrated partner service operated by **Trifacta** and based on their industry-leading data preparation solution. With Dataprep, you can leverage hundreds of transformation functions available for performing tasks such as aggregation, joins, union, extraction, and merge. In addition, thanks to its proprietary inference algorithm, Dataprep can interpret the data transformation intent of a user's data selection and suggest patterns for the selections. Once you've defined your sequence of transformations through an easy-to-use UI, Cloud Dataprep uses Cloud Dataflow under the hood to run the data transformation pipeline. You can work with both structured and unstructured datasets of virtually any size.

The primary value offered by this service is its intelligence. For example, Dataprep automatically detects schemas, data types, possible joins, and anomalies, such as missing values or duplicates. Such features help offload from data analysts some of the time-consuming work of assessing and preparing data. As a serverless service offering predictive transformations via an easy-to-use interface, you should consider it an excellent value-added service to be incorporated into your big data solutions. It can significantly reduce management and operations overhead and enable agility. Documentation for this service is available at `https://docs.trifacta.com/display/dp/`.

Finally, one last service to discuss is **Data Catalog**. This is a fully managed and scalable **data discovery** and **metadata management** service. It provides an API and UI built with the same search technology as Gmail to empower users to find or tag data. The data can be on BigQuery, Pub/Sub, Cloud Storage, or many external data sources with the provided connectors. As a metadata management service, it is very useful for cataloging and classifying data assets. With native integration with Cloud **Data Loss Prevention** (**DLP**), you can use it to tag sensitive data to manage your data security.

Tagging data with metadata and searching for data assets are the two main ways in which you interact with Data Catalog. The integrated DLP feature can also automatically identify and tag sensitive data. Data Catalog can catalog the *native* metadata on data assets from the following sources:

- BigQuery datasets, tables, and views
- Pub/Sub topics

Using the Data Catalog APIs, you can create and manage entries for custom data resource types. Once data is cataloged, you can add your own metadata using tags. Metadata can be of two types: *technical metadata* and *business metadata*.

Technical metadata includes information such as the following:

- GCP project name and ID
- Data asset name and description
- GCP resource labels
- Schema name and description (for BigQuery tables and views)

On the other hand, business metadata is the user-generated metadata applied to the asset using Data Catalog tags. For example, this could be a data sensitivity level, data owner, or other relevant information from a business and data governance perspective. In the context of Data Catalog, you can think of a *tag* as synonymous with *business metadata*.

To start tagging data, you first create one or more tag templates containing a group of metadata key-value pairs (called *fields*). Creating a template is akin to defining a database schema for your metadata. One common practice would be to structure your tags by topic. For example, a *data governance* tag may contain fields for data owner, retention date, deletion date, and data classification. In contrast, a *data quality* tag may contain fields for update frequency, SLO information, and suchlike.

The ability to catalog and tag your data assets has limited value without searching and discovering them efficiently. Therefore, Data Catalog also offers powerful, structured search capabilities and predicate-based filtering over metadata. You can search for data assets directly from the Data Catalog page in the console or use its APIs. Documentation relating to the search syntax, including predicates and logical operators, is available at `https://cloud.google.com/data-catalog/docs/how-to/search-reference`.

If you're not familiar with data analytics services, it's easy to feel overwhelmed with the variety of services and features on GCP in that space. The following table presents a summary of the services discussed in this section:

Service	Description	When to use it
Dataflow	Stream and batch processing service based on Apache Beam	You need to read, transform, and ingest data You're already familiar with Apache Beam
Pub/Sub	A publish-subscribe messaging service where senders and receivers are decoupled	As message-oriented middleware Asynchronous messaging Service integration and decoupling
Data Fusion	Visual point-and-click interface for code-free deployment of ETL data pipelines	Less-complex ETL data pipelines Quick and code-free data transformations
IoT Core	Service to connect, manage, and ingest data from globally dispersed devices	IoT scenarios
Composer	Workflow orchestration service based on Apache Airflow	You need to build, automate, and monitor workflows to manage and organize ETL pipelines Pipeline orchestration
Dataprep	Data service based on Trifacta for visually exploring, cleaning, and preparing data	Data "wrangling" cases for gathering and transforming data for exploration Data lake analytics
Data Catalog	Data discovery and metadata management service	Data cataloging and classification DLP

You've learned so far about the big data ecosystem on GCP, and you probably now have a good grasp of what is possible to do. Next, we're going to explore how to approach the design of a data pipeline, before you get hands-on experience with big data on GCP.

Designing pipelines

To start designing data pipelines, you need to ask yourself the following questions:

- What/where are my data sources and sinks?
- Does my pipeline need to support batch and/or streaming data?
- What data transformations will be needed?
- Are there existing no-operation solutions that support the transformations I need to do?

In addition to these questions, you may also want to understand what programming languages and technologies are most suitable based on your team's existing skillset. It's not uncommon to have different data pipeline solutions for different needs. The following diagram illustrates a typical enterprise data pipeline landscape:

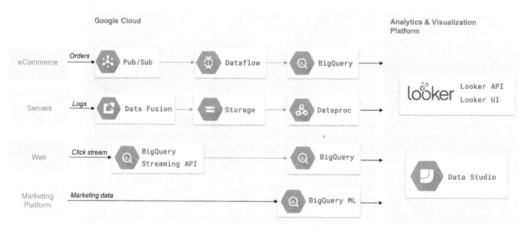

Figure 8.15 – Enterprise big data landscape

A combination of Cloud Pub/Sub, Cloud Dataflow, and/or Cloud BigQuery covers the majority of use cases, with Data Fusion potentially replacing Dataflow in simpler cases. Advanced analytics and AI/machine learning cases often find a fitting BigQuery feature.

As a first step, identify which data sources you have and whether they need a batch or streaming ingestion. For data sources on GCP, check for and leverage native integration options. For external sources, or when you have multiple sources that you wish to aggregate into a single batch or stream, use Pub/Sub as the intermediate messaging layer. Consider whether Dataprep and/or Data Catalog would add value by providing data discovery and preparation capabilities.

Once the underlying infrastructure is defined, identify what set of transformations you need to apply to your data and how to lay them out in your tool of choice. Typically, data analysts would perform this task, but in many instances, a cloud architect may be involved in defining the pipeline architecture. For example, data transformation actions that you can perform with Apache Beam to run on Dataflow include the following:

- Reading and filtering data

- Partitioning data

- Joining/flattening data

- Performing generic parallel processing (*Map*)

- Performing generic grouping/combining (*Reduce*)

With the Apache Beam framework, you can define a **ParDo** (short for **Parallel Do**) type of transform to run parallel processing similar to the Map phase of the MapReduce model. For example, you can use ParDo to apply a filter or format to a dataset, convert each element's type, or count the occurrence of each element in the dataset. Instead of carrying out these tasks sequentially, the ParDo action will parallelize it. Then, you can use a **GroupByKey** transform for processing collections of key-value pairs. This is a parallel reduction operation, similar to the Shuffle stage of the Reduce phase in MapReduce.

CoGroupByKey is a similar type of transform that applies to collections with key-value pairs and joins values with the same *key*. Finally, the **Combine** transform corresponds to the Reduce stage and computes the specified aggregate function (such as total and average).

In the code directory for this chapter, an Apache Beam program written in Python counts how often specified words appear at least once in lines of an input text. An example is provided with the book *Frankenstein; or, the Modern Prometheus* as an input text file, with the words *Frankenstein* and *Margaret* to be counted. To run it yourself, do the following:

1. Open a Cloud Shell session. You can optionally use a local terminal if you have Python 3 installed.

2. Clone the repository if you haven't already done so and then navigate to the ch8/ apache-beam directory:

    ```
    $ git clone https://github.com/PacktPublishing/
    Architecting-Google-Cloud-Solutions
    $ cd Architecting-Google-Cloud-Solutions/ch8/apache-beam
    ```

3. Then, install the Apache Beam library by running the following command:

    ```
    $ pip3 install -r requirements.txt
    ```

4. Now, run the application:

    ```
    $ python3 word_count_pipeline.py
    ```

5. After it finishes (it should only take a few seconds), inspect the output by running the following command:

    ```
    $ cat tmp/output-00000-of-00001
    ```

    The output files are generated under the tmp subdirectory and automatically sharded. Because we're running this simple example, there should be a single output file named output-00000-of-00001. The output should look as follows:

    ```
    ('Frankenstein', 30)
    ('Margaret', 10)
    ```

6. You can optionally rerun the program and provide your own comma-separated list of words to count by using the --words argument, as in the following example:

    ```
    $ python3 word_count_pipeline.py --words
    the,that,this,though
    ```

    You may also provide your own input file by specifying the path using the --input argument.

7. Spend some time inspecting the code to see how this Apache Beam pipeline was constructed. Notice how just a few lines define a MapReduce pipeline that can work on any input text file, at any scale. However, because you ran this in Cloud Shell as a local deployment (within the Cloud Shell instance), you're not actually leveraging the power of a distributed filesystem and all the capabilities of Cloud Dataflow.

    As a challenge to you, try to deploy this code as a dataflow pipeline. You can upload the text file to Cloud Storage and modify the value of input to be the Cloud Storage endpoint URI for the file (starting with `gs://`). Do the same for the `output_ prefix` path, defining it as a Cloud Storage path so that your output is written there.

By now you should have a good idea of how to design a data pipeline and how to leverage GCP services for each of your data needs. If you're feeling warmed up, it's time to solve a big data case study that brings together many of the concepts discussed so far to give you some more hands-on practice.

Getting hands-on – a big data case study

An unnamed company wants to build a *data analytics pipeline* for their *IoT data* and has turned to you for guidance on running a **proof of concept** on GCP. This company (your client) has a team of analysts who already work with Apache Beam, and they wish to keep using the same framework to avoid a steep learning curve. Your client's IoT devices produce semi-structured data, and they also want to have a data warehouse solution for storing all of it. They expect the number of devices and telemetry data generated to scale nearly exponentially as they expand in the next few years, so they want to ensure that the solution is highly scalable and future-proof.

You come up with the following design decisions:

Component/Layer	Service
Device message aggregation and ingestion	Cloud IoT Core
Message streaming	Cloud Pub/Sub
Data pipeline	Cloud Dataflow
Data warehouse	Cloud BigQuery

To prepare a proof of concept, you then perform the following steps:

1. Go to the GCP console (`console.cloud.google.com`), and then click on the shell icon in the top-right corner of the screen to activate Cloud Shell.

2. In the Cloud Shell terminal, run the following command:

    ```
    $ gcloud projects create --name chapter-8 --set-as-
    default
    ```

    Type *Y* and hit *Enter* to confirm the autogenerated project ID.

3. Associate a billing account with your project by running the following command:

    ```
    $ gcloud beta billing projects link [PROJECT_ID]
    --billing-account [ACCOUNT_ID]
    ```

    PROJECT_ID is the ID generated for your project in the previous step, while ACCOUNT_ID is your billing account ID. You can check your billing account ID by running the `gcloud beta billing accounts list`.

    > **Important note**
    > Never include brackets in the command arguments. They were added here to let you know that it's an input to be replaced/defined by you.

4. Enable the required APIs by running the following commands:

    ```
    $ gcloud services enable cloudiot.googleapis.com
    $ gcloud services enable pubsub.googleapis.com
    $ gcloud services enable dataflow.googleapis.com
    ```

5. To make things easier, define environment variables to hold your project ID and preferred region:

    ```
    $ export PROJECT_ID=[YOUR_PROJECT_ID]
    $ export REGION=[YOUR_REGION]
    ```

    To prevent a lack of service availability, choose one of `us-central1`, `europe-west1`, or `asia-east1` for the region.

6. Start by creating the Pub/Sub topic that will be used by the IoT devices to publish messages to. Run the following command:

    ```
    $ gcloud pubsub topics create iot-topic
    ```

7. Since the IoT Core service will publish messages, you need to assign to the IoT Core service account the Publisher role on the topic. You do this by running the following command:

```
$ gcloud pubsub topics add-iam-policy-binding iot-topic
--member=serviceAccount:cloud-iot@system.gserviceaccount.
com --role='roles/pubsub.publisher'
```

8. Next, create an IoT device registry:

```
$ gcloud iot registries create iot-dev-registry
--project=$PROJECT_ID --region=$REGION --event-
notification-config=topic=projects/$PROJECT_ID/topics/
iot-topic
```

A device registry is a container of devices with shared properties. Every device needs to be added to a registry, which is why you must have at least one. With the preceding command, you've created a registry called iot-dev-registry. Since this is a proof of concept, you don't necessarily need to use real physical devices, so we will use a virtual device simulator, which is a Python program provided by Google. You will do this later. Let's now finish setting up the implementation of our data architecture.

9. Create a BigQuery dataset:

```
bq --location=$REGION mk -d \
--default_table_expiration 3600 \
--description "IoT dataset" \
iotdataset
```

10. Then, create a table and table schema:

```
bq mk --table iotdataset.telemetrytable
timestamp:TIMESTAMP,device:STRING,temperature:FLOAT
```

The schema defined in the preceding command specifies three columns a timestamp, containing the timestamp of the device's reading; device, which identifies the device; and temperature, containing a float value of a temperature reading from the device.

11. Create a Cloud Storage bucket to store temporary files that are going to be used by Cloud Dataflow. Run the following command:

```
$ gsutil mb -l [LOCATION] gs://BUCKET_NAME
```

According to the region you chose previously, choose one of the multi-region locations, such as US, EU, or Asia, for the location. The bucket's name needs to be unique. Therefore, you will need to pick one that is not in use. If it is in use, the command will fail, and you will have to repeat the command with a new bucket name. Once you have successfully created one, export its value to an environment variable as follows:

```
$ export BUCKET_NAME=[BUCKET_NAME]
```

12. Create a Cloud Dataflow pipeline by running the following command:

```
$ gcloud dataflow jobs run iotpipelinejob --gcs-location
gs://dataflow-templates-$REGION/latest/PubSub_to_BigQuery
--region $REGION --staging-location gs://$BUCKET_NAME/
temp --parameters inputTopic=projects/$PROJECT_ID/
topics/iot-topic,outputTableSpec=$PROJECT_ID:iotdataset.
telemetrytable
```

The preceding command is creating a Dataflow pipeline from a pre-defined template (called PubSub_to_BigQuery) that streams data from a Pub/Sub topic, converting each message into a table row, and flattening (merging) it before writing it to BigQuery. It also includes handling for error events. The following diagram shows the architectural diagram for this pipeline template:

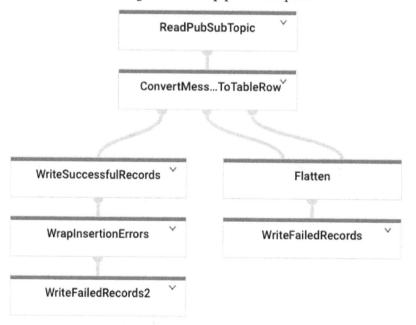

Figure 8.16 – Dataflow streaming pipeline template for Pub/Sub and BigQuery

The command also defines the storage bucket you've created as the temporary (staging) location for data, the Pub/Sub topic as the source topic, and the BigQuery table as the data sink for the output collection.

You have now successfully set up the streaming data pipeline based on your client's requirements. However, to complete the proof of concept, you will need to test the pipeline by ingesting messages from at least two distinct devices and see whether you successfully receive data on BigQuery.

In the next few steps, you will create two small VM instances that will each run a virtual device simulator:

1. Run the following two commands to create two VM instances in two separate regions:

    ```
    $ gcloud compute instances create ch8vm01 \
            --machine-type n1-standard-1 \
            --network default \
            --zone us-east1-c \
            --image-project debian-cloud \
            --image-family debian-10

     $ gcloud compute instances create ch8vm02 \
            --machine-type n1-standard-1 \
            --network default \
            --zone europe-west1-b \
            --image-project debian-cloud \
            --image-family debian-10
    ```

2. In the console, navigate to **Compute Engine | VM Instances**. Click on the **SSH** button next to ch8vm01 to open an SSH terminal in your browser. In the SSH terminal, run the following commands to install required packages, remove the default Cloud SDK installation, and install its latest version:

    ```
    $ sudo apt-get install python3-pip openssl git wget -y
    $ python3 -m pip install -U pip
    $ pip3 install -U pyjwt paho-mqtt cryptography virtualenv
    $ sudo apt-get remove google-cloud-sdk -y
    $ curl https://sdk.cloud.google.com | bash
    ```

3. Now, close the SSH terminal for ch8vm01, and open a new terminal by clicking again on the **SSH** button in the console's VM instances page. You need to reinitialize the shell in order for the changes to take effect, which is why you need to reopen the terminal. Once the terminal loads up again, run the following command:

    ```
    $ gcloud auth login
    ```

    If you're prompted, `Are you sure you want to authenticate with your personal account?` type `Y` and hit *Enter*. Go to the URL shown in the output using your browser and follow the prompts to authenticate your user (the same you've been using for this project). This is to run a `gcloud` command to create a device in the IoT registry, which you will do next.

    Once authenticated, make sure you are in the `chapter-8` project. If not, run `gcloud config set project [PROJECT_ID]` to change it. Also, before proceeding, make sure you set environment variables (as you did previously for Cloud Shell) inside this VM, with your project ID and region of choice:

    ```
    $ export PROJECT_ID=[PROJECT_ID]
    $ export REGION=[REGION]
    ```

4. Next, you will create a device in your device registry. Devices need a way to authenticate (otherwise anyone with the right URL would be able to send messages to your IoT service). For that reason, you will first create an SSH key pair and then provide the public key part to the device registry. Still from the VM's SSH terminal, run the following commands to create a device using an SSH key pair for authentication:

    ```
    $ git clone https://github.com/PacktPublishing/
    Architecting-Google-Cloud-Solutions
    $ cd Architecting-Google-Cloud-Solutions/ch8/iot
    $ openssl req -x509 -newkey rsa:2048 -keyout rsa_private.
    pem -nodes -out rsa_cert.pem -subj "/CN=unused"
    $ wget https://pki.google.com/roots.pem
    $ gcloud iot devices create temp-sensor-01 \
      --project=$PROJECT_ID \
      --region=$REGION \
      --registry=iot-dev-registry \
      --public-key path=rsa_cert.pem,type=rs256
    ```

5. Finally, after successfully creating the device, run the following command to run the simulation program:

```
$ python3 cloudiot_mqtt_example_json.py \
    --project_id=$PROJECT_ID \
    --cloud_region=$REGION \
    --registry_id=iot-dev-registry \
    --device_id=temp-sensor-01 \
    --private_key_file=rsa_private.pem \
    --message_type=event \
    --algorithm=RS256
```

This program will publish 100 messages containing simulated temperature data. While this is running, repeat *steps 2 through 5* for ch8vm02, replacing temp-sensor-01 with temp-sensor-02 in *steps 4 and 5*.

Once you have the second VM up and running and run the Python program, you can optionally rerun the program in ch8vm01 (parallel to the run of ch8vm02). This is a good way to test the solution's ability to handle multiple incoming device messages, at least to a small extent.

6. Now, the final step is to visualize the entries in BigQuery. Go to the console, and then navigate to **Big Data | BigQuery**. In the **Query editor** window, paste in the following query:

```
SELECT timestamp, device, temperature from iotdataset.
telemetrytable
ORDER BY timestamp DESC
LIMIT 100
```

7. Click on **Run**. You should see in the **Results** tab several rows for temperature readings from both devices, as shown in the following screenshot:

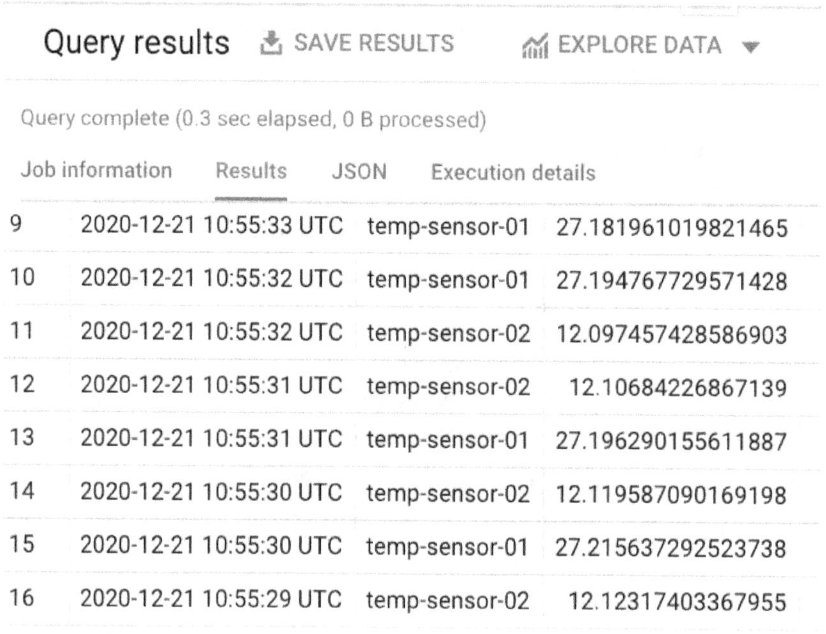

Query results		SAVE RESULTS	EXPLORE DATA ▼

Query complete (0.3 sec elapsed, 0 B processed)

Job information   Results   JSON   Execution details

9	2020-12-21 10:55:33 UTC	temp-sensor-01	27.181961019821465
10	2020-12-21 10:55:32 UTC	temp-sensor-01	27.194767729571428
11	2020-12-21 10:55:32 UTC	temp-sensor-02	12.097457428586903
12	2020-12-21 10:55:31 UTC	temp-sensor-02	12.10684226867139
13	2020-12-21 10:55:31 UTC	temp-sensor-01	27.196290155611887
14	2020-12-21 10:55:30 UTC	temp-sensor-02	12.119587090169198
15	2020-12-21 10:55:30 UTC	temp-sensor-01	27.215637292523738
16	2020-12-21 10:55:29 UTC	temp-sensor-02	12.12317403367955

Figure 8.17 – Query results for an IoT telemetry table

This successfully completes the proof of concept.

You report back to your client saying that the proof-of-concept setup successfully got messages from two different IoT devices in two different regions, streaming them through a Pub/Sub topic and then a Dataflow pipeline that flattens all telemetry data into BigQuery. You then point out to your client that the next steps will be as follows:

1. Define a **Role-Based Access Control** (**RBAC**) strategy for determining which groups of individuals should be assigned which role(s).

2. Test the solution with real IoT devices, adapting the simulation program to read real sensor data using device-specific libraries, and then send it to Cloud IoT Core, either directly or via a gateway. Optionally, modify BigQuery's table schema to include other data columns.

3. Build the visualization layer with either Cloud Data Studio, Looker, or any third-party tool of choice for building charts, dashboards, and reports.

To clean up all the resources, delete the project created for this chapter:

```
$ gcloud projects delete [PROJECT_ID]
```

Summary

In this chapter, you learned about some of the fundamental concepts surrounding big data, including data lakes, data warehouses, and data integration. You also then learned about the services on GCP with which you can build big data and data analytics solutions. You've understood what problems are solved by a message-oriented architecture and why and when you would build data pipelines. We then discussed some common architectural patterns, and how to choose the right services for your solution. Finally, you got some hands-on practice with a use case involving an IoT data analytics pipeline, where you built a solution using Cloud IoT Core, Pub/Sub, Dataflow, and BigQuery.

You should now possess the foundational knowledge and skills to design big data solutions for modern enterprises that can unlock business value from large volumes of data.

In the next chapter, you will learn about another crucial pillar of modern enterprise solutions architecture: automation and **Site Reliability Engineering** (**SRE**).

9
Jumping on the DevOps Bandwagon with Site Reliability Engineering (SRE)

Modern enterprises have learned that siloed ways of working and conflicting priorities between development and operations teams hinder their ability to deliver applications and services at high velocity and quality. **DevOps** emerged to solve this problem with a set of principles and working philosophies to foster collaboration and goal alignment.

In this chapter, you will learn about the five key pillars of DevOps, its cultural principles, and the motivations for incorporating it into a cloud adoption and digital transformation project. You will also learn about the practical ways in which DevOps can be implemented with **Site Reliability Engineering** (**SRE**) practices. You will learn about the SRE practices you can drive as a cloud architect and get hands-on experience with infrastructure automation and **continuous integration and continuous delivery** (**CI/CD**) on GCP. Finally, you will learn some best practices for the practical implementation of SRE in an organization and the forming of SRE teams. By the end of this chapter, you will understand what DevOps fundamentally is, how SRE differs from DevOps, and how to apply it to consistently deliver high-quality, reliable services.

In this chapter, we're going to cover the following main topics:

- Understanding DevOps and SRE

- Automating all things

- Applying SRE

Technical requirements

For the hands-on activities in this chapter, you will need a billing-enabled Google Cloud account and optionally the Google Cloud SDK installed (if you don't have it, you can use Cloud Shell from a browser). Helper scripts and code for this chapter can be found at `https://github.com/PacktPublishing/Architecting-Google-Cloud-Solutions/tree/master/ch9`. For this chapter, you will also need a personal GitHub account.

Check out the following link to see the Code in Action video: `https://bit.ly/3kN7aqj`

Understanding DevOps and SRE

In recent years, DevOps has become a loaded term with diverse interpretations and perspectives. To fundamentally understand what it is, you need to first understand the context in which it arose and what problem it was meant to solve.

Traditionally, IT teams consisted of developers and operators. Developers were solely responsible for creating and deploying software systems on IT infrastructure, whereas operators were responsible for ensuring that infrastructure and systems worked reliably. While developers were expected to be agile and push new code and features as quickly as possible, operators were expected to carefully plan any changes to reduce the risk of disruption and keep the systems stable. This resulted in developers delivering software code (or, as the metaphor often goes, "throwing it over the wall") for operators to run in production and worry about its reliability. Understandably, the conflicting priorities between these two teams caused tension and often resulted in unsustainable ways of working. As a way to close the gap between developers and operators and align their priorities with the needs of the business, DevOps was born as a *culture* and *set of practices*. Google identifies five key pillars within DevOps:

1. **Reduce organizational silos**: Break down barriers across teams to foster collaboration.

2. **Accept failure as normal**: Computer systems are inherently unreliable, and humans are inherently prone to making mistakes. Failure will always happen and must be accepted as normal.

3. **Implement gradual change**: Small, incremental changes are easier to review, deploy, and recover from in case of mistakes.

4. **Leverage tooling and automation**: Automating manual repetitive tasks will help teams work efficiently and focus on what matters.

5. **Measure everything**: There's no way to tell whether what you're doing is working or not if you have no way to measure it.

The essential common theme underlying it all is that DevOps is not a development methodology or technology – it's a philosophy, a way of working. DevOps also doesn't provide prescriptive guidance on *how* exactly organizations can successfully implement DevOps practices. That's where SRE comes in.

SRE is a particular implementation of DevOps practiced at Google, although it started and has evolved separately from it. The principles are very similar, which is why the two terms – and their associated job roles – are often used interchangeably. However, SRE differs from DevOps in some ways. It goes beyond the cultural foundation and includes practical, technical practices that are generally aligned with DevOps' five key pillars, as represented in the following table:

DevOps principle	How Google does it with SRE
Reduce organizational silos	Share ownership
Accept failure as normal	Blamelessness
Implement gradual change	Reduce the cost of failure
Leverage tooling and automation	Toil automation
Measure everything	Measure toil and reliability

In general, an SRE team is responsible for the **availability**, **latency**, **performance**, **efficiency**, **change management**, **monitoring**, **emergency response**, and **capacity planning** of their services. Because these are all crucial pillars of cloud solutions architecture, as you've been learning throughout this book, you will need to understand how to approach these SRE practices within your organization and how to foster a DevOps culture that is able to sustain consistently high standards across all these areas.

We will delve into each one of these five SRE practices next.

Blameless postmortems

In *Chapter 6, Configuring Services for Observability*, we discussed the importance of observability and the concepts of **Service-Level Indicators (SLIs)**, **Service-Level Objectives (SLOs)**, and **Service-Level Agreements (SLAs)**. SRE engineers learn to eliminate ambiguity through well-designed and well-implemented observability and monitoring in the platform. They learn to become comfortable with failure thanks to the supporting structure and disambiguation from SLIs, SLOs, and SLAs. They help establish a common language and understanding across teams, with SLOs being the main focus within SRE as they indicate the objectives that everybody should aim for. On the flip side, SLOs also determine the **error budget**, which teams can use to confidently drive changes and innovation. Error budgets reframe errors as not something to be avoided at all costs, but something to be consumed within a limit – akin to a monetary expense budget. As a reminder, here are the definitions for each of these terms:

- **SLI**: A quantifiable *measure* of service reliability

- **SLO**: A reliability *target* for an SLI, representing the desired experience from a user's perspective

- **SLA**: A reliability target *commitment* with the paying customers

You can refer back to *Chapter 6, Configuring Services for Observability*, for a more in-depth exploration of these concepts. In that chapter, we also highlighted the importance of an **incident response** strategy. SRE teams focus on documenting and learning from outages and taking steps to ensure that similar ones don't happen again in the same way. They do this by performing a **postmortem**, or retrospective, which aims to identify and provide a written record of the following:

- Details and timeline of the incident

- Actions taken to mitigate or resolve it

- The incident's quantifiable impact

- The incident's trigger and root cause(s)

- The follow-up actions to be taken to prevent its recurrence

Because the focus is on the system- or process-related root causes and not on individuals or teams responsible for an outage, these are also commonly called **blameless postmortems**. In fact, calling them *blameless* postmortems makes it very clear from the beginning that blame is out of the picture and the focus is fully on handling the problem. It creates a psychological safety net for **Site Reliability Engineers (SREs)** to not fear failure. Beyond fixing the issue and identifying the root cause, postmortems have important goals that are often neglected by IT teams. For example, they help ensure that the root causes are properly understood by the team(s) involved. They also help define what effective actions can be taken to prevent the incident from occurring again, reducing the likelihood of similar outages. In the long run, this is a key quality-of-life factor for engineers, since it improves the system's hygiene and allows them to spend less time dealing with incidents and more time on value-adding work. The supporting philosophy behind blameless postmortems is that, if a "human error" caused a severe outage, the human is not the one at fault but the poorly implemented *processes* and automation that failed to prevent it.

Finally, blameless postmortems help avoid the growth of complexity in the system. Quick fixes are often not the ideal, long-term solution. Although quick fixes and workarounds are often necessary to immediately remediate an incident, teams that focus solely on doing so but not learning from the experience and defining follow-up steps will soon be dealing with an overly complex system. That is because quick fixes and "patches" stack on top of each other and make the systems less maintainable, eventually increasing the likelihood of future failures.

Experienced SREs learn from their mistakes and those of others. They are *constructive pessimists* and learn to rely on past failure experiences. By practicing blameless postmortems in your organization and fostering a culture of collaboration and acceptance of failure, you and your teams will be able to work more effectively.

If you feel like it's a daunting task to change the ways of working in your organization, consider pitching an SRE-focused training delivered by a Google training partner. Or, simply start small within your team and, once you're able to show that it's been working well, you might be able to more confidently drive larger changes or get executive buy-in on the idea. The good thing about the blameless postmortem practice (or any SRE practice, for that matter) is that it doesn't require any special tool, and it most certainly doesn't require a large budget to be implemented.

Share ownership

SRE promotes the culture of shared ownership. This can be achieved through a few different practices that have the common goal of reducing organizational silos and the metaphorical wall between developers and operators. In particular, defining SLOs and error budgets are the main overarching practices in SRE for fostering shared ownership.

As discussed previously, SRE gets everyone to agree on how to measure and target reliability metrics, establishing a common language for engineers, product teams, and business executives alike. Moreover, within SRE, the responsibility for the reliability of the systems is shared. SLOs are defined based on a user-centric view of reliability, that is, a threshold below which the service level is deemed unsatisfactory for users. For distributed systems, this is irrespective of there being individual server or component failures, if they don't affect the overall service reliability. Beyond defining a model of shared understanding with SLOs, having an error budget helps motivate teams to push new changes and features, while still holding them accountable for violating SLOs (or overrunning the budget).

The error budget is the difference between the SLI and the SLO quantities when the former is higher than the latter. In other words, SRE teams don't "care" about keeping reliability levels any higher than SLOs dictate. By definition, when SLOs are met, users are happy – regardless of the actual SLI. For example, suppose your application's availability SLO was set at 99.95%, as illustrated in the following figure:

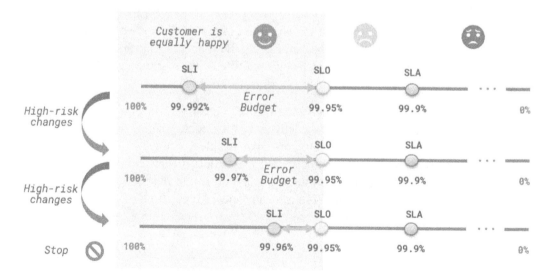

Figure 9.1 – Example use of an error budget

Whether your *actual* availability measures (that is, the SLI) is at 99.99%, or 99.992%, or 99.97%, it won't truly matter. There will be only a marginal, if any, increase in user satisfaction. In addition, if your service's actual performance is much better than its stated SLO, users will come to expect and rely on its current performance. Google is known to have deliberately planned outages to prevent this from happening to some of its services.

This is the premise of error budgets: if there's no good reason to keep reliability levels as high as possible beyond SLO levels, then why not take advantage of that wiggle room to implement new features or try new things? Conversely, if SLIs are dangerously low and too close to their corresponding SLOs, it's time to put changes on hold until the next evaluation period. The point here is that a single team (the SRE team) is making all the decisions – when to push new changes and when to hold back. There are no conflicting priorities held by siloed development and operations teams that are evaluated on different metrics. There is only one common incentive: keep reliability levels above SLOs, but *not much higher* at the expense of slowing down changes. Even if there are different functional teams, such as application and platform operations teams, the idea of shared responsibility and common incentives still remains, effectively still reducing organizational silos.

Reduce the cost of failure

The DevOps pillar of implementing gradual change is practically implemented within SRE in a few ways that aim at reducing the cost of failure. Although changes are risky, they're more manageable and less disruptive to users when they're *small* in scope and *frequent*. The practices of **continuous integration (CI)** and **continuous delivery (CD)** are common among SRE teams and help realize this ideal.

CI is the practice of integrating code into a shared central repository frequently, often several times a day. Each code integration is automatically verified by a build pipeline that usually (and ideally) incorporates *automated testing*. The higher the quality of the pipeline construct and its baked-in tests, and the less human intervention the process requires, the earlier issues can be detected and remediated, and the higher the pace at which quality-assured software can be delivered. In addition, critical issues can be avoided, effectively reducing the associated risks and costs of a production incident.

CD is the practice of deploying to production frequently or having the capability to do so at any time, even if choosing not to. It's typically implemented in practice with release pipelines that deploy the latest successful build either automatically upon build completion, or manually upon approval or another human-mediated trigger. *Continuous deployment* is a term often used to differentiate these two options, with continuous delivery referring to the manual deployment scenario, whereas continuous deployment refers to the case when deployment is fully automated. Businesses can decide on the actual pace of deployment but, ideally, they should happen almost as frequently as new builds happen. There's a saying in DevOps that goes:

"If it hurts, do it more often."

The idea is that the more often you make changes, the smaller and more easily reversible they will tend to be, accelerating the feedback cycle. Consequently, the more comfortable teams will feel with releasing changes, and the experience of doing so will be less "painful." As with any activity, we improve at deploying changes by practicing and doing more of it. Teams will naturally get better at deploying new releases by doing it more often.

The following figure illustrates the concepts of CI, CD, and continuous deployment:

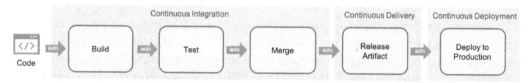

Figure 9.2 – Continuous integration, delivery, and deployment

In general, the combined practices of CI/CD help you achieve the following:

- Reduce human error
- Promote higher code quality
- Recover more easily from breaking changes
- Enable automation and agility for faster time to market
- Improve visibility on software projects

All these benefits contribute to the enablement of gradual, incremental changes and, ultimately, the reduction of failures and their costs.

Another practice that can be combined with CI/CD for the purpose of reducing costs of failure even further is that of **canarying**. The name comes from a traditional method used by coal miners to detect the presence of carbon monoxide. They would release canaries into the mine and, since these birds succumb to high levels of carbon monoxide much faster than humans do, they would use them as an alert to the danger. If canaries died, they knew they had to react, but they also knew that they would have time to do so. The impact was minimized (at least from the perspective of the humans). The same principle applies well to software releases. A canary release means that you release a new version of the software, with new features and tentative bug fixes, to only a small subset of your users. If this new release causes issues in production, the changes can be reverted with "minimal" damage because only a small fraction of the userbase was affected. If things work, you can gradually roll out the changes to more users. A balance must be struck between keeping the canary population small enough that the impact is minimized but also large enough to be a representative subset of the entire population. The following figure illustrates the concept of canarying:

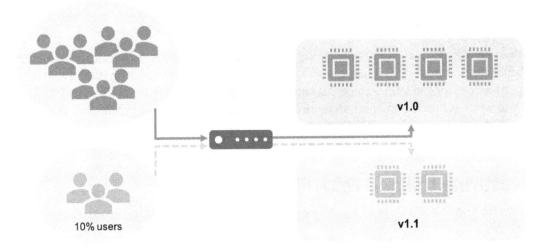

Figure 9.3 – Canary release

In the diagram, a new software version (**v1.1**) is released to only 10% of the users, while the majority of users still "see" the non-updated application (**v1.0**).

The canarying practice is only effective if it is very clear what specific changes are being evaluated by canarying, and the process for reverting them if necessary.

Design thinking and prototyping

With gradual change practices such as CI/CD and canarying, teams are empowered to become more innovative. For that reason, **design thinking** and **prototyping** are key aspects of SRE culture. It is an effective approach to solving complex problems by combining creativity and structure through five different phases:

- **Empathize**: Observe closely your intended users to learn about them and gain insights into their behavior and needs.

- **Define**: Define the problem to be solved, framing it from the point of view of users. By taking a user-centric perspective of the problem, you will be better able to identify ways to deliver real value.

- **Ideate**: Generate ideas for solutions, in a brainstorming manner. This is the time to think outside the box and exercise imagination.

- **Prototype**: Get the ideas out of your head and the realm of imagination and into the concrete, experimenting with alternative solutions and gathering feedback.

- **Test**: Test the idea in a real-world setting with the intended users.

With a prototype-driven culture, teams are encouraged to try and test more ideas, leading to better innovation. Prototyping doesn't need to steer developers away from their main responsibilities for too long. Prototypes can be as rough as a paper drawing. Testing it in the real world is crucial, however, to more accurately gauge the success potential of the idea. With practices such as CI/CD and canarying, you can quickly test it and ascertain how ideas are received while minimizing impact.

Measuring toil and reliability

In the SRE book (available at `https://sre.google/books`), **toil** is defined as:

> *"the kind of work tied to running a production service that tends to be manual, repetitive, automatable, tactical, devoid of enduring value, and that scales linearly as a service grows."*

To put it simply, toil is work that doesn't consist of the best possible use of an engineer's time. Google's SRE organization has an advertised goal of keeping toil below 50% of each SRE's time. In other words, at least 50% of their time is aimed at *engineering project work* that will either reduce future toil or add value to the service. This proactive stance on limiting toil is a crucial SRE practice that prevents toil from expanding and filling nearly 100% of everyone's time. It helps keep the team's focus on engineering, value-adding work, that is, the kind of work that intrinsically requires *human judgment* and produces a *permanent improvement* in the service. Engineering work is typically guided by a strategy, is frequently creative and innovative in nature, and takes a design-driven approach to solving problems. In the long run, the cumulative output of this type of work is what enables SRE organizations to handle larger services (or more services) with the same level of staffing – in other words, it allows them to scale the engineering teams sub-linearly with service size. That's the motivation for measuring toil in addition to reliability as the second-best surrogate metric to measure an SRE team's success.

So, how can toil be measured in practice? With a good understanding of what toil is and what it *is not*, individual SREs can measure how much time they spend on it. It's not uncommon for organizations to have an employee time management tool used for tracking and billing purposes. These same tools can be used as long as there is an easy way to tell toil from engineering work. The SRE book's chapter on toil, available at `https://sre.google/sre-book/eliminating-toil/`, provides a deeper explanation of what constitutes toil and what constitutes engineering work from Google's SRE experience. It's not as straightforward as it may sound, since in a lot of cases it depends on the context.

In *Chapter 6, Configuring Services for Observability*, we discussed the architectural best practices for monitoring and observability. We also discussed the differences between white-, black- and gray-box monitoring. These are all enabling mechanisms for the DevOps principle entitled "measure everything." As important as measuring things is being able to understand, analyze, and act on data. That is why the **SLI-SLO-SLA** approach, together with the practice of measuring toil, is a useful and concrete way to quantify success – the way you define it. Ultimately, measuring this way enables teams to remove ambiguity, identify necessary actions from data, and make better decisions.

In summary, this DevOps principle translates to the following SRE practices:

- **Measure reliability**: Use SLIs, SLOs, and error budgets to measure reliability, define reliability targets, and encourage change and innovation. Choose metrics that reflect whether the users are happy, that is, metrics strongly correlated with the service's reliability, not that of individual servers and components.

- **Measure toil**: Identify and measure toil with an appropriate unit of measure, such as minutes, hours, and number of tickets. Do it in a simple way to not create too much overhead (and additional toil). An estimate often works. Track these measurements continuously, making it a habit within the team to think about toil. This will often trigger a toil reduction effort and empower SREs to find ways to prevent future toil.

- **Monitor**: Design for observability by collecting logs and metrics centrally. Define an alert and incident management strategy that clearly determines when incidents should be declared and what is the action plan. Refer back to *Chapter 6, Configuring Services for Observability*, for practical guidance on achieving this.

Finally, you need to build these practices on a foundational culture of transparency and **data-driven decision making**. If you're a leader, strive to set goals and **key performance indicators (KPIs)**, decide what to measure and how, and make decisions based on data available to everyone, not based on individual hunches. For example, Google sets goals and measure KPIs internally by using an **Objectives and Key Results (OKRs)** grading system. A workshop recording that goes through this strategy in detail is available at `https://library.gv.com/how-google-sets-goals-okrs-a1f69b0b72c7`. If you currently don't have data-driven goal setting and performance measurement processes in your organization, OKRs may serve as a reference and starting point for you to implement them within your team. In general, as you start making more informed decisions based on data you have gathered, you close the feedback loop that this practice intends to create, as illustrated in the following figure:

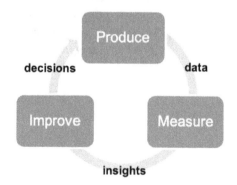

Figure 9.4 – Continuous improvement feedback loop

Numbers allow much less room for ambiguity than vague goals or principles. Engineers tend to work more effectively when they're up against concrete metrics as opposed to loosely defined intents.

Toil automation

This last practice reflects the DevOps principle entitled "leverage tooling and automation." It's the only principle that has any mentioning of the word *tooling*, though it doesn't specify any specific type – because it doesn't matter as much as the idea itself of leveraging the rights tools *for your needs*. Which tools are best and even when and where to use them will strongly depend on your specific situation.

As mentioned previously, toil is work that is repetitive, manual, tactical, without enduring value, and *automatable*. Note that this definition of toil doesn't include administrative work or things that you don't like to do. Some of these types of work may be truly necessary and require human judgment. They're *overheads*, not toil. Still, as many system administrators and IT professionals know, a lot of the non-overhead work they do can be scripted or automated in some way. The more repetitive and time-consuming the work is, the higher the potential value of automating it. In general, the less time is spent on toil, the greater the team's value output. This is the reason why toil automation is one key SRE practice.

Automating toil is not only about optimizing the execution of certain tasks. It has a clear benefit on *systems*, for sure, but there's also a psychological benefit on *people* that should be considered. Excessive toil can lead to low morale, career stagnation, and low quality of life for team members. Nobody likes to be constantly handling incidents, putting out "fires," or doing grunt work. Small amounts of these types of tasks are unavoidable and can be well tolerated (some people may even enjoy them). However, they should not constitute the majority of an SRE's time, hence the 50% cap on toil that we discussed previously as being one good strategy. Automation also provides the following benefits:

- **Consistency**: Machines execute tasks consistently no matter how many times they need to be performed. Contrary to humans, who can make mistakes (especially when a task is repeated several times across several components), automation tools can deploy the exact same configuration set across different environments, clusters, or IT subsystems.

- **Faster action and repair**: Automation tools can apply configuration changes to several systems nearly simultaneously, and at a much faster pace than humans can. This is useful in both pushing new configurations and fixing mistakes much more quickly. Automated monitoring and failover systems can also identify and remediate issues much sooner than human operators can, resulting in improved reliability.

- **Centralized platform**: Any updates or fixes that need to be made to an automation script or tool can be done centrally, which is not always the case with manually configured systems. Automation provides a central platform that can be extended and applied to more systems. Moreover, relevant metrics can be more easily exported from this one single platform.

- **Time saver**: Although it may take a considerable amount of time and effort to automate certain types of work, once it's done the system can be reused multiple times and continue to work reliably even if the system scales or if team members switch roles. It eliminates the need for continuous training on the administration of automated systems.

- **24/7**: Automation jobs can run at any time, not only during business hours. Machines don't get tired or psychologically stressed, and they certainly don't need to sleep. Certain tasks that can have a performance impact on applications can be scheduled to run at times of low activity.

The first step toward automating toil is deciding *what* to automate and *how* to automate it. If automation has not consistently been a common practice in your organization, there might be so much toil that it won't be very straightforward to determine what should be automated first. A simple and intuitive rule is to start with the biggest "return-on-investment" potential, that is, tasks that, if automated, will reduce toil the most. Typically, these are tasks that consume a lot of time, are very repetitive, and/or produce very little value, if any. As to how to automate it, it's better to start simple with scripts and/or accessible tools at your team's disposal. Go for the quick wins, before setting out to implement a fully fledged automation solution. Embracing the culture and practice of automation is most important, and deciding on specific tooling should come later when you're able to identify which tools best suit your needs.

The following table presents a non-exhaustive list of some useful automation tools, for reference purposes:

Area	Tools
Runtime configuration/scripting	Bash
	PowerShell
	Python
Code build and integration	Maven
	Make
	Ninja
	Jenkins
	Travis CI
Infrastructure deployment and orchestration	Octopus Deploy
	Cloud Deployment Manager (GCP)
	Terraform
	Ansible
	Chef
	Puppet
Monitoring	Grafana
	Prometheus
	Cloud Monitoring (GCP)
	Cloud Logging (GCP)
	Cloud Trace (GCP)
	Cloud Profiler (GCP)
	Logstash
Incident and IT service management	VictorOps
	Jira Ops
	ServiceNow
	Opsgenie
	Jira ServiceDesk

Several of these tools are free and open source, and there are many more that can be found. As an SRE best practice, you should set a target for how much toil you want your SREs to have as a maximum, then measure it continuously. Only then will you be able to gauge whether automation – and the choice of tooling – is having a positive, lasting impact. The goal is to keep your SREs mostly engaged with engineering work, as illustrated in the following figure:

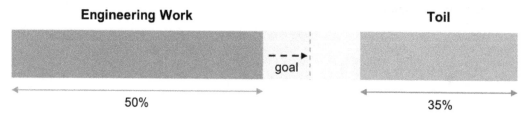

Figure 9.5 – Prioritizing engineering work over toil

A few common use cases for automation are listed here:

- User account creation
- Software installation and/or setup
- Runtime configuration changes
- Copying files and application artifacts to multiple destinations

As you identify toil within your team(s), automation opportunities can certainly be uncovered.

In this section, you have learned about the cultural principles of DevOps and their associated practices in SRE. These are broad organizational changes that can have a lasting and profound impact but also take time to put into practice. And these are not the kinds of changes that you can drive alone. They require a team effort and sometimes also executive buy-in. However, any one individual can reach for the low-hanging fruits, start a conversation, and perhaps take the first step toward the shift to an SRE way of working. As a cloud or solutions architect, there's plenty you can do. A broad digital transformation effort driven by cloud adoption may provide the kind of momentum and motivation needed to get everyone on board with embracing DevOps and SRE practices. On the other hand, there are also solutions design practices that incorporate SRE. In the next section, you will learn how to implement automation across your cloud infrastructure by leveraging GCP-native tools.

Automating all things

The cloud enables automation by offering serverless and event-based compute services, some with built-in scheduling and automation capabilities. It also facilitates many types of infrastructure automation by providing programmatic capabilities and APIs for performing administrative actions on the platform. In other words, the cloud enables infrastructure to be treated like *software*. In Google Cloud, the **Cloud Deployment Manager** allows you to specify all GCP resources needed in a declarative format to implement **Infrastructure as Code (IaC)**, a concept discussed a few times in this book. In addition, **Cloud Build** offers a serverless CI/CD platform for building, testing, and deploying code. We will explore these services and other GCP automation capabilities in this section.

Infrastructure as Code (IaC) with Deployment Manager

IaC is an approach to managing infrastructure by declaratively defining *all* infrastructure components (networks, virtual machines, databases, firewall rules, and so on) using source-controlled descriptive models. It has evolved to solve the problem of *environment drift*, where configuration changes cause different infrastructure environments to deviate from their baseline configuration and become unique. This drifting state tends to aggravate over time, causing the applications' behavior to be unpredictable across different environments since they're no longer exactly the same. Application developers know all too well how even minor differences between two environments can cause an application to work flawlessly in one, yet fail to run altogether in another. Furthermore, when changes to the infrastructure are done manually without a source control mechanism, it becomes very difficult to troubleshoot and find the root causes of issues when they occur due to a configuration change.

The idea behind IaC is to handle infrastructure in the same way as applications: you define it in *code* once, from which a binary artifact is *built* and subsequently *released and deployed*. Any changes are made to the code and pushed to a code repository, from where it is reviewed, rebuilt, and redeployed. No matter how many times you build the source code, if the source hasn't changed, the same resulting binary will be produced. This allows IaC frameworks to be designed for *idempotence*. This property refers to the fact that infrastructure code will always set the target environment with the same configuration, *regardless of its starting state*. Idempotence is a prerequisite property for **immutable infrastructure**. With the immutable infrastructure approach, the infrastructure is redeployed entirely with any new change – be it to incorporate new resources, update or remove existing configurations, or simply as part of a daily deployment that prevents environment drift by rogue manual changes. In fact, redeploying infrastructure periodically and idempotently is a great governance strategy to enforce the principle of code-only infrastructure and remediate any accidental environment drift.

This approach has the added benefit of strongly enforcing security, as it prevents any deviation from the baseline caused by either intentional (by hackers, potentially) or unintentional changes to security configurations. No misconfiguration would live more than a certain number of hours, depending on how often you run the deployments.

The benefits of IaC go beyond solving environment drift and allowing for immutable deployments. Some of the benefits are similar to those of automation in general:

- Improves the consistency of deployments and infrastructure reliability

- Improves agility by allowing the faster delivery of infrastructure changes

- Facilitates change management with source-controlled templates and "pull request" workflows

- Facilitates identifying bugs and reverting changes with code history and CI/CD pipelines

- Enables the repeatability of deployments with reusable templates

Google Cloud Deployment Manager allows you to write flexible template and configuration files to define and deploy your infrastructure consisting of GCP resources. A set of resources can then be managed as a unit, called a *deployment*. For example, a set of resources consisting of **virtual machines (VMs)** and a Cloud SQL database can be defined in a file and deployed with Deployment Manager. This file can be included in a code repository to be managed along with application code. Cloud Deployment Manager uses **YAML** (a recursive acronym short for **YAML Ain't Markup Language**) as the syntax language for its configuration files, and Jinja2 or Python for templating and parametrizing the configuration. Parametrization is essential to make templates reusable and your different deployments consistent across different environments by changing input values only.

You will learn later in this section how to approach parameterization. If you're unfamiliar with YAML or Jinja2, an in-depth discussion of which is beyond the scope of this book, refer to `yaml.org` and `https://jinja.palletsprojects.com/` as the official sources and reference documentations. That being said, YAML was designed with human readability as its core goal so it is, in fact, a format that is easy to read and understand. It relies on indentation to define nested content, as opposed to things such as curly braces, which makes for a cleaner look. YAML is straightforward to grasp as a language since it only defines the structure, not what the actual content schema should look like. In that way, it is very similar to JSON. Deployment Manager has its own syntax and that is what you may need to spend more time understanding. The reference syntax documentation is available at `https://cloud.google.com/deployment-manager/docs/configuration/syntax-reference`.

Deployment Manager is probably best understood with a concrete example. The following YAML-based configuration defines a Compute Engine VM instance:

```
resources:
- type: compute.v1.instance
  name: testvm-01
  properties:
    zone: europe-west1-b
    # Replace [PROJECT_ID] with your project ID
    machineType: https://www.googleapis.com/compute/v1/
projects/[PROJECT_ID]/zones/europe-west1-b/machineTypes/f1-
micro
    disks:
    - deviceName: boot
      type: PERSISTENT
      boot: true
      autoDelete: true
      initializeParams:
        sourceImage: https://www.googleapis.com/compute/v1/
projects/debian-cloud/global/images/family/debian-10
    # Replace [PROJECT_ID] with your project ID
    networkInterfaces:
    - network: https://www.googleapis.com/compute/v1/projects/
[PROJECT_ID]/global/networks/default
      # The configuration below is required to give the
instance a public IP address
      accessConfigs:
      - name: External NAT
        type: ONE_TO_ONE_NAT
```

Note how the Deployment Manager YAML file defines a list of **resources** (with a single resource in this example). Each resource has a **type** and a **name** as well as a **properties** configuration block. The properties of the resource depend on the resource type. Naturally, while a VM has things such as disks and network interfaces, a database or a firewall rule would contain completely different properties. You will need to check each resource type's reference API to see what attributes are included. A complete list of supported resource types and a link to their API documentation is available at `https://cloud.google.com/deployment-manager/docs/configuration/supported-resource-types`.

Typically, people have an easier time working with and understanding Deployment Manager files by using examples. You can find examples similar to what you want to build, modify it to your needs, and occasionally peek into the API documentation if you need to define a property you can't find in examples. Luckily, Google Cloud maintains a Cloud Foundation Toolkit, an open repository containing production-ready templates. A list of available examples is at `https://cloud.google.com/deployment-manager/docs/reference/cloud-foundation-toolkit`. In the same code repository, you will be able to find templates written for **Terraform**, if you prefer that alternative. If you're not comfortable working with the Python and Jinja languages, you may find it difficult to use Deployment Manager effectively. However, they can also be empowering since they give you the full flexibility and capabilities of a programming language (Python) or of a feature-rich templating language (Jinja).

To understand the usefulness of templating, you need to understand the importance of parametrization. Suppose you have development, test, and production infrastructure environments, and you wish to deploy a similar type of VM to these environments but with the following differences:

Property	Value		
	Development	Test	Production
name	dev-instance-01	test-instance-01	prod-instance-01
machineType	f1-micro	n1-standard	n1-standard
diskType	pd-standard	pd-ssd	pd-ssd
network	dev-network	test-network	prod-network

All other properties, such as zone, boot disk configuration, and public IP configuration, are supposed to be the same in all environments. You could approach this by creating three different files very similar to the example given previously, only with the properties listed in the preceding table having different values in different files. However, this is not ideal for a few reasons:

- The common set of parameters is now replicated across three different files, increasing code complexity unnecessarily.

- It becomes more difficult to maintain consistency since a change can be accidentally made to a shared parameter in only one of the files.

- Every time a change needs to be made to a parameter, it needs to be applied to all three files.

- The files are not reusable since they hardcode all properties into them. If the VM were to be deployed to an entirely new environment, a new file containing the entire config set would need to be created and modified to suit the new environment.

Wouldn't it be better to have a single VM file with all the common properties hardcoded in it, while all *environment-specific properties* are set as parameters to be defined at deploy time? That's where templates come in. Instead of having three different configuration files, you will have a single template file and three or more simpler and smaller deployment-specific input files that would look like this:

```
imports:
  - path: path/to/instance/template/file
    name: instanceTemplate.py


resources:
  - name: dev-instance-01
    type: instanceTemplate.py
    properties:
      machineType: f1-micro
      diskType: pd-standard
      networks:
        - network: dev-network
```

Test and production environments will have similar input files, with their properties in them. You still have multiple files per environment, but this time you ensure that they only contain properties and configurations that are not common across environments and are uniquely defined for each deployment. If changes need to be made to a *common* parameter, such as a new deployment zone for all VMs, you can apply this change to a single template file. Furthermore, adding a new environment to reuse the template on is much easier and less error-prone with this approach.

The template can be written in Python or in Jinja. Jinja maps more closely to the YAML syntax, so you may find it easier to write templates in Jinja if you are more familiar with YAML than you are with Python. On the other hand, Python would allow you to define more complex logic and programmatic constructs to generate parts of your templates.

To get some hands-on experience and make sense of all of this, let's deploy a VM instance using a YAML configuration file and Deployment Manager. Next, we will deploy two other VM instances using a basic VM Jinja template and two input YAML files:

1. To start, go to the GCP console (`console.cloud.google.com`), and then click on the shell icon on the top-right corner of the screen to activate Cloud Shell.

2. In the Cloud Shell terminal, create a new project for this chapter and link a billing account by running this:

    ```
    $ gcloud projects create --name chapter-9 --set-as-
    default
    ```
    ```
    $ gcloud beta billing projects link [PROJECT_ID]
    --billing-account [ACCOUNT_ID]
    ```

    PROJECT_ID is the ID generated for your project after the first command, while ACCOUNT_ID is your billing account ID. You can check your billing account ID by running gcloud beta billing accounts list.

    > **Important note**
    >
    > Never include the brackets in the command arguments. They were added to let you know that it's an input to be replaced/defined by you.

3. Since we will be deploying Compute Engine instances, enable the API:

    ```
    $ gcloud services enable deploymentmanager.googleapis.com
    $ gcloud services enable compute.googleapis.com
    ```

4. Next, clone the repository and navigate to this activity's directory:

    ```
    $ git clone https://github.com/PacktPublishing/
    Architecting-Google-Cloud-Solutions/
    $ cd Architecting-Google-Cloud-Solutions/ch9/deployment-
    manager
    ```

5. Using an editor such as vim or nano, modify the instance-01.yaml file by replacing [PROJECT_ID] with your project ID in the two places where it occurs. This file's content is the same as the example shown previously.

6. Next, run the following to deploy the VM from the YAML file:

    ```
    $ gcloud deployment-manager deployments create
    vm-deployment-01 --config instance-01.yaml
    ```

7. Once the deployment has completed, you can check the deployed instance's configuration by running this:

```
$ gcloud compute instances describe testvm-01 --zone
europe-west1-b
```

You've now deployed a VM defined entirely in a configuration file. This file can be placed in a code repository for version control (in fact, it already has been – you just pulled it from GitHub). Now, we're going to deploy two additional VMs using a Jinja template. Still in the Cloud Shell terminal, perform the following steps:

1. Inspect the `instance-template.jinja` file. Notice how it looks almost exactly the same as the previous YAML file, except for the existence of parameters inside double curly braces, { { } }. There are two types of parameters in this template: environment variables (using the `env` function) and `properties`. Deployment Manager creates pre-defined environment variables that contain information inferred from your deployment. These include deployment name, project ID, current time, and current user, among a few others. In this template, we're using the `project` environment variable, which contains the inferred project ID (from your *gcloud* context). Therefore, this time you won't need to write your project ID in the file.

2. Now, inspect the `instance-02.input.yaml` file. It contains the values for the parameters we defined with the `properties` function in the template. These values define a particular deployment, that is, a particular instance. Go ahead and deploy this instance by running this:

```
$ gcloud projects add-iam-policy-binding [PROJECT_ID]
--role roles/editor --member serviceAccount:[PROJECT_
NUMBER]@cloudservices.gserviceaccount.com
$ gcloud deployment-manager deployments create
vm-deployment-02 --config instance-02.input.yaml
```

To check your project ID and project number, you can run `gcloud projects list`.

3. Inspect `instance-03.input.yaml`, which has different property values, and then deploy this other instance by running this command:

```
$ gcloud deployment-manager deployments create
vm-deployment-03 --config instance-03.input.yaml
```

4. Check the configurations of the two new instances:

```
$ gcloud compute instances describe testvm-02 --zone
europe-west1-b
$ gcloud compute instances describe testvm-03 --zone
europe-west1-b
```

Now you've deployed instances using a template and deployment-specific configuration files. Notice how the deployment YAML files became simpler. Someone without knowledge of Deployment Manager syntax can more easily create a new deployment by copying one of these files and modifying the values because parameterization has also the advantage of simplifying input. For example, Deployment Manager requires that the machine type be defined by its full URI. So, this is how it's written in the template:

```
machineType: https://www.googleapis.com/compute/v1/projects/
{{ env["project"] }}/zones/europe-west1-b/machineTypes/{{
properties["machineType"] }}
```

However, instead of requiring the full URI to be set in each deployment-specific configuration file, the template can contain the full URI with parameters inserted in the parts that "matter" for a new deployment; in this example, only the GCP project (as an environment variable) and the actual *name* of the machine type. That way, the input files will just need to include the following:

```
machineType: f1-micro
```

If the API URL or the deployment project changes, a new URI will likely be needed for all deployments. Therefore, being able to modify it only in the template and not everywhere is also an advantage.

Important note

As an optional exercise, can you figure out how you would modify the template to parametrize the VM source image? Try to do that and then deploy a new instance with a different source image (for example, `debian-9`).

To clean up your deployments, you could delete the instances you've created. However, because you've deployed them using Deployment Manager, a better way to delete them is to run this:

```
$ gcloud deployment-manager deployments delete vm-deployment-01
$ gcloud deployment-manager deployments delete vm-deployment-02
$ gcloud deployment-manager deployments delete vm-deployment-03
```

In this simple example, it doesn't make much difference. But suppose you had several resources within the same *deployment*, such as VMs, database, and firewall rules. If you deploy them as a unit, you can also delete them as a unit. Deployment Manager makes it easier for you to group resources that share the same life cycle (for example, infrastructure resources used by the same application) and manage them together as a unit of deployment.

You now have hands-on experience with Deployment Manager and IaC on GCP. Feel free to browse the Cloud Foundation Toolkit if you're eager to see more examples, or examples with templates using Python. But don't delete your project just yet; we will continue with hands-on practice.

CI/CD with Cloud Build

Cloud Build is a serverless CI/CD platform in Google Cloud that allows you to execute a build to your specifications and produce artifacts ready to be deployed. You write a build config file (in YAML or JSON format) to provide instructions to Cloud Build on what tasks to perform. The build is executed as a series of steps, where each step is run in a platform-managed Docker container. Executing build steps is analogous to executing commands in a script, providing you with the flexibility of executing arbitrary instructions as part of your build process. Cloud Build has also published a set of supported open source build steps for common languages and tasks at `https://github.com/ GoogleCloudPlatform/cloud-builders`.

You can manually start builds using *gcloud* or the Cloud Build API; however, the real value lies in its **build triggers** feature. With build triggers, you can create a CI/CD workflow that starts new builds in response to, for example, code changes to the main branch. Cloud Build integrates with many code repositories, including **Cloud Source Repositories** and GitHub. Cloud Source Repositories is a managed source repository service offered within GCP. It offers private Git repositories that integrate with many GCP services, including Cloud Monitoring and Logging. That offers a useful and seamless way to centralize audit logs for actions performed on the repository in the same location where platform logs are sent to. If you're doing IaC, your infrastructure is defined entirely in code, which means the code repository's audit logs become crucially important for change tracking and security audits. That being said, if you currently already use GitHub or other supported repository services, you can leverage Cloud Build's integration capabilities.

To get a feel for how it works, you will learn next how you can use Cloud Build to implement CI/CD for your App Engine deployments.

Automating App Engine deployments using Cloud Build

In this hands-on activity, you will automate the deployment of an App Engine web application. The goal is that every time you push new code changes to the repository, a new version of the app will be deployed automatically:

1. Go to the GCP console (`console.cloud.google.com`), and then click on the shell icon on the top-right corner of the screen to activate Cloud Shell.

2. Set the current project as the project for this chapter you created previously:

    ```
    $ gcloud config set project [PROJECT_ID]
    ```

    If you don't remember your project ID, run `gcloud projects list` to find it.

3. Enable the App Engine and Cloud Build APIs on your project:

    ```
    $ gcloud services enable cloudbuild.googleapis.com
    $ gcloud services enable appengine.googleapis.com
    ```

4. Next, you need to grant Cloud Build's service account the **App Engine Admin** role. Do this by running the following:

    ```
    $ gcloud projects add-iam-policy-binding [PROJECT_ID]
    --member=serviceAccount:[PROJECT_NUMBER] @cloudbuild.
    gserviceaccount.com --role=roles/appengine.appAdmin
    $ gcloud iam service-accounts add-iam-policy-binding \
        [PROJECT_ID]@appspot.gserviceaccount.com \
        --member=serviceAccount:[PROJECT_NUMBER]@cloudbuild.
    gserviceaccount.com \
        --role=roles/iam.serviceAccountUser \
        --project=[PROJECT_ID]
    ```

    Replace PROJECT_ID and PROJECT_NUMBER with your project ID and number, respectively. You can see your project number by running `gcloud projects describe [PROJECT_ID]`.

5. Create an App Engine instance in your project:

    ```
    $ gcloud app create --region [REGION]
    ```

    Replace REGION with an App Engine location of your choice, such as `us-central` or `europe-west`.

6. You will now need to fork the repository for this book into your own GitHub account. To do so, go to `https://github.com/PacktPublishing/Architecting-Google-Cloud-Solutions` and click on **Fork**.

7. Let's now switch to the console. Make sure you select **chapter-9** as your project on the project selection dropdown in the top bar. Navigate to **Cloud Build**, which is located under **Tools** on the left-side menu.

8. Click on **Triggers**, then on **Manage Repositories**. Finally, click on **Connect Repository**.

9. Select the **GitHub (Cloud Build GitHub App)** option and click on **Continue**. Follow the onscreen instructions to connect your GitHub account, install the Cloud Build app, and authorize it to access code in your repository. Make sure to select **Only select repositories** when prompted and select the **Architecting-Google-Cloud-Solutions** repository within your GitHub account. Once this is done, select the repository and the consent checkbox and click on **Connect repository**, as shown in the following figure:

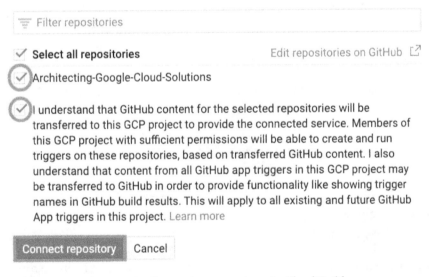

Figure 9.6 – Connecting a repository in Cloud Build

10. Click on **Create Trigger**. In the **name** field, type in `ci-trigger`. Leave other options with their default values.

Under **Build configuration**, select **Cloud Build configuration file (YAML or JSON)**. In the **Cloud Build configuration file location** field, type `/ch9/cloud-build/cloudbuild.yaml`, as shown in the following screenshot:

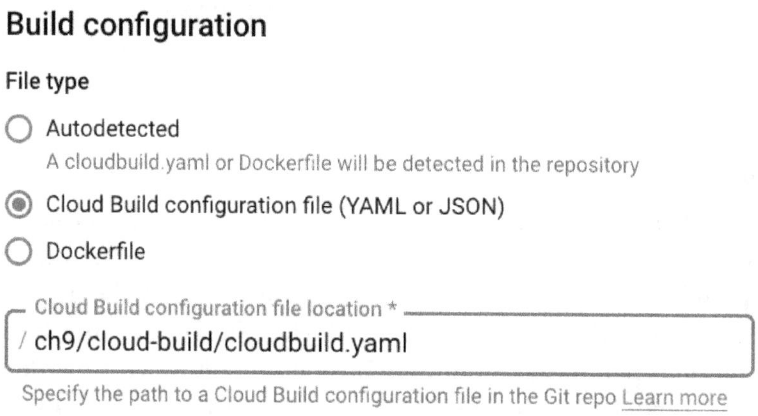

Build configuration

File type

○ Autodetected
  A cloudbuild.yaml or Dockerfile will be detected in the repository

◉ Cloud Build configuration file (YAML or JSON)

○ Dockerfile

Cloud Build configuration file location *
```
/ ch9/cloud-build/cloudbuild.yaml
```
Specify the path to a Cloud Build configuration file in the Git repo Learn more

Figure 9.7 – Setting the build configuration

Then, click on **Create**.

11. Click on **Run** next to your build trigger and then **Run trigger** to manually trigger a build now. Then navigate to **History** and check the new build entry. Click on the build ID to see the build logs being generated.

12. Once the build has completed, navigate to your app by running `gcloud app browse` in Cloud Shell, or copy the app URL from the build log output and paste it in your browser.

13. In Cloud Shell, clone your repository and navigate to the application's source code directory:

```
$ git clone https://github.com/[GITHUB_USERNAME]/
Architecting-Google-Cloud-Solutions
$ cd ch9/cloud-build/src
```

14. Using a text editor such as vim or nano, modify the `main.py` file or the `app.yaml` file (for example, replace the custom environment variable with the public URL of an image of your choice). Commit your changes to the master branch and push them to the remote repository:

```
$ git clone https://github.com/[GITHUB_USERNAME]/
Architecting-Google-Cloud-Solutions
cd Architecting-Google-Cloud-Solutions/ch9/cloud-build/
src
```

```
## NOTE: Either remove the existing directory cloned from
Packt or clone this repository to another directory in
Cloud Shell
$ git config --global user.email "YOUR_GITHUB_EMAIL"
git config --global user.name "YOUR_NAME"
```

15. Navigate back to Cloud Build's **History** page. You should see that a new build was created as a result of your code push. Wait until it has finished and navigate to the app URL again (you may need to refresh the page a few times in case the content you modified was cached in your browser). You should see the changes you've made.

You have now implemented a *continuous deployment* solution for a web app on GCP. Although it was a simple use case and example, it successfully demonstrates how to enable agility by automating the deployment process of your code. It wouldn't be hard to extend this to include infrastructure code, such as what you worked on previously to deploy VMs. In a real production scenario, you should consider including build steps for automated tests.

To clean up the resources created for this chapter, delete the project by running this:

```
$ gcloud projects delete [PROJECT_ID]
```

So far, we haven't discussed the subject of security in the context of DevOps. We will delve into this next.

DevSecOps

While DevOps was successful in helping organizations reduce silos and creating a culture of shared responsibility, security was a topic left out of the early discussions – and indeed was never mentioned in any of the principles. The SRE practices don't seem to include security as one of their core goals either. Enterprise architects have since learned that security too is a shared responsibility and must be implemented as early as possible in the process. After all, the costs of fixing security incidents are often higher than those of fixing breaking infrastructure changes or application bugs. Therefore, it made sense to find and prevent security-related defects early in the software and infrastructure delivery processes. This practice, commonly referred to as *shifting left*, is illustrated in the following figure:

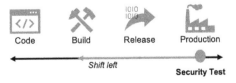

Figure 9.8 – Shifting security left

If the different stages of development are placed side by side in a timeline, the *left* refers to the early stages, where the *cost of failure is the lowest*. This idea was already embraced in DevOps and SRE practices for quality (development) and reliability (operations). By integrating security as another DevOps pillar as opposed to a sidelined consideration, the term **DevSecOps** was coined and became a new paradigm.

DevSecOps means thinking early about application and infrastructure security. The principles previously mentioned for DevOps still stand. This means security is a shared responsibility to be continuously measured and improved, with changes implemented gradually and often and automated when possible, and where incidents are to be expected and learned from. Leveraging tooling to automate things such as security checks, scans, reporting, and even remediation actions is crucial to implement DevSecOps without slowing down the end-to-end workflow. **Security as Code** is the new implementation approach and toolset of resources that enable the secure delivery pipelines. Security policies and checks defined as code can be source-controlled, and their life cycles approached in the same way as application and codified infrastructure.

Thankfully, cloud-native services lend themselves well to DevSecOps. In *Chapter 7, Designing for Security and Compliance*, we discussed policy-driven security and the programmatic capabilities in Google Cloud that enable you to secure your infrastructure from the ground up. We also discussed incorporating automated checks in your pipelines as a best practice. However, crucial to any successful DevSecOps organization is to foster collaboration and make security a team effort. Security teams may still exist, but their goals will be aligned to those of developers and operators, in the same way as previously achieved by DevOps and SRE.

To effectively implement Security as Code, think of the following questions:

- What checks can I do on my *code* to ensure it follows security best practices? Examples: the presence of plain-text passwords and/or connection strings, the absence of crucial security configuration, and deviations from a baseline policy set.

- What checks can I do on my *build artifacts* to ensure it's a secured build? Examples: deviation from a baseline configuration in VM or container images, undesired security changes in Terraform plans, and the presence of known vulnerabilities.

- What checks/tests can I run once it's *deployed* to an environment? Examples: real-time vulnerability detection, and policy compliance status.

The earlier you detect defects, the lower the cost of addressing them. Therefore, aim to implement as many code- and artifact-level checks as possible. These types of checks are often referred to as *static analysis – or static application security testing (SAST)* – since they happen before anything is actually deployed and running. Other types of security tests are **dynamic application security testing (DAST)**, in which tests are performed against running applications; **interactive application security testing (IAST)**, in which code is analyzed while the app is being run by an automation tool; and **runtime application self-protection (RASP)**, which leverages runtime instrumentation to detect and block security attacks while the application is running. The following is a list of some useful open source and commercial Security as Code tools for infrastructure:

- **Checkov**: `https://checkov.io`.
- **Terraform-compliance**: `https://terraform-compliance.com`.
- **Tfsec**: `https://www.tfsec.dev`
- **Aqua Security**: `https://www.aquasec.com/`
- **Qualys**: `https://www.qualys.com/`

Security can be overwhelming. It's easy to want to delegate this responsibility to a "security team" and have them handle all aspects of it. However, remember that DevOps saying, *"if it hurts, do it more often."* As the culture of collaboration and shared responsibility evolves, more people can get involved with security practices. As more people practice more security and do it more often, the easier and less "painful" it will become. And the better everyone will get at it too. Start small with easy picks for your infrastructure code and grow gradually from there. A strong governance foundation with organizational policies plus a few pipeline security validations will go a long way.

Job scheduling with Cloud Scheduler

Automation often relies on the ability to schedule jobs to run at a certain time. On GCP, you can leverage **Cloud Scheduler**, which is a fully managed enterprise-grade **cron** job scheduler. It supports a variety of **cron** job targets, allowing you to automate virtually anything. For example, you can trigger an App Engine app, send a message via Pub/Sub, or call an arbitrary HTTP endpoint. With Cloud Scheduler, you get guaranteed at-least-once delivery and a configurable retry policy for cases of error or failure. Even if you are inexperienced with **cron** or **crontab**, it provides a simple UI and command-line interface using which you can manage cron jobs. The schedule, or the frequency of execution, can be defined using a Unix-based cron string format.

You create a scheduled job by defining a name, a cron-based frequency, a time zone, and a target. The target can be one of the following:

- **HTTP**: Requires URL, an HTTP method (POST, GET, PUT, and so on), and an optional body

- **Pub/Sub**: Requires a Pub/Sub topic and a payload (message content)

- **App Engine HTTP**: Requires the relative HTTP URL of an App Engine app and optional fields such as service name, HTTP method, version, instance, and HTTP body

The job will run according to the cron schedule and, since it's a serverless service, the underlying resources and their availability will be managed for you. You can also trigger a job manually at any time.

There can be many scenarios in which you can leverage Cloud Scheduler. A few examples are as follows:

- Trigger Cloud Function on a schedule to run a batch job.

- Schedule data exports by calling a database export API.

- Trigger a function to start and/or stop Compute Engine instances.

- Trigger an application once a day to check for expired user accounts and delete them.

If you have existing cron jobs set up on VM instances, you may want to consider using Cloud Scheduler instead as a fully managed service that offers better availability and delivery guarantees. Current executable scripts running on VMs can be either rewritten for Cloud Function or as a web script with an HTTP endpoint.

So far, you've learned about the DevOps principles, the SRE practices, the enabling GCP services, and you even got some hands-on experience with deployment automation and CI/CD pipelines. In the next and final section, we will take a step back and look at ways to apply SRE in your organization.

Applying SRE

As you've learned throughout this chapter, DevOps is a set of *principles* and a working *culture*. On the other hand, SRE is a set of technical *practices* where many of the underlying principles are similar to those of DevOps. An analogy to object-oriented programming is often made to describe SRE: if DevOps is a class, SRE is an object that instantiates the class. In other words, SRE is a practical implementation of an otherwise abstract set of principles. Moreover, it "extends" the class to include its own unique methodologies.

It doesn't make much sense to start a DevOps journey by hiring "DevOps engineers" and procuring tools. Even the role of a DevOps engineer shouldn't yet exist unless you have already established a basic DevOps foundation. It's easy to fall into the trap of thinking that simply hiring engineers who are well versed in the DevOps ways of working will bring DevOps to your organization. It might help you get there to a certain extent, but it almost certainly won't be enough. Even though SRE is different in that it is much more practical, it can't be established properly simply by hiring SRE professionals either. That being said, there are some recommendations and guidance on how to apply it to your organization, which we shall explore next. These are useful to learn even if you're not a leader in your organization. By being an SRE champion, you may eventually be able to influence the leadership toward SRE adoption and will likely be consulted on how best to approach it.

Creating an SRE foundation

As with any large transformation endeavor, the first step should be to assess the organizational maturity level for adopting SRE. The level will be *low* if none of the SRE principles, practices, or underlying cultures are present in your organization. Conversely, it will be *high* if there is a well-established SRE team (even if they're not called SRE) that widely embraces the SRE principles and practices. Then, of course, it can be anywhere in between. To understand where exactly you are, think of the concrete practices you've learned about in this chapter and ascertain whether or not they exist in your organization. Consider these characteristics, for example:

- Existing teams don't have conflicting priorities (that is, they are not measured on different metrics and/or have different goals).

- There are documented user-centric SLOs for each critical service.

- There is an error budget in conjunction with each SLO that is used to increase the pace of change in a controlled manner.

- Blameless retrospectives (postmortems) are conducted after each incident.

- Your team has a low tolerance for toil and continually works on ways to reduce it (for example, by leveraging tooling and automation).

- Quality and reliability (and potentially security) are continuously measured and improved.

- Your team leverages strategies such as automated testing and canarying to reduce the cost of failure.

Beyond these technical practices, think of cultural elements and whether or not they are present and well understood across teams:

- Psychological safety around failures

- Collaboration culture

- Design thinking and prototyping mentality

- Goal setting and data-driven decision making

Once you understand what is currently already present and what is not, you should have a much better idea of where you are. Most importantly, you will be able to identify the first steps to take toward higher SRE maturity. If you're starting from zero or coming from a low maturity level, Google recommends applying SRE on both technical and cultural fronts in the following order:

Technical	Cultural
Set SLOs, error budgets, and a postmortem practice. Form an SRE team.	Psychological safety Shared vision Collaboration
Implement automation practices such as CI/CD, canarying, and toil automation.	Design thinking and prototyping Change management
Measure toil and reliability. Implement comprehensive monitoring.	Goal-setting culture Data-driven decision making Transparency

Ultimately, however, SRE is practiced by *people* and its success will depend on certain *skills*. Team members must be knowledgeable on both development and operations practices, which are not often taught together in universities or IT courses. For that reason, training and upskilling are essential to ensure that your SREs will be able to develop a generalized skillset. For example, you can offer software engineering training to your system administrators and/or IT operations training to your software engineers as a starting point. The goal is not to try to transform operations engineers into software developers or vice versa. The goal is to give both teams a common frame of reference.

Google recommends the following essential training for new SRE teams:

- Operations and software engineering
- Monitoring systems
- Production automation
- System architecture
- Troubleshooting
- Culture of trust
- Incident management

If you start with setting SLOs plus error budgets and postmortem practices, then by forming an SRE team that is offered basic training on these subjects, you will have a great foundation on which to grow an SRE organization. A culture of fostering collaboration and psychological safety will help create the necessary momentum for the team to move forward and embrace the other practices. In particular, as your team starts to automate toil away, there will likely be greater motivation for further automation – ultimately leading to more reliable systems and a better quality of life for engineers.

Another useful resource for assessing your team's current DevOps status is to take the **DevOps Research and Assessment (DORA)** quick check at `https://www.devops-research.com/quickcheck.html`. It's a short questionnaire that will quickly allow you to assess where you stand compared to others in the same industry.

Now that you know the basics for getting started with SRE, let's now delve into some of the practical ways to form and approach SRE teams.

Forming SRE teams

The best way to structure your team(s) will depend on the size of your organization and your maturity level. Google recommends six different models for SRE teams' implementations:

1. **Kitchen sink, or "everything SRE"**: In this approach, there's a single team with unbounded scope. It is a good starting point for a first SRE team and recommended for organizations with few applications. The primary disadvantage of this model is that it risks overloading the team, especially as the organization grows in size and complexity.

2. **Infrastructure**: An infrastructure team works to help make other team's jobs easier by maintaining shared infrastructure services. This approach is recommended for organizations with multiple development teams as it helps define a common IT standard. This approach puts the focus on highly reliable infrastructure, while other DevOps-oriented development teams focus on continuous improvement of software. The primary disadvantage of this approach is that it may lead to a disconnect between this team and the customer experience, and improvements the team makes may not be tied to real business value.

3. **Tools**: A tools-focused SRE team builds software and tools to help developers with SRE work. This is recommended for organizations that need highly specialized reliability-related tooling such as monitoring and measuring software, automation tools, or capacity planning tools. The main disadvantage of this approach is that there is a risk of increased toil and overall workload on the team.

4. **Product/Application**: A product- or application-oriented SRE team works to improve the reliability of a critical application. This approach is recommended for organizations that have applications with high reliability needs and also already have a kitchen sink, infrastructure, or tools SRE team. This helps provide a clear focus and priority for the team's effort. The main disadvantage is that it can lead to the duplication of work with infrastructure teams or to the divergence of practices.

5. **Embedded**: This team has SREs that are embedded with developers, working closely with them to help them achieve SRE-related goals. These relationships tend to be project- or time-bound. During engagements, SREs work very hands-on by changing code and the configuration of services to maintain reliability objectives and/or make use of error budgets. This model is recommended for organizations that are starting an SRE function and need it for a period of time. This approach can be a very effective teaching method as it allows side-by-side collaboration and demonstration of SRE practices. The disadvantage is that it can cause a lack of standardization between teams and a consequent divergence in practice.

6. **Consulting**: Similar to an embedded team, a consulting team works closely with other teams to help drive SRE practices. However, it typically does not involve hands-on activities such as a change in code and configurations. This is recommended for organizations with greater complexity and size to help existing SRE teams scale their positive impact. Being decoupled from coding and tooling, this team can focus on improving practices and processes. On the flip side, its disadvantage is that it may lack sufficient context to offer useful guidance.

Remember, only once you have assessed your SRE maturity level and started with some basic practices and training should you be forming a first SRE team. Over time, and as your maturity level and scale increase, you will likely have a combination of two or more of these team models.

Finally, consider leveraging SRE-focused training and guidance provided by Google's professional services team or partner. As a cloud or solutions architect, you may want to read through the SRE book and workbook available at `https://sre.google/books/`. In particular, check out real-world SLO engineering case studies at `https://sre.google/workbook/slo-engineering-case-studies/` to see examples of how SRE has been implemented in practice. You may not be in the capacity of leading an SRE transformation in your organization, but by acquiring these skills you will be able to support them by building DevOps-oriented cloud solutions with an automation and "shift left" mentality.

Summary

In this chapter, you've learned about the problems DevOps emerged to solve and its five backbone principles. You've then learned about SRE, which is a practical implementation of DevOps. You've learned how you can incorporate SRE, from broad cultural changes to specific technical practices. In particular, you've learned about the motivations for automation and the importance of measuring and automating toil. You got hands-on experience in using GCP to automate infrastructure deployments and implement a serverless CI/CD pipeline.

Finally, you've learned a few practical ways to apply SRE to your organization and form SRE teams. You should be able to apply many of the concepts learned in this chapter to design modern enterprise solutions with the perfect balance between reliability and innovation agility to support organizations in their DevOps journey.

In the next chapter, you will learn how to design a scalable microservices architecture on GCP.

10
Re-Architecting with Microservices

Microservices have almost become the de facto architecture pattern in modern scalable application design. It's a concept that aligns well with DevOps and **Site Reliability Engineering (SRE)**. However, like all new technologies and design patterns, it's not necessarily the right solution for all scenarios and certainly doesn't come without its set of challenges. A cloud architect must understand the pros and cons of microservices architectures, when to adopt them, and how to make the best use of them.

In this chapter, you will learn what problems microservices solve – and what problems they create. You will learn how to design modern application architectures that leverage microservices and common design patterns. You will then learn about the enabling technologies in Google Cloud to deploy microservices and manage **APIs**. In particular, you will get hands-on experience in decomposing a monolithic application into microservices and deploying them on **Google Kubernetes Engine (GKE)**. Finally, you will be presented with a case study to test your knowledge of microservices architecture. The skills you acquire in this chapter will empower you to design modern microservices-oriented enterprise solutions at any scale.

In this chapter, we're going to cover the following main topics:

- Understanding microservices and when to adopt them
- Building microservices with Kubernetes
- Designing and managing APIs for microservices
- Testing your knowledge – microservices design case study

Technical requirements

For the hands-on activities in this chapter, you will need a billing-enabled Google Cloud account and optionally the Google Cloud SDK installed (if you don't have it, you can use Cloud Shell from a browser). Helper scripts and code for this chapter can be found at `https://github.com/PacktPublishing/Architecting-Google-Cloud-Solutions/tree/master/ch10`.

Check out the following link to see the Code in Action video: `https://bit.ly/2MONxlk`

Understanding microservices and when to adopt them

As with all good buzzwords, there's no single view on what exactly microservices are. However, there's good consensus on the general idea behind it. That is, *an architectural style and approach to designing applications as suites of independently deployable and loosely coupled services*. These services are "small" and specialized, and the communication protocols are lightweight (typically an HTTP resource API). Furthermore, services can be written in different programming languages and use different storage technologies. You may have already heard these things or already know this much about microservices. So, what's all the fuss about, and why should you use microservices? Let's take a more in-depth look.

Why microservices?

A microservices architecture is perhaps best understood when contrasted with the traditional *monolithic* style that it is meant to replace. A monolithic application is designed without modularity and as a self-contained application. A typical enterprise web application using this style is built in three strongly coupled layers: a client-facing presentation layer (the frontend), a server-side application layer (the backend), and a data layer (the databases). The strong coupling results from the fact that these different components are designed as a service unit, responsible for every function of a web application. For example, the backend component of a typical web application handles HTTP requests coming through the frontend, executes business domain logic, manipulates data in the database, and selects and populates web views to be presented at the frontend. All this logic runs in a single process.

Consequently, any change made to any part of the application requires the entire monolith to be rebuilt and redeployed. This hinders development agility and innovation, making it difficult for teams to deliver new features at high velocity. Because of the lack of modularity, changes made to one component may negatively affect other parts of the application's behavior, impacting its overall reliability.

On the other hand, microservices architectures seek to "break down" monoliths into loosely coupled services. They generally present the following differentiating characteristics:

- Componentization and modularization via *independent* services.
- Services organized around *business capabilities* and functions.
- Services are networked and communicate using a technology-agnostic *lightweight protocol*.
- Services are small and *specialized in scope, bounded by contexts, independently deployable*, and *decentralized*.
- They favor the "*smart endpoints and dump pipes*" architectural approach, that is, having self-contained endpoints that own their entire domain logic and lightweight messaging between them (with no features beyond message routing).

Such characteristics help explain what microservices are and how they differ from the traditional monoliths. But what are the practical benefits? And when should they be used?

The main value proposition of a microservices architecture is that different components can be independently developed and thus *managed by different teams*. This enables teams to work at their own cadence and decouple strong ties between components. Consequently, these various components can scale more easily and independently – you no longer need to increase resource capacity for the entire monolith just because one of its parts hit a limit. Therefore, your application can be more *resource-efficient* by allowing you to define the resource specifications for each application service more granularly. With loose coupling and message-oriented architectures that leverage asynchronous messaging, as we will see later in this chapter, the application can reach much greater scalability potential.

Because microservices own their domain logic, each microservice must define a clear interface through which other microservices and clients (internal or external) can "consume" it. This interface helps establish an agreement on how the service is to be used while abstracting internal implementation details. As long as the interface is respected, teams can push changes and implement new functionalities to evolve their service without having its clients make any change.

As teams become more independent, they're also able to specialize and focus on their respective services to make them do the one thing they're supposed to do – and do it well. In fact, from a strategy perspective, microservices architectures follow the known Unix design philosophy captured in the sentence: "*do one thing and do it well.*" The following figure illustrates the high-level differences between monolithic and microservices architecture:

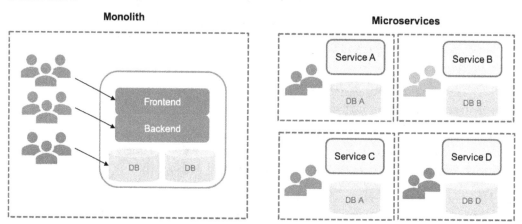

Figure 10.1 – Monolith versus microservices

Crucial to success in increasing delivery agility with microservices is embracing deployment **automation**. In *Chapter 9, Jumping on the DevOps Bandwagon with Site Reliability Engineering (SRE)*, we discussed **continuous integration** and **continuous delivery (CI/CD)** as well as the DevOps principles and SRE practices that enable teams to deliver high-quality software at high velocity. There's a reason that chapter came before this one. If your organization has not reached a reasonable level of DevOps maturity, with most deployments automated via CI/CD pipelines, then it may not be ready for microservices yet. Decomposing an application results in several parallel software life cycles to manage and several components to build and deploy where there was previously only one. Moreover, working with microservices requires cross-functional teams that are capable of owning the end-to-end life cycle of the application's development and across all its infrastructure stack. For that reason, having organizational practices that reflect the DevOps principle of shared ownership and collaboration is fundamental for adopting microservices.

In light of what the microservices architectural pattern is and what it helps you achieve, we can now turn to the question of *when* to use it. The following are the typical scenarios where you can consider using microservices architectures:

- Your application has components with clearly defined boundaries around business capabilities. These different components don't write to the same database table.

- Different components would be able to work with a strong degree of independence, providing their capabilities as networked services only.

- You have the necessary infrastructure automation capabilities and DevOps maturity level to support the development of a complex distributed system.

- Your application relies heavily on integrations with other applications via web services or message brokers.

- Your primary goals are scalability, agility, and manageability of applications.

Microservices architectures are great in many ways, but they're also complex solutions to complex problems. If your organization doesn't have these problems or doesn't have yet the required conditions just mentioned, microservices might be overkill. There are still software patterns with which you can build robust monolithic application architectures. As professionals working in IT, we must sometimes make an effort not to be lured by the newest and "shiniest" tool (a common occurrence in the field) for the sake of not missing out.

With the *when* out of the way, we'll delve next into the *how*.

How to decompose a monolith

To clarify what a microservices architecture looks like in practice, consider the example of a typical online web shop. In this application, users can browse products on a website, place an order for one or more products, and then pay for the order with a credit card. They can then follow the order status, including shipping information and estimated delivery date. This entire application would fit into a three-tier architecture in a monolithic approach, with an application backend owning most of the domain logic. In a microservices architecture, this web application can, for example, be split by the following business capabilities:

- **Order service**: Responsible for taking a new order and processing it
- **Catalog service**: Responsible for checking and maintaining product inventory
- **Payment service**: Responsible for managing credit card payments
- **Shipping service**: Responsible for managing product shipments.

Other services that would likely be present include an authorization service responsible for authorizing registered customers and a cart service to manage user carts. But let's focus on these listed services, which are represented in the following diagram:

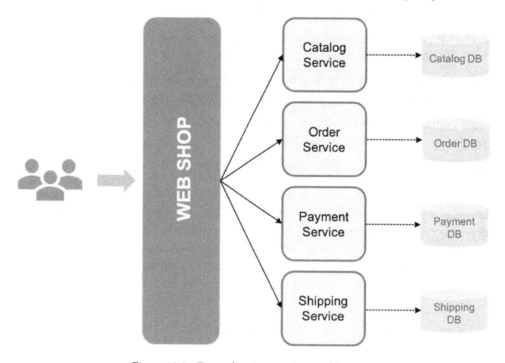

Figure 10.2 – Example microservices architecture

In this architecture, when a user places an order, a series of API calls happen to each affected service so they can do what they're responsible for. That also includes any validations that the service needs to perform. For example, the catalog service is requested to check and confirm whether the ordered products are available. Once confirmed, the payment service is called to process and validate the payment. Once that is completed, the order service processes the order and updates the order status to "confirmed" before a request for shipment is placed on the shipping service. Finally, the catalog service updates the inventory accordingly. When the user requests the order status, the order service and the shipping service can be queried for order and shipping status, respectively. You get the idea. Each component specializes in one functionality (or *business capability*), and interactions between them happen over the network, whereas previously, these operations would have occurred within a program.

The capability-oriented aspect of microservices is an essential design principle. A common anti-pattern is to base microservices on the different *layers* of the application stack, such as frontend, backend, and database. That achieves very little in terms of the benefits discussed previously. You should think in terms of the *logical domains* of your application, not architectural layers. In fact, a microservice may, through its own internal design, implement a layered architecture. It's often the case that teams run into such anti-patterns because they decompose a monolith in a way that precisely matches the organizational structure – a common setting in many organizations is to have a UI team, an application development team, and a database team. Hence, splitting the services this way feels more natural. However, most successful organizations have cross-functional, full stack development teams responsible for each microservice when working with microservices architectures. Amazon captured this idea best with its famous adage: "*you build it, you run it.*" In this case, each microservice encapsulates an entire domain logic containing the full stack of infrastructure components it requires (from the user interface to the databases). This approach to segregating components is commonly referred to as domain-driven design in software development.

Another useful guiding principle for decomposing monoliths is to isolate services that provide shared functionality, for example, an authentication service that centralizes all authentication functions or a reporting service that performs all the reporting. It is sometimes useful to logically group services by categories such as "frontend services,", "backend services," or "utility services."

The microservices architectural approach does come with its downsides. Remote calls over the network are not as fast and efficient as in-process calls. In addition, it is more challenging to move functionalities and responsibilities from one service to another than it is to do so within a monolith (by, for example, moving them across classes or namespaces). Decomposing an application *improves individual component complexity at the expense of greater overall system complexity*.

If not approached correctly, these added complexities may not justify the choice of microservices. In fact, you may even be thinking: with all this communication going on between microservices, aren't they still somewhat strongly coupled, except now at *runtime*? That would be true with a poorly designed microservices architecture that doesn't isolate functionalities properly or that relies too heavily on **synchronous communication** patterns. When building microservices, an essential guiding principle should be that communication between microservices must be kept to a minimum and done exclusively via services' exposed interfaces. As much as possible, a microservice should operate on its own and not depend on other services to do its work and function properly. A microservice may need to know about another service's state, but neither affect it nor depend on it to execute its domain logic. If these qualities are not present, it's a sign that functionalities are tightly coupled and that what you're deploying instead is a *complex distributed monolith*.

That being said, communication between microservices does happen. Therefore, it's crucial to understand the differences between **asynchronous** and synchronous **messaging patterns** to understand one of the pillars of scalable microservices architectures. Next, we will delve into this topic before looking at other challenges of microservices architectures and design patterns that help overcome them.

Asynchronous messaging

A good analogy to understand the difference between synchronous and asynchronous messaging paradigms is within human communication. When two individuals are talking face to face with each other, the communication is *synchronous* because one individual is always talking while the other is only listening (for the sake of this example, these are polite people). Once the first individual stops talking, they expect the second to respond more or less immediately after. On the other hand, *asynchronous* communication is akin to texting or sending an email. One individual sends a message to another but doesn't expect an immediate answer – or, for that matter, that the other party is ready to read it.

The same idea applies to software programming and communication protocols. In synchronous messaging, different programs (or servers, applications, and so on) communicate with each other by sending messages and *actively waiting* for a reply. The HTTP protocol, for example, is synchronous. When you type in a URL on your browser (the HTTP client), it waits for the server to reply back with the web content. That state of "waiting" means that whichever process thread originated that request is not terminated and doesn't do anything else until it gets a reply. In programming jargon, that thread is said to be *blocked*. In contrast, an asynchronous protocol such as **AJAX** (short for **Asynchronous JavaScript and XML**) allows protocol clients to send requests without blocking.

For example, web applications can use AJAX to send and retrieve data from a server asynchronously without slowing down the display of the web page or interfering with it. In plain language, asynchronous requests usually translate to "do this in the background while I work on other stuff and let me know when it's ready." In the context of computer processes, this difference is illustrated in the following figure:

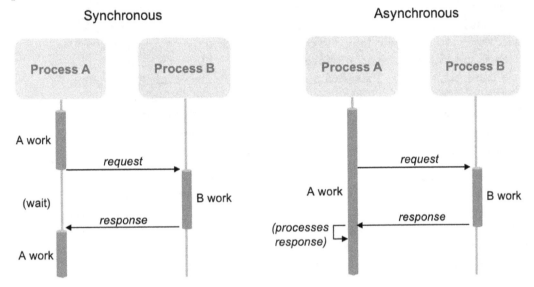

Figure 10.3 – Synchronous versus asynchronous communication

You can begin to see how microservices may benefit from an asynchronous messaging pattern. In our previous example, the shipping service and the catalog service could probably process their requests asynchronously. In other words, the order service can immediately proceed to process an order without waiting for these services to do their bit, since they're not crucial to the order service's operation (if they were, this would have been a suboptimal microservices architecture to begin with). The order service can periodically ask these two other services for their status and update its own status accordingly. And what if something goes wrong somewhere?

For example, suppose the shipping service determines during its internal validation that one of the items cannot be shipped to the requested location. In this case, the order service will need to kick off a refund process for that particular item and notify the customer. This is one drawback of decoupling via asynchronous communication: you need to design around the fact that your services won't get immediate feedback from other services when working asynchronously and may need to act to revert operations already done. That being said, for a properly designed solution and with the help of specific design patterns, this should not be a problem. You will learn more about this shortly.

An important distinction to be made regarding messaging patterns is between that which is used by protocols and that which is used at the *service integration* layer. The fact that HTTP is a synchronous protocol doesn't mean you can't design asynchronous service integrations with it. For example, with multithread parallel programming, a service can initiate a synchronous communication process to request data from another service, and then work on something else at the same time (in parallel) while that first thread is blocked. As long as the main request/response cycle of the service is never blocked by the service's internal communication with other services, then the messaging pattern between services is still effectively asynchronous at a higher level. When you're loading a website on a browser tab, that tab's associated process thread may be waiting for a response from the web server, but the browser is still fully operational – for instance, you're able to load other pages. It's the same principle. You could argue that building asynchronous systems on top of synchronous protocols is not as optimal a solution as using underlying asynchronous protocols, but it does work well in most cases.

Asynchronous messaging allows for much greater decoupling and, consequently, better scalability. However, it will not solve all the potential service integration challenges that may arise in microservices architectures. Two particularly problematic scenarios are when services need to handle transactions using relational databases or when cross-service requests are common. Luckily, design patterns have emerged to tackle these and other challenges. You will learn next what they are.

Common design patterns

Many of the challenges of microservices architectures derive from the fact that multiple services operate independently but somewhat in tandem. Although a well-designed solution will have microservices that are isolated and self-contained entities, there will always be a degree of dependency – or, perhaps more precisely, a degree of *coordination* – between them *at higher layers*. For example, users buying products from our online shop will rely not only on all the services (cart, order, payment, and so on) to be fully functional but also properly orchestrated to avoid any inconsistencies. An example of inconsistency would be having the payment confirmed while the order status is forever stuck on "pending" – and products are never delivered. Moreover, since each service typically owns its data model and has its dedicated database, ensuring the overall consistency of business transactions becomes difficult.

The Saga pattern

When each service has its own database, but a transaction spans multiple microservices, how to ensure data consistency across services? If each database performs its own local ACID transaction without knowledge of other related transactions, it can't be possible.

> **Important note**
>
> ACID refers to the four key properties of database transactions: atomicity, consistency, isolation, and durability. Each of these properties was discussed in detail in *Chapter 5, Architecting Storage and Data Infrastructure*.

The Saga pattern tackles this issue by breaking down a request into several local transactions. Local transactions are then executed sequentially, each one proceeding only after a previous one has been completed. Building on our e-commerce example, the Saga pattern could be incorporated as shown in the following figure:

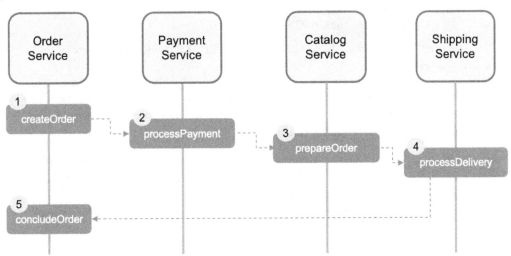

Figure 10.4 – The Saga pattern

Each local transaction happens in reaction to a previous transaction (except for the first one, which initiates the flow). Each transaction also needs to have a *compensating transaction* that gets executed if and when the request fails. The Saga pattern is generally implemented using one of two approaches:

- **Choreography**: With no central coordination, each service producing and reacting to other services' events to decide whether or not to take an action. This is an event-based implementation.

- **Orchestration**: With a central orchestrator/coordinator service being responsible for centralizing the decision making and sequencing logic.

With the choreography approach, an example flow could look like this:

1. The order service creates a new order and generates the ORDER_CREATED event.

2. The payment service reacts to the ORDER_CREATED event by processing the payment and then generating a PAYMENT_CONFIRMED event.

3. The catalog service reacts to the PAYMENT_CONFIRMED event by executing its order preparation function, at which point it identifies that the product is no longer in stock. It generates the OUT_OF_STOCK event.

4. The order service listens to the OUT_OF_STOCK event and process an order cancellation. It generates the ORDER_CANCELLED event.

5. The payment service reacts to the ORDER_CANCELLED event and executes a payment refund.

There could be other ways of "choreographing" these services, but the fundamental idea is to design the flow of events in such a way that it always ends in a consistent manner and every possible scenario is accounted for.

The orchestration approach would instead involve one orchestrator service responsible for telling each participant service exactly what to do and when. In the previous example, each operation would happen in a request-response style between the orchestrator and each service. This way, the orchestrator has visibility into every step and is able to make decisions and coordinate rollbacks if necessary.

The Command Query Responsibility Segregation (CQRS) pattern

When database queries require joint data from multiple services, how can this be achieved efficiently with microservices?

The CQRS pattern suggests splitting the application into a *command* model and a *query* model. The command model handles the *creation*, *updating*, and *deletion* of data records. The query model exclusively handles the *read* operations by using materialized views. There's flexibility as to how "models" can be practically implemented – they can be different processes, different interfaces, and/or different databases. A common approach – and most relevant for the context of microservices – is to implement the query model as a separate, read-only replica database that contains multiple denormalized views. The application keeps the replica up to date by listening to domain events published by the service that owns the data.

For example, the order, shipping, and payment services in our e-commerce scenario could be used to build a read-only *order history* database that aggregates relevant data from each. A history record could contain order, payment, and delivery information as "pre-computed" views to be queried by the application. For example, when the user wishes to browse their order history. An update to either one of the source data records (for example, a change in the order status) triggers an update to the view. This pattern is illustrated in the following figure:

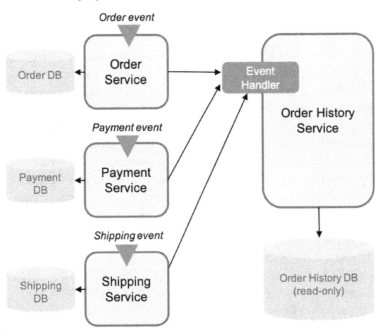

Figure 10.5 – The CQRS pattern

In the diagram, **Order History Service** introduced handles events from the various services, manages the materialized views, and serves queries. Queries never write to the database. Only commands do.

In this pattern, commands are task-oriented instead of reflecting granular data-level operations. For example, commands may be defined as `createOrder` or `executePayment` instead of "set `orderStatus` field to `processing`." A command may encapsulate several data operations and handle data objects at a granularity that matches that of the domain. In other words, this pattern suggests you care less about individual data fields and more about the *tasks* or domain-level data updates being performed.

One caveat of CQRS is that this approach tends to compromise strong consistency. That is, read operations may return "stale" data for a brief period of time. However, in many cases, this sort of eventual consistency is acceptable for read queries that span multiple services. Moreover, this approach offers additional benefits such as improved performance and scalability due to the separation of reads and writes, the optimization of read databases for queries (for example, with materialized views), and the possibility to scale *out* read replicas.

The API Gateway pattern

When our web shop user makes a purchase or browses information about orders and products, the code that executes such operations needs to fetch information from various services. Therefore, there's a *granularity mismatch* between individual services' APIs and the API that a client needs. While microservices typically provide domain-specific, fine-grained APIs, users require less granular APIs that encapsulate broader business logic. For example, a purchase on the website is a single request from the user´s perspective. However, that request is broken down into several downstream requests spanning multiple services, such as **create order**, **check inventory**, and **execute payment** Moreover, if the web shop has a mobile client app, client-to-microservice requests can result in several round trips over unstable network connections.

The **API Gateway** pattern creates a single point of entry for requests. It helps solve the challenge of orchestrating multi-service operations and reduce chatty communications between clients and backend services. It works similar to a proxy service, routing requests to the affected microservices while abstracting the complexity of the services' distribution. This pattern is similar to the *façade pattern* commonly used in object-oriented software design but applied to a distributed system. The gateway is the mediator that translates business logic to an aggregate sequence of microservices API calls, potentially performing protocol translations as illustrated in the following figure:

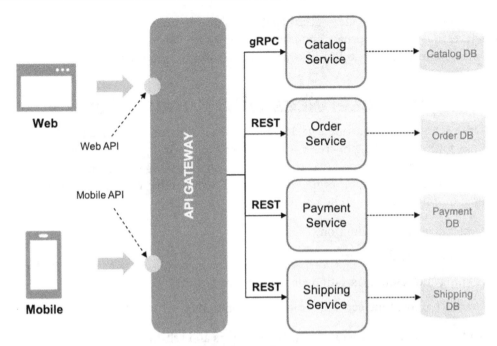

Figure 10.6 – The API Gateway pattern

In this pattern, the API gateway typically exposes a different API for each client type (such as a web browser and mobile app). This is so each API can be designed to best suit each client's requirements and include client-specific features.

A separate API gateway is used for each type of client in a common variation of this pattern known as the **Backends For Frontends (BFF)** pattern. This creates better isolation and separation of concerns, allowing, for example, mobile and web teams to work more independently. It also allows the API gateway to be fine-tuned and optimized for each client from both software and infrastructure perspectives.

Consider this pattern if your application serves different clients and has sufficient complexity to justify the added overhead. You must be careful when implementing the API Gateway pattern, as it can be "abused" to the point of it acting as a *monolithic aggregator*, creating strong coupling and thus violating microservice autonomy. You can use it to dispatch client requests to several internal microservices requests with the main goal of reducing "chattiness" between the client apps and the backend APIs, but not with the goal of coupling together microservices that aren't capable of working on their own. Think of it this way: if your application cannot work at all without including an API gateway in its design, you're probably doing something wrong.

Now that you have a general idea of the benefits and drawbacks of microservices architectures and how to approach monolith decomposition and design patterns for common scenarios, we will explore how to *build* microservices in practice.

Building microservices with Kubernetes

Microservices and Kubernetes are a great combination. Containers are not a required technology for implementing microservices – no technology is – but they're certainly a great fit, especially when properly orchestrated by software such as Kubernetes. For example, the following are some of the features of Kubernetes that make it particularly well suited for microservices architectures:

- Declarative service definition

- Built-in service discovery

- Naming and resource isolation via namespaces

- Granular autoscaling capabilities for pods/containers

We can add abstraction of several infrastructure layers and self-healing capabilities as extra bonuses to this list. Because Kubernetes (and a *managed* Kubernetes service, particularly) enables teams to focus more on customer-facing functionalities and less on undifferentiated "heavy lifting," it allows for the agility required to scale microservices deployments. Earlier, we discussed how a microservices architecture favors lower individual service complexity over lower system complexity. Therefore, having technologies that deliver system abstractions and automation capabilities is beneficial. **Google Kubernetes Engine (GKE)** is one such technology, along with the others you learned about in *Chapter 9, Jumping on the DevOps Bandwagon with Site Reliability Engineering (SRE)*, concerning **deployment automation** and **Infrastructure as Code (IaC)**. Alternatively, you can also leverage **Google App Engine (GAE)** as a perfectly viable platform for microservices deployments. GAE also delivers autoscaling capabilities and different applications are naturally isolated from an infrastructure and deployment management perspective.

Moreover, GAE applications can either use a native runtime (such as supported versions of Java, Node.js, or Python) or be packaged as a Docker container for any custom runtime configuration.

A simplified, generic microservices solution on GCP is captured in the following figure:

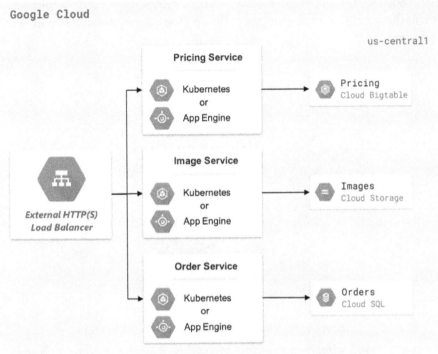

Figure 10.7 – Generic microservices solution on GCP

The solution shown in the preceding figure is regional but could easily be extended to span several regions. This could be achieved by replicating services to other regions and using a global HTTP(S) load balancer to route users based on their location or some HTTP header.

The number and kind of microservices will vary based on the business capabilities (the preceding example being specifically a small e-commerce solution), but the general architecture will likely be similar. Microservices architectures are built to be easily expandable by adding new services without requiring re-architecting or disrupting existing services. Ideally, all state is stored externally using fully managed data services. With the right service decomposition strategy, this solution allows for service decoupling and elastic scaling. A messaging service such as **Cloud Pub/Sub** and/or an API service such as **API Gateway** can be used for service integrations, allowing for greater scale as the applications grow and become more complex. We will explore the use of Google Cloud's API Gateway service in the next section. Before we do, let's get hands-on with microservices and put some of what you've learned so far into practice.

Deploying a microservices web application to GKE

In the code repository for this chapter, you will find a Python-based monolithic web application in the `monolith` sub-directory. The application architecture is shown in the following figure:

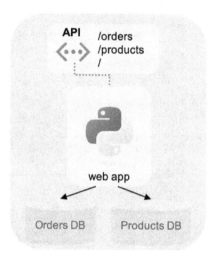

Figure 10.8 – Monolith application architecture

In the microservices sub-directory, the same application has been decomposed and re-architected as shown in the following figure:

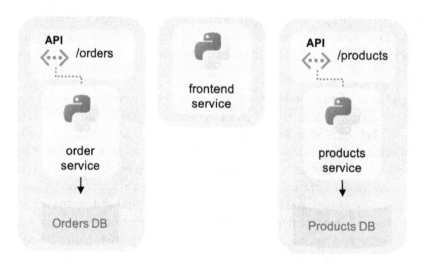

Figure 10.9 – Microservices application architecture

In this hands-on activity, you will build a Kubernetes cluster, configure Deployments and Services, and then deploy the application to the cluster. As a refresher on Kubernetes concepts, which were discussed in *Chapter 4, Architecting Compute Infrastructure*, the following are the things we're going to be working with:

- **Cluster**: The cluster is the foundational infrastructure on which Kubernetes runs. When you deploy a cluster, you get a set of worker machines ("nodes"), a control plane that manages the worker nodes and workloads, and various agents that run in the background to allow the control plane's components to detect and respond to cluster events and make global decisions about the cluster.

- **Nodes**: The nodes are the worker machines that run containerized applications. Each node hosts one or more Pods that are the components of the application workload.

- **Pods**: A Pod is the smallest deployment unit in Kubernetes. It is a logical host for containers and provides shared network and storage resources for them. The most common scenario is that a single container runs on each Pod, except for a few situations where an application component benefits from being further decomposed into tightly coupled sub-components running on separate containers. Pods are *non-permanent* resources and get created and destroyed dynamically.

- **Deployments**: A Deployment provides declarative updates for Pods. You describe a *desired state*, and the Deployment controller will enforce it on Pods at a controlled rate. In a Deployment config, you determine things such as the minimum number of replicas that should be running at all times and the Pods' specifications, including the source container images and network ports they listen to. A Deployment automatically creates and manages a **ReplicaSet**, another Kubernetes component, which is the one responsible for maintaining a stable set of replica Pods running at any given time. For example, if you configure your deployment to have a minimum of three replicas (desired state), the deployment will create a **ReplicaSet** to enforce that minimum. The **ReplicaSet** controller will continuously monitor your Pods, and if a Pod crashes or is terminated for whatever reason, a new one will be created.

- **Services**: A Service provides an abstract way to expose an application over the network with a static IP address (which can be public or private, depending on the service type) and an underlying load balancer. A Service's configuration defines a logical set of Pods, usually determined by a *selector*, and a policy by which to access them. The controller for the Service selector continuously scans for Pods that match its selector, updating the load-balanced pool accordingly. A Service can be of a few different types:

  — **ClusterIP**: The default Service type. It gives you a Service accessible from within your cluster but not externally. The IP address and DNS name you get are known only to the cluster.

  — **NodePort**: This Service type allows you to get external traffic to your Service by opening a specific network port on all nodes, and then forwarding any traffic sent to this port to the Service. Therefore, you get a one-to-one mapping of node (VM) port to Service. Whichever external clients can access those node ports can access the Service. You can only use ports in the range `30000-32767`.

  — **LoadBalancer**: This type is usually the most commonly used to expose a Service to the internet. You get a load balancer with an external IP address that forwards all traffic to your backends. On GCP, this Service type is backed by a Network Load Balancer. Because each Service gets its load balancer instance and dedicated external IP address, it can be an expensive solution if you have many of them.

  — **Ingress**: Not exactly a type of Service, the Ingress sits on a category of its own. It acts as a layer 7 router and entry point into your Services. Different ingress controllers have different capabilities. On GCP, the default ingress controller is backed by an HTTP(S) Load Balancer, thus delivering the same kind of features (such as URL-based routing and SSL offloading) available with this service. It's the most powerful way to expose your Services and is especially useful for large-scale, global applications.

If you want to dig a little deeper into these concepts, a great resource is `https://kubernetes.io/docs/concepts`.

The following figure illustrates how each of these components come together in an example Deployment and *LoadBalancer*-type Service configuration:

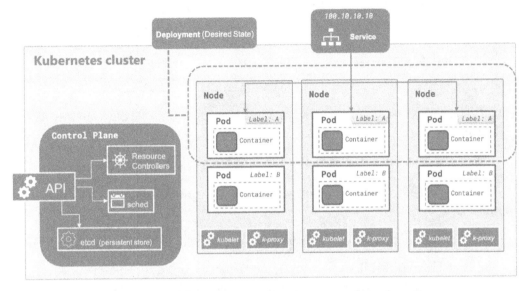

Figure 10.10 – Kubernetes components in an example configuration

In this example, the highlighted Deployment specifies a minimum of three replicas for an application labeled as **Label: A**. The Service then uses this label as a selector to expose this application as a load-balanced external endpoint (with an IP address of 100.10.10.10). The control plane elements are responsible for enforcing the desired state and orchestrating infrastructure resources.

To start with the hands-on activity, do the following to set up a project, link a billing account, enable the required API, and set up a cluster:

1. Go to the GCP console (console.cloud.google.com), and then click on the shell icon on the top-right corner of the screen to activate Cloud Shell.

2. In the Cloud Shell terminal, create a new project for this chapter and link a billing account by running the following:

```
$ gcloud projects create --name chapter-10 --set-as-
default
$ gcloud beta billing projects link [PROJECT_ID]
--billing-account [ACCOUNT_ID]
```

PROJECT_ID is the ID generated for your project after the first command, while ACCOUNT_ID is your billing account ID. You can check your billing account ID by running gcloud beta billing accounts list.

> **Important note**
>
> Never include the brackets in the command arguments. They were added to let you know that it's an input to be replaced/defined by you.

3. Since we will be working with containers and Kubernetes, enable the container API by running this command:

```
$ gcloud services enable container.googleapis.com
```

4. Next, set a default zone for compute services in your project with the following command:

```
$ gcloud config set compute/zone [ZONE]
```

The available zones are listed at https://cloud.google.com/compute/docs/regions-zones#available. The zone you define will be the default one where compute resources will be deployed to.

5. Now, create a GKE cluster named ch10-cluster with the following command:

```
$ gcloud container clusters create ch10-cluster
```

The creation of the cluster will take a few minutes. The platform is setting up VM instances and all the infrastructure required to run Kubernetes.

6. Once the cluster has been created, clone the repository and navigate to this activity's directory:

```
$ git clone https://github.com/PacktPublishing/
Architecting-Google-Cloud-Solutions/
$ cd Architecting-Google-Cloud-Solutions/ch10/monolith
```

7. This directory contains a simple monolithic application consisting of a Python Flask web app, and JSON files stored locally to represent the databases. In this directory, you will also see a file named `Dockerfile`. This is a text document that contains the sequence of commands to assemble a container image. It effectively contains the build steps that result in a container image for our application. If you're familiar with Docker and wish to build this image locally and test it locally, feel free to do so. For the purpose of this assignment, however, an image has already been built for you and is publicly available in the Docker hub (`hub.docker.com`). You don't need to do anything to retrieve it; the image's URL is included in the manifest files.

In the `manifests` sub-directory, there are two YAML files: `deployment.yml` and `service.yml`. The former holds the declarative configuration for a Kubernetes deployment, including the location of the container image, while the latter contains the Service definition, which specifies a frontend port of `80`, a backend port of `8080`, and a service type of `LoadBalancer`. Feel free to spend a few minutes inspecting the contents of these files. Note how the selector field was used to specify which Pods are "served" by the Service, that is, to which Pods the Service's underlying load balancer directs traffic.

When you're ready, run the following to deploy this application to Kubernetes:

```
$ kubectl apply -f manifests
```

> **Important note**
> `kubectl` is Kubernetes' command-line tool that lets you control and inspect Kubernetes clusters. The `kubectl apply` command manages applications through configuration files (often referred to as *manifests*) that define Kubernetes resources. The `-f` command-line argument lets you specify a path where the files are located.

8. Next, run the following to inspect the newly created Pod:

```
$ kubectl get pods
```

9. Then, run the following to inspect the Service:

```
$ kubectl get services
```

In the output, you will see a column named EXTERNAL-IP in the results. If the value for this column under the monolith service entry shows <pending>, wait a few seconds and run the command again. Eventually, once the load balancer is set up, an external IP address will be listed. Copy that IP address and paste it on your browser's URL field. You should see a simple welcome page that looks like this:

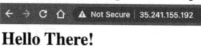

Hello There!

Figure 10.11 – Web app front page

10. Still on the browser, append to the URL the /orders path. You should now see some JSON output containing some fake order data. Next, replace /orders with /products. You should now see some fake products for our fictitious online shop. These are the two APIs present in this application (besides the frontend). As a monolith, everything runs as a single process and is coupled together as a single Service. Also, the two databases are maintained by this same application process.

11. You can also check the newly created Deployment and Service resources on the GCP console. Navigate to **Kubernetes Engine**, and then click on **Workloads** or **Services & Ingress**. You should see the following:

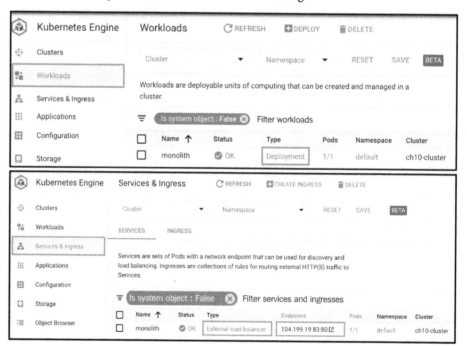

Figure 10.12 – Viewing Deployments and Services in the console

You have now deployed the monolithic version of the application to Kubernetes. You have a single Service hosting a few different APIs.

In the next few steps, you will be deploying the same application, except this time it has been re-architected as microservices. This means you will be creating three different Services: *frontend*, *orders*, and *products*:

1. Back in Cloud Shell, navigate to the `microservices` sub-directory by running the following (from the `monolith` sub-directory):

   ```
   $ cd ../microservices
   ```

2. Run the next three commands in sequence to deploy the three microservices:

   ```
   $ kubectl apply -f src/frontend/manifests/
   $ kubectl apply -f src/orders/manifests/
   $ kubectl apply -f src/products/manifests/
   ```

3. Once again, run the following:

   ```
   $ kubectl get pods
   ```

   You may need to wait a few seconds for the Pods to go from a `Creating` state to a `Running` state. Your output should eventually look similar to the following:

NAME	READY	STATUS	RESTARTS	AGE
frontend-66cc44cb8d-kgh7v	1/1	Running	0	65s
monolith-74486b59d8-qg984	1/1	Running	0	9m53s
orders-8d9cb544c-8k7f5	1/1	Running	0	60s
products-694d7fb476-rb9jk	1/1	Running	0	59s

Figure 10.13 – Output of kubectl get pods

4. Then, run the following to inspect the Service:

   ```
   $ kubectl get services
   ```

   Again, you may need to wait a minute or two for the load balancers to be set up with external IP addresses. The output should look similar to the following:

NAME	TYPE	CLUSTER-IP	EXTERNAL-IP	PORT(S)	AGE
frontend	LoadBalancer	10.107.240.183	35.241.133.27	80:30139/TCP	2m34s
kubernetes	ClusterIP	10.107.240.1	<none>	443/TCP	20m
monolith	LoadBalancer	10.107.243.212	35.241.155.192	80:31212/TCP	11m
orders	LoadBalancer	10.107.247.43	34.76.33.217	80:30421/TCP	2m30s
products	LoadBalancer	10.107.251.22	34.78.231.63	80:31428/TCP	2m29s

Figure 10.14 – Output of kubectl get services

Note the different external IP addresses assigned to your services. Copy the one shown for the *frontend* microservice and paste it on your browser's URL field. You should see the same welcome page as before. Now, if you try to append /orders or /products to the URL, you will get an HTTP 404 (page not found) error, because the frontend Service has no knowledge of orders or products and doesn't serve these APIs.

5. Next, copy the external IP address assigned to your *orders* microservice. Paste it in your browser with the /orders URL suffix appended. You can also try / orders/1 to request a specific order (by its ID, which is 1 in this case). What you'll see is the *orders* microservice doing what it's supposed to do: serving information about orders exclusively. Repeat this step for the *products* microservice (getting its external IP address and appending /products path). Now you should see results for products, but if you were to try to append either / (to access the *frontend* API) or /orders (to access the *orders* API) to this microservice, you'd get nothing.

Congratulations! You have deployed microservices on Kubernetes. Each Service is hosted on its own Pod, contains its own code (which could have been written in a different language), and has its own data store. Inspect the directory structure and the files under the microservices sub-directory and see how it compares to the monolith scenario.

> **Important note**
>
> If you want to explore and learn more about Kubernetes, try modifying the manifest files to different configurations. For example, can you figure out how to recreate a Deployment with a minimum of three Pod replicas?

This example is somewhat crude and meant for demonstration of the microservices architecture – and how easy it is to host it on Kubernetes. In larger-scale scenarios, you would need components that integrate your services and perhaps a façade through which customers would be able to purchase products without having their client (for example, browser or mobile app) make several direct API calls. Also, the databases would ideally be database services external to the microservices' Pods. But the point is hopefully well illustrated with this example.

If you want to play around with a more robust and realistic-looking demo, including many more microservices written in different languages, check out Google's microservices demo code available at https://github.com/GoogleCloudPlatform/ microservices-demo.

To clean up the resources created for this chapter, delete the project by running this command:

```
$ gcloud projects delete [PROJECT_ID]
```

In this activity, you were able to make a few API calls because you were told exactly what they look like. What if you weren't? Would you need to peek into the source code to see what they are? Each microservice needs a clearly defined interface that provides a "contract" for users. This contractual agreement is essential for this type of architecture to work reliably. Also, as mentioned previously, having a way to manage and orchestrate API calls through a single point of entry is a good design pattern that helps solve a few challenges. In the next section, we will explore how to approach microservices APIs on GCP.

Designing and managing APIs for microservices

You've learned that each microservice should only be invoked from its interface. But when we design interfaces for our services, how can we let others know how to use them? Considering the fact that different teams may be managing different microservices and that microservices can be exposed as public APIs for others to consume, how can we implement a "contract" so that everyone knows what to expect? Better yet, is there a standard used by many others that we can also adhere to? That's what an API definition language such as **OpenAPI** (previously **Swagger**) helps accomplish. The OpenAPI specification (https://www.openapis.org/) is a "broadly adopted industry standard for describing modern APIs," as stated on its website. It's a vendor-neutral description format developed under the Linux Foundation. Another API specification language also backed by a large open source community is **RAML** (https://raml.org/), short for **RESTful API Modeling Language**. The main value of a standardized API specification is that it *allows humans and tools to understand how to use a service without needing its source code.*

Consider our online bookshop from the previous section, which had three services:

- Frontend service, serving requests at /*
- Orders service, serving requests at /orders/*
- Products service, serving requests at /products/*

The following is a snippet of an Open API 2.0 specification file for our bookshop API:

```
swagger: "2.0"
info:
  title: microservices
  description: "Get orders and products of the online
bookshop"
  version: "1.0.0"
host: "apigateway-bc3pwx5e.ew.gateway.dev"
schemes:
- "http"
paths:
  "/orders":
    get:
      description: "Get orders."
      operationId: "getOrders"
      x-google-backend:
        address: http://orders.example.com/orders
      responses:
        200:
          description: "Success."
          schema:
            type: string
  "/products":
    get:
      description: "Get products."
      operationId: "getProducts"
      x-google-backend:
        address: http://products.example.com/products
      responses:
        200:
          description: "Success."
          schema:
            type: string
```

Note the `x-google-backend` parameter included in it. This is Google's Open
API extension that allows you to specify local or remote backends to route requests
to (typically within GCP). You can also configure things such as authentication and
timeouts for each backend using this parameter. You'll likely be using it when managing
APIs on GCP. In the example specification, the addresses `orders.example.com` and
`products.example.com` were used to represent the distinct DNS names of the *orders*
and *products* services, respectively. As you may recall from the previous hands-on activity,
these services had their own external IP addresses.

This specification is simplified, but other relevant information includes supported media
types, various HTTP status codes, authentication methods, and even things such as
license and contact information. Because the specification can be extended, different
hosting providers or software companies may include additional information specific to
their service.

Google has published an API Design Guide document, available at `https://cloud.`
`google.com/apis/design`, which provides several recommendations for API
developers based on the way Google has been designing their own APIs since 2014. For
example, it includes information on resource naming, versioning, and design patterns for
APIs. In particular, the versioning strategy is a crucial component of API design worth
spending some time on. Versioning allows you to evolve your service without breaking
existing integrations.

Each version establishes a contract, and for as long as clients remain using the same
version, you should ideally guarantee that the API specification and the system behavior
will not change even as you add new versions to your service. You may eventually
deprecate older versions when your systems have evolved to the point of being unable to
offer backward compatibility. But you should never change the specification of the API for
an existing version. You can also use major and minor version numbers to signal to clients
whether a change made to the service was substantial or minor (for example, an update
from v1.0 to v2.0 implies bigger changes and disruption potential than an update from
v1.0 to v.1.1). The linked API Design Guide is a great reference for this and many other
considerations you should have when designing your APIs.

In our specification example, you may have noticed the **host** field with the value of
`apigateway-bc3pwx5e.ew.gateway.dev`. This field represents the API host or the
entry point for clients. This value is the public address of an API gateway on GCP that was
deployed for this example. We'll explore this and other API services next and how they
can be used to manage APIs on GCP.

API Gateway, Cloud Endpoints, and Apigee

The main service offerings for API management on GCP are **API Gateway**, **Cloud Endpoints**, and **Apigee**.

API Gateway allows you to implement the pattern of the same name we discussed earlier. It's a newer service (at the time of this writing, it's in beta release) than Cloud Endpoints, which have similar functionalities.

Cloud Endpoints is a distributed API management system that provides an API console, hosting, logging, monitoring, and a few other features to manage and secure APIs. It's a **service proxy** that uses Google's general-purpose **Extensible Service Proxy** (**ESP**), based on NGINX or the newer **ESPv2** (open sourced at `https://github.com/GoogleCloudPlatform/esp-v2`), which is based on Envoy (`https://www.envoyproxy.io/docs/envoy/latest/`). With ESPv2, you can use Cloud Endpoints with any GCP compute service. When run with Kubernetes Engine, it gets deployed as a side-car container in front of the API service application container. To understand more about the Cloud Endpoints architecture, refer to `https://cloud.google.com/endpoints/docs/openapi/architecture-overview`.

On the other hand, API Gateway is a fully managed and *serverless* solution that provides a single interface and secure access for multiple backend services. You start with an API configuration, where you define a publicly available API endpoint that clients use and a backend endpoint that the API uses to connect to backend services. The gateway is an Envoy-based, scalable proxy that hosts the deployed API config. This service was created to provide a more seamless API management experience. For example, with the following three simple steps, an API Gateway instance can be created to manage the APIs of our microservices deployment from the previous section:

1. Enable the service's API on GCP and create a gateway resource.

2. Upload an Open API 2.0 specification file with the gateway's address in the `host` field.

3. Deploy the API specification to the gateway.

As a result, navigating to the gateway's address (a public DNS name), and appending the `/orders` or `/products` paths will route you to the corresponding service. The following screenshot shows the API gateway's response after calling the `/orders` API:

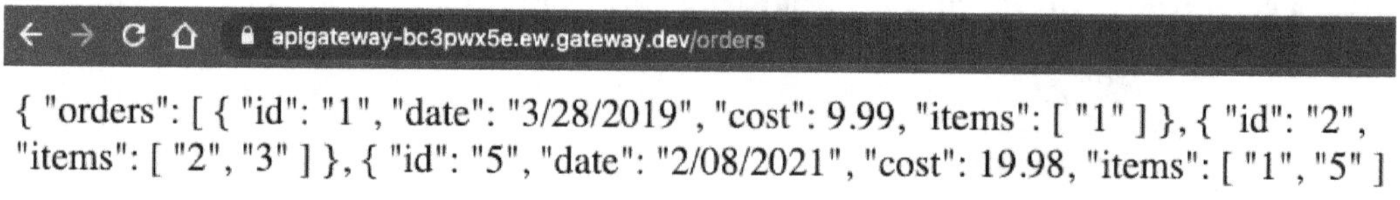

```
{ "orders": [ { "id": "1", "date": "3/28/2019", "cost": 9.99, "items": [ "1" ] }, { "id": "2",
"items": [ "2", "3" ] }, { "id": "5", "date": "2/08/2021", "cost": 19.98, "items": [ "1", "5" ]
```

Figure 10.15 – Response after API Gateway implementation

This is the simplest use case of the API Gateway pattern, that of request routing. It's worth noting that the specification doesn't accept IP addresses for the backend hosts, so a public DNS name must be created for the services' endpoints (which I did for this example using my domain registrar).

Another API management service that you can use on GCP is **Apigee**. Apigee is a more comprehensive solution for API management, geared for large enterprise customers (and not free, like the other two services). It contains more advanced features, such as a customizable portal for onboarding partners and developers as well as monetization and analytics capabilities. Security features are also more robust. Moreover, the runtime plane can be extended to on-premises or another cloud provider environment to support hybrid scenarios. To learn more about Apigee, check out the documentation at `https://cloud.google.com/apigee/docs`. It's possible to request a demo from Google sales before committing to purchasing it. If your use cases are simpler, API Gateway is likely to be a more cost-effective solution with a significantly smaller learning curve. However, if you're more serious about API management and APIs have higher complexity and business criticality in your organization, Apigee is a powerful platform well worth exploring.

Understanding the enabling technologies for building robust microservices solutions is essential for cloud architects. However, even more important is understanding the conceptual building blocks that make up great microservices designs. The technology landscape changes very often, but the fundamental principles almost always remain. In the next and final section, you will get to test your knowledge and exercise your design thinking around microservices.

Testing your knowledge – microservices design case study

The twelve-factor app (`https://12factor.net/`) is a broadly endorsed set of best practices for software applications – and software-as-a-service applications in particular. As such, it is a very useful reference for those designing microservices. Several of the 12 best practices mentioned in the list were already discussed in some way or another in this book, but there are still other useful concepts in there that are worth a read. It summarizes brilliantly what the fundamental factors for designing robust service-oriented applications are. For that reason, it's a resource worth referring to from time to time.

To test the knowledge you acquired in this chapter, let's wrap up with a design case study. You can use the twelve-factor app as a reference too. In this case study, you will be presented with a fictitious application and its current state and you'll be asked to recommend improvements for it.

Case study

An unnamed company has developed an e-commerce application with the following capabilities:

- It has a web UI and a mobile UI for web and mobile users.

- Users can sign up and log in. There's a database dedicated to user profiles.

- Users can shop for various products the company offers by adding/removing items to a cart and then placing an order.

- Payment is made exclusively via third-party payment providers.

- Relevant purchase data is stored in a data warehouse for analytics and reports.

- The application is built in a three-tier architecture and runs on virtual machines.

Lately, this company has been facing the following challenges:

- Performance issues due to an inability to scale quickly to meet demand spikes.

- Changes take a long time to be deployed to production.

- Changes often introduce bugs that take the teams a long time to remediate.

- Sometimes newly introduced changes break existing integrations (for example, with third-party partner products).

This company has turned to you for guidance in solving these challenges. They expect both a high-level design diagram as well as general suggestions on the choice of technologies and ways of working to help them improve their situation. They would prefer that you think long term, even if the changes may take a lot of time and effort to put into place.

Come up with a design sketch of how you think this application can be redesigned. Start with a high-level design, including application components and communication patterns. Then, refine your recommendation by including specific technologies that you'd suggest for each component of your design. What suggestions can you give this client?

Once you have your solution, you can compare it to the answer provided at https://github.com/PacktPublishing/Architecting-Google-Cloud-Solutions/tree/master/ch10/case-study. Note that there's no single right answer to this problem – the requirements given were intentionally somewhat vague, as real-world problems invariably are – and the solution provided may not be better than yours.

Summary

In this chapter, you've discovered the underlying principles of microservices architectures. You've learned the motivations for adopting microservices as well as the potential drawbacks of this architectural style. You then learned about ways to go about decomposing monoliths and designing and building microservices, and how to leverage common design patterns. In particular, you got hands-on experience with building microservices on Kubernetes, a popular platform for this type of architecture. Then, you've learned about API design and specific technologies on GCP to manage microservices APIs. Finally, you got to test your knowledge and your design skills with a case study reflecting a typical real-world scenario.

In the next chapter, you will learn about **Machine Learning** (**ML**) and **Artificial Intelligence** (**AI**), technologies that the most successful modern enterprises use to gain valuable insights from their data.

11
Applying Machine Learning and Artificial Intelligence

The subject of **Artificial Intelligence** (**AI**) is no longer exclusive to research and innovation. It's here and now. In fact, it's been around for quite some time. With the advancements in **Machine Learning** (**ML**) science and techniques, along with the increase in hardware capacity and data availability, the entry barrier has never been lower. Modern and data-driven enterprises can now leverage cloud-based AI to unlock insights from their data.

In this chapter, you will learn how to leverage **Google Cloud Platform's** (**GCP's**) AI services and prebuilt ML models. You will learn how these cloud-based solutions can add business value and discover real-world use cases. Then, we're going to explore how to build, train, and run custom models on GCP and even look at ways to do so without any coding or data science experience. Finally, you will learn how to apply MLOps to automate ML pipelines and productionize ML applications with agility and efficiency. By the end of this chapter, you will have gained the foundational skills that will enable you to incorporate AI into your Google Cloud solutions effectively.

In this chapter, we're going to cover the following main topics:

- Making the business case for AI and ML

- Leveraging pretrained models on GCP with ML APIs

- Building custom ML models with Cloud AI Platform and BigQuery ML

- Productionizing custom ML models with MLOps

Technical requirements

For the hands-on activities in this chapter, you will need a billing-enabled Google Cloud account and optionally the Google Cloud SDK installed (if you don't have it, you can use Cloud Shell from a browser).

Helper scripts and codes for this chapter can be found at the following site:

```
https://github.com/PacktPublishing/Architecting-Google-Cloud-
Solutions/tree/master/ch11
```

Check out the following link to see the Code in Action video: `https://bit.ly/3qir9ye`

Making the business case for AI and ML

The field of AI has seen a significant rise in popularity in the past decade or two. Still, it is often considered by many as a purely academic and scientific subject. The reason for this may be due to the *AI effect*, a phenomenon in which feats of AI often get removed from the definition of AI once they become a routine technology. What was once considered an impressive achievement and a demonstration of artificially intelligent behavior becomes a normal machine task and is no longer thought of as AI.

For example, **optical character recognition** (**OCR**) is a technology so pervasive now that it is not thought of as an AI application as often as it used to be. The *AI effect* sometimes misleads businesses into thinking that AI belongs to the realm of research and it's not something worth investing too heavily in. But that couldn't be further from the truth. Beyond leveraging existing AI technologies – whether we think of them as AI or not – organizations can also derive value from their unique set of data by applying ML techniques. AI can also open up new revenue streams and give organizations a competitive edge. Fortunately, as you shall learn in this chapter, that doesn't always require hiring a team of specialized ML data scientists.

Before exploring the AI landscape with GCP, let's briefly clarify a few concepts.

Understanding AI and ML concepts

In its simplest definition, AI refers to the intelligence demonstrated by machines. It's also a branch of computer science and a scientific discipline that studies techniques for simulating human-like intelligence. Whereas AI is the broader *discipline* concerning machine intelligence, ML is the *concrete toolset* that includes algorithms and methods to *architect* intelligence in software. In other words, ML is an approach to achieve AI. Therefore, when we speak of *applying* AI or *doing* AI, we're most often referring to ML. In general, ML techniques help us find patterns in complex datasets to solve complex problems.

In particular, **deep learning** is one very popular subfield of ML that is used for a wide variety of problems. Deep learning's algorithms are inspired by the human brain's structure and function. An artificial neural network is the name given to the logical network that simulates the biological network of neurons inside our skulls. A typical artificial neural network is illustrated as follows:

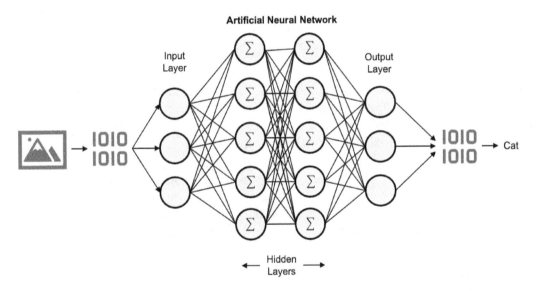

Figure 11.1 – Artificial neural network

The network consists of different layers, each consisting of different *nodes* (or *neurons*). The **input layer** is where data is fed – initially for training and then for predictions. What makes deep learning so powerful and so popular is the fact that input data can be either **structured** or **unstructured**. That allows machines to see and detect patterns within images or videos, for example.

The intermediate layers (referred to as **hidden layers**) of the neural network represent mathematical functions with weights and **parameters** that the algorithm learns by itself during the training process. Nothing is coded in an artificial neural network other than the initial network architecture, which among other things determines the number of hidden layers and the number of nodes in each layer. Instead, the algorithm learns and adapts on its own by adjusting its internal parameters in a structured way.

The **output layer** of the neural network represents the numerical result (which may translate to a category). For example, the output for a previously unseen picture of a pet fed to a classification model may be cat or dog with varying degrees of confidence. This particular example is the one illustrated in the preceding figure. Deep learning is not the only ML tool in existence, but it's extremely versatile and very commonly used. Hence, it's the main technique powering several cloud ML services.

In ML, several properties of the learning process itself, such as **learning rate** and **batch size**, can be adjusted to refine the model and improve its learning performance. These are referred to as **hyperparameters**. Once an algorithm is trained, it generates a so-called **model**. A model is a representation of reality that the machine now possesses. Provide unlabeled, previously unseen data to the model, and it will spit out a result based on its internal model parameters.

There are three main types of learning techniques: **supervised**, **unsupervised**, and **reinforcement** learning. Supervised learning refers to the fact that training data is provided with the expected outcome for each data point, such as a category in a classification problem or a value in a regression problem. In contrast, unsupervised learning doesn't require labels and is used in specific types of ML problems that allow machines to learn from "scratch." Finally, reinforcement learning is an area of ML that includes the notion of a reward, making machines learn by maximizing the cumulative reward obtained through trial and error. The primary focus of this chapter will be on the supervised machine learning technique, which is the most common in the enterprise space.

There are also a few different types of ML problems. These are summarized in the following table along with their use cases:

ML Problem Type	Typical ML Technique	Description	Example Use Cases
Classification	Supervised learning	Identify the class of object in an image (that is, what is this an image of?)	Identify an animal in an image (cat, dog, or mouse) Identify digits in an image (0, 1, 2, ...)
Regression	Supervised learning	Predict numerical values	Estimate housing prices Estimate click-through rate
Clustering	Unsupervised learning	Group different examples by the degree of similarity between them	Identify fake news Spam filtering Fraud detection
Association rule learning	Unsupervised	Infer likely associations	Recommendation systems (if you buy this product, you're likely to buy these...)
Structured output (or structured prediction)	Supervised	Predict structured (rather than scalar) objects	Translating a natural language sentence into a parse tree representing the predicted syntax
Ranking	Supervised, semi-supervised, or reinforcement learning	Identify position (rank) on a scale	Ranking of search results Sentiment analysis

A good overview of different ML techniques and problems is given at https://developers.google.com/machine-learning/problem-framing/cases.

In the case of **supervised learning**, the input training data consists of *labeled* data, that is, the data plus the expected result for each individual data entry. For example, in an image classification problem, that could consist of images of cats along with the label *cat* and images of dogs with the label *dog*. Supervised learning therefore requires more than just raw data: the data must also be annotated by humans.

During the evaluation phase of an ML model, **metrics** and **losses** are computed to gauge the performance of the model. This is typically done by letting the model analyze a separate set of labeled data (that is, a set not used for training) and evaluating its performance against specific loss functions and metrics that are appropriate for the type of problem. For example, a classification algorithm's success can be measured by its *accuracy*, which is defined by the number of correctly predicted data points divided by the total number of data points. *Precision* is another common metric for classification problems and is defined by the number of correct positive results (true positives) divided by the total number of positive results (true and false positives). Regression problems, such as that of estimating prices or other numerical quantities, are typically evaluated by the statistical computation of **Mean Squared Error (MSE)** or **Mean Absolute Error (MAE)** values. Seeking the internal parameter configuration that minimizes errors and/or improves performance metrics is how an ML program constructs its model – that is, how it *learns*. The most common mathematical technique for doing so is *gradient descent*, explained in more detail at `https://developers.google.com/machine-learning/crash-course/reducing-loss/gradient-descent`.

What makes ML programs fundamentally different from traditional software programs is that their precise behavior is not coded. Whereas a traditional program codes a set of logical `if-then` statements that attempt to capture in advance all possible usage patterns and behavior of the application, an ML algorithm is designed to learn by itself what all the relevant patterns are, how to distinguish them, and how to use them to make inferences on new input. This capability uncovers a broad set of problems that would otherwise have been impossible to solve with traditional computational techniques. We can feed a model many examples, tune some hyperparameters, and the model learns by itself – through its internal parameters and various algorithmic functions – how to reason about what you subsequently input into it. From that perspective, a model is like a black box, an idea that is illustrated in the following figure:

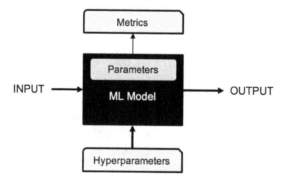

Figure 11.2 – ML model as a black box

ML is a very broad and complex area and an in-depth discussion of ML techniques and concepts is outside of the scope of this book. The theory discussed in this section covers the concepts you'll hear the most when approaching ML problems and throughout this chapter. Therefore, they're the most important ones to understand at least at a fundamental level. In summary, the following are the basics that you need to know for this chapter:

- AI refers to the discipline, philosophy, and science of machine intelligence.

- ML is a subset of AI that consists of tools and techniques for developing a *model*, a machine's learned representation of reality. An ML model can draw inferences from previously unseen data that bears some resemblance to the data used for training.

- An ML model is mathematical in nature and is represented primarily by its internal *parameters*.

- An ML model's learning ability is affected by the choice of *hyperparameters* and its performance is measured by *metrics* and *losses*.

- Deep learning is a subset of ML that uses algorithms inspired by the human brain's structure and function.

- There are three main branches of ML: supervised, unsupervised, and reinforcement learning. Supervised learning is the most commonly used technique today and requires *labeled data*.

If you wish to deepen your knowledge of ML, a great crash course is provided by Google at https://developers.google.com/machine-learning/crash-course.

Beyond the ability to tell cats from dogs, there are several ML applications that can help organizations unlock value from their data. We will dive next into some of the business motivations for ML and how you can make the case for it when you're working with modern, data-driven enterprises.

Making the case for ML

ML is not a new science. In fact, even deep learning has been around for decades. However, for many years, ML hasn't been able to take off because we lacked, among other things, the amount of data and the hardware capacity for it to be useful (or affordable). One caveat of ML, at least as ML science currently stands today, is that it requires a vast amount of training data to produce accurate results. Certain classes of problems, especially those involving images and large unstructured data, can require immense computational power. Fortunately, barriers to entry have lowered significantly, thanks primarily to three factors:

- Increased availability of data (and the emergence of big data)
- Increased maturity and democratization of ML science and algorithms
- Increased power of hardware and software

Google has been one of the main enablers on all three fronts. With its expertise in AI technologies, big data supremacy, and distributed, hyperscale cloud infrastructure, ML is now within reach of many organizations. Furthermore, with several ML **Platform-as-a-Service (PaaS)** options currently available on GCP, businesses can leverage the power of deep learning and other robust techniques in a cost-effective manner.

The primary value-deriving use cases for enterprises are the following:

- **Predictive insights**: Supporting decision-making. For example, a predicted demand surge in a certain region leading to an anticipated price raise.

- **Pattern detection on unstructured data**: For example, detecting objects within images for automatic classification.

- **Human speech understanding**: For example, in voice-enabled products and online assistants.

- **Human text understanding**: For example, delivering AI-powered customer service chatbots.

Some other niche applications include autonomous vehicles (self-driving cars), game playing (such as Chess or Go), and medical diagnosis. The list can extend well beyond the length of this page, but the preceding scenarios cover most of the enterprise AI landscape. In research done by MIT in partnership with Google Cloud (the research report is available at `https://lp.google-mkto.com/rs/248-TPC-286/images/ MIT_TechReview_MachineLearning.pdf`), it's been found that the adoption of ML results in *2x more data-driven decisions, 5x faster decision-making*, and *3x faster execution*. Though the business case for ML and its benefits may often be clear to data-driven organizations, the journey to adoption is frequently a challenging one. For that reason, Google has developed the Google Cloud's AI Adoption Framework whitepaper, available at `https://services.google.com/fh/files/misc/ai_adoption_ framework_whitepaper.pdf`, to help organizations create value through AI by approaching its adoption in the right way.

Later in this chapter, you will learn about **Cloud AI Platform (Unified)**, a cohesive platform bringing together a suite of AI-enabled GCP services: **AI Platform (classic)**, **AutoML**, and **MLOps**. At the time of this writing, AI Platform (Unified) is in *preview* stage and not generally available. The qualifying *unified* in the name helps differentiate it from the *classic* AI Platform service, whose capabilities are now consolidated into AI Platform (Unified). However, before we delve into this service, we'll look at the several pretrained models available in Google Cloud. These services allow you to leverage Google's unparalleled access to vast amounts of data that, for many years, have fed their ML models to deliver very robust AI technologies that are available through GCP.

Leveraging pretrained models on GCP with ML APIs

Google's pretrained models are offered as a suite of ready-to-consume APIs. These are described in the following table:

Service	Description	Use cases
Cloud Translation API	Translate content between languages using Google's translation model. Supports more than 100 languages.	Document translation. Document language detection. User interface text translation.
Cloud Vision API	Integrate vision detection features within an application.	Image labeling, face detection, OCR, explicit content tagging.
Cloud Speech-to-Text API	Convert speech into text.	Real-time or batch speech content transcription. Search service for audio. Call center analytics. Voice-controlled IoT devices.
Cloud Text-to-Speech API	Convert text into natural-sounding speech.	Contact center voice bots. IoT device voice generation. App accessibility.
Cloud Video Intelligence API	Enable video content discovery.	Video object recognition. Video annotation service. Surveillance apps.
Cloud Natural Language API	Use ML to reveal the structure and meaning of text.	Document information extraction. Content classification. Receipt and invoice understanding.

These services can often be combined to deliver an ML-powered solution. For example, you could combine the **Speech-to-Text** and **Natural Language** APIs to extract meaning from audio conversations. Or you could combine the **Vision** and **Translation** APIs to detect and translate text content within images.

The main appeal behind these services is that they're easy to consume. For example, the Text-to-Speech API has a demo available at `https://cloud.google.com/text-to-speech`. You can experiment using different texts and voice parameters and listen to the result. By clicking on **Show JSON**, you can see the underlying (and relatively uncomplicated) API call, as shown in the following screenshot:

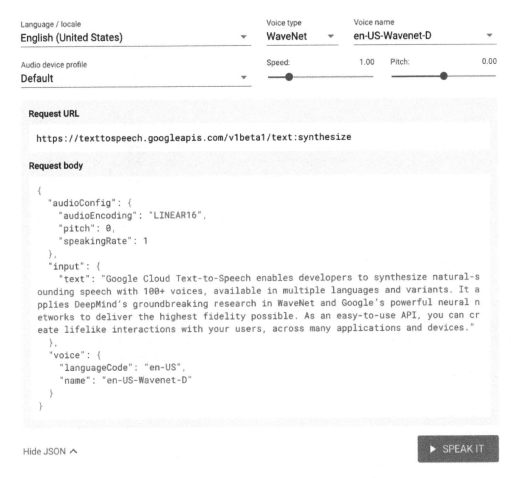

Figure 11.3 – Text-to-Speech API usage example

As another example, the following are the few steps needed to set up and use the Translation API:

1. Set up a project, enable the Cloud Translation API, and create service account credentials to make authenticated calls. Instructions are available at `https://cloud.google.com/translate/docs/setup`.

2. Write a request JSON body such as the one shown in the following example:

```
{
    "sourceLanguageCode": "en",
    "targetLanguageCode": "ru",
    "contents": ["Friends don't let friends reinvent
translation"],
```

```
    "mimeType": "text/plain"
}
```

3. Submit an authenticated HTTP POST request to the Translation API, containing the request JSON body. For example, here we are using `curl`:

```
curl -X POST \
-H "Authorization: Bearer "$(gcloud auth application-
default print-access-token) \
-H "Content-Type: application/json; charset=utf-8" \
-d @request.json \
https://translation.googleapis.com/v3/projects/project-
number-or-id:translateText
```

(This requires the GOOGLE_APPLICATION_CREDENTIAL environment variable to be set with a service account's private key file path.)

Naturally, that last step could be executed from within an application using libraries from any of the supported languages: C#, Go, Java, Node.js, Python, or Ruby. You can easily find language-specific usage instructions for each of these APIs on GCP's documentation pages. The following figure illustrates a scenario where two client applications consume a combination of GCP's ML APIs to get prediction results for various data:

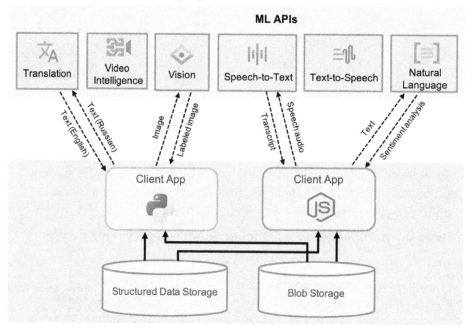

Figure 11.4 – Consuming Google Cloud's ML APIs

Beyond these APIs, there are other Google Cloud services that are also powered by ML, such as **Cloud Data Loss Prevention** (**DLP**) and Dialogflow, a natural language understanding platform. They all provide pretrained models; that is, you don't have to provide data and train a model yourself – a huge burden off your back. The ML APIs are powered by Google's models, trained with data that Google has access to. Google has both volumes of data and hardware capacity that far exceed those of most other organizations. Moreover, these models have been refined over time and continue to improve as more data and technology become available. Therefore, by using these services, you're leveraging state-of-the-art ML models. Whenever Google Cloud's ML APIs suit your use cases, you should consider using and experimenting with them before setting out to build your own models.

However, while these services are very easy to use and have robust performance, they may not suit your business needs. For example, if your organization belongs to a niche domain where a specific type of content is generated that is unlike normal content (the kind that may have been used to train Google's models), you might not obtain good results from them. Or, you may simply have access to unique data that better reflects the situation you want machine intelligence for. Therefore, in these cases, building your own model using your unique data is often a better decision.

Let's see how a cloud architect can approach custom model building on GCP.

Building custom ML models with Cloud AI Platform and BigQuery ML

Before getting to the different components and capabilities within Cloud AI Platform (Unified) – hereafter referred to as AI Platform – it's useful to understand the **ML workflow** stages. A typical production-ready workflow for a supervised ML application is represented in the following diagram:

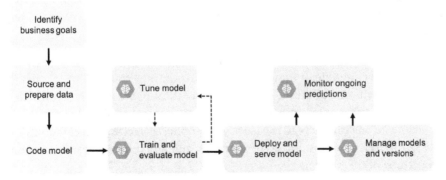

Figure 11.5 – The ML workflow

Let's break this down.

The first and most fundamental step is that of identifying the **business goals** and formulating the business case. Ensure the problem is well defined by answering the following two questions at a minimum:

1. What information are you trying to get out of the model?
2. Why will this information be useful?

Sometimes these questions generate hypotheses to be tested. Therefore, you must determine the project's feasibility and whether you can afford to fall short of achieving the outcomes. A machine learning project is typically iterative, and you may move back and forth between different stages as you obtain more information and validate assumptions. From a business case perspective, you need to also probe the problem by asking whether ML is indeed the best solution for it. As discussed earlier, ML algorithms need a sizable volume of data to obtain an accurate model. The exact amount will depend on several variables, such as the type and dimensionality of the problem, the quality of the data, and the choice of algorithm. But the more data attributes (or **features**, in ML jargon) you include in your model, the more training data records you need to properly train the model.

For example, consider the problem of predicting housing prices in a particular region. A simplified model for this problem may include only three features: *size, number of rooms,* and *location.* This model may give you a rough predictive power of house prices. However, if you require more precise inferences, you may need to include several additional features such as *year of construction, street name, whether it's been recently renovated, number of windows, crime rates in the neighborhood, type of floor material,* and so on. The idea is that the more data attributes there are (that influence buying decision), the better your chance of obtaining better predictions from your model. However, since the addition of all these new attributes will increase the complexity and dimensions of the problem, your model will need substantially more training data. Identifying which features to capture and balancing that against the size of the data set is part of the discipline referred to as **feature engineering**.

Another common challenge of working with ML problems is knowing when the model development phase is complete. It may be tempting to continue to refine the model for a long time to obtain better results, but there's a point of diminishing returns at which more time and effort only generates marginal improvements, if any at all. For that reason, it's essential to define *beforehand* how to measure your model's success. You can do this by defining the **key metrics**, **acceptable error margins**, and any other relevant criteria for a successful outcome of the project.

Provided you have gone through these probing questions and decided to build an ML model, the next step concerns **data sourcing**. At this stage, you confirm the availability of data in terms of *quantity* and *quality*. Data governance questions may be elicited at this point, such as who owns the data, who has access to it, what the appropriate usage of the data is, and whether there are any compliance-related restrictions to be aware of. During your data sourcing stage, you should also leverage data visualization tools to identify patterns and gain a *deeper understanding* of your data. This process is described as **exploratory data analysis (EDA)**, which you can learn more about at `https://www.itl.nist.gov/div898/handbook/eda/section1/eda11.htm`.

Next comes the process of **data preparation**. In the beginning, this process will be exploratory. You'll need to discover what *union, join*, and/or *merge* operations you will need to do to collect your data in the right place and format. In *Chapter 8, Approaching Big Data and Data Pipelines*, you've learned several techniques for building a data lake to consolidate data from multiple sources and how to leverage data transformation and exploration tools on GCP. In an ML context, you may design a data pipeline to perform, for example, the following preprocessing steps:

1. Join data from multiple sources.

2. Clean the data to remove anomalous values caused by errors in data input or bad measurements.

3. Normalize numerical data to a common scale.

4. Apply formatting rules to data.

Beyond data consolidation, a common objective of data preparation is to get data in a suitable format that is optimal for ML. The services you might leverage at this stage include **Cloud Dataprep**, **Cloud Dataflow**, **Cloud Dataproc**, and/or **Cloud BigQuery**. It is a good practice to start simple and evolve your data preparation pipeline and workflows incrementally. By leveraging GCP's fully managed and highly scalable services, you will be able to do so in a cost-effective manner, since you pay only for the infrastructure resources you use.

The next step after getting the data ready is to **code your model**. There are several languages and frameworks supported on GCP that you can use to code ML models, including **TensorFlow**, originally developed by Google and one of the most popular open source ML frameworks. You can opt for **TensorFlow Enterprise** (`https://cloud.google.com/tensorflow-enterprise`), a GCP-exclusive version that offers enterprise-grade support and features such as security patching and bug fixes. A great resource for learning TensorFlow is the URL `https://www.tensorflow.org/tutorials`, where you can find tutorials for beginners and experts. Other popular options you can use for coding models on AI Platform include **scikit-learn** (`https://scikit-learn.org/stable/getting_started.html`) and **XGBoost** (`https://xgboost.readthedocs.io/en/latest/`). All these frameworks provide libraries and abstractions for several ML algorithms, helping you get started with building custom models easily. However, refining and building robust models still requires a basic knowledge of data science and computer programming. Even with all the abstractions that come with these frameworks, they are not very forgiving if you lack either. On the other hand, if you're allergic to code or data science, AI Platform has you covered with **AutoML**. You'll learn more about this powerful service later in this section.

So far, we've discussed data sourcing, preparation, and model coding. The following diagram is an example of the ML workflow up to this point:

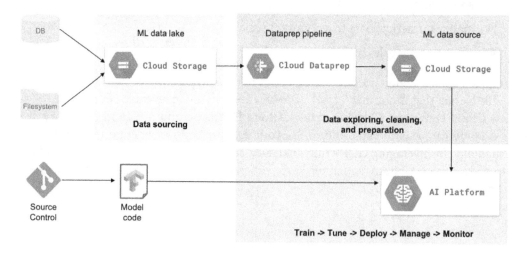

Figure 11.6 – Data sourcing, preparation, and model coding

For the remaining stages of the workflow, AI Platform provides a suite of managed services and APIs that help you build, test, and run models by taking care of the infrastructure-related heavy lifting for you. We'll next explore each of these stages and how you can use AI Platform to execute them successfully. You'll also get hands-on experience with an ML project that leverages AutoML to train and serve a model without any coding.

Training, evaluating, and tuning ML models

This is probably the most important and often most time-consuming stage of the ML workflow. Training a model consists of feeding it data for which you already know the value of the data attribute that you targeted for prediction (that is, the **label**). In our housing prices example, the label is the *price*. Therefore, training a model to predict housing prices would mean feeding the model *many* data points such as the following:

Size (sqft)	Num. of rooms	Num. of bedrooms	Location	Price (USD)
800	3	2	-122.24, 37.84	322100

In this particular example, four feature columns are provided along with the label (price) column. This is a **regression** problem, meaning that the predicted output will be a continuous value. In contrast, a **classification** problem (also referred to as a **multi-class regression** problem) would have produced an output that is a discrete category. When a classification problem has a binary output (that is, only two possible labels, such as yes or no), then it is referred to as a **logistic regression** model type. The same data can be used for those different problem types. For example, we could use the same housing prices data set to classify houses into three large categories such as "expensive", "medium", and "cheap."

A crucial practice at the start of model training is **splitting the data set** into three groups: a *training* set, a *validation* set, and (optionally) a *test* set. The training set is the data samples used to train the model. The validation set is also used to train the model, but it is used by the ML algorithm to evaluate its learning performance during training. The test set is a separate sample of data meant to replicate real-world data and provide an unbiased evaluation of the final model. Typically, all three sets come from the same source and most ML frameworks offer library functions for splitting the data automatically. You want your training set to be the biggest set (typically anywhere between 60% and 90% of your data), while the validation and test sets may be smaller subsets.

One key consideration when splitting data is to ensure you don't introduce **bias** by doing so, and that your splitting strategy creates **reproducible data sets**. Consider the example of housing prices data. You could easily split the data by, for example, randomly taking 80% of all entries as your training set, then 10% as validation and 10% as test. However, each time you would run this program, completely different sets would be generated. This makes it difficult to refine your model, since it's hard to know if a model is improving (or not) due to better learning and hyperparameter tuning or just by chance as a result of using a different training set. This is especially problematic if you collaborate with different individuals, who won't be able to reproduce your data split and your results. To solve this, it may be tempting to split the data instead by taking, for example, the 80% lowest price houses for the training set, then the next lowest 10% for the validation set and the remaining 10% for the test set. You eliminate randomness by doing this, but now you're potentially introducing bias. Why? Because your model will learn how to predict house prices only for the subset of cheap houses. When tested against more expensive houses, it will potentially perform badly.

Simply put, you want all your data sets to be as diverse as possible, that is, as representative of as many different combinations of feature values as possible. Therefore, splitting the data by any particular column is often a bad idea, *unless that data column is not correlated with the label*. For example, if our housing data contained an ID column, referring to a generic numerical identifier for each data point with no bearing on the price, you could use it to split your data set by. There are strategies commonly used when such a column is not present that essentially involve creating one (by, for example, concatenating several column values into one identifier column, and taking a hash of the resulting value). You can read more about data set splits at `https://developers.google.com/machine-learning/crash-course/training-and-test-sets/splitting-data`.

Once you have obtained a reproducible data set split (or are comfortable with not having one), it's time to train and refine your model. On AI Platform, you can do this by uploading your code package and dependencies to a Cloud Storage bucket, then running your code on either a pre-built container or a container you provide with a custom runtime. A list of readily available runtimes for pre-built containers is provided at `https://cloud.google.com/ai-platform-unified/docs/training/pre-built-containers`. You can then determine hyperparameters and inference settings and start training. AI Platform will provide and manage the underlying infrastructure and also handle scalability for you.

At this stage, you will be looking at the evaluation metrics you defined and working to improve your model. Alternatively, you can use AutoML for code-free model training and automated tuning. In this case, you only provide the source data and AutoML will take care of all these steps for you. Both options are illustrated in the following diagram:

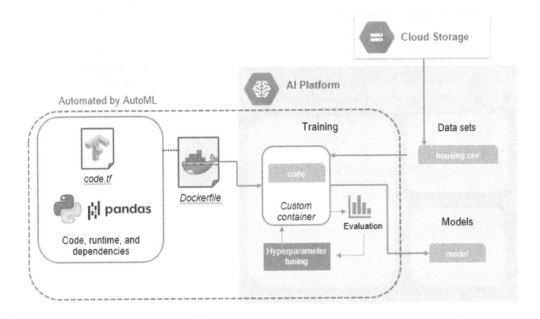

Figure 11.7 – Training, tuning, and deploying a model on AI Platform

When testing and evaluating your model, do it in a context as close as possible to your final production use case. As mentioned before, having a dedicated, separate test set can be very helpful. When the model is ready and its performance is acceptable based on your predefined criteria, the next step is to deploy the model and start serving requests.

Serving, monitoring, and managing models

A model deployed on AI Platform is ready to serve requests. There are two ways to serve predictions from trained models: **online prediction** and **batch prediction**. As the names suggest, the former allows you to continuously serve prediction requests over the web as an HTTP endpoint, whereas the latter is tailored for batch prediction requests. As a fully managed platform, you don't need to manage and operate any underlying infrastructure in either case.

Once your model is up and running and serving requests, AI Platform also provides interfaces for managing your model and versions using the console, its REST API and *gcloud* commands. You close the loop of the ML workflow by monitoring and evaluating the performance of your model in production *against the expected business outcomes* for the project. This is the time to reflect on whether the project was successful based on your definition of success done at the early stages.

Even if performance is above expectations, a continuous improvement cycle should be in place to ensure the model doesn't become obsolete. The performance may start to decrease over time as the model fails to capture new ways in which the data space may have evolved. For example, an economic crisis may hit the real estate market suddenly and cause prices to go down, rendering your model – which was trained with pre-crisis data – less performant. You may also start facing competition, and your competitors may come up with better models for the same problem. Either way, continuously monitoring and improving your models will ensure better chances of success.

Now that you know the high-level capabilities of AI Platform, let's put some of what you learned into practice.

Getting hands-on – training, deploying, and serving a model using AutoML

Google Cloud's AutoML service automates all aspects of ML model training (including feature engineering, choice of learning architecture, and hyperparameter tuning) to enable you to build state-of-the-art custom models easily. All you need to do is provide the data, either structured or unstructured. The various AutoML products specific to each data type are documented at `https://cloud.google.com/automl/docs`. The entire AutoML portfolio has been consolidated into AI Platform and made even easier to use, as you will get to experience now.

In this activity, you will use AI Platform and AutoML to predict apartment prices in the city of Stockholm, Sweden. A data set has been provided in this chapter's code repository as a CSV file. The schema of this file is as follows:

Field	Type	Description
street_name	String	The street name
num_of_rooms	Float	The total number of rooms, including bedrooms
size	Integer	Size in square meters
location	String	The name of the area where the house is located
sold_year	Integer	The year the apartment was sold
initial_price	Integer	The starting price for the bid
floor_num	Integer	The apartment's floor number
year_built	Integer	The year the apartment's building was built
final_price	Integer	The price the apartment was sold for

In Stockholm, houses are advertised with a starting price and sold through a bidding process. The ML model you're going to build will try to predict the final price (post-bidding) of new apartment advertisements. Therefore, final_price will be the *label* in our data set, that is, the prediction target. You may have noticed and found it odd that the num_of_rooms field, which reflects the total number of rooms in the apartment, is a float number type. That is because in Sweden an apartment can have what is considered to be a half-room, and therefore this number may have values such as 2.5 or 3.5.

To start with this hands-on activity, do the following to set up a project, link billing account, enable the required API, and set up a cluster:

1. Go to the GCP console (console.cloud.google.com), then click on the shell icon on the top-right corner of the screen to activate Cloud Shell.

2. In the Cloud Shell terminal, create a new project for this chapter and link a billing account by running the following:

    ```
    $ gcloud projects create --name chapter-11 --set-as-
    default
    $ gcloud beta billing projects link [PROJECT_ID]
    --billing-account [ACCOUNT_ID]
    ```

    PROJECT_ID is the ID generated for your project after the first command, while ACCOUNT_ID is your billing account ID. You can check your billing account ID by running gcloud beta billing accounts list.

    > **Important Note**
    > Never include the brackets in the command arguments. They were added to let you know that it's an input to be replaced/defined by you.

3. Clone the Git repository and navigate to this activity's directory:

```
$ git clone https://github.com/PacktPublishing/
Architecting-Google-Cloud-Solutions
$ cd Architecting-Google-Cloud-Solutions/ch11/automl
```

This directory contains a file called `stockholm-house-prices.csv`. This is going to be our data set.

4. Run the following to create a Cloud Storage bucket and upload the CSV file to it:

```
$ gsutil mb gs://[PROJECT_ID]
$ gsutil cp stockholm-house-prices.csv gs://[PROJECT_ID]
```

The first command creates a bucket named after your project ID. This guarantees that the name is unique, which is a requirement for naming storage buckets. The second command uploads the file from your Cloud Shell instance to the bucket.

5. You can now close the Cloud Shell terminal and switch to the console. First, make sure you select the newly created project for this chapter in the project selection menu on the top bar. Then, using the navigation menu on the left, scroll down to the **Artificial Intelligence** sub-group and click on **AI Platform (Unified)**, as shown in following the screenshot:

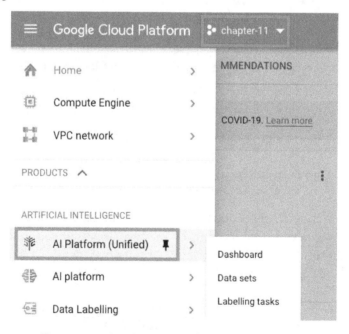

Figure 11.8 – Accessing AI Platform from the console

6. Click on **Enable AI Platform API**. Wait a few seconds until the API is enabled.

7. On the left-side navigation menu, click on **Data sets**. Then, click on **Create** at the top of the page.

8. For **Data set name**, type `stockholm-housing-dataset`. Under **Select an objective**, click on **Tabular**. Leave **Regression/classification** selected and other options with their default values. Click on **Create**.

9. On the next page, select **Select CSV files from Cloud Storage**. Click on **Browse**, then double-click on the storage bucket named after your project ID and click on the `stockholm-house-prices.csv` file. Click on **Select**.

10. Click on **Continue**.

11. On the left-side navigation menu, click on **Training**. Then, click on **Create**.

12. Under **Dataset** drop-down menu, select **stockholm-housing-dataset**. Under **Objective**, select **Regression**. Select **AutoML**, then click on **Continue**.

13. In the **Define your model** page, type in `stockholm-housing-model` under **Model name**. For the target column, select **final_price**. Click on **Continue**.

14. On the next page, you should see all the columns from the CSV file listed, with the option **Auto** under the **Transformation** column. Click on **Advanced Options** to expand the **Optimization objective** selection. Select **MAE**, as shown in the following screenshot:

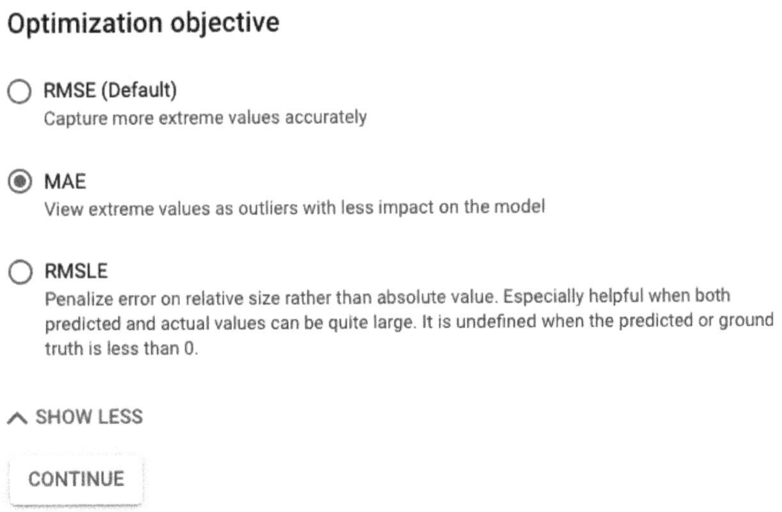

Optimization objective

○ RMSE (Default)
Capture more extreme values accurately

◉ MAE
View extreme values as outliers with less impact on the model

○ RMSLE
Penalize error on relative size rather than absolute value. Especially helpful when both predicted and actual values can be quite large. It is undefined when the predicted or ground truth is less than 0.

∧ SHOW LESS

CONTINUE

Figure 11.9 – Choosing optimization objective for ML problem

The MAE is a loss function commonly used for regression models. MAE represents the sum of absolute differences between actual and predicted values. Therefore, it measures the magnitude of errors without considering positive or negative directions. This type of loss function tends to lower the impact of outliers (unusually high or unusually low prices, in our example). It doesn't mean it's better than other functions, since it may, in fact, lead to worse training performance. It always depends on the data set. However, when you have a data set that is noisy in the sense of having several outliers (or if you suspect that's the case without knowing the data), it is often a good choice to start with.

15. On the next page, type 1 in the **Budget** field to limit the training budget to 1 node hour. This dictates the amount of resources that will be consumed by your model for training. Leave **Enable early stopping** enabled. Click on **Start Training**.

The training process will take one hour or less. It might be a good time for a coffee or tea break. In the next few steps, you will be deploying the model as an HTTP endpoint to be served online. When the model is ready, you can continue with the following steps:

1. Still on the **AI Platform (Unified)** console page, click on **Models**.

2. You should see your newly trained model named **stockholm-housing-model**. Click on it.

3. Under the **Evaluate** tab, you can see the evaluation results of the model you just trained as shown in the following screenshot:

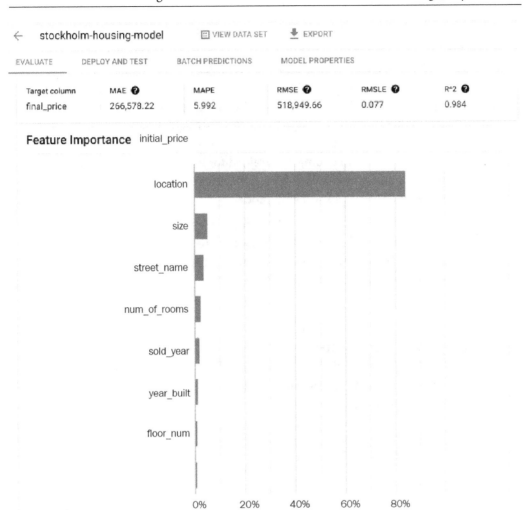

Figure 11.10 – Model evaluation

Your results will likely differ, since the data set split was randomized for this model (the default option in AutoML). But you'll likely see a very similar evaluation under **Feature Importance**. The bar chart shows the relative contribution (or weight) of each feature in obtaining the target predicted value. As you can see, the initial price for the bidding had a much stronger effect than anything else, probably because these prices were set by real estate agencies that took into account many more features (and real-world experience) to establish a price. Unsurprisingly to anyone who ever went house hunting, location topped the contribution among the other features.

You can see the values for MAE, RMSE, and other loss metrics in the preceding screenshot. MAE and RMSE values reflect the actual price values in Swedish currency (SEK). Since 1 USD equals roughly 8.32 SEK, an MAE of 266,578 SEK would correspond to 32,000 USD. That is the mean error of the model; that is, the model is typically some 32,000 USD off when making predictions. It may seem high but considering these are house prices in the Swedish capital, where typical values are between 200,000 USD and 600,000 USD, it's not a terrible loss value, especially for a model that required no coding and trained for less than one hour. But this would be the kind of key metric for which to have a threshold defined in advance determining whether this is a successful model.

4. Now that we have a model, we can deploy it for serving predictions. To do this, click on the **Deploy and Test** tab. Then, click on **Deploy to Endpoint**. Give the endpoint a name, and leave **Traffic split** at **100**. For **Machine type**, choose **n1-standard-2**. Leave other settings with their default values. Click on **Done** to confirm the model settings.

5. Click on **Deploy** to deploy the endpoint.

6. Wait until the endpoint is created (it may take several minutes). When ready, click on the shell icon on the top-right corner of the console to open a Cloud Shell terminal. Note the **ID** and the **Region** of the endpoint shown in the console, as highlighted in the following screenshot:

Figure 11.11 – Model endpoint

7. In Cloud Shell, make sure you're in the project created for this chapter. If not, run `gcloud config set project [PROJECT_ID]`. Run the following to set environment variables for your project ID, endpoint ID, and endpoint region:

```
$ export ENDPOINT_ID=[ENDPOINT_ID]
$ export PROJECT_ID=[PROJECT_ID]
$ export REGION=[REGION]
```

Substitute [ENDPOINT_ID] with the ID you see in the console for your endpoint and [REGION] with the region value.

8. Next, navigate to this activity's directory where there's a file called `input.json`:

```
$ cd Architecting-Google-Cloud-Solutions/ch11/automl
```

This file contains two fictional input entries for Stockholm apartments, previously unseen by the model, that we will use to make price predictions.

9. Run the following to make predictions for the sample input data:

```
$ curl -X POST \
-H "Authorization: Bearer $(gcloud auth print-access-
token)" \
-H "Content-Type: application/json" \
https://${REGION}-prediction-aiplatform.googleapis.com/
v1alpha1/projects/${PROJECT_ID}/locations/us-central1/
endpoints/${ENDPOINT_ID}:predict
\ -d "@input.json"
```

Your output should look similar to the following:

```
{
    "predictions": [
        {
            "upper_bound": 3090748.75,
            "value": 2471487.5,
            "lower_bound": 2097346.25
        },
        {
            "value": 3782161.75,
            "upper_bound": 4434672,
            "lower_bound": 3270429.75
        }
    ],
    "deployedModelId": "550881713794842624"
}
```

Figure 11.12 – Prediction output

According to this model shown in the screenshot, we should expect the two apartments to cost 3,090,748.75 SEK (about 370,971 USD) and 3,270,429.75 SEK (about 392,408 USD) respectively.

Congratulations! You created a production-ready ML model in just a little over an hour to predict house prices in the Swedish capital. You provided the data, and AutoML trained the model for you. No coding required. Then, you deployed an HTTP endpoint to serve your model online – no infrastructure to be managed either.

If you are comfortable with ML coding and would like to try what AI Platform has to offer, feel free to spend some time exploring. The flow would be similar if you're using custom code instead of AutoML, except when creating a training pipeline, you'd choose **Custom training (advanced)** option. You also have the option to upload a container that packages your code and all its libraries and dependencies.

Cloud AI Platform is the most robust GCP service available for custom ML model building. However, it's not the only one. You can also use **BigQuery ML**, as you shall see next.

BigQuery ML

In *Chapter 8, Approaching Big Data and Data Pipelines*, we've explored BigQuery as a data warehouse solution platform. BigQuery ML is an extra BigQuery feature that allows you to create, train, and get predictions from machine learning models using standard and familiar SQL queries. BigQuery ML is part of Google's vision to democratize ML by lowering its entry barrier for SQL practitioners and empowering them to apply ML through existing SQL tools and skills.

BigQuery ML supports a large number of different models. These include linear regression, binary logistic regression, multiclass logistic regression, time series, matrix factorization, K-means clustering, and a few others.

Compared to AI Platform, BigQuery ML offers the following advantages:

- No need to program an ML solution.
- Adopts familiar SQL syntax.
- Simpler and quicker to get started with.
- If all source data is in BigQuery, it removes the need to move data out of it, increasing the speed of experimentation.

Put simply, if there's no need for increased power of customization and model *programming*, and no requirement for model types not supported by BigQuery, then BigQuery ML may be a better fit than AI Platform. Especially the case in the lack of a data science team or teams with specialized ML skillset.

To showcase how you can quickly train, deploy, and serve a model using BigQuery ML, we will repeat the exact same problem you've worked on using AI Platform, this time on BigQuery ML.

Getting hands-on – training, deploying, and serving a model using BigQuery ML

In this activity, we will again deploy a linear regression model using the same data set of Stockholm housing prices provided in the repository. That way, you will be able to compare the experience of using BigQuery ML with that of using AI Platform for the same ML problem:

1. To start, open the GCP console (`console.cloud.google.com`).

2. In the console, make sure the project for this chapter is selected on the top bar, and click on **BigQuery** on the left-side menu.

3. On the **SQL workspace page**, under **Explorer**, click on your project's ID. Then, click on **Create Dataset**.

4. For **Dataset ID**, type in `housing_dataset`. Choose **United States (US)** in the **Data location** drop-down selection field and leave the other fields with their default options. Click on **Create dataset**.

5. Under **Explorer**, click on **housing_dataset**. Click on **Create Table** next to the plus sign on the top-right corner of the workspace.

6. Under **Source**, select **Google Cloud Storage** in the **Create table from** drop-down selection field. Under **Select file from GCS bucket**, click on **Browse**. Double-click on the bucket named after your project's ID, then select **stockholm-house-prices. csv** and click on **Select**. Under **Destination**, type in `housing` in the **Table name** field. Under **Schema**, check the box **Schema and input parameters** under **Auto-detect**. Leave all other fields with their default values. Click on **Create table**.

7. Under **Explorer**, click on **housing** to navigate to the newly created table. Then, on the top-right corner of the workspace, click on **Compose New Query**.

8. On the query editor, paste in the following:

```
CREATE MODEL `housing_dataset.housing_model`
OPTIONS
   (model_type='linear_reg',
     input_label_cols=['final_price']) AS
SELECT
   street_name,
   num_of_rooms,
   size,
   location,
```

```
        final_price,
        sold_year,
        initial_price,
        floor_num,
        year_built
    FROM
        `housing_dataset.housing`
    WHERE
        RAND() < 0.001
```

This command creates a linear regression model called `housing_model` using the housing table as the data source, the `final_price` column as the label, and all other columns (under the `SELECT` statement) as feature columns for training. The last part of the SQL statement (`RAND() < 0.001`) was introduced so that only a small sample of the table is used, so the model won't take long to train.

9. Click on **Run** to run this query. In a few minutes, you'll be able to navigate to the model called `housing_model` when it shows up under the **Explorer** pane. In there, you can see details of the model and various statistics. Explore the **Training** tab within the workspace of the model. You should see something similar to the following:

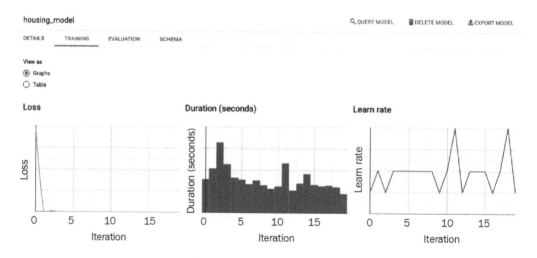

Figure 11.13 – Model training statistics

Then, explore the **Evaluation** tab, which should show present statistics as shown in the following figure (your values may differ):

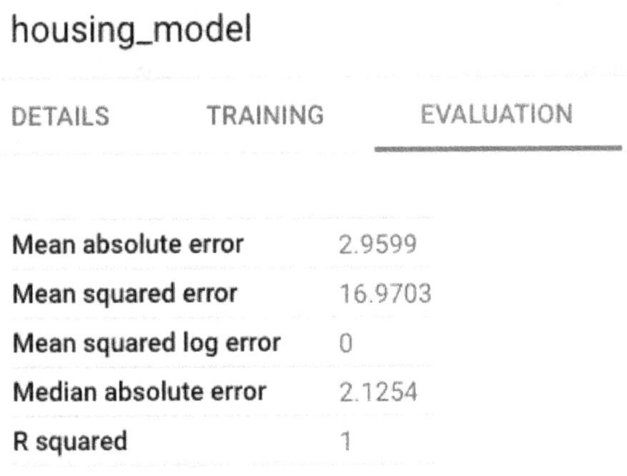

housing_model

DETAILS   TRAINING   EVALUATION   SCHEMA

Mean absolute error	2.9599
Mean squared error	16.9703
Mean squared log error	0
Median absolute error	2.1254
R squared	1

Figure 11.14 – Model evaluation statistics

10. Before we can get predictions from the model, we need to have unlabeled input data. To do so, we're going to upload a new CSV file to Cloud Storage, then create a new table in BigQuery using that CSV file. Keep the current console page open and click on the shell icon on the top-right corner of the console to open a Cloud Shell terminal.

11. In Cloud Shell, make sure you're in the project for this chapter. If not, run `gcloud config set project [PROJECT_ID]`. Then, run the following commands:

```
$ cd Architecting-Google-Cloud-Solutions/ch11/bigqueryml
$ gsutil cp stockholm-house-predictions.csv gs://
[PROJECT_ID]
```

This command uploads the CSV file to the same bucket created in the previous activity. This file contains two entries for prediction: the exact same two entries used in the previous activity (as a JSON input file).

You can now close Cloud Shell.

12. Back on the BigQuery page in the console, under **Explorer**, click on **housing_dataset** to navigate back to the data set. Then, click on **Create Table**.

13. Repeat step 6, this time selecting the `stockholm-house-predictions.csv` CSV file and naming your table `housing_predictions`.

14. Click on **Compose New Query** in the top-right corner of the workspace. Paste in the following query:

```
SELECT
  predicted_final_price
```

```
FROM
    ML.PREDICT(MODEL `housing_dataset.housing_model`,
    (
    SELECT
        street_name,
        num_of_rooms,
        size,
        location,
        sold_year,
        initial_price,
        floor_num,
        year_built
    FROM
        `housing_dataset.housing_predictions`))
```

15. Click on **Run** to run the query. Under the **Query results** pane, you should see a similar output to that shown in the following figure:

Figure 11.15 – Prediction query results

These are the two predicted prices for the two apartments listed in the CSV file provided. Note how wildly different (and likely off) these are compared to the previous activity. This is simply because we took a very small sample of data for training this time (to quickly get the model up and running), so the model is likely much less accurate. This showcases the importance of having a lot of training data!

In this activity, you've imported data into BigQuery from Cloud Storage, created a linear regression model by running a SQL query, and, with another SQL query, obtained predictions from your model. You have now gained hands-on experience with ML using BigQuery. Regardless of your ML skill level, BigQuery ML can get you up to speed in no time and is a powerful tool to incorporate into your projects.

The Google Cloud documentation page for BigQuery ML includes several tutorials for different types of ML problems, such as these:

- Predict birth weight (`https://cloud.google.com/bigquery-ml/docs/bigqueryml-natality`)

- Predict movie recommendations (`https://cloud.google.com/bigquery-ml/docs/bigqueryml-mf-explicit-tutorial`)

- Predict website content for visitors (`https://cloud.google.com/bigquery-ml/docs/bigqueryml-mf-implicit-tutorial`)

- Single time-series forecasting (`https://cloud.google.com/bigquery-ml/docs/arima-single-time-series-forecasting-tutorial`)

- Multiple time-series forecasting (`https://cloud.google.com/bigquery-ml/docs/arima-multiple-time-series-forecasting-tutorial`)

If you wish to continue to experiment with BigQuery ML and expand your skills to other classes of ML problems, I encourage you to check out some of these tutorials. Otherwise, to clean up the resources created for this chapter, open a Cloud Shell terminal and delete the project by running the following:

```
$ gcloud projects delete [PROJECT_ID]
```

You've learned about ML APIs on GCP, AI Platform and its suite of services, and BigQuery ML. The following figure summarizes all the services discussed so far and where they fit in terms of power of customization versus ease of implementation:

Figure 11.16 – GCP AI ecosystem

Next, we're going to discuss how you can improve agility and operations efficiency for your ML workflows by drawing on some of the principles from DevOps.

Productionizing custom ML models with MLOps

ML systems have unique characteristics that differentiate them from traditional software. They require the testing and validation of both code and *data*, they have unique ways of measuring quality and evaluating performance, and deployed ML models typically degrade over time if they don't continuously evolve. Moreover, observability becomes difficult since systems can underperform without throwing errors or showing signs of it. Therefore, managing and operating ML models can be challenging.

In *Chapter 9, Jumping on the DevOps Bandwagon with Site Reliability Engineering (SRE)*, we've discussed DevOps principles and how they can help improve the reliability of systems and shorten development cycles. As data science and ML became crucially important capabilities for modern enterprises, applying a similar set of principles to ML systems has become a priority for many. Hence, the **Machine Learning Operations (MLOps)** paradigm emerged. MLOps is an engineering culture and practice similar to DevOps but tailored to solve ML-specific problems. MLOps still advocates for automation and monitoring at all steps, including the automation and codification of infrastructure deployments, and the elimination of silos. However, it differs from DevOps in a few ways:

- MLOps is concerned not only with testing code but testing and validating data, data schemas, and models.

- MLOps practices consider the whole system (the ML workflow and pipeline) as opposed to individual software packages and services.

- Whereas in DevOps software grows incrementally in a feature-oriented fashion, MLOps software requires continuous retraining and rebuilding. **Continuous Training (CT)** is a unique MLOps practice.

- ML is experimental in nature and involves heavy data analysis. MLOps systems are iterative and must be supported by data analysis tools.

The code of an ML system is typically only a small fraction of the whole. In many cases, the code is not even present (when you're using services such as AutoML or BigQuery ML). The real challenge lies in orchestrating all the dependencies and processes around it, such as data collection, data verification, feature engineering, model evaluation, monitoring, and so on. Therefore, being able to efficiently operationalize these parts and automate as many steps as possible is a key differentiator for businesses. Let's look at some concrete ways with which you can help implement an MLOps model in your organization.

Identifying MLOps maturity level

Firstly, you must identify and detail all the steps in your ML workflow. For each step, identify also what is its expected outcome (or output). A typical breakdown is shown in the following table:

Step	Description	Output
Data extraction	Select data from various sources and integrate relevant data in a single place.	List of data sources and integration operations.
Data analysis	Perform data analysis using, for example, exploratory data analysis (EDA) to understand the data.	Description of the data schema and characteristics. Identification of the data preparation and feature engineering steps that will be needed.
Data preparation	Clean and prepare the data for the ML task. Split data into training, validation, and test sets.	Cleaned and transformed training, test, and validation data sets.
Model training	Implement and run different training algorithms against a prepared training data set. Perform hyperparameter tuning to improve ML model performance against a validation set.	Trained model.
Model evaluation	Evaluate model quality against a test set.	Metrics that quantify the quality of the model.
Model business validation	Assess model's validity for deployment – actual predictive performance versus success baseline	Go/no go decision. If no go, the step from which to reiterate.
Model deployment and serving	Deploy the validated model to a target environment in a format ready serve predictions.	Deployed model on a suitable infrastructure and with a serving endpoint (for example, an HTTP endpoint on AI Platform).
Model monitoring	The model's predictive performance is continuously monitored.	Set of monitoring metrics and periodic assessment on whether to invoke a new iteration.

You may wish to extend this workflow description to include finer-grained details of implementation for each step as you implement them. The maturity of your ML process will be defined by the level of automation you have. Google defines three levels of MLOps maturity:

- **Level 0**: Manual process
- **Level 1**: ML pipeline automation
- **Level 2**: CI/CD pipeline automation.

At level 0, all steps are manual. ML development and operations are disconnected, release iterations are infrequent, and there's little to no automation beyond scripted processes. Continuous integration, continuous training, and continuous delivery are not present.

At level 1, you have an automated ML pipeline and continuous training. At this level of maturity, you should have the following enabled:

- Rapid experimentation.
- CT in production.
- Same pipeline implementation for the development/test and staging/production environments.
- Modularized and reproducible code for components and pipelines. While data exploration tools and code can live outside of the source repository, the source code for pipeline components (executable, artifacts, pipeline steps) must be defined in code and reusable as much as possible.
- CD in production (automatically serve newly trained models).

The availability of new data triggers the ML pipeline and the training of a new model. The existing CT pipeline is executed; that is, no new pipeline components are deployed. This scenario is illustrated in the following diagram:

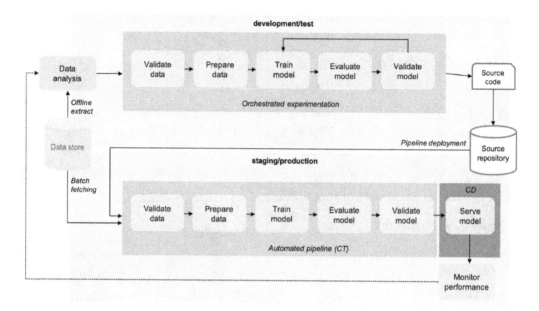

Figure 11.17 – MLOps ML pipeline automation

Finally, the highest level of maturity (level 3) is when data scientists can rapidly experiment and explore new model architectures, hyperparameter sets, and feature engineering techniques to evolve the ML pipeline continuously. As these new ideas are implemented, the resulting pipeline components are automatically built, tested, and deployed to the target environment.

At this level, a CT pipeline is continuously deployed and run through a CI/CD pipeline, providing the highest level of development and experimentation agility. The following diagram captures this scenario:

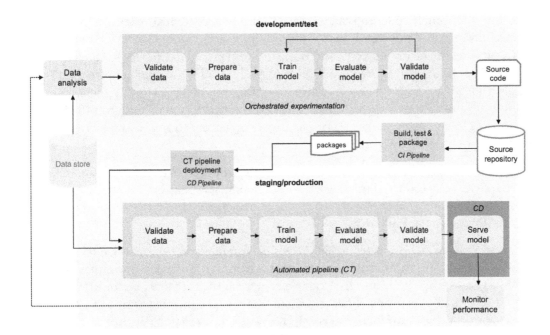

Figure 11.18 – MLOps CI/CD pipeline automation

More detailed information on MLOps maturity levels and best practices is well documented at https://cloud.google.com/solutions/machine-learning/mlops-continuous-delivery-and-automation-pipelines-in-machine-learning.

MLOps and CI/CD for ML on GCP

Your action plan toward improving your MLOps maturity will depend on where you currently are. At each level, you can work your way up by incrementally automating each step of the ML workflow.

On GCP, AI Platform provides some useful MLOps enabling features, such as a Continuous Evaluation service (https://cloud.google.com/ai-platform/prediction/docs/continuous-evaluation), monitoring capabilities (including integration with Cloud Monitoring), and easy ways to publish new code and data into the platform. AI Platform also provides **Jupyter Notebook**, an open source web-based platform for code experimentation and visualization. Google is continuously improving the AI Platform service by adding new features. Since it's still in beta at the time of writing, it wouldn't be surprising if several new capabilities beyond those discussed in this chapter are now available when you read this.

For hosting your source code, you can leverage **Cloud Source Repositories**, which provides fully managed private Git repositories with integrations for CI/CD capabilities. Your CI pipeline can be hosted on **Cloud Build**, as we explored in *Chapter 9, Jumping on the DevOps Bandwagon with Site Reliability Engineering (SRE)*. Containers are great candidates for ML artifacts, since you're able to package the runtime entirely, including dependencies and custom libraries. You can leverage Google Cloud's **Container Registry** (`https://cloud.google.com/container-registry/docs`) as a service to store, manage and secure Docker container images.

Finally, your ML system can be orchestrated using **Kubeflow** pipelines. Kubeflow is an open source Kubernetes-based framework for developing and running ML workloads. You can run Kubeflow pipelines with little management and operational overhead on **Google Kubernetes Engine (GKE)**.

For a great resource on how to set up an MLOps environment on GCP, check out `https://cloud.google.com/solutions/machine-learning/setting-up-an-mlops-environment`. An example comprehensive architecture for MLOps using TensorFlow, Kubeflow pipelines and Cloud Build is documented at `https://cloud.google.com/solutions/machine-learning/architecture-for-mlops-using-tfx-kubeflow-pipelines-and-cloud-build`.

As you can see, Google has no shortage of good reference architecture documentation and resources for you to incorporate ML into your solutions. ML can be an overwhelmingly complex area and services evolve quickly. For that reason, there's much more to learn and explore than what was presented in this condensed chapter, so I do encourage you to check out the resources linked. And keep an eye out for new AI Platform developments on GCP.

Summary

In this chapter, you've learned some fundamental concepts in the field of AI and the motivations for ML. You then learned about the many pretrained models that are readily available on GCP for consumption and how you can leverage them for different business use cases. With a good grasp of the AI landscape on GCP, we explored options for building custom models, and you learned about and got hands-on experience with AI Platform and BigQuery ML. In particular, you've learned how you can deploy and serve state-of-the-art models without any ML coding experience. Finally, we briefly discussed MLOps and best practices for productionizing ML models and improving agility and operational efficiency of ML workflows on GCP. These are all essential and yet relatively scarce skills among cloud professionals. And you're now equipped to use AI and ML to incorporate modern and data-driven enterprise architecture practices into your cloud solutions.

In the next chapter, you will learn about the last – but no less important – pillar of great cloud solutions, which is that of operational excellence.

12
Achieving Operational Excellence

The cloud is not just someone else's data center. It's a new **operating model** for IT. And in all cloud adoption efforts, **operational excellence** is crucial for long-term success. In fact, it's one of the pillars in Google's **Architecture Framework**, a collection of best practices created by seasoned experts at Google Cloud. These are practices to consider before, during, and after cloud adoption. It is a continuous and iterative effort, with many ways to start but with no finish line.

In this final chapter, you will begin by learning the strategies and guiding principles of operational excellence. You will then learn how to apply Google Cloud's Architecture Framework best practices to your solutions and incorporate design strategies and guiding principles to improve operational efficiency. Finally, you will also learn how you can use Cloud Operations Sandbox to put this knowledge into practice in Google Cloud. By the end of this chapter, you will have learned how to define a cloud operating model based on a broader cloud strategy, and how to apply the best practices for operational excellence to efficiently run production workloads on GCP.

In this chapter, we're going to cover the following main topics:

- Starting with a cloud strategy

- Learning and applying operations best practices

- Bringing it all together with Cloud Operations Sandbox

Technical requirements

For the suggested hands-on activity in this chapter, you will need a billing-enabled Google Cloud account.

Starting with a cloud strategy

The major hyperscale cloud providers (such as Microsoft, Amazon, and Google) may disagree on a few things when it comes to the best ways to build and operate workloads in the cloud. But one of the things they agree on is that **operational excellence** makes up one of the pillars of well-architected cloud solutions. Operational excellence is a business function and set of practices that include design and governance decisions to achieve the following goals:

- Develop and run workloads effectively

- Manage resources and efficiently monitor their operations

- Continuously improve processes that support systems' reliability and workload efficiency

When *operations* is perceived as an isolated function, as it has been in traditional IT models, these goals are challenging to achieve. Indeed, operational excellence goes hand in hand with the principles and practices you've learned in *Chapter 9, Jumping on the DevOps Bandwagon with Site Reliability Engineering (SRE)*. It encompasses a broad set of strategies at the organization level and, at the same time, a set of practices and design principles at the workload level.

A clear **strategy** is the foundation of any cloud adoption and operational excellence effort. It helps determine the motivations and the expected outcomes, which in turn help determine the right processes and design decisions that drive those outcomes. In *Chapter 1, An Introduction to Google Cloud for Architects*, we introduced these ideas in the context of making a business case for cloud adoption. We've now come full circle to explore how a well-defined strategy that supports the architectural concepts and best practices discussed throughout this book can enable operational excellence.

A strategy can be manifested in different ways and expressed in various formats, but generally, the following are the key focus areas that must be determined and *understood*:

- The priorities and motivations
- The operating model
- The organizational culture

Let's explore each of these briefly before getting to operational excellence practices.

Setting priorities

In *Chapter 9, Jumping on the DevOps Bandwagon with Site Reliability Engineering (SRE)*, we discussed the importance of having a **shared understanding** and **alignment** culture in an organization. Well-defined organization priorities help establish common business goals and eliminate ambiguity. In **Site Reliability Engineering** (**SRE**), these are expressed primarily in the form of **Service-Level Objectives** (**SLO**), which offer a user-centric definition of successful outcomes.

More generally, the following are a few guiding steps you can work through to elicit your organization's priorities:

- **Evaluating customer needs**: Determine what customers value about your business and what defines a successful business and customer outcomes. Involve key stakeholders, including business, engineering, and operations teams, to identify customer needs and determine where to focus efforts *for the greatest impact* on meeting those needs. Make it a shared goal and understanding across stakeholders.

  For example, you may decide on an SRE-based approach and reflect customer needs using SLOs. Once you determine the SLOs that capture user satisfaction for your services, you may decide to focus your improvement efforts on areas such as workload performance, runbook automation (toil reduction), observability, and incident response.

- **Evaluating governance and compliance requirements**: Your organization may have guidelines and regulations to adhere to depending on the industry it operates in and the type of data it handles. Validate that you have mechanisms and processes to identify compliance and changes that may affect governance decisions.

  For example, if your organization processes card payments and is subject to the **Payment Card Industry Data Security Standard (PCI DSS)** regulations, you need to validate that you have employed mechanisms such as organization policies, data encryption, access control, and other security- and compliance-related practices as discussed in *Chapter 7, Designing for Security and Compliance.*

- **Evaluating security requirements and the threat landscape**: Assess the potential threats to the business and validate that you have mechanisms and processes in place to continuously monitor and mitigate those threats.

  For example, you may have highlighted *identity theft* and *data exfiltration* as the main risks in your threat model. In this case, ensure that you have strong identity security policies and that you review audit logs regularly; also, that you have data encryption and data access settings enforced at, for example, the infrastructure pipeline level.

- **Evaluating trade-offs and benefits versus risks**: When faced with trade-offs between competing approaches, lean on the broader organization priorities to help make informed decisions about where to focus effort.

  For example, if service reliability and user experience are a priority, you may decide on a less risky design approach – where the alternative approach is to deliver newer features to the customers. In SRE, this relates to the concept of an error budget. If you've burned through your error budget and don't have much room for experimentation, reducing risk at the expense of added benefits is a choice that is better *aligned with the priorities* (SLOs in this case).

As you may have noticed, a lot of these examples draw on SRE practices as well as security and governance principles you have learned about in previous chapters.

Once you have identified the priorities and the governance decisions that support them, the next step is to determine the cloud operating model.

Determining the cloud operating model

The cloud operating model is the high-level representation of processes that help realize the broader cloud strategy. In the cloud, the hardware is removed as a unit of operations, and the focus shifts to digital assets and managed services. Therefore, there are two main operation areas: application (*workload*) and virtual cloud infrastructure (*platform*). The latter tends to be a very limited function in a model that favors managed services. Moreover, cloud providers such as Google Cloud consistently put out guidelines and best practices that you can leverage in many scenarios. Hence, a cloud operating model is likely to differ significantly from that of traditional IT and converge toward modern and democratized best practices.

Smaller companies may have a bias toward action and prioritize putting workloads into production quickly, but larger and more mature enterprises typically prefer a top-down strategy approach that first invests in defining a cloud operating model before any workloads are deployed. There are a number of factors that go into defining an operating model, but some common ones are the following:

- The organization of teams
- Change management (adoption) processes
- Operations management
- Governance, compliance, and security

What an operating model ultimately helps define is *who is responsible for what* and *who is accountable for what decisions*, that is, the **ownership** and **responsibility** structure. The following are some common cloud operating models:

- Fully separated: segregated responsibilities for application engineering, platform engineering, application operations, and platform operations
- Application engineering and operations separate from platform engineering and operations (*you build it, you run it*), with centralized or decentralized governance
- Enterprise operations with **Cloud Center of Excellence (CCoE)**
- Distributed operations

Some overlapping and variations may occur among these models. But to help illustrate the general differences between them, the following image represents each of these models according to an *engineering* and *operations* versus a *workload* and *platform* responsibility quadrant:

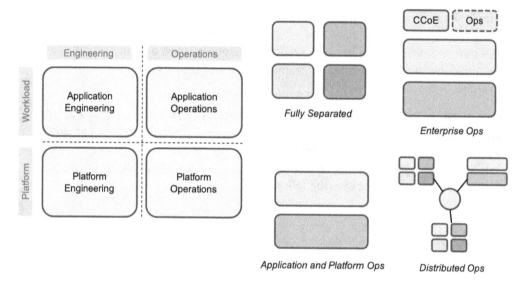

Figure 12.1 – Operating model responsibility quadrant

Any of these models may include any degree of managed services adoption (that is, Platform-as-a-Service and Software-as-a-Service services) from Google Cloud and, therefore, the platform operations function may be limited or removed altogether. No particular model is recommended over others as a one-size-fits-all solution. Organizations can in fact be successful with any of these, as long as it best suits their structure and their cloud adoption phase.

In the fully separated model, separate teams exist and are responsible for each of the quadrants shown on the left-hand side of the preceding diagram. Typically, work is passed between teams through work requests, tickets, or other such mechanisms. This approach creates *greater segregation of duties* but increases *complexity* and creates bottlenecks. Moreover, there is a higher risk of *misalignment* since engineering and operations teams may work toward separate goals and be evaluated on different metrics. This can cause teams to focus on their specific responsibilities instead of working toward achieving business outcomes. This model prioritizes *control* and the *continuation of traditional operational processes.* Organizations doing a lift-and-shift from an on-premises data center may find this model adds the least friction to their cloud migration effort.

An evolution from that model is when engineering and operations are merged together similar to the DevOps or SRE way of working (*you build it, you run it*). Separation still exists between workloads and platforms, but not between engineering and operations. In this model, governance can be centralized or decentralized. With centralized governance, standards are defined centrally (often by the platform team) and shared with other teams. In contrast, the decentralized governance model allows different teams to have more autonomy and define their standards. The choice of governance structure is a trade-off between speed of innovation and control. This operating model is a strong enabler for microservices-oriented (or product-oriented) solutions and rearchitecture/modernization efforts. It prioritizes *autonomy* and *agility* over *control*.

A very similar model and one that modern enterprises tend to converge on is the *enterprise operations* model. This model (named somewhat arbitrarily by Microsoft) provides similar democratization of decisions and more autonomy and responsibility to application teams. At the same time, it includes a CCoE team to replace the traditional central IT team as a more facilitative – rather than controlling – function. A CCoE team helps define standards and best practices and holds other teams accountable for decisions without limiting their actions. A central operations team can also be created to maintain workloads that require increased security, compliance, and/or stable operations. These two extra functions (the latter being optional) are included in the enterprise operations scenario illustrated in the top-right corner of the diagram. This model provides a good balance between *control* and *innovation*. However, if not accompanied by the right cultural shift, it may not deliver on its advantages. You will learn in the next section what the important supporting cultural elements are.

Finally, the distributed operations model involves a combination of other models for more complex IT portfolios. This approach requires the integration of different models (and possibly different partners or service providers). It has a greater risk of business misalignments, but it also offers higher scalability and flexibility for larger organizations, allowing them to fit the best operating model to different organizational segments.

For any choice of operating model, aim to validate the following:

- Resources and processes have identified owners
- Operations activities have identified owners
- Team members know what they are responsible for
- There are mechanisms in place to identify responsibility and ownership as well as request additions, changes, and exceptions

Understanding priorities and establishing the operating model will provide the kind of clarity that enables teams to work efficiently toward common goals. However, that won't yet be sufficient to drive operational excellence if a supporting organizational culture is not present. Next, we'll explore this final component.

Establishing the organizational culture

The organizational culture is once again a theme that relates to SRE and DevOps. Some of the important cultural elements that are crucial for driving operational excellence are the following:

- **Empowerment and blamelessness**: When team members are empowered to take action and, at the same time, feel they have a safety net created by a culture of tolerance toward mistakes and failures

- **Communication**: When mechanisms exist for teams to communicate, and when they're encouraged to express concerns and speak up about any issues

- **Experimentation**: When team members are encouraged to experiment, that is, spend time on engineering work and also have some autonomy on what they work on

- **Continuous learning**: When team members are encouraged to learn and given the time and the resources for training and upskilling

The open communication culture and the reduction of silos are particularly important in models that merge engineering and operations functions, such as those inspired by SRE. The organizational culture is not just about providing psychological benefits to employees, but they have a measurable impact on operational performance, as successful DevOps and SRE organizations have demonstrated over the years. The preceding cultural elements are the building blocks for **continuous improvement**, which is fundamental for sustainable and successful growth.

To sum up the strategic areas for operational excellence, you must define and understand the priorities, the IT operating model, and the organizational culture. These three components comprise the foundation. As a cloud or solutions architect, you may or may not have influence over them, but they're still fundamentally important markers of success to look out for. The following image illustrates the idea of having these strategies as the foundation on which best practices can be built to drive operational excellence:

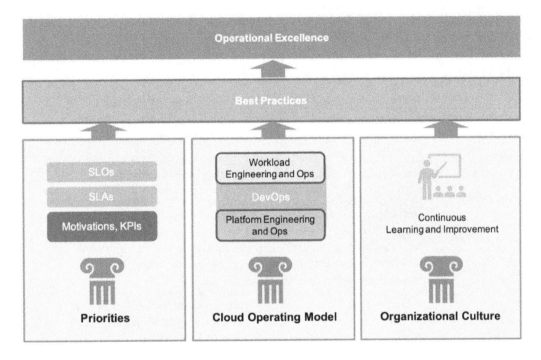

Figure 12.2 – The foundational strategy for operational excellence

Next, let's dive into the concrete best practices that you can apply.

Learning and applying operations best practices

Google Cloud's **Architecture Framework** describes best practices and provides implementation recommendations for products and services on GCP. A part of the framework is dedicated to operational excellence and is documented at https:// cloud.google.com/architecture/framework/operational-excellence.

In this section, we'll break down these guiding principles and recommendations, elaborate on them, and relate them to concrete examples as well as architectural concepts you've learned in this book.

The framework sets forth the following strategies (guiding principles):

- Automate, build, test, and deploy
- Monitor business objective metrics
- Conduct **disaster recovery** (**DR**) testing

In short, they encapsulate the SRE practices of **automation**, **observability**, and **designing for failure**. As strategies, they must be embraced as overarching guiding principles that teams must not deviate from. Therefore, have these strategies clearly defined and communicated.

As an example of how you can approach defining these strategies in practice as your organization's guiding principles, the following table shows how they could be documented:

Guiding principle	Description	Baseline implementation
Automation	Every production infrastructure and application deployment must be reviewed and executed through **continuous integration and continuous delivery (CI/CD)** pipelines.	Every change must happen in a source repository and through a **pull request** (**PR**) workflow. A PR must have two mandatory reviewers and no user can approve its own PR. CI pipelines must at a minimum contain automated unit tests, automated integration tests, and automated security checks. CD pipelines must release application and infrastructure artifacts (binaries and Terraform plans) associated with a tag in the Git repository. Deployment to a production environment requires the approval of one member of the platform team.
Observability	All relevant business metrics must be measured and have associated alerts.	Application uptime, response time, number of errors, number of requests, and traffic load must be measured for all applications. Alerts must be set according to thresholds defined by SLOs and SLAs.
Disaster recovery	Periodically conduct DR testing	Once every quarter, conduct a DR drill and measure performance against **recovery time objectives (RTOs)** and **recovery point objectives (RPOs)**.

In this example, a baseline implementation is provided as the skeleton design for how the strategy must be implemented. It establishes a minimum level of implementation guidance.

The framework also defines best practices around these guiding principles. We'll explore them in detail.

Increasing development and release velocity

As you learned in *Chapter 9, Jumping on the DevOps Bandwagon with Site Reliability Engineering (SRE)*, it is a good practice to use **Infrastructure-as-Code (IaC)** to codify your infrastructure and have a source repository be your *single source of truth*. Taking this even further, strongly discourage and even *disallow* manual changes entirely. Then, use CI/CD pipelines with automated testing to increase velocity without hurting reliability. To do this, establish a set of **testing criteria** that builds must meet before they're released. Make the tests and validations comprehensive enough for developers and infrastructure engineers to feel confident to make more frequent (and smaller-scoped) changes. Breaking changes will have a smaller impact and will be easier to reverse if they're small. This idea is illustrated in the diagram image and applies to both application and infrastructure code:

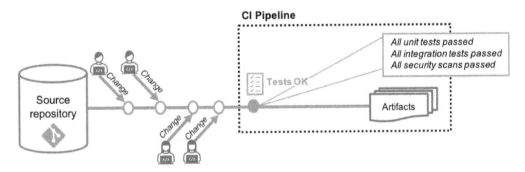

Figure 12.3 – Making frequent, small releases with automated testing

Ensure you also version your build configurations, environment configurations, and any other application- or infrastructure-related configurations that can be coded – including operations tools. For example, suppose your environment has VMs that use a standard marketplace image but have a sequence of post-deployment configuration steps. In that case, have a source-controlled *startup script* that runs automatically upon every VM creation instead of making it a manual configuration process. You can have *operations as code* too. Say you perform periodic OS security patches on your VMs. Instead of that being executed manually, have it executed by a configuration automation tool such as Chef, Puppet, or Ansible, and have the associated configuration playbooks in the source repository. *Automation always trumps manual work in terms of consistency and efficiency.* In addition, IaC helps eliminate **environment drift** and allows for better manageability and **change tracking**.

Testing is a crucial component of any development cycle, too, and no exception to the automation-trumps-manual-work rule. Therefore, it is also a good practice to incorporate testing activities into CI pipelines. They help ensure reliability and security by automating software and system tests as well as security checks and scans. There are several types of application tests, such as the following:

- **Unit testing**: Consists of tests for individual methods and functions of software programs.

- **Integration testing**: Verifies that different software components (modules or classes) or services work well together, that is, that individual changes don't impact existing integrations.

- **Functional testing**: Tests that focus on the business requirements and functionalities of the application. Typically involves real-world scenarios and validates a service's behavior and its actual response values. Also referred to as **acceptance testing**, in which case business requirements are captured in the form of *acceptance criteria*.

- **System testing**: Tests the fully integrated product or service, including dependencies and runtime.

- **Performance testing**: Validates that the system meets performance and scalability requirements under load. Also referred to as **load testing** or **stress testing**.

- **Smoke testing**: Tests meant to check and quickly validate the business requirements and the functionalities of the application. Useful as a first post-build test to decide whether or not the build successfully meets the basic requirements.

- **Security testing**: Tests that check for security vulnerabilities and/or violations from a baseline. As discussed in *Chapter 9, Jumping on the DevOps Bandwagon with Site Reliability Engineering (SRE)*, these can be **static-, dynamic-, interactive-, or runtime-based application security tests** (**SAST**, **DAST**, **IAST**, and **RASP**, respectively).

It is not straightforward to apply these testing methodologies to *infrastructure* code. However, there are a few tests and validations that you can run against infrastructure templates and code, some of which will depend on the capabilities of the specific IaC tool you choose. For example, **Cloud Deployment Manager** offers a *preview* feature that allows you to analyze the target configuration before deploying a template.

Terraform has a `plan` command that has a similar function. You can use it to do dry-run tests and automate certain checks against their outputs, such as the presence of specific attributes or resources. Terraform also offers testing plugins and other useful testing features you can learn about in the guidance provided at `https://www.terraform.io/docs/extend/best-practices/testing.html`. In particular, you can read about how to approach infrastructure unit and acceptance testing with Terraform at `https://www.terraform.io/docs/extend/testing/unit-testing.html` and `https://www.terraform.io/docs/extend/testing/acceptance-tests/index.html`.

You can also extend security testing to your infrastructure by incorporating **policy constraints** at the pipeline stage, a practice we discussed in *Chapter 7, Designing for Security and Compliance*. For example, you can define organization policies in code that restrict resource deployment location and allowed GCP services. You can also leverage some of the tools referenced in *Chapter 9, Jumping on the DevOps Bandwagon with Site Reliability Engineering (SRE)*, for static security analysis of infrastructure code.

At the stage of deployment, it's a best practice to perform **canary testing** (discussed in *Chapter 9, Jumping on the DevOps Bandwagon with Site Reliability Engineering (SRE)*). This ties to the SRE principle of reducing the cost of failure. On GCP, you can deploy workloads to **managed instance groups (MIGs)**, App Engine, or Kubernetes Engine to do A/B or canary testing easily. Having a **rollback procedure** is also crucially important. A rollback is most often done in two ways:

- Rolling back code changes, and pushing code again as a new release that gets subsequently deployed
- Re-releasing the previous build and deleting the defective build, before reverting the code changes

A **branching strategy** that defines a single main branch and several smaller feature branches seems to work best in most cases (true of both application and infrastructure code). A good guidance on this type of branching strategy for Git is provided by Microsoft at `https://docs.microsoft.com/en-us/azure/devops/repos/git/git-branching-guidance`.

Finally, as already highlighted as of one of the guiding principles, ensure the CI/CD pipeline is the only way to deploy to production. In addition, ensure that every code change goes through a **pull request (PR)** workflow that requires **peer review**. Two reviewers is the optimal number according to a research study published at `https://www.microsoft.com/en-us/research/publication/convergent-software-peer-review-practices/`. If you're not familiar with the PR workflow, a good tutorial is available at `https://www.atlassian.com/git/tutorials/making-a-pull-request`.

This practice is illustrated in the following workflow:

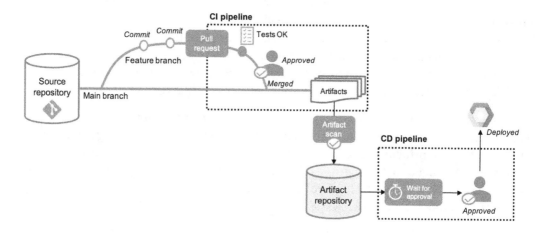

Figure 12.4 – CI/CD pipelines with PR workflow

As shown in the figure, you can optionally set approval gates at the deploy stage in the CD pipeline for production environments, to ensure someone reviews and approves the deployment. This is an example where you don't have continuous deployment enabled, reducing agility but providing greater control. This method is most useful for platform pipelines, since infrastructure changes tend to happen much less often – and have a much higher impact.

Now that you have a grip on the best practices for increasing deployment and release velocity, we'll look at some key enabling services and tools.

Key services and tools

The following are key services and tools on GCP, or otherwise available as open source software that you can use to enable deployment velocity:

Service / Tool	Description	How it helps
Cloud Source Repositories	Fully-featured, private Git repository service.	It can be used to host and source-control all your application and infrastructure code. It provides standard Git change control features such as pull requests. It is hosted on GCP and fully managed, thus requiring no operations.
Container Registry	A fully-managed Docker image repository with access control and vulnerability analysis.	It can be used as a single place for hosting all your container-based artifacts. Built-in CI/CD integrations make it easy to incorporate into your pipelines. Security features enable DevSecOps.
Cloud Build	Fully-managed CI platform on GCP.	Can be used for your CI needs by continuously executing your builds. Can be integrated with Cloud Source Repositories, GitHub, and other sources.
Jenkins	Free and open source CI/CD automation software for building, testing, and deploying applications.	Can be used for all your CI/CD needs. Can be leveraged by teams already familiar with this software. Guidance for setting up on Google Kubernetes Engine (for high availability and scalability) available at `https://cloud.google.com/solutions/jenkins-on-kubernetes-engine-tutorial`.
Terraform	Open source IaC software.	Can be used as your IaC framework to codify infrastructure resources. Can also be leveraged for static testing and automated validations for infrastructure changes. Terraform Validator (`https://github.com/GoogleCloudPlatform/terraform-validator`) can be leveraged as well to enforce policies on configurations. Guidance on using Terraform with Google Cloud is available at `https://cloud.google.com/docs/terraform`.

Next, we'll explore the best practices concerning monitoring.

Monitoring system health and business health

In *Chapter 6, Configuring Services for Observability*, we discussed the different types of monitoring and the importance of observability for your cloud solutions. In addition, you learned about the *four golden signals* to monitor your systems, according to Google's SRE. Namely, these are the following:

- **Latency**: The time it takes to service a request

- **Traffic**: A measure of how much demand is being placed on your system

- **Errors**: The rate of requests that fail

- **Saturation**: A measure of how full the service is

These are the main signals that will help you learn crucially important information about your *systems*. That information helps you understand whether they are operating correctly and according to requirements. In turn, this enables you to analyze trends, evaluate changes, perform security analytics, and so on. Therefore, it's a recommended practice to monitor these signals for all your systems, including VMs, databases, application platforms, APIs, and endpoints.

While improving your systems' observability is an excellent win, you can gain further insights from gathering *business-driven metrics*. These are the kinds of metrics that help you understand how your *business* is performing. For example, you can look at the number of products sold or the time a customer spends on your website. These metrics help you gauge the impact of things such as sales campaigns or application changes on your customers' behavior. In *Chapter 6, Configuring Services for Observability*, we also discussed how you can instrument applications with **custom metrics** that can be analyzed in cloud monitoring.

Also crucial to your overall observability is logging various system events. **Logs** may contain valuable information for **debugging** and **troubleshooting** and also serve as a basis for security and compliance analysis. On GCP, you can also use logs to build metrics for monitoring and you can also export logs to external services.

Finally, by leveraging visualization tools such as **charts** and **dashboards**, you can focus on the most relevant monitoring data for your systems with an at-a-glance view of their state. But another fundamentally important aspect of monitoring that can't be overlooked is that of **alerting**. Having the right alerting strategy will allow you to quickly react to important events and, accompanied by a well-defined incident response strategy, quickly remediate issues. Therefore, make sure you create *actionable* alerts for relevant system components. Ensure that you *learn from all failures* by performing **postmortems** and work to prevent the same issues from reoccurring. Work iteratively on fine-tuning your alert thresholds if alerts become more noise than signal or if they fail to capture real issues.

To summarize, the following are the recommendations to follow:

- Choose relevant system and business-driven metrics. Create custom metrics if necessary.
- Ensure logging is configured for all relevant log entries. Create custom metrics from logs if useful.
- Use Cloud Monitoring and Cloud Logging and leverage built-in chart and dashboard features.
- Define actionable alerts for important events.
- Have an incident response strategy that includes an escalation path and a clearly defined plan of action.
- Learn from issues and mistakes and refine operations procedures frequently.

Let's now look at some key enabling services and tools.

Key services and tools

The following are key services and tools on GCP or otherwise available as open source software that you can use to enable observability and monitoring:

Service/Tool	Description	How it helps
Cloud Monitoring	GCP's monitoring service, which provides metrics aggregation, dashboards, and alerts.	Cloud Monitoring offers you a single pane of glass through which to collect and analyze metrics. You can also use it to create charts and dashboards and set up alerts. You can leverage integrations with the entire GPC service landscape and external sources.
Cloud Logging	GCP's logging service, which provides log collection and aggregation and lets you search, visualize, filter, and export logs.	Cloud Logging can be used for your logging needs. You can leverage integrations with the entire GCP service landscape and external sources. You can use it to aggregate and analyze logs and also export them to a storage service for long retention.
Cloud Debugger	A service that allows you to inspect the state of your application without stopping it or slowing it down.	This service can be used to provide greater observability and insights into your applications' behavior. It can help troubleshoot software bugs and speed up remediation.
Error Reporting	Aggregates and displays errors produced by various cloud services and your applications.	This service can be used to notify you when errors are detected to help you react quickly.

Service/Tool	Description	How it helps
Cloud Trace	A service that provides distributed tracing for your applications, collecting latency data and displaying them in near real time in the console.	It can be very useful to provide insights on request latency for your various applications' components. It gives you one of the four golden signals.
Cloud Profiler	A low-overhead profiling service that continuously gathers performance information (such as CPU and memory usage) from your applications.	It can be used to continuously measure the performance of your application and help you identify bottlenecks and performance issues quickly.
Grafana	An open source observability platform that provides analytics and interactive visualization.	Can be used as a feature-rich alternative to Cloud Monitoring. It's a useful platform to aggregate charts, create dashboards, and create powerful visualizations. Can be useful in hybrid- or multi-cloud solutions. Find out more at `https://grafana.com/`.
OpenTelemetry	An open source observability framework.	This framework provides tools, APIs, and SDKs for various languages that you can use to instrument and export telemetry data (including metrics, logs, and traces). Can be used in conjunction with Cloud Trace.
Prometheus	An open source monitoring and alerting system that offers several client libraries and visualization capabilities.	Can be used as a great monitoring and alerting solution alternative, particularly for Kubernetes deployments.

Monitoring and alerting practices will help you *react* to failures. However, one equally important component is *anticipating* failure and preparing accordingly. We'll delve into this complementary practice next.

Designing for failure and practicing disaster recovery

Even when you do everything right, disasters and events outside of your control can happen. Anticipating failure scenarios and designing your systems to handle these scenarios will help ensure business continuity. However, it's hardly enough to simply incorporate redundancy and backups to your infrastructure components. You may think that everything looks good on paper, but you can never know for sure until you try. Therefore, aim to not only plan for DR but also regularly *test* it.

DR planning typically revolves around two crucial business metrics:

- **Recovery time objective (RTO)**, representing the maximum period of *application downtime* your business can tolerate.

- **Recovery point objective (RPO)**, representing the maximum amount of *application-related data loss* your business can tolerate, measured in length of time.

So, for example, your RTOs and RPOs may look like the following in practice:

Workload/Service	RTO	Associated Data	RPO
Web UI	6 hours	User profile	4 hours
Web Shop	2 hours	Transactions	10 minutes
Analytics	24 hours	Offline data warehouse	12 hours

Naturally, the smaller your RTO value, the higher the costs associated with the application's operation. These costs result from architectural decisions, such as infrastructure redundancy and replication across different zones or regions, and from human labor, since operations personnel may need to be available at all times. Similarly, the smaller the RPO level, the higher the costs of operating the associated datastores. These typically result from backup frequency and redundancy, which increase the price of data storage, but may include labor costs as well for manual restores that operations personnel may need to be available for.

RTO and RPO are closely tied to SLOs and SLAs. As you may recall from *Chapter 6, Configuring Services for Observability*, the SLA represents a contractual agreement that, if breached, may incur monetary compensation. The SLO, as discussed then and revisited earlier in this chapter, reflects the organization's priorities from the point of view of the service's quality and reliability (as perceived by end users). Therefore, RTOs and RPOs may be considered either SLOs or SLAs within an SRE model.

Designing systems and services for DR has traditionally been a difficult task. However, the cloud operating model facilitates the implementation of DR-ready designs thanks to the global scale and the lack of hardware operations. You can leverage GCP's global network and redundant infrastructure to improve the resiliency and reliability of your systems. Throughout this book, you've learned several ways to design your network, compute, storage, and big data solutions for **high availability (HA)**. As a reminder, the following are a few recommended design strategies we've discussed in this book:

Domain	Recommendations
Network	Leverage global networking by deploying different subnetworks on different regions.
	Use regional or global load balancing services.
	Use hybrid connectivity services in HA configuration.
Compute	Deploy VM clusters across different zones behind a regional load balancer.
	Deploy VM clusters across different regions behind a global load balancer.
	Use regional **Managed Instance Groups (MIGs)**.
	Leverage fully-managed compute platforms such as App Engine, Cloud Functions, and Cloud Run.
Storage	Set up Cloud SQL as a regional instance in HA and failover configuration.
	Set up read replicas for SQL databases.
	Configure backups and point-in-time recovery for Cloud SQL.
	Leverage Cloud Spanner for relational data.
	Leverage regional or multi-regional non-relational and unstructured datastores (Cloud Bigtable, Cloud Firestore, Cloud Memorystore, Cloud Storage).
Big data	Use BigQuery for data warehousing.
	Leverage fully-managed and highly available big data services (Cloud Storage, Cloud Dataflow, Cloud Pub/Sub, Cloud IoT Core, Cloud Dataprep).
AI and **Machine Learning (ML)**	Leverage fully-managed, highly available ML services (AI Platform, AutoML, BigQuery ML).

Finally, ensure you test your DR plan. Google's Architectural Framework recommends you do it at least once a year. However, the faster the rate of changes in your environment (and architectural changes, in particular) the more often you should do it. Once a quarter works well for many organizations. Remember that DevOps saying, *if it hurts, do it more often*.

A practice that can help with your DR drills and resiliency testing in general is that of **chaos engineering**. Chaos engineering is the discipline and set of practices aimed at purposefully injecting or simulating faults into your systems, in a controlled manner, in order to test its resiliency. The website `https://principlesofchaos.org/` offers a great and concise summary of the principles of chaos engineering and how you can apply it. Probably the most famous example application of this is Netflix's *Chaos Monkey*, a service (available at `https://netflix.github.io/chaosmonkey/`) responsible for deliberately terminating instances at random in your *production* environment as a way to test it against failure. The idea is illustrated in the following figure:

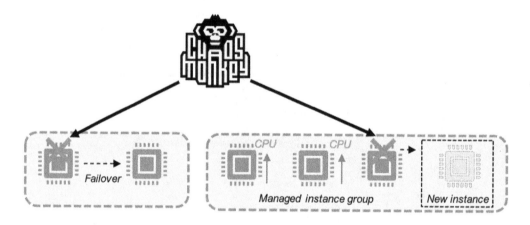

Figure 12.5 – Using Chaos Monkey to randomly terminate production instances

By terminating instances in a way that simulates real fault scenarios, you train everyone's failure muscles by forcing them to design for failure from the start, since failure will always be expected. In general, think of possible ways your systems could fail, identify and eliminate single points of failure, then design your solution in a way that RTOs and RPOs can be realistically achieved. A great DR planning guide is provided at `https://cloud.google.com/solutions/dr-scenarios-planning-guide`.

Next, we'll look at the key enabling services and tools.

Key services and tools

The following are key services and tools on GCP or otherwise available as open source software that can help you design for failure and plan or test DR:

Service/Tool	Description	How it helps
Persistent Disk	Storage disk for VM instances	You can leverage the snapshot feature of Persistent Disk, which allows you to perform incremental backups or snapshots of VM disks. Backups and snapshots can be copied across regions and used to recreate disks.
Live Migration	A Compute Engine feature that allows you to keep your VM instances running in the event of maintenance	This service migrates running instances (hence live migration) to another host in the same zone to prevent your VMs from being rebooted due to maintenance events.
Cloud Storage	Object store service	You can leverage low-cost storage classes such as Nearline, Coldline, or Archive, to retain data and backups that are not meant to be accessed frequently. You can have data placed in separate regions from that of the original data source.
Cloud DNS	DNS service on GCP	You can leverage Cloud DNS programmatic capabilities to automatically update DNS records in the event of a disaster and following an automated recovery process.
Chaos Monkey	An open source chaos engineering software tool	You can use Chaos Monkey to simulate random failure events. This will help you test the resiliency of your Compute solution.

You've now learned about some of the best practices and concepts related to operational excellence in Google Cloud. Armed with this knowledge, you should be able to deliver robust solutions with a good balance between *agility* and *reliability*.

You may be feeling discouraged about the fact that it's one thing to have all that information, but another entirely to have *actual experience* with these practices. I wouldn't blame you. Learning operations is hard and, as with most technical skills, many people can only internalize its concepts by *doing*. Although only real-world experience operating large-scale distributed systems will give you true confidence, luckily, Google has recently released the **Cloud Operations Sandbox** to give you an opportunity to put this knowledge into practice without messing up anyone's production environment. Let's learn how in the next section.

Bringing it all together with Cloud Operations Sandbox

Cloud Operations Sandbox is an open source tool developed by Google to help you learn SRE-based operations with hands-on practice. It's available at `https://cloud-ops-sandbox.dev`.

Cloud Operations Sandbox includes the following:

- A demo application built using **microservices** architecture
- An automated script for deploying and configuring the demo environment on GCP, including Cloud Monitoring, Cloud Tracing with OpenTelemetry, Cloud Profiling, Logging, Error Reporting, and Debugging
- A load generator to simulate production traffic on the service
- A set of pre-built chaos engineering tasks that introduce intentional errors in the app for you to find the root cause through GCP operations tools
- An interactive walk-through

Using the sandbox is very easy. You can simply go to the preceding URL and click on **Open in Google Cloud Shell**. This will create a new Google Cloud project and immediately kick off a Terraform script that sets up the environment. An interactive walk-through window will also be displayed. The microservices application provided is pre-instrumented with logging, monitoring, tracing, debugging, and profiling. If you wish to understand how, you can check out the source code at `https://github.com/GoogleCloudPlatform/cloud-ops-sandbox` (the application's source code is under the `src` directory). At this GitHub URL, you can also learn more about the demo service's architecture and detailed information about each microservice. This is an online shop, built similarly to our fictional webshop from *Chapter 10, Re-Architecting with Microservices.*

The setup script automatically creates a custom dashboard that displays metrics related to the four golden signals of monitoring. For example, the following screenshot shows some of the charts included in the dashboard for the *cart* service:

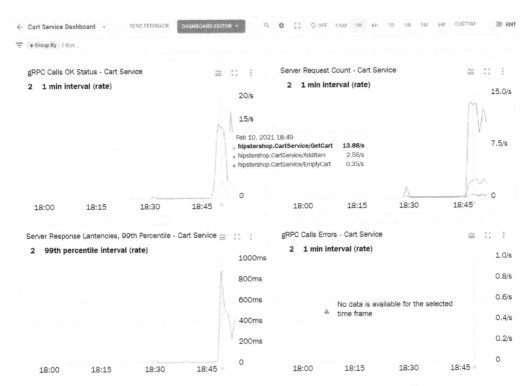

Figure 12.6 – Custom dashboards from Cloud Operations Sandbox

In this environment, production load was simulated shortly after the **18:45** time mark. This dashboard is capturing **gRPC Calls** and **Server Request Count** (which help us measure saturation), and **Server Response Latencies** (the latency signal measure) and **gRPC Calls Errors** (none present yet in the chart, but a measure of request errors). These pre-built dashboards will give you a good idea of what observability best practices look like when implemented.

The script also automatically configures *service monitoring* (SLOs and SLIs) with associated alerts, as shown in the following screenshot (SLOs are expanded for the *cart* service):

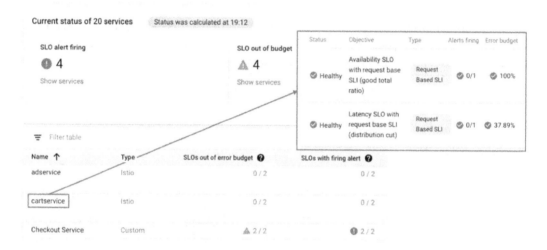

Figure 12.7 – SLOs and alerts from Cloud Operations Sandbox

The load generator tool, shown in the next screenshot, allows you to simulate real users browsing the website and buying products:

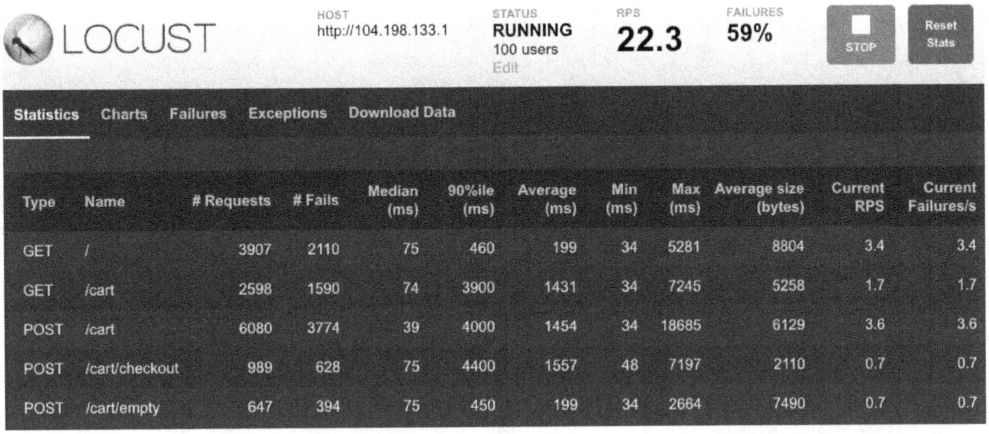

Figure 12.8 – Load generator tool from Cloud Operations Sandbox

As far as demo applications go, this one sets up a reasonably complex environment and helps you generate a realistic load. That gives you a decent picture of a real-world production scenario, which is why Cloud Operations Sandbox is a great learning tool.

I encourage you to spend some time with it, read through the guide, and work through the steps to learn the SRE concepts it teaches you. Even if you don't see yourself as an operations person, having this kind of hands-on knowledge and experience with production-like applications will improve your cloud operational skills, which tend to translate over to other areas.

Summary

In this chapter, you learned about the fundamentals of defining a cloud strategy that supports operational excellence, including understanding motivations and priorities, the operating model, and the organizational culture. Then, you learned about the best practices and recommendations from Google Cloud's Architecture Framework for operational excellence. We explored and expanded the guiding principles and best practices and summarized recommendations and the key enabling services for each area. Finally, you learned about Cloud Operations Sandbox, a tool designed to teach SRE and operational excellence principles on GCP.

This chapter concludes *Section 3, Designing for the Modern Enterprise*, with the proven principles and practices for long-term cloud adoption success. This also concludes this book, and my hope is that you're now armed with the knowledge and confidence to future-proof your Google Cloud solutions and bring value and insights to discussions ranging from cloud strategy to architecture and operations.

`Packt.com`

Subscribe to our online digital library for full access to over 7,000 books and videos, as well as industry leading tools to help you plan your personal development and advance your career. For more information, please visit our website.

Why subscribe?

- Spend less time learning and more time coding with practical eBooks and Videos from over 4,000 industry professionals

- Improve your learning with Skill Plans built especially for you

- Get a free eBook or video every month

- Fully searchable for easy access to vital information

- Copy and paste, print, and bookmark content

Did you know that Packt offers eBook versions of every book published, with PDF and ePub files available? You can upgrade to the eBook version at `packt.com` and as a print book customer, you are entitled to a discount on the eBook copy. Get in touch with us at `customercare@packtpub.com` for more details.

At `www.packt.com`, you can also read a collection of free technical articles, sign up for a range of free newsletters, and receive exclusive discounts and offers on Packt books and eBooks.

Other Books You May Enjoy

If you enjoyed this book, you may be interested in these other books by Packt:

Google Cloud Platform for Developers

Ted Hunter and Steven Porter

ISBN: 978-1-78883-767-5

- Understand the various service offerings on GCP

- Deploy and run services on managed platforms such as App Engine and Container Engine

- Securely maintain application states with Cloud Storage, Datastore, and Bigtable

- Leverage StackDriver monitoring and debugging to minimize downtime and mitigate issues without impacting users

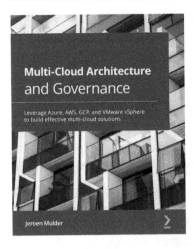

Multi-Cloud Architecture and Governance

Jeroen Mulder

ISBN: 978-1-80020-319-8

- Get to grips with the core functions of multiple cloud platforms

- Deploy, automate, and secure different cloud solutions

- Design network strategy and get to grips with identity and access management for multi-cloud

- Design a landing zone spanning multiple cloud platforms

- Use automation, monitoring, and management tools for multi-cloud

- Understand multi-cloud management with the principles of BaseOps, FinOps, SecOps, and DevOps

- Define multi-cloud security policies and use cloud security tools

Packt is searching for authors like you

If you're interested in becoming an author for Packt, please visit authors. packtpub.com and apply today. We have worked with thousands of developers and tech professionals, just like you, to help them share their insight with the global tech community. You can make a general application, apply for a specific hot topic that we are recruiting an author for, or submit your own idea.

Leave a review - let other readers know what you think

Please share your thoughts on this book with others by leaving a review on the site that you bought it from. If you purchased the book from Amazon, please leave us an honest review on this book's Amazon page. This is vital so that other potential readers can see and use your unbiased opinion to make purchasing decisions, we can understand what our customers think about our products, and our authors can see your feedback on the title that they have worked with Packt to create. It will only take a few minutes of your time, but is valuable to other potential customers, our authors, and Packt. Thank you!

Index

M

N

CPSIA information can be obtained
at www.ICGtesting.com
Printed in the USA
JSHW012119211222
35288JS00007B/110